SUPERIORITY
AND
SOCIAL
INTEREST

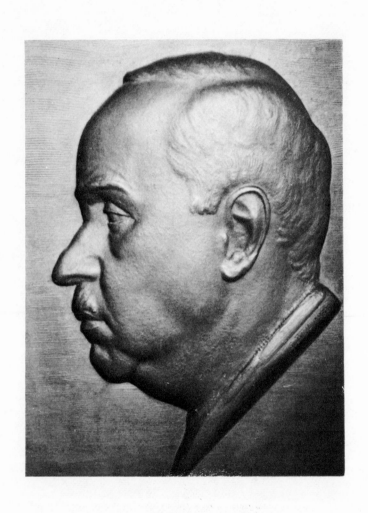

Alfred Adler

SUPERIORITY
AND
SOCIAL
INTEREST

A Collection of Later Writings

Edited by Heinz L. Ansbacher
and Rowena R. Ansbacher

WITH A BIOGRAPHICAL ESSAY BY CARL FURTMÜLLER

AND ADLER BIBLIOGRAPHY

Third Revised Edition

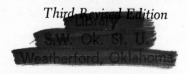

THE VIKING PRESS | NEW YORK

THE PLAQUE of Adler reproduced as the frontispiece is the work of the brilliant Yugoslav portrait sculptor Slavko Bril (1900-1943) who had been a student and assistant of the famous Ivan Meštrović. Bril died in a Croatian concentration camp during the Nazi occupation. The work had been commissioned by the Individual Psychology group in Zagreb, Yugoslavia, and its leader, Dr. Benno Stein, introduced Bril to Adler on the occasion of a visit by Adler in January 1932. We are indebted for this information to Mrs. Vera Stein-Ehrlich, widow of Dr. Stein. The plaque is in the possession of Dr. Kurt Adler. The photograph is by courtesy of Dr. O. Peter Radl.

Preface

Eight years ago the editors of the present volume published a systematic presentation of the Individual Psychology of Alfred Adler in selections from his writings (A1956b).[1] Such a volume was considered necessary from the viewpoint of historical accuracy and because of what Adler's works still had to offer.

At that time the name of Adler appeared relatively infrequently in the literature of psychology and psychiatry, although thinking in the areas of personality theory and psychotherapy was moving in the direction Adler had been pointing out against much opposition and disparagement from professional circles of his day. We explained this paradox as due in large part to the unsystematic manner of Adler's writing which was likely to leave the professional reader unsatisfied.

The purpose of the earlier volume then, as stated in its preface, was "to make Adler's contributions to the theory and practice of psychology available in a systematic and at the same time authentic form. To this end we made selections from his writings and organized them with the aim of approximating the general presentation of a college textbook. Because every word in the main body of the work is Adler's, the outcome of our efforts . . . should be the equivalent of a textbook by Adler" (A1956b, p. v). Important excerpts from Adler's writings, beginning with 1907 until his death in 1937, were selected and arranged so as to show the development of his thinking; his theories of personality, of mental disorder and psychotherapy; his views and methods of child guidance; and his views in various other

1. See Part VII, Bibliography of Alfred Adler, p. 417.

problem areas. An introductory chapter by the editors showed Adler's Individual Psychology in relation to other systems of psychology. This integrative effort was continued throughout the volume by means of editorial comments.

Since that time there has been an increasing recognition of Adler, the extent and nature of which are reviewed in the introductory chapter to the present book. This increase is largely due to the continuing change in the climate of personality theory and psychotherapy favorable to Adlerian thinking. To some extent, however, it may also have been helped by the appearance of the earlier volume which, it is believed, has enabled others "to examine Adler's system, to polish, correct, or change it and, thus, has made it viable." [2]

Due to this new interest it was felt that the time had come to supplement the first volume with a second, presenting Adler's important later writings which had not heretofore appeared in book form.

Thus the present book came into being. It contains essentially 21 papers by Adler, of which 17 are dated between 1931 and 1937, two are dated 1928 and 1929, and two are undated. Nine of these papers are original translations, one from an unpublished manuscript.

The method of presentation differs from that in the earlier book as follows: there we aimed at showing systematically the development of Adler's thinking, and the many areas to which his interests eventually extended, by piecing together brief excerpts from all his writings. The present volume is limited to selections from Adler's last period but gives these in full, thereby conveying more of his approach and style. In addition, the present book includes a new biographical essay on Adler and an exhaustive bibliography.

Specifically, the present book supplements the earlier one in the following ways:

Part I, General Assumptions and Principles, supplements the earlier Chapters 4 to 6 by further discussion of the striving for superiority, social interest, inferiority feelings, degree of activity, typology, and the concept of the complex. It is interesting to note that of the seven selections included here, five are new translations. Apparently such

ᴧᴧᴧᴧᴧᴧᴧᴧᴧᴧᴧᴧᴧ

2. Ford, Donald H., & Urban, Hugh B. *Systems of psychotherapy: a comparative study.* New York: John Wiley, 1963, p. 306.

papers, of less direct interest to the practitioner, had a slighter chance of being translated.

Part II, Theory of the Neuroses, consists of three selections supplementary to the earlier Chapters 9 to 12. Unlike the papers in Part I, all three had been previously translated. In fact they were published in Adler's American journal, while it was still under his editorship.

Part III, Case Interpretation and Treatment, presents three case discussions at length and a relatively short section on Technique of Treatment. This would supplement Chapter 13 in the first book, especially with regard to the case material which had to be held to a minimum there due to space limitations.

Part IV, Various Topics, opens with a summary by Adler on his differences from Freud; the beginnings and the dramatic climax of this historic controversy are found in Chapter 2 of the first book. This is followed by five papers on various behavior disorders, all but one supplementing the earlier Chapter 12. It concludes with a paper on delinquency which is supplementary to the earlier Chapter 17.

Part V consists of Adler's essay on religion, which originally appeared in a small volume, the coauthor of which was the Reverend Ernst Jahn who has now kindly supplied a new preface to this essay. This supplements material briefly introduced at the end of the first book, the last part of Chapter 19.

Part VI is the first publication of a biographical essay on Adler by his earliest important co-worker, Carl Furtmüller, who was a member of the Freudian circle, which he left, with Adler, in 1911. Supplied with numerous documentary footnotes by the editors, this represents the first attempt at a *documented* biography of Adler. The earlier book contained a few pages of biographical material at the end of Chapter 7.

Part VII, a bibliography of some 350 entries, is an extension of the earlier bibliography of 100 entries. The latter included only titles to which reference was made in the text, while the new bibliography is an exhaustive one. In this way it becomes a biographical document as well, showing Adler as an untiring worker whose ideas were widely disseminated, who gave interviews to popular magazines and daily newspapers, and who was interested in public health and health education even before he became interested in psychology.

In addition to the selection, and translation where needed, of the papers by Adler, the editors have provided for each a brief introductory note, except for the case discussion in Part III where existing introductions by Rudolf Dreikurs and F. G. Crookshank were used. Also, nearly all of the subheadings have been provided by the editors. In the papers which had been previously translated, occasional changes were made, mostly for the sake of consistency of terminology within this volume and with the earlier volume. This refers particularly to *Gemeinschaftsgefühl*, the key term in Adler's writings, for which a number of possible translations have been used by the various translators. We have chosen "social interest," as in the previous volume, which also seems to have been Adler's preferred translation, while occasionally we used "social feeling" where this seemed more appropriate in the specific context.

Our particular hope for the present book is that in addition to strengthening the knowledge of Adler's psychology, it will convey to the reader an appreciation of his theory and practice as having been formulated by a man who perhaps more than any other in his field felt the great responsibility of the psychologist toward mankind and who was untiring in meeting this responsibility. That the person, the theory, and the practice of Adler are all of the same cloth, the reader should be able to learn from this volume. As one author recently expressed it: "Adler in his own life was a strong believer in social causes and democratic principles, indicating . . . a theorist who appears to have lived much more closely by his theory than have some of the others." [3]

Adler also was the rare combination of a "plain" man who was a sophisticated theoretician ahead of his time, an astute practitioner, and a fervent propagandist for an optimistic, constructive world philosophy which he had found to be associated with better mental health, better personal and group morale. In his theories he felt he had forged a useful tool in the fight against cynicism and discouragement. And yet these theories are free from any mysticism, from any speculative concepts lending themselves to reification, but rest essentially on an operational, scientifically sound basis.

In his final development, as expounded in this volume, Adler stands

~~~~~~~~~~~~~~~~

3. Bischof, Ledford J. *Interpreting personality theories.* New York: Harper & Row, 1964, p. 251.

far from the false cliché of the will-to-power and from the simple inferiority feeling-compensation paradigm that were at one time associated with his name. Instead, he saw man, like all living creatures, as incessantly striving. The striving of man is toward some kind of individually conceived superiority, perfection, or success. When it is directed toward a narrow, self-centered goal, it provides the precondition for the various forms of failure in life. In the mentally healthy the focus is broad and shares in the "common sense," and the superiority which is aimed for is not over other persons but over general difficulties, the overcoming of which will benefit others as well. Hence—"Superiority *and* Social Interest."

University of Vermont   H. L. A.
Burlington, Vermont   R. R. A.
April 23, 1964

Note on the Second Edition

Factual changes in this second edition are, with a few exceptions, limited to Parts VI and VII, the biography and bibliography of Adler. In the five years since the first printing, certain new biographical information has become available, especially through the efforts of Dr. H. A. Beckh-Widmanstetter of Vienna. The bibliography has grown by some 38 titles, about ten per cent, through the publication of Volume 2 of the *Minutes of the Vienna Psychoanalytic Society, 1908–1910*, through some other newly found material, and through further reprinting of the works of Adler.

We should also like to observe that this new printing shortly anticipates the 100th anniversary of Adler's birth on February 7, 1870.

September, 1969   H. L. A.

NOTE ON THE COMPASS EDITION

In updating the Introduction several footnotes have been added and one older reference and paragraph have been omitted. Throughout the main text a few translations have been improved and footnotes added which are marked by a letter in addition to the numeral. A few items have also been added to the main bibliography of Alfred Adler.

June, 1972   H.L.A.

Acknowledgments

We are glad to express our sincere thanks to Mr. Robert Erwin, formerly of the Northwestern University Press, for his initiating suggestion for a book of the later works of Adler which might not be readily accessible to the English reading public, and for having stood by patiently and faithfully while the idea remained dormant with us for several years. We wish to thank him also for the great stimulation we finally received through his suggestion. Without his inspiration this volume would not have come into existence.

We are very grateful to Dr. Alexandra Adler and Dr. Kurt A. Adler for their continuing warm friendship and support. They made available and entrusted to us numerous of their father's unpublished manuscripts, two of which are used in this volume. They also kindly read the manuscript of our Introduction and of the biography by Furtmüller. Dr. Kurt Adler, furthermore, brought to light a number of early titles for the bibliography of his father.

It was a pleasure to correspond with Mrs. Leah C. Furtmüller in connection with her late husband's biography of Adler on which she had worked with him originally. Her keen interest, helpfulness, and friendly understanding extended beyond the biography and were most valuable. Some of the bibliographical material was found or verified by her. For all this we wish to express our sincere thanks.

We are also thankful to Miss Godelieve Vercruysse for her contribution to the bibliography. She gave it a painstaking, critical reading and suggested several valuable additions. Dr. Josef Rattner helped us by obtaining for us material from Switzerland.

We take pleasure in acknowledging permissions from the following to reprint or translate selections:

The Estate of Alfred Adler for "Religion und Individualpsychologie," for the five articles from the *Internationale Zeitschrift für Individualpsychologie,* and for the two unpublished manuscripts mentioned above.

Mr. Sydney M. Roth, publisher, for the six articles from the *International Journal of Individual Psychology.*

Individual Psychology Association of Chicago, Inc., for the four articles from the *Individual Psychology Bulletin.*

C. W. Daniel Co., Ltd. for an article from *Individual Psychology Pamphlets.*

Mrs. Danica Deutsch, editor, for an article from *Mitteilungsblatt für Individualpsychologische Veranstaltungen.*

The *Journal of Individual Psychology* for two articles.

We are also indebted to the following journals for two articles: *Pädagogische Warte* and *Schweizer Erziehungs Rundschau*

Although there are essentially twenty-one selections, in Selections 2 and 14 three additional sources are used to the extent that we wished to acknowledge them. Thus the above acknowledgments add up to twenty-four.

Contents

INTRODUCTION. THE INCREASING RECOGNITION OF ADLER

BY HEINZ L. ANSBACHER

PART I. GENERAL ASSUMPTIONS AND PRINCIPLES

PART II. THEORY OF THE NEUROSES

PART III. CASE INTERPRETATION AND TREATMENT

Part V. Religion and Mental Health

Part VI. Alfred Adler: A Biographical Essay
BY CARL FURTMÜLLER

Bibliographical Note

Bibliographical references are presented as follows:

a) Special lists of references are given at the end of the Introduction (pp. 18–20) and at the end of Part VI (pp. 391–94), the biographical essay by Furtmüller, where this procedure seemed indicated by the special nature of the material.

b) *All references to works by Adler*—throughout the entire book—are found in Part VII, the Adler bibliography (pp. 397–419). Wherever in the text or a footnote a notation appears, consisting of a capital A, the year of publication, and an identifying letter, without the name of an author, e.g., A1908b, this refers to the Adler bibliography.

c) Some additional references are given in the footnotes.

INTRODUCTION

The Increasing Recognition of Adler
by Heinz L. Ansbacher

In this introduction some of the evidence is reviewed for the significance which is today attributed to Alfred Adler. It covers the areas of personality theory in general, existential psychology and psychiatry, neo-Freudian psychoanalysis, Freudian psychoanalysis, personality diagnosis including dream interpretation, practice of psychotherapy, and theory of positive mental health. The recognition of the importance of Adler's concepts for anthropology is also discussed. But before presenting this review, a few historical statements would seem to be indicated for general orientation.

Adler was born in Vienna, February 7, 1870, and received his medical degree there in 1895. An early co-worker of Freud's, Adler was best known during the 1920's and 1930's. With Freud and Jung he was generally mentioned as one of the founders of "depth" psychology, a term which he rejected (A1927c, preface). Also, the term "inferiority complex" associated with his name was in fashion. Numerous popular books by him were available in inexpensive editions and in many languages. His school of psychology and psychotherapy, known as Individual Psychology, was organized internationally and had 34 local associations, mainly in Central Europe. There were some 30 Adlerian child guidance clinics in Vienna. A bimonthly journal of Individual Psychology was edited by Adler in German, and in 1935 an American quarterly was added. In 1931 an English periodical had also been started, by a group of medical men.

Adler's impact was greatest in personal contact and general lectures. He was imbued with the conviction that basic psychological and mental health knowledge should be imparted to everyone. In his opinion, psychology had "for its proper goal the understanding of human nature by every human being" (Bottome, 1957, p. 255). Accordingly, he was indefatigable in lecturing before physicians, teachers, clergy, or any interested group, and in holding demonstration clinics and informal discussion meetings with small groups of students. On his last lecture tour, which he made from the United States to Europe and which was to have lasted from April through July, 1937, his schedule called for over 100 lectures (Bottome, 1957, pp. 252 & 286; Orgler, 1963, pp. 200–201). He died on May 28, 1937, of a heart attack in Aberdeen, Scotland.

With the advent of Hitler nearly all the Central European associations disappeared and a sizable number of Adlerians emigrated, many of them to the United States. With the death of Adler the German and American journals ceased publication, and the English periodical was also eventually discontinued.

The great many publications Adler left behind were essentially lectures; even his books were almost all collections of lectures. There is considerable overlap to be found in them. Furthermore, since Adler was largely concerned with basic principles on the one hand, and the individual case on the other hand, his theories never became as differentiated as one is accustomed to finding in other systems. Since he urgently wanted to stay close to real life and create a psychology which could be grasped, understood, and used by all, he also shunned technical jargon and avoided coining new technical terms. Thus he was accused by many professionals of popularization and over-simplification.

For all these reasons, after his death his name faded for a number of years, except within small circles of Adlerians. This, however, did not mean at all that Adler's ideas had become antiquated. Quite on the contrary, many were simply ahead of their time, and were subsequently rediscovered and restated from other quarters. Many others lived on as part of the "common sense," without Adler's name attached to them. As Ruth Munroe (1955, p. 335) so aptly phrased it: "Adler's fate is like that of Heine, whose little masterpiece *The*

Lorelei attained such prompt popularity that when he himself asked a group of people singing it for the name of the author, he was told, 'why nobody wrote it—it's a folk song.' "

During the last several years, the trend has changed. In the words of Julian B. Rotter (1962, p. 3): "Recently there appears to be an increasing recognition of Adler's contribution to personality theory and to the practice of psychotherapy. . . . The nature of these shifts can be summarized quite briefly: (a) denial of the importance of instincts for the explanation of behavior, (b) denial of the primacy of the sexual drive in the explanation of all psychopathology, (c) greater emphasis on what is typically referred to as ego needs and ego defenses, (d) greater desire to look upon man from a moral or ethical point of view, (e) recognition that psychotherapeutic techniques should include an explicitly stated set of ethical values, since values play an implicit role in any case in all therapy. . . . Along with this increased recognition of Adler's contributions to the practice of psychotherapy there has been some but perhaps not as great, reawakened interest in teaching Adler's theory in university psychology departments."

Quite logically, a good many of the authors who will be quoted in this review are among those whom A. H. Maslow (1962) has designated as a presently emerging "third force" in psychology, this force representing a counterweight against the two comprehensive theories of human nature which have most influenced American psychology, namely, the Freudian and the experimental-positivistic-behavioristic theories. Maslow quite correctly lists Adlerians first among the "third force." The following review includes only statements from non-Adlerians.

PERSONALITY THEORY IN GENERAL

As a sign of the place in personality theory which is beginning to be attributed to Adler, we may perhaps take the introductory psychology textbook by Paul Swartz (1963). Here Adler's Individual Psychology is selected as one of three major viewpoints considered worthy of inclusion, the other two being those of Freud and G. W. Allport.

The nucleus of Adler's personality theory is the concept of a unitary, goal-directed, creative self which in the healthy state is in a positive, constructive, i.e., ethical, relationship to his fellow men. The idea of the unitary self was formulated by Adler in the term "style of life," that of the normal positive social relationship in the term "social interest." Both concepts have within the last ten years come into prominence.

Life style. Regarding style of life, Allport (1961, pp. 565–566) writes in his new textbook on personality that "Many of the ideas we have surveyed in this [last] chapter can be viewed under the inclusive concept of *life-style*," that "Adlerian psychology . . . centers in the concept of the life-style," and that this concept, although difficult to define, "will have to be dealt with by psychology in the future." Frederick C. Thorne (1961, pp. 65–68) speaks of the "Adlerian *style of life*" as the principle of unification and the organizing factor in personality.

A reviewer of Adler's works in the London *Times* (Anonymous, 1958, pp. 665–666), although rather critical of him, summed up the situation: "There has been a marked tendency to distrust the more analytical approach to problems of personality and to stress once again the unitary, coherent, and purposeful character of human conduct. This outlook, well represented in the writings of Gordon Allport and Gardner Murphy, undoubtedly owes something to Adler's insistence upon the study of the whole individual and his characteristic 'life-style.' To this extent at least, Adler anticipated an influential standpoint in present-day psychology."

The life style, according to Adler, is ultimately the individual's own creation, the product of his creative power. Adler attributed this creative power to every individual, not only a chosen few. Hall and Lindzey (1957, p. 124) consider this concept of the creative power "Adler's crowning achievement as a personality theorist."

All psychological processes come under the influence of the individual's life style; not only his actions, motives and emotions, but particularly also his cognitive processes. In fact, the former are subordinated to the cognitive processes, the individual's schema of apperception, his picture of the world, his opinion of himself and the world. Thus Robert W. Leeper (1963, p. 369), presenting a modern "cognitive" approach to problems of personality and learning, acknowledges: "Among the important workers in the field of personality upon whom I have depended are, especially, Adler, Sullivan, Horney, Rogers, and Diamond."

Social interest. For Gladys L. Anderson (1961, p. 481), social interest—as realized by the creative self in social interaction—is the key phrase in Adlerian psychology. On account of this, she considers that "Alfred Adler's theories of thirty years ago are quite contemporary today . . . psychologists are catching up with Adler. . . ."

As to the ethical factor implied in the concept of social interest, the psychiatrist Thomas S. Szasz (1961, pp. 266–267) has called attention to Adler: "The notions of democracy, equality, reciprocity, and cooperation were never discussed in Freud's writings. . . . In contrast, Adler freely expressed his concept of the morally desirable or 'mentally healthy' human relationship. It was characterized to a high degree by *social interest* and *cooperativeness*. . . . The point that I wish to make is that I believe Adler was ahead of his time in openly acknowledging the role of values—and moral problems, generally—in human psychology and psychotherapy. At the beginning of this century, it was bad enough to study sexual behavior. The scientific study of ethical behavior was completely impossible. Only during the past several decades—and only because of the rapid growth of the social sciences—has it become possible to undertake a scientifically respectable study of moral problems as an integral part of human behavior."

Adler's concept of social interest is an integral part of his view of man as not confronted by, but firmly embedded in society. Adler refused "to recognize and examine an isolated human being" (A1956b, p. 2) and spoke of "the iron logic of communal life." Thus, in his survey of the history of modern psychology, Gardner Murphy (1949, p. 341) finds that "Adler's was the first psychological system in the history of psychology that was developed in what we should today call a social-science direction."

EXISTENTIAL PSYCHOLOGY AND PSYCHIATRY

A significant development during the last years is the growing influence of the thinking of the existentialists on psychology and psychiatry. Existential psychology sees man as a unique being, fundamentally concerned with the meaning of his existence and with plans and projects to solve his existential problems. In order to understand a person we must try to see his situation as much as possible from his own point of view. Existential psychology is a movement away from a mechanistic, deterministic, and analytical approach to man. All these basic points for which existential psychology stands were also very central in Adler's system. It is therefore not surprising that the existential psychologist Wilson M. Van Dusen (1959, p. 156) discovered that Adler's system "translates rather directly" into existential psychology.

One of the first to point out the similarity between existentialism and Adlerian psychology was the philosopher Alfred Stern, analyzing the work of Jean-Paul Sartre. Stern (1958, p. 38) states that "Sartre is much more Adlerian than he might know or want to admit," while many of the differences which Sartre stresses are only apparent.

The chief theorist behind the existentialist movement in psychiatry is Martin Heidegger. Pointing out his "abstruse, semi-poetic, nearly mystical metaphysics" the psychologist Joseph Lyons (1961, p. 149) maintains that instead of Heidegger, "On the basis of his lectures and writings, Adler ought to have been the first source rediscovered by adherents of the new existentialist emphasis in psychology and psychiatry."

But there are also direct personal lines of descent from Adlerian psychology to existential psychology. Viktor E. Frankl, one of the leading European existential psychiatrists, started out with Adler, and his main contribution has been described as an extension of Adler's views to human situations of suffering and aging (Birnbaum, 1961). Rollo May, one of the outstanding existential psychologists in the United States, also started with Adler. Of one of May's early books, recently reprinted (1959), a reviewer said: "Alfred Adler is the book's *élan vital*" (Hall, 1959).

Henri F. Ellenberger (1955), coeditor with May and Angel of the current American standard work on existential psychology (May *et al.*, 1958), becomes quite explicit regarding the lineage from Adler. In the historical part of a paper on existential analysis Ellenberger discusses the various key concepts of Adler and finds that they "constitute in several respects an interesting prefiguration of those of existential analysis." He demonstrates this by drawing a number of parallels between the concepts of Adler and of Binswanger.

In contrast, Freud is considered farthest removed from existentialism among the founders of modern psychotherapy. This, despite the fact that so many existential psychotherapists attempt to reconcile their position with that of Freud. According to Harold Kelman (1962, p. 120), a leader of the Horney group: "Of existentialism there is least in Freud, somewhat more in Jung and Rank, and the most in Adler and Ferenczi." "While for Freud, society was a fixed coordinate to which the individual should adjust, Adler focused on man as a social being. In defining the individual's life style and the movement from below to above and for completion, his ideas flow in the current of phenomenology. If we speak of social beingness as the individual's unique way of being-in-this-world, his thinking is existentialistic" (p. 115).

May we conclude this part with the observation by Van Dusen (1958): "One almost wonders if the existential analytic movement is not a revolt against Freud which would not have been so imperative if the main analytic current in Europe had followed Adler instead of Freud."

NEO-FREUDIAN PSYCHOANALYSIS

The position of the neo-Freudians may be briefly described as stressing social relations rather than biological factors, the self rather than the id and the superego, the striving for self-actualization rather than the sex instinct, and the present situation rather than early experiences. A number of neo-Freudians have come very close to existential psychology.

The similarity of all these points of emphasis to those of Adler serves as another confirmation of—and helps explain the revived interest in—his concepts. Actually, the question has frequently been raised whether these later deviators from Freud should not be called neo-Adlerians. In his textbook on psychological theories, Benjamin B. Wolman (1960, p. 298) remarks: "It has to be said that Adler's influence is much greater than is usually admitted. The entire neo-psychoanalytic school, including Horney, Fromm, and Sullivan, is no less neo-Adlerian than it is neo-Freudian. Adler's concepts of sociability, self-assertion, security, self, and creativeness permeated the theories of the neo-analysts."

Sundberg and Tyler (1962, p. 394) also point out the neo-Freudian—neo-Adlerian equation. They further observe: "It is an interesting fact that . . . the essential ideas of Adlerian psychology crop up again and again in the writings of other psychologists, often persons who begin with a Freudian psychoanalytic orientation. . . . It is as though other persons, when they reach a certain stage in their development, feel a need to break with Freud on essentially the same grounds that Adler originally did" (p. 360).

Earlier, Munroe (1955, p. 334) had made the same point. She finds that, although Horney, Sullivan, and Fromm owe no direct allegiance to Adler and, historically, represent new revolts from Freud, nevertheless their theoretical additions seem to belong in the section with Adler rather than in the Freudian section. This pattern is followed by Hall and Lindzey (1957, pp. 114–156) who regard Adler as the ancestral figure of the "new social psychological look" in psychoanalytic theory, by which they mean Horney, Fromm, and Sullivan.

The late Clara Thompson (1950, pp. 160–161), who is herself counted among the neo-Freudians, says about Adler that "he anticipated by several years a more general acceptance of several similar ideas. He was a pioneer in applying psychoanalysis to the total personality. . . . He was the first person to describe a part of the role of the Ego in producing neurosis and to show that the direction in which a person is going, that is, his goals, significantly contribute to his neurotic difficulties."

FREUDIAN PSYCHOANALYSIS

The recent developments in Freudian circles proper also point toward Adler. Since the death of Freud, even his closest followers have tended to place more emphasis on the role of the ego in the total personality. It is exactly this emphasis which Adler placed on the self and the unity of personality which was one of the issues that in 1911 led to his parting from Freud, who accused him of being interested merely in ego psychology. In this and certain other connections

Robert W. White (1957a) stated: "In certain respects it is indeed legitimate to say that Freudian psychology is in process of catching up with Adler." Elsewhere, White (1957b, p. 114) agrees with Munroe in affirming that "the first pioneering steps toward an ego psychology within psychoanalysis were taken by Alfred Adler." This is also the judgment of Martin Hoffman (1962, p. 231) who goes further, to point out that Adler's pioneering development of ego psychology was "later taken up by Freud and his disciples."

Recalling that Adler's theory was at first denounced by Freud and his followers for being essentially an ego psychology, O. H. Mowrer (1959) asks, "What is the New Look in psychoanalysis itself?" and gives the answer, "Ego psychology!"

The behavioristically oriented psychologist, John Dollard (1956), who believes that Freud's system is mainly right, at the same time holds that to perfect and complete it "there is most to be gained by reviewing the work of Alfred Adler."

COMPARISON WITH OTHER PERSONALITY THEORIES

Adler's theory has come out well in two studies comparing current personality theories through cluster analysis and factor analysis. The studies used quite different sets of data: the first, purely theoretical; the second, more applied.

Hall and Lindzey (1957, pp. 539–550) rated 17 personality theories on 18 dimensions. These ratings were subjected by Taft (1958) to a cluster analysis. He found, among other interesting results, that with regard to "most similarity in factors to the 16 other theories," Adler's came first among the top three, which included Freud's and H. A. Murray's. From this Taft concludes that these three theories "are either very eclectic . . . or have had a major influence on other theories. Let the reader decide for himself."

Farberow and Shneidman (1961, pp. 306–313) asked theoreticians of six different orientations to appraise one case of attempted suicide, in a "blind" analysis, by the Q-sort technique. The outcome was subjected to a factor analysis by H. Gulliksen (Kelly, 1963). The theories represented were those of Freud, Jung, Adler, Sullivan, Kelly, and Rogers. The Adlerian Q-sort yielded the highest communality of any of these theories.

Both studies would indicate that the Adlerian theory contains a greater part of the common core of all personality theories, better represents their consensus, than any other theory in these studies.[1]

PERSONALITY DIAGNOSIS

In addition to the interview and keen observation in general, Adler relied on three methods of diagnosis which he originated: early recollections, the birth-order position in the family constellation, and his form of dream interpretation. All three have found more general recognition only recently.

Regarding early recollections, Munroe (1955, pp. 428–429 n.) remarked correctly, "It seems to me that Adler's routine request for a first memory was actually the first approach toward the projective-test methodology now so widely used. Adler knew very well that the first memory is realistically often incorrect, that its chronology is often suspect. His idea was that the item selected as 'first' was creatively selected, and could be interpreted in relation to the total personality . . . the very core of contemporary projective techniques." Since then a considerable research literature on early recollections has been developing and several large research projects are under way.

As to ordinal position as a diagnostic concept, this has now also been brought to the very center of psychological research interest through the work of Stanley Schachter (1959). A second, rather speculative book on the same subject matter by Walter Toman (1961, p. vi) points out Adler's "early emphasis on character structure and sibling positions."

Adler's theory of dream interpretation has been discussed by Montague Ullman (1962) in the light of his own thinking, which takes the recent work of Kleitman and associates on the physiology of sleeping and dreaming into account. Ullman agrees with Adler that, contrary to Freud, there is no systematic difference between the conscious and the unconscious, that the aim of the dream is not

ᴡᴡᴡᴡᴡᴡᴡᴡᴡᴡᴡ

1. As to classification, Adler is today grouped among others with those advancing a "fulfillment" model of man, rather than a conflict or consistency model (Maddi, 1972), or a "pilot" rather than robot model (Ford and Urban, 1963, p. 597).

limited to the gratification of desires, and that the motivation is not exclusively sexual. On the positive side, he agrees with the following main insights of Adler: (a) Dream explanation must not offend common sense. (b) Dreams are the product of a particular life style and in turn build up and enforce this style. (c) Dreams must be understood in terms of the individual's orientation to his own future. In the light of these major agreements, certain points on which Ullman differs from Adler are of secondary consequence.

Thus a new appreciation of Adler's methodology, in addition to his theory (closely related as these are), has become a factor in the revived interest in his work.

PRACTICE OF PSYCHOTHERAPY

The psychiatrist Joseph Wilder (1959, p. xv) has coined the sentence, "The proper question is not whether one is Adlerian but how much of an Adlerian one is." He was led to this statement through the realization that by now most observations and ideas of Adler have subtly and quietly permeated modern psychological thinking.[2]

Rotter (1960, p. 383), surveying the literature in psychotherapy from April, 1958, to April, 1959, found that current advances in psychoanalysis all have in general an Adlerian flavor, and he notes that "theorists for the last 20 years have been writing books re-expressing many of Adler's concepts without reference to Adler, although sometimes twisting and turning considerably in order to prove that these ideas were accepted by Freud." R. R. Mezer (1957), a psychiatrist, states plainly: "Present-day psychoanalysis in practice is an

---

2. Lewis R. Wolberg (1970), Dean, Postgraduate Center for Mental Health, New York, stated on the occasion of the 100th anniversary of Adler's birth: "It is a matter of great amazement to discover, from the inspired writings of Adler, how many so-called modern trends in mental health parallel Adlerian theories and methods. Our present-day focus on community mental health embodies a good deal of emphasis that Adler gave to social vectors. Similarly, educational methodologies, family therapy, and social therapy . . . have been elaborated in detail by Adler."

Henri F. Ellenberger (1970), in his monumental *The Discovery of the Unconscious*, concludes, "It would not be easy to find another author from whom so much has been borrowed from all sides without acknowledgment than Alfred Adler" (p. 645).

ego psychology not too discrepant from Adler's Individual Psychology."

Sundberg and Tyler (1962, p. 42), in their textbook on clinical psychology, credit Adler with anticipating two approaches to psychotherapy, among the seven kinds which they distinguish. These two are psychotherapy as change in concepts and values, and psychotherapy as interpersonal relations and communications, i.e., the cognitive and interpersonal approaches to psychotherapy. The authors hold that "the lead in both these lines . . . was taken by Alfred Adler."

Ford and Urban (1963, p. 365), in their textbook comparing ten systems of psychotherapy as such, also credit Adler with being the first to emphasize the role of interpersonal experience. They also point out his primacy in recognizing the importance of the building and maintenance of the self-image, and in taking the subjectivistic, phenomenological position which has become so popular in more recent therapy theory. By the extensive thoroughness of their account of Adler's system they confirm their expressed judgment, "This system is to be highly regarded for its contributions to the developing field of therapy theory."

The psychotherapist Albert Ellis (1962, p. 323), who developed his own system of a Rational Psychotherapy, concludes a comparison of his system with that of Adler with these words: "That Alfred Adler should have had a half century start in stating some of the main elements of a theory of personality and psychotherapy which was independently derived from a different framework and perspective is a remarkable tribute to his perspicacity and clinical judgment." [3]

THEORY OF POSITIVE MENTAL HEALTH

There is increasing appreciation today that Adler offered a very workable, positive concept of mental health, while Freud's theory was, at best, that of mental disorder. In the words of R. W. White (1957b, p. 114), "Adler was the first person to see that something had to be added to Freud's analytic penetrations if one were to account for recovery from neurosis and for the healthy functions of personality."

wwwwwwwwww

3. The Fourth Brief Psychotherapy Conference, sponsored by the Department of Psychiatry, Chicago Medical School, March 24–25, 1972, in Chicago, was given entirely to Adlerian techniques (*J. Indiv. Psychol.*, 1972, 28, No. 2). It celebrated the centennial of Adler's birth and honored the proponents of his teachings, especially the late Rudolf Dreikurs.

According to Hoffman (1962, p. 233), Adler also supplied a program for mental health action: "For Adler, we need to construct a society which stresses education for harmonious group life by encouraging the development of 'social interest.' For those who are not able to develop this capacity in the usual course of their upbringing, re-education (that is, psychotherapy) is the answer."

When Maslow (1954, p. 217) studied people of ideal mental health, he found that one of their characteristics was *Gemeinschaftsgefühl* (social interest), which was Adler's criterion for mental health. "This word, invented by Alfred Adler, is the only one available that describes well the flavor of the feelings for mankind expressed by self-actualizing subjects. They have for human beings in general a deep feeling of identification, sympathy, and affection in spite of occasional anger, impatience, or disgust. . . . They have a genuine desire to help the human race. It is as if they were all members of a single family."

Being close to Maslow in his views, Sidney M. Jourard (1963, p. 21) has incorporated the idea of social interest in his definition of mental health: "[The mentally healthy individual] can take himself more or less for granted and devote his energies and thoughts to socially meaningful interests and problems beyond security, or lovability, or status." Jourard appreciates that "Adler's writings have been influential in psychiatry and in education, though perhaps less widely recognized than those of Freud. The concept of social feeling accords with the highest precepts of ethics and religion and represents a wholesome corrective to the more pathology-oriented psychoanalytic writings" (p. 8).

The mental health aspect of Adler's theory is also brought out by Hall and Lindzey (1957, p. 125): "Adler fashioned a humanistic theory of personality which was the antithesis of Freud's conception of man. By endowing man with altruism, humanitarianism, cooperation, creativity, uniqueness, and awareness, he restored to man a sense of dignity and worth that psychoanalysis had pretty largely destroyed. In place of the dreary materialistic picture which horrified and repelled many readers of Freud, Adler offered a portrait of man which was more satisfying, more hopeful, and far more complimentary to man. Adler's conception of the nature of personality coincided with the popular idea that man can be the master, and not the victim, of his fate."

The reviewer in the London *Times* (Anonymous, 1958), mentioned before, concludes: "This more optimistic view of organized society is undoubtedly the real reason for the present revival of interest in Adler. Both he and our modern neo-Freudians share a belief not only in the therapeutic function of the group but in the ultimate betterment of society itself. Neurosis, they seem to say, is the price paid not for civilization but for its lack."

ANTHROPOLOGY

The anthropologist Ashley Montagu has for some time been explicit in his regard for Adler's concept of social interest. Montagu (1955, p. 185) applies this concept to the mother-child relationship, to education, and to man's relatedness in general, in support of his own view that "life is social and man is born to be social, that is cooperative—an interdependent part of a whole."

A recent development is the central significance attributed to Adler by another anthropologist, Ernest Becker (1962). He holds that the need for self-esteem, for overcoming inferiority feelings, for establishing and maintaining his worth in his own eyes, is the most specific characteristic of man, which becomes evident throughout the diversity of cultures.

Becker accuses Freud of having retarded the development of the social sciences by his instinct theory, and by his contentions of innate aggression and of essential individual-society antagonism. Becker speaks of "the straight jacket in which Freud has held social scientists" (p. 133) for a half-century. Today, "Freud's physiological-drive invariants have been all but wholly discredited by researchers in a variety of disciplines. . . . Most of the major invariants which Freud derived from his theory of human development are spurious" (p. 162).

Becker then makes the astoundingly forceful statement: "We shall make no real progress in social science until we accept the symbolic nature of human striving upon which Adler—who early abandoned the concept of aggression—insisted long ago" (p. 134). And finally he adds his own protest to the growing number of protests by others, over the temporary historical eclipse of Adler: "It is incredible that human behavior can be discussed from a psychoanalytic point of view without mentioning Adler's name. Or that some so-called 'neo-Freudians' can deliver ostensibly 'fresh' ideas with an air of discovery, when many of these ideas were adumbrated by Adler over a half-century ago. Freud set a precedent for ignoring Adler's dangerously competitive brilliance, which has been continued ever since their formal split" (p. 200).

ACTIVITIES OF ADLERIANS

The period which marks the low point of Adlerian psychology in the United States, as well as elsewhere, was around 1940, according to Rudolf Dreikurs (1956), one of the leaders in Individual Psychology today. It was in this year that he founded the *Individual Psychology Bulletin*, which eventually evolved into the current *Journal of Individual Psychology*, and which he edited until 1956. The purpose of the present journal, published by the American Society of Adlerian Psychology, is to be the scientific medium of all those concerned with the study of the individual person, conceived as being unique, self-consistent, active, and creative; always oriented and motivated toward a goal of success which lies ahead of him; and endowed with an innate potentiality for social living and contribution. In this sense the journal endeavours to continue the tradition of Adler.

Since the low point, Adlerian psychologists and psychiatrists have reconstituted themselves in a number of places. Today there are regional associations in New York, Chicago, and Los Angeles which maintain training institutes and mental hygiene centers. There are also several clinics and groups elsewhere. The central organization is the American Society of Adlerian Psychology which conducts annual meetings and publishes the above-mentioned journal.

In addition there are Adlerian groups in Austria, England, France, Holland, Israel, and Switzerland. Together with the American Society, they form the International Association of Individual Psychology which publishes the *Individual Psychology News Letter*, Paul Rom, editor, and has been holding international congresses every three years.

The present-day work of Adlerians is best reflected in two publications. R. Dreikurs, R. Corsini, R. Lowe, and M. Sonstegard (1959) have edited a manual for counseling centers to which fourteen individuals have contributed.[4] The second publication is a volume edited by Kurt A. Adler and Danica Deutsch (1959), to which 48 Adlerians, mostly from the New York City area, have contributed. Finally, for a recent survey of the contributions of Adlerians since 1955 the reader is referred to a paper by Helene and Ernst Papanek (1961).

REFERENCES

Adler, K. A., & Deutsch, Danica (Eds.). *Essays in Individual Psychology: contemporary applications of Alfred Adler's theories.* New York: Grove Press, 1959.

Allen, T.W. (Ed.) "Individual Psychology: the legacy of Alfred Adler." *Counsel. Psychol.,* 1972, 3, No. 1.

Allport, G. W. *Pattern and growth of personality.* New York: Holt, Rinehart & Winston, 1961.

Anderson, Gladys L. Review of K. A. Adler & Danica Deutsch (Eds.), Essays in Individual Psychology. New York: Grove Press, 1959. *Int. J. Group Psychother.,* 1961, 11, 481–482.

Anonymous, Review of A. Adler, The Individual Psychology of Alfred Adler, London: Allen & Unwin, 1958. *The Times (London) Literary Suppl.,* Nov. 21, 1958, 665–666.

Arnold, M.R. "Let 'em fight: how to rear kids and stay sane." *Nat. Observer,* January 1, 1972, 1 and 14.

Becker, E. *The birth and death of meaning: a perspective in psychiatry and anthropology.* New York: Free Press of Glencoe, 1962.

Birnbaum, F. "Frankl's existential psychology from the viewpoint of Individual Psychology (1947)." *J. Indiv. Psychol.,* 1961, 17, 162–166.

Bottome, Phyllis. *Alfred Adler: a portrait from life.* 3rd ed. New York: Vanguard Press, 1957.

Dollard, J. Review of I. Progoff, The death and rebirth of psychology, New York: Julian Press, 1956. *N. Y. Times Book Rev.,* Dec. 16, 1956, Pp. 6 & 20.

Dreikurs, R. Editorial. *Amer. J. Indiv. Psychol.,* 1956, 12, 177–179.

Dreikurs, R., Corsini, R., Lowe, R., & Sonstegard, M. *Adlerian family counseling: a manual for counseling centers.* Eugene, Oregon: Univer. Oregon Press, 1959.

Ellenberger, H. "Analyse existentielle." In H. Ey (Ed.), *Encyclopédie médico-chirurgicale.* Vol. 3. *Psychiatrie.* Paris: Ed. Encyclopédie Médico-Chirurgicale, 1955. Pp. 1–4.

〰〰〰〰〰〰〰〰〰

4. Educational counseling, as well as family education, under the leadership of Dreikurs, has experienced a particularly vigorous development, as evidenced, respectively, by a special issue of *The Counseling Psychologist,* edited by T.W. Allen (1972), and a leading article in the *National Observer* by Arnold (1972). Dr. Dreikurs died on May 25, 1972.

Ellenberger, H. F. *The discovery of the unconscious: the history and evolution of dynamic psychiatry.* New York: Basic Books, 1970.

Ellis, A. *Reason and emotion in psychotherapy.* New York: Lyle Stuart, 1962.

Farberow, N. L., & Shneidman, E. S. (Eds.). *The cry for help.* New York: McGraw-Hill, 1961.

Ford, D. H., & Urban, H. B. *Systems of psychotherapy: a comparative study.* New York: Wiley, 1963.

Hall, C. S. Review of R. May, The art of counseling, New York: Abingdon Press, 1959. *Contemp. Psychol.*, 1959, 4, 263.

Hall, C. S., & Lindzey, G. *Theories of personality.* New York: Wiley, 1957.

Hoffman, M. "A note on the origins of ego psychology." *Amer. J. Psychother.*, 1962, 16, 230–234.

Jourard, S. M. *Personal adjustment: an approach through the study of healthy personality.* 2nd ed. New York: Macmillan, 1963.

Kelly, G. A. "Nonparametric factor analysis of personality theories." *J. Indiv. Psychol.*, 1963, 19, 115–147. Also in B. Maher (Ed.), *Clinical psychology and personality: the selected papers of George Kelly.* New York: Wiley, 1969. Pp. 301–322.

Kelman, H. "Psychoanalysis and existentialism." In L. Salzman & J. H. Masserman (Eds.), *Modern concepts of psychoanalysis.* New York: Phil. Libr., 1962. Pp. 115–126.

Leeper, R. W. "Learning and the fields of perception, motivation, and personality." In S. Koch (Ed.), *Psychology: a study of a science.* Vol. 5. New York: McGraw-Hill, 1963. Pp. 365–487.

Lyons, J. "Heidegger, Adler, and the paradox of fame." *J. Indiv. Psychol.*, 1961, 17, 149–161.

Maddi, S. R. *Personality theories: a comparative analysis.* Rev. ed. Homewood, Ill.: Dorsey Press, 1972.

Maslow, A. H. *Motivation and personality.* New York: Harper, 1954.

Maslow, A. H. *Toward a psychology of being.* Princeton, N. J.: Van Nostrand, 1962.

May, R. *The art of counseling* (1939). New York: Abingdon Press, 1959.

May, R., Angel, E., & Ellenberger, H. F. (Eds.). *Existence: a new dimension in psychiatry and psychology.* New York: Basic Books, 1958.

Mezer, R. R. Review of A. Adler, The Individual Psychology of Alfred Adler, New York: Basic Books, 1956. *Amer. J. Sociol.*, 1957, 532–533.

Montagu, A. *The direction of human development: biological and social bases.* New York: Harper, 1955.

Mowrer, O. H. "Comments on Trude Weiss-Rosmarin's 'Adler's psychology and the Jewish tradition.' " *J. Indiv. Psychol.*, 1959, 15, 128–129.

Munroe, Ruth L. *Schools of psychoanalytic thought.* New York: Dryden, 1955.

Murphy, G. *Historical introduction to modern psychology.* Rev. ed. New York: Harper, 1949.

Orgler, Hertha. *Alfred Adler: the man and his work.* New York: Liveright, 1963.

Papanek, Helene, & Papanek, E. "Individual Psychology today." *Amer. J. Psychother.*, 1961, 15, 4–26.

Rotter, J. B. "Psychotherapy." *Annu. Rev. Psychol.*, 1960, 11, 381–414.

Rotter, J. B. "An analysis of Adlerian psychology from a research orientation." *J. Indiv. Psychol.*, 1962, 18, 3–11.

Schachter, S. *The psychology of affiliation*. Stanford, Calif.: Stanford Univer. Press, 1959.

Stern, A. "Existential psychoanalysis and Individual Psychology." *J. Indiv. Psychol.*, 1958, 14, 38–50.

Sundberg, N. D., & Tyler, Leona E. *Clinical psychology: an introduction to research and practice*. New York: Appleton-Century-Crofts, 1962.

Swartz, P. *Psychology: the study of behavior*. Princeton, N. J.: Van Nostrand, 1963.

Szasz, T. S. *The myth of mental illness*. New York: Hoeber-Harper, 1961.

Taft, R. "A cluster analysis for Hall and Lindzey." *Contemp. Psychol.*, 1958, 3, 143–144.

Thompson, Clara. *Psychoanalysis: evolution and development*. New York: Hermitage House, 1950.

Thorne, F. C. *Personality: a clinical eclectic viewpoint*. Brandon, Vermont: J. Clin. Psychol., 1961.

Toman, W. *Family constellation: theory and practice of a psychological game*. New York: Springer, 1961.

Ullman, M. "Dreaming, life style, and physiology: a comment on Adler's view of the dream." *J. Indiv. Psychol.*, 1962, 18, 18–25.

Van Dusen, W. Review of R. May, E. Angel, & H. Ellenberger (Eds.), Existence: a new dimension in psychiatry and psychology. New York: Basic Books, 1958. *J. Indiv. Psychol.*, 1958, 14, 188–189.

Van Dusen, W. "The ontology of Adlerian psychodynamics." *J. Indiv. Psychol.*, 1959, 15, 143–156.

White, R. W. Review of A. Adler, The Individual Psychology of Alfred Adler. New York: Basic Books, 1956. *Contemp. Psychol.*, 1957, 2, 1–4. (a)

White, R. W. "Adler and the future of ego psychology." *J. Indiv. Psychol.*, 1957, 13, 112–124. (b)

Wilder, J. Introduction. In K. A. Adler & Danica Deutsch (Eds.), *Essays in Individual Psychology*. New York: Grove Press, 1959. Pp. xv–xvii.

Wolberg, L.R. In "Tributes to Alfred Adler on his 100th birthday." *J. Indiv. Psychol.*, 1970, 26, 16.

Wolman, B. B. *Contemporary theories and systems in psychology*. New York: Harper, 1960.

PART I

General Assumptions
and Principles

I

The Progress of Mankind
$\left(1937\right)^{1}$

The following selection would certainly seem appropriate for the opening of a volume of later papers of Alfred Adler. It was published the year of his death and deals with a topic which was both his personal credo throughout his life and the foundation of his psychology —the optimistic idea of progress.

It contains a final summary of his Individual Psychology in the form of six assumptions, which are: the *organismic* unity of the individual; the importance of the individual's subjective, *phenomenological* world, his opinion; a *unitary dynamics*, named here the striving for success; the *uniqueness* of the individual, formulated in the concept of style of life; his partial *self-determination* attributed to his creativity; and man's *positive social orientation*, expressed as his potentiality for social interest.

The paper is also most characteristic of Adler's general approach and style in that he supports his thesis of the advancement of social interest by homely considerations, appealing to the "common sense."

—*Eds.*

The question of whether progress of mankind is possible, probable, impossible, or certain moves everyone today more than ever. But even

---

1. A1937g. Reprinted from translation, A1957c.

regarding the meaning of progress there is disagreement. The explanation for this is probably that people in general tend to overlook the larger contexts, and to regard all problems, including scientific ones, from their own, usually too narrow, personal perspective. This is also true for the problem of progress.

Everyone subordinates all experiences and problems to his own conception. This conception is usually a tacit assumption and as such unknown to the person. Yet he lives and dies for the inferences he draws from such a conception. It is amusing, and sad at the same time, to see how even scientists—especially philosophers, sociologists and psychologists—are caught in this net. In that it also has its assumptions, its conception of life, its style of life, Individual Psychology is no exception. But it differs in that it is well aware of this fact.

BASIC ASSUMPTIONS OF INDIVIDUAL PSYCHOLOGY

Individual Psychology was the first school of psychology to break with the assumption of inner forces, such as instincts, drives, unconsciousness, etc., as irrational material. When it comes to the understanding and appraisal of an individual or a group, this break has proved most helpful. On the positive side, Individual Psychology makes the following assumptions.

Individual Psychology has established the presupposition, against which no argument can be found, of the *unity and self-consistency of the personality*.

Individual Psychology finds its firm, rational field of activity in the manner in which the always unique individual behaves towards the changing problems of life. Decisive for his behavior is the individual's *opinion of himself and of the environment* with which he has to cope.

Individual Psychology assumes further the individual's *striving for success* in the solution of his problems, this striving being anchored in the very structure of life. But the judgment of what constitutes success is again left to the opinion of the individual.

Our criterion for appraising a specific variant, whether a given individual or a group, is always the direction towards the ascending development and welfare of mankind. In other words, it is the degree and kind of *social interest* necessary to arrive at this goal of general welfare and upward development. The weightiest reason for this assumption is our finding that the individual is faced exclusively with such problems as can be solved only with sufficient social interest. He may have had this from childhood, or may have acquired it later. All problems of life merge into the three social problems of neighborly love, work, and sexual love. One finds a degree of social interest, although this is usually inadequate, in all men, with the exception of idiots, and even in animals. We therefore feel justified in assuming that this social interest which is demonstrated throughout life is rooted in the germ cell. But it is rooted as a potentiality, not as an actual ability.

Social interest, like all innate human potentialities, will develop in accordance with the individual's self-consistent *style of life.*

The style of life arises in the child out of his *creative power,* i.e., from the way he perceives the world and from what appears to him as success.

Such a foundation of a psychology greatly supports the certainty of the observer. Firstly, since the assumptions are made explicit, he gains certainty in that he knows and understands them well and can check them at any time. Secondly, he is especially protected from false conclusions and mistaken appraisals regarding an individual or a group, because he is forced to seek the existing degree of social interest in all the expressive movements, personality traits, and symptoms. This latter advantage he owes to the basic view of the unity and self-consistency of the personality in thinking, feeling, willing, and acting.

THE IDEA OF PROGRESS

From our basic assumptions there follows an important conclusion bearing on the problem of the progress of mankind.

We may define human progress as a function of a higher development of social interest. Admittedly the level of social interest is presently still low, as indicated by such phrases as "Why should I love my neighbor?" and "After me the deluge." But social interest is continually pressing and growing. For this reason, no matter how dark the times may be, in the long-range view there is the assurance of the higher development of the individual and the group. Social interest is continually growing; human progress is a function of the higher development of social interest; therefore, human progress will be inevitable as long as mankind exists.

THREE PROSPECTIVE CONSIDERATIONS

In the following we wish to argue through three brief prospects that evolution leads to the success of social interest. This gives Individual Psychology the imprint of a gay and optimistic science.[2]

1. The first prospect is in the nature of an anecdote. I once read it in an American article, the author of which I have unfortunately forgotten, and it has moved me very strongly.[2a] A multimillionaire who had spent a hard youth in poverty and misery wanted to protect his descendants from similar deprivations. He consulted a lawyer and told him the size of his fortune, as well as that he wanted to protect his descendants to approximately the tenth generation. The lawyer took his pen and began to figure. When he was finished he turned to his client and said: "Your fortune is so great that it is completely sufficient to provide for your descendants adequately up to the tenth generation. But do you know that if you do this, you are protecting children, each of whom is related to over 1,000 persons of your generation as closely as he is related to you?"

It follows from this consideration, if we widen our view to include 100 and more generations, that everything that people have contributed, even if only in the apparent interest of their own family, is irrevocably for the benefit of the whole of mankind. This "equalization process" may be slowed down at times for lack of useful contributions, but it cannot be stopped.

2. A consideration from my forthcoming book, *Der Sinn des Lebens* (A1933b), supplements the first prospect. I raise the question, "What do we find when we are born into this world?" The answer is: We find all the previous useful contributions which have been supplied by our forebears. We find human beings in their bodily and mental development, social institutions, art, science, lasting traditions,

2. The expression of "gay science" is undoubtedly borrowed from Nietzsche's book of that title.

2a. The author is Harry Stillwell Edwards (1855–1938), American novelist and writer of magazine stories (Editorial, *J. Indiv. Psychol.*, 1966, 22, 237–238).

social relations, values, schooling, etc. We receive all these and build upon them, advancing, improving, and changing, always in the sense of a further durability. This is the inheritance from our forebears which falls to us for administration. It is their contribution in which their spirit lives on immortally after the body has fallen.

What happened to the earthly life of those who contributed nothing, or who interfered with the developmental process? The answer is: It has disappeared. Nothing from their lives can be found. Does this not appear like an inviolable law aimed against all who supply no contributions for later generations? Their trace on earth is lost forever.

This train of thought, against which it would be difficult to find any counter-argument, is closely related to my findings that the life of the individual as well as of the group presents itself as a "compensation process." This process attempts to overcome felt or alleged "inferiorities," in a physical or psychological manner. One goal of this compensatory striving is the steadily growing culture of mankind which collects all useful and productive contributions of the various generations and passes them on.

The power of social interest which is inherent to the life of mankind, which as innate aptitude determines human nature in great part, and which is lacking only in the feeble-minded, comes to life and becomes productive through the creative power of the child, as pointed out above. Although not strong enough at present to solve human difficulties for the benefit of the entire human family, the existing social interest is nevertheless so powerful that individuals and groups must refer to it. Human judgment can do no more than consider whether the line of a proposed movement will ultimately merge into the well-being of man in general. Political movements, the utilization of the advances of science and technology, laws, and social norms are included in this evaluation. Claims of interest in the well-being of the community, however, have power in the long run only if their professed accord with the general well-being finds confirmation.

3. A third prospect has a much more serious background but leads to the same result, namely, that progress is forced upon men. This consideration is that the finality of the individual life merges into the progress of mankind. Even though we are tragically affected by

withered and rapidly withering life, we realize that its rejuvenation in the next generation, enriched by the earlier generation, forces new contributions and progress. Rejuvenation raises new problems and meets them. No heredity has matured for these problems because they have never arisen before. Again and again the creative power of the child and of the adult come under new tensions until new solutions have been brought into being and useless ones have been removed.

Each new generation struggles afresh with old and new tasks and, pitted against the environment, is forced as a whole to maintain its equilibrium (Cannon) physically and psychologically with growing senses and growing understanding. This equilibrium can be gained only if the sum of the energies of the individual, supported through the growth of a rational picture of the world, is successful in bringing the problems of the environment closer to a solution.

In the holistic relationship between man and cosmos progress will rule until the decline of the human family. "The environment molds man, but man molds the environment" (Pestalozzi). With the limitation of our senses and our understanding of the ultimate things, rational science speaks the last word. At this point, a strong word is spoken by Individual Psychology with its emphasis on the whole and on social interest.

2

On the Origin of the Striving
for Superiority and of Social Interest
(1933)[1,2]

As an organismic, holistic theory, Individual Psychology requires a unitary theory of motivation, which postulates either one master motive or merely the force of life itself as the dynamic principle. Adler essentially chose the second alternative, and when he named a master motive, it was actually only to describe the form which the force of life takes in man. Adler's assumption of the life force remained a constant, while the names he gave to the human master motive varied over the years, within a certain range. In the previous paper (written in 1937) he speaks merely of striving for success. In the present paper (prepared in 1933) he speaks variously of a striving for perfection, superiority, overcoming, an upward striving, a coercion to carry out a better adaptation, "innate as something which belongs to life."

As a holistic theory, Individual Psychology also assumes an essential cooperative harmony between individual and society, with conflict an erroneous condition. This harmony is assumed to be based on an "innate substratum of social interest" which must be consciously developed. Social interest is not a second dynamic force, but gives

~~~~~~~~~~~~~~~

1. From a paper read at the Vienna Medical Society for Individual Psychology, with the exception of the "Summary" which was read at the Individual Psychology Association, Vienna.

2. Original translation of A1933i₁, and A1933i₂ (the present "Summary").

direction to the striving for superiority, just as any other developed
potentiality would influence the direction of the striving. As a
direction-giving factor, social interest also becomes a normative ideal.
                                                                —Eds.

It sounds almost like a timely problem to speak on the striving for
perfection and the roots of social interest. For Individual Psychology,
however, it is an old problem. I may well say that in these two
questions and their solution rests the entire value and the entire
significance of Individual Psychology.

The emphasis on these two questions has never been lacking in our
work, but you, like myself, will probably have felt the need to have the
questions for once treated in a fundamental form, so that we can
avoid the vacillation and uncertainty which we have met occasionally
among our friends, still more often among our opponents. I don't
believe that outside our circle it is very well known what we
understand by striving for perfection. I am obliged to add further
supplements to the knowledge up to now. This knowledge cannot be
comprehended immediately; it cannot be found through an analysis
of the visible phenomena and facts, as, altogether, something new can
never be created through analysis. Here we would have parts in our
hands instead of the whole. To us Individual Psychologists, the whole
tells much more than the analysis of the parts. Also, nothing new can
emerge through synthesis if one simply puts the parts together.

THE STRIVING FOR PERFECTION

Where must we begin with our considerations, if we want to get
beyond the position of what has already been reached? Regarding the
striving for perfection, or as it manifests itself sometimes, the striving
for superiority, or the striving for power which authors of less
understanding sometimes attribute to us, some few have always
known about it. But their knowledge was not so thorough that they
could communicate it to a larger number, or could illuminate the

fundamental significance of this striving for the structure of the entire personality. It took Individual Psychology to point out that every individual is seized by this striving for perfection, that we find it in every individual. It is not at all necessary first to inoculate man with the desire to develop into superman, as the daring attempt of Nietzsche has maintained. Individual Psychology has shown that every individual is seized by the striving for perfection, by the upward striving. He who can read between the lines will have realized that we are continuously aware of the fundamental importance of the striving for perfection. In the consideration of a case of illness we have always uncovered the individual direction of this striving.

And yet one question remains which always returns whenever this problem appears, a question emphasized by friends and opponents, a question which perhaps in our circle as well has not yet been completely clarified. I shall attempt today to bring it nearer to a solution because I have always considered it necessary to create on this point clarity for all.

Part of Evolutionary Principle

Thus I should first of all like to stress that the striving for perfection is innate. However, it is not innate in a concrete way, since we find it again and again in the various individuals in thousandfold variation. It is not innate in the sense of a drive which would later in life be capable of bringing everything to completion and which only needs to unfold itself. Rather, the striving for perfection is innate as something which belongs to life, a striving, an urge, a developing, a something without which one could not even conceive of life.

The scientists, especially the biological scientists, have always stressed this evolutionary principle in the body. Especially since Darwin, Lamarck, and others, it is a matter of course to take the evolutionary thought into account. If we go a step further here and emphasize more strongly what these ingenious researchers envisioned, we want to state: To live means to develop.

The human mind is accustomed to bring all flow into a form, to regard not the movement but the frozen movement, movement which has become form. However, we have always been intent to resolve into movement what we comprehend as form. Thus we must ascertain for the single individual of our time as well as for the development of living creatures in general that to live means to develop. Everyone knows that the complete man originates from an ovular cell. But one should also properly understand that in this ovular cell rest the fundaments for the development.

How life came on this earth is an uncertain matter; possibly we shall never reach a final answer. We could assume that there is life even in inanimate matter, as for example the ingenius attempt of Smuts[3] has done. Such a view becomes quite plausible through modern physics which shows that the electrons move around the proton. Whether this view will be further vindicated, we do not know. But it is certain that our concept of life as development can no longer be doubted. Thereby movement is ascertained at the same time, movement toward self-preservation, procreation, contact with the surrounding world, victorious contact in order not to perish. We must take our point of departure from this path of development, of a continuous active adaptation to the demands of the external world, if we want to understand in which direction life moves.

We must keep in mind that we are dealing here with something primary, something which adhered already to primordial life. It is always a matter of overcoming, of the existence of the individual and the human race, of establishing a favorable relationship between the individual and the surrounding world. *This coercion to carry out a better adaptation can never end.* Herein lies the foundation for our view of the striving for superiority.

Probably much of what I have just discussed seems familiar, and it certainly was also known to others. Individual Psychology has only the one merit, to have established a connection and to have shown which form this force, called life, takes in each single individual and how it prevails. We are in the midst of the stream of evolution but notice it as little as the rotation of the earth. In this cosmic relation, in which the life of the single individual is a part, the striving for *victorious adaptation to the external world is a precondition.* Even if one doubted that the striving for superiority existed already at the beginning of life, the course of the billions of years puts it clearly

3. Smuts, J. C. *Holism and evolution.* New York: Macmillan, 1926.

before us that today the striving for perfection is an innate factor which is present in every man.

Individual Conceptions of Perfection

This consideration may show us something else. None of us knows which is the only correct way to perfection. Mankind has variously made the attempt to imagine this final goal of human development. The best conception gained so far of this ideal elevation of mankind is the concept of God (Jahn and Adler).[4] There is no question but that the concept of God actually includes this movement toward perfection in the form of a goal, and that as a concrete goal of perfection it corresponds best to man's dark longing to reach perfection. Of course, it seems to me that each person imagines his God differently. Thus there are conceptions of God which from the outset are not equal to the principle of perfection. But of the purest formulation of God we can say: Here the concrete formulation of the goal of perfection has been accomplished.

There are, of course, countless attempts among men to imagine this goal of perfection differently. We physicians who deal with failures, with persons who have fallen sick from a neurosis or psychosis, who have become delinquents, alcoholics, etc., we see this goal of superiority in them also, but in another direction, one which contradicts reason in so far as we cannot acknowledge in it a correct goal of perfection. When, for example, someone attempts to concretize this goal by wanting to dominate over others, such a goal of perfection appears to us incapable to steer the individual and the group. The reason is that not every one could make this goal of perfection his task, because he would be forced to come into conflict with the coercion of evolution, to violate reality, and to defend himself full of anxiety against the truth and its confessors. When we find persons who have set themselves as a goal of perfection to lean on others, this goal of perfection also appears to us to contradict reason. When someone perhaps finds the goal of perfection in leaving the tasks of life unsolved in order not to suffer *certain defeats which would be the opposite of the goal of perfection,* this goal also appears to us

4. See Part V.

altogether unsuited, although it appears to many persons as acceptable.

Let us enlarge our prospect and raise the question: What has become of those creatures who posited for themselves an incorrect goal of perfection, whose active adaptation has not succeeded because they took the incorrect path, who did not find the path toward the advancement of all (*Sinn des Lebens* [A1933b])? Here the extinction of species, races, tribes, families, and thousands of individual persons of whom nothing has remained, teaches us how necessary it is for the individual to find a halfway correct path to the goal of some kind of perfection. After all, it is understood in our day and by the individual among us that the goal of perfection gives the direction for the development of his entire personality, for all his expressive movements, his perceiving, his thinking, his feeling, his view of the world. It is equally clear and understandable for every Individual Psychologist that a direction which deviates in a considerable degree from the truth must turn out to the detriment of the one in question, if not to his doom. This being the case, it would be a lucky find if we knew more about the direction which we have to take since we are, after all, embedded in the stream of evolution and must follow it. Here as well, Individual Psychology has performed a great achievement, as it has with the ascertainment of the general striving for perfection. From thousandfold experience it has gained a view which is capable of understanding to some degree the direction toward ideal perfection, through its ascertainment of the norms of *social interest*.

SOCIAL INTEREST

Regarding social interest, you will also have observed certain fluctuations in the Individual Psychology literature, and it is for this reason that I wanted to talk about it. I do not wish to say much about the usual and thoughtless case which is occasionally found within our circle among beginners, and outside our circle—the mistake of understanding what we call community as a private circle of our time, or a larger circle which one should join. Social interest means much more. Particularly it means *feeling with the whole, sub specie aeternitatis,* under the aspect of eternity. It means a striving for a form of community which must be thought of as everlasting, as it could be thought of if mankind had reached the goal of perfection. It is never a present-day community or society, nor a political or religious form. Rather the goal which is best suited for perfection would have to be a goal which signifies the ideal community of all mankind, the ultimate fulfillment of evolution.

Normative Ideal

Of course, one will ask, how do I know this? Certainly not from immediate experience. I must admit that those who find a piece of metaphysics in Individual Psychology are right. Some praise this, other criticize it. Unfortunately, there are many who have an erroneous view of metaphysics, who would like to see everything eliminated from the life of mankind which they cannot comprehend immediately. But by doing so we would interfere with the possibilities of development, prevent every new thought. Every new idea lies beyond immediate experience; immediate experiences never yield anything new. Only a synthesizing idea can do this. Whether you call it speculation or transcendentalism, there is no science which does not have to enter the realm of metaphysics. I see no reason to be afraid of metaphysics; it has had a very great influence on human life and development. We are not blessed with the possession of the absolute truth, and on that account we are compelled to form theories for ourselves about our future, about the results of our actions, etc.

We conceive the idea of social interest, social feeling, as the ultimate form of mankind, a condition in which we imagine all questions of life, all relationship to the external world as solved. It is a normative ideal, a direction-giving goal. This goal of perfection must contain the goal of an ideal community, because everything we find valuable in life, what exists and what will remain, is forever a product of this social feeling.

I want to repeat what I have mentioned in another connection. The newborn child always finds in life only what the others have contributed to life, to welfare, to security. What we find when we enter our life is always the contribution of our forebears. This one fact alone could enlighten us as to how life will move on: We shall approach a condition of larger contributions, of greater ability to cooperate, where every individual presents himself more fully as a part of the whole—a condition for which of course all forms of our societal movement are trials, preliminary trials, and only those will endure which are situated in the direction of this ideal community.

We do not want to judge; only one thing we can say: A movement of the individual or a movement of the masses can for us pass as valuable only if it creates values for eternity, for the higher development of all mankind. Maybe you will understand this fact better if I raise once more the question: What happens to those persons who have contributed nothing? They have disappeared, have become extinct. There you see again how the force of evolution, how this urge to achieve a higher stage physically and mentally, how this urge extinguishes everything which does not go along and contributes nothing.

If one is a friend of formulations, one could say there is a basic law in development which calls to those who are negating: Away with you; you do not understand what counts! Thus duration emphasizes itself, the eternal duration of the contribution of persons who have done something for the common good. Of course we are thoughtful enough not to assume that we have the key for telling in each case exactly what is calculated for eternity and what not. We are convinced that we can err, that only a very exact, objective investigation can decide, often also only the course of events. It is perhaps already a great step that we can avoid what does not contribute to the striving for perfection.

Social Context

I could talk more about this and show how all our functions are calculated not to disturb the community of man, to connect the individual with the community. To see means to receive, to make fertile that which falls on the retina. This is not only a physiological process; it shows the person as part of the whole, who takes and gives. In seeing, hearing, speaking we connect ourselves with the others. Thus all functions of our organs are correctly developed only if they are not detrimental to the social interest.

We speak of virtue, and mean that one participates in the game; of vice, and mean that one disturbs cooperation. I could also point out how everything which signifies a failure is a failure because it disturbs the development of the community, whether we are dealing with problem children, neurotics, criminals, or cases of suicide. In all cases you see that the contribution is lacking.

In the entire history of mankind you will find no isolated persons. The development of mankind was possible only because mankind was a community and in striving for perfection strove for an ideal community. All movements, all functions of a person express whether or not he has found this direction in the stream of evolution which is characterized by the community ideal. The reason is that man is inviolably guided by the community ideal. He becomes impeded, punished, praised, and advanced by it, so that each individual becomes not only responsible for each deviation but must also suffer for it. This is a hard law, virtually a cruel law. Those who have already developed in themselves a strong social feeling constantly endeavour to ameliorate the hardships of anyone who proceeds erroneously. They do this as if they knew that here is a man who has missed the way for reasons which only Individual Psychology is able to demonstrate. If a man understood how he erred, stepping out of the way of evolution, he would leave this course and join general humanity.

Innate Substratum

Finally, I should like to submit a thought which has much in its favor and which I should like you to consider. If you agree with my arguments, you will have to raise the question: Is social interest innate or must one bring it to man? Of course it is also innate, like the striving for perfection, except that it must be developed and can be developed only when the child is already in the midst of life.

Like the character traits which depend on it, social interest can come to life only in the social context. By social context, of course, is meant the child's subjective understanding of the same. The decision [as to how he will interpret the essentially ambiguous social context] rests in the creative power of the child, which, however, is guided by the environment and educational measures, and influenced by the experience and evaluation of his body.[5] At the present stage of

5. By "experience and evaluation of his body," Adler means that the child is not directly influenced by his physique but by how he subjectively experiences and evaluates it. Thus a beautiful girl who feels that boys are attracted by her beauty rather than by her brains (for which she would like to be admired) will evaluate her beauty negatively.

mankind's psychological and possibly also physical development, we must consider the innate substratum of the social interest as too small, as not strong enough, to become effective or to develop without the benefit of social understanding. This is in contrast to abilities and functions which succeed almost all on their own, such as breathing. But with social interest we are far from having reached this stage. We have not developed it to the same extent as breathing. And yet we must expect the development of social interest so strongly in the ultimate goal of perfection that mankind of the future will possess and activate it like breathing.

CONCLUSION

What we have to do in the present critical state follows automatically. Unquestionably this consideration gives us a certain and firm foundation not only for the evaluation of a person and for the education of a child but also for the improvement and guidance of one who has gone astray. But this succeeds only through explanation and understanding. We must talk about it, because we are not certain whether every child and every adult knows where the way leads. This is why one must talk about it so long until perhaps in the course of thousands of years talking also will have become superfluous, as perhaps it has today become superfluous to talk about correct breathing.

The talking about social interest as belonging to the evolution of man, as a part of human life, and the awakening of the corresponding understanding is today being attended to by Individual Psychology. This is its fundamental significance, its claim to existence, and this is what represents its strength. Today everybody speaks about community and community feeling. We were not the very first, but we are the first to have strongly emphasized the basic nature of the social feelings.

The concept of community and community feeling can also be abused. But one who has properly understood knows that in the nature of community and community feeling rests an evolutionary factor which turns against everything which resists this direction. He will be able to avoid the abuse of the concept of the community or to let himself be abused by others in its name.

This represents the practical value and the significance of Individual

Psychology: It has clarified the fundamental significance of social interest for the development, the higher development, of the individual and of the whole of mankind.

SUMMARY

Individual Psychology has shown that the striving for superiority and perfection is not limited to the characterization of *certain* individuals, nor is it *brought to them from the outside*; rather, it is given to *every* person and must be understood as *innate*, as a *necessary and general foundation of the development of every person.*

The originators of the concept of evolution in the field of general organic life, such as Darwin and Lamarck, have pointed out that life must be understood as *movement toward a goal*, and that this goal—the preservation of the individual and the species—is attained through the overcoming of resistances with which the environment confronts the organism. Thus *mastery of the environment* appears to be inseparably connected with the concept of evolution. If this striving were not innate to the organism, no form of life could preserve itself.

The goal of mastering the environment in a superior way, which one can call the striving for perfection, consequently also characterizes the development of man. It is expressed most clearly in the concept of God. In the individual case, however, the striving for superiority takes on very different concrete forms. Typical is, e.g., the striving *to master one's fellow man.* Exactly this form was shown by Individual Psychology to be erroneous, contradicting the concept of evolution. Individual Psychology has uncovered the fact that the deviations and failures of the human character—neurosis, psychosis, crime, drug addiction etc.—are nothing but forms of expression and symptoms of the striving for superiority directed against fellowmanship,[6] which presents itself in one case as striving for power, in another case as an evasion of accomplishments by which another might benefit. Such erroneous striving leads to the psychological decline and fall of the individual, as any biological erroneous striving has led to the physical decline and fall of entire species and races.

6. The German original for fellowmanship is *Mitmenschlichkeit*, meaning "being a fellow man," as well as "co-humaneness."

Individual Psychology has found a special formula for the correct striving for perfection of man: The goal which the individual must pursue must lie in the direction which leads to the perfection of *all of mankind sub specie aeternitatis.* "Virtue" means advancement, "vice" means disturbance of the common work which aims at perfection. Never can the individual be the goal of the ideal of perfection, but only mankind as a *cooperating community.* A *partial community* of any kind—perhaps groups that are associated through certain political, religious, or other ideals—is also not sufficient. Neither do we mean the *existing* society, but an *ideal* society yet to be developed, which comprises *all* men, all filled by the common striving for perfection.

This is how the Individual Psychology concept of social interest (*Gemeinschaftsgefühl*) is to be understood. This is to be considered as *innate*—"innate" also in the categorical (metaphysical) sense, namely as the necessary and general premise for human cultural development. Every human being brings the disposition for social interest with him; but then it must be *developed* through *upbringing,* especially through correct guidance of the *creative power* of the individual. We can assume that the innate substratum of the ability to cooperate will become increasingly stronger through the training of the generations.

An important aid in this training is that the individual become *conscious* of the importance of social interest as the form of the striving for perfection which is appropriate for man. Exactly in this work of information rests the foremost practical task of Individual Psychology.

3

Brief Comments on Reason, Intelligence, and Feeble-Mindedness (1928)[1]

Gemeinschaftsgefühl, probably Adler's most significant concept, has offered difficulty not only to translation but also to understanding. The most general translation today is *social interest*, followed by *social feeling*. As to its meaning, the previous paper has shown that social interest gives direction to the striving for superiority and perfection. It must certainly not be understood as an altruistic motivational force which would counterbalance egoistic urges. This would violate the principle of unitary motivation required by a holistic theory. Social interest acquires motivational properties only secondarily.

In the present paper Adler describes social interest more clearly than on any other occasion. It becomes practically equated with identification and empathy, both cognitive functions. Its primary cognitive nature becomes most evident from its tendency to combine with intelligence, changing the latter from "private intelligence" to reason or "common sense."   —Eds.

1. Original translation of A1928f, with some rearrangements.

To be sure, one can disagree on terminology and one can introduce other names, but what I should like to emphasize is a fundamental difference that I have increasingly noted between two abilities, namely, between reason and [mere] intelligence. The question has, of course, been approached from various sides before, but from our viewpoint one may perhaps gain a deeper insight.

SOCIAL INTEREST, IDENTIFICATION, EMPATHY

We must understand by reason a *generally valid* category which is altogether related to *social interest*. It seems necessary that we clarify this conception of reason more and more, and formulate it more precisely.

Our conception of social interest or feeling differs from that of other authors. When we say it is a feeling, we are certainly justified in doing so. But it is more than this, it is a form of life (*Lebensform*). It is a quite different form of life from what we find in persons whom we call antisocial. This is not to be understood as only a superficial life form, as if it were only the expression of a mechanically acquired form of life. It is much more. I am not in the position to define it quite unequivocally, but I have found in an English author a phrase which expresses clearly what could contribute to our explanation: "To see with the eyes of another, to hear with the ears of another, to feel with the heart of another." For the time being this seems to me an admissible definition of what we call social feeling. We see at first glance that this gift coincides in part with another which we call identification or empathy (Lipps). This identification occurs always according to the degree of social interest.

The term "identification" has different meanings. With Individual Psychology it has one meaning, with Freud another. When a child aims to become like his father, wants to see with the eyes of the father, etc., "understands" him, and has a useful goal before his eyes, we call this identification. Freud unknowingly comprehends this concept as usurping the role of another in order to arrive at a "personal" advantage.

Identification is absolutely necessary in order to arrive at a social life. Sympathy is merely a partial expression of identification which, in turn, is one aspect of social interest. We can understand only if we identify, and so reason appears as a social ability. We identify with a picture by regarding it. We identify also with all other inanimate objects. E.g., in playing pool or bowling, the player follows the ball with his eyes and makes the movement which he hopes the ball will make. In the theatre every spectator empathizes and participates. This is identification in our sense—not to usurp the role of the father. Empathy plays an enormous role in dreams, also in the group mind.

Herder, Novalis, and Jean Paul were acquainted with the process of empathy, described it, and considered it important. Later Wundt, Volkelt, and especially Lipps stressed empathy as a fundamental fact of our experience. Lipps, Dilthey, Müller-Freienfels, and others described the relationship of empathy and understanding. Individual Psychology may claim as its contribution to have pointed out that empathy and understanding are facts of social feeling, of being in harmony with the universe.

REASON, COMMON SENSE

The ability to identify must be trained. This can be done only if a person grows up in a connection with others and feels himself a part of the whole. He must sense that not only the comforts of life belong to him, but also its discomforts. He must feel at home on this earth with all its advantages and disadvantages. This feeling at home is directly a part of social interest. His life on this poor earthcrust takes its course "as if he were at home." Thus there arises for him a quite specific form of life in which he regards the adversities of life not as an injustice inflicted upon him. Here we see that the fact of fellowship is added to social interest. We shall also find in this life form all other forces which serve to overcome the adversities of life. Thus he is a part of the whole who proves himself in correspondence with the community and useful to it.

All this taken together is a way of acting and behaving which we designate as "reasonable." Reasonable is what one understands by "common sense." [2] Incidentally the common sense is not unchange-

wwwwwwwwww

2. The English phrase "common sense" is used in the German original.

able, but is the meaning of all forms of expression, the content of all behavior which we find advances the community. With this view we also come closer to the understanding of what we call reason.

Thus we arrive at Kant's conclusion: Reason has general validity. This would mean at the same time that we comprehend under reason all actions, behaviors, and forms of expression which depend on a goal of superiority in which the common welfare finds expression. This goal would have to be present.

Intelligence is the broader concept. Reason is that intelligence in which social interest is contained, which accordingly is limited to the side of the generally useful.

In psychotherapy we are occupied mainly with persons who have a goal of *personal* superiority and in this way transgress the borders which in the course of the cultural development of mankind have come to signify the common sense.

In the common sense we shall continuously find new turns. I do not know if Socrates was the first who regarded a coat full of holes no longer as a sign of humility but of vanity. However, assuming he was the first, he did thereby enrich the common sense. He showed that a thing can be its own opposite and that we can comprehend the meaning of an expressive movement only from its context. I wanted to show by this that the common sense can change. It is not something fixed; it is the sum of all recognized psychological movements which are in accord with reason, are generally recognized, and are connected with the continuance of the culture.

PRIVATE INTELLIGENCE

We now want to consider intelligence as we find it in neurotics. The neurotic acts completely correctly. He acts so correctly that, as in compulsion neurosis, he notices and states the difference between his personal intelligence and the common sense.[2a] Whatever he does is

2a. Here Adler apparently followed Kant, who had stated: "The only character-istic common to all mental disorders is the loss of common sense (*sensus communis*), and the development instead of a unique, private sense (*sensus privatus*)."

(Ansbacher, H. L. "Sensus privatus versus sensus communis." *J. Indiv. Psychol.*, 1965, 21, 48–50).

"intelligent." But this fact of "personal intelligence" must be further elaborated. A criminal says: "I killed him because he was a Jew." This man has the notion that as a Christian he possesses a certain superiority and therefore may dispose freely of those of another creed, e.g., over a despised Jew. His goal is to take possession of the property of this Jew. He acts according to this goal. "Intelligence" will facilitate his way, will bring him closer to his goal, as we see it clearly in problem children. Since his goal, which is to rob, is fixed, he uses arguments which facilitate reaching this goal. This facilitation actually sets in.

Another robber-murderer expresses himself similarly. "This young man had beautiful suits and I had none. That is why I killed him." This is quite intelligent thinking and acting. Since he is not confident that he is able to acquire suits in the *generally usual manner,* on the generally useful side of life, he can in fact attain beautiful suits only by robbing. To do this he must kill the other person.

Thus we find in all criminals the attempt through some "intelligent" arguments to come closer to their goal. With cases of suicide we can make similar observations. After long training these individuals dismiss any interest in life; they are permeated by the idea of arousing general attention by their suicide and, like the murderer, of having an elation of superiority. ("I have done something not everybody could do. Formerly nobody paid any attention to me, but now . . .") Being master over life and death brings them near to God, as it does the murderer who disposes over the life of others. They will always find arguments which are completely "intelligent"; since they want to kill themselves, they argue, nothing is of interest to them. They will always find arguments by which they reach their goal, deceive themselves, poison themselves. These arguments are "intelligent" in respect to the goal of personal superiority on the useless side of life.

This private intelligence is to be sharply differentiated from what one must call reason, common sense. We find "intelligence" in both cases, but we call reason only the kind of intelligence which is connected with social interest.

If we regard the alcoholic we find, unless it is a case of feeble-mindedness, that he also argues intelligently: Life brings worries, but there are means by which one can surmount its difficulties. Thus his action is intelligent in regard to the goal, which is to surmount difficulties in an easy, personal manner, not to solve them in the sense of the community. Anyone who agreed with this goal would act like the alcoholic.

The same holds true in perversions. When, for reasons we know from Individual Psychology, a male homosexual excludes a part of humanity he will attempt to pursue the goal which he has set for himself with logic and intelligence. He will always judge intelligently, he will always cite such considerations by which he justifies himself. In the question of love he has a goal on the useless side; but corresponding to this goal he will judge and act absolutely correctly.

The basic idea is that we must make a sharp distinction between reason, which has general validity, which *therefore* corresponds to the common welfare, and the isolated intelligence of the neurotic ("all or nothing," wanting to have the successful result at the beginning, etc.), in short, the intelligence of the failures with whom we are always occupied.

FEEBLE-MINDEDNESS

In this manner one should arrive at a significant differentiation between the feeble-minded and normally thinking persons. In the feeble-minded the above "intelligent" arguments directed toward a goal of superiority appear to be lacking, so that the thinking shows a certain disregard for logic.

Feeble-mindedness is not [only] a lower form of intelligence, but a different form of thinking. Pure feeble-mindedness is cold towards the demands of reason and abides by them at best through force. [But in addition,] the shaping of a life style is lacking, which is never so in the reasonable and intelligent person. The feeble-minded has no life style; his forms of life are wholly removed from the understanding of any connection. Also, we miss the respect for the common sense, which [even] in the cases of private intelligence still plays a part, namely, in the form of excuses, justifications, comparisons, etc.

The feeble-minded does not arrive at the formation of a life plan. In his case, when we place him in a new situation we cannot guess what he will do, aside from mechanical movements, because he lacks planned procedure. With the really feeble-minded one cannot identify. He is characterized by coldness and lack of respect for reason. He is not subject to the laws of the common sense nor does he have the intelligence which expresses itself in a goal of personal superiority.

In pseudofeeble-mindedness, on the other hand, an ideal goal can be found with which another can identify. The styled, self-consistent aspect of a life style is found, although on the useless side, in paranoia. A decidedly intelligent although not reasonable chain of thought is found in melancholia; the patient experiences in a fiction the elevation of his self-esteem. I have been able to observe that catatonics play the *role* of a doll, a dead person, a hero, etc. But one cannot empathize with the sequence of thought of a feeble-minded person; at best one can guess at it from without.

CONCLUDING STATEMENTS

We call virtuous, wise, reasonable, valuable only that which takes place on the side of general usefulness. Our judgment is also guided in this manner and every person in his full senses distinguishes approximately according to the same classification principle. Even one who moves on the useless side of life, such as a problem child, neurotic, criminal, suicide, alcoholic, pervert, etc., will be aware of the difference, will be able to distinguish between good and bad, and will attempt to defend his own work against [reproaches from] reason and from virtue. But he will continue on his useless path as long as he has not separated himself from his ideal goal of a personal superiority, useless for the community. He will separate himself from it only when he has comprehended the principle of reason with his private intelligence; i.e., when he has recognized the erroneous prototype from his childhood, his increased inferiority feeling, his striving for personal superiority, and the significance of social interest for the development of courage, reason, and feeling of worth.

Thus we shall find in all problem persons, in so far as we can exclude feeble-mindedness, that all partial movements are "intelligent," but that their goal of personal power striving has miscarried. They will strike us as abnormal because they contradict reason, "which joins us all," [3] and the common sense. But they will always be correctly integrated in a system on the useless side of life. Therefore they will also be lacking the degree of a developed social interest and the courage which are required for the useful solution of the problems of life.

Here are some examples:

1. A child who feels displaced from his pampered situation by a younger sibling will usually pursue a goal to regain the center of attention and will, in a belligerent attitude, disturb the order of the house. According to his goal he acts intelligently, but according to the demand of the community, unreasonably.

2. An anxiety neurotic who from childhood on has used his anxiety as a means to draw another into his service, to "prescribe to him the laws of his action," acts intelligently, but not in accordance with the common sense.

3. A murderer who slays someone for the sake of his possessions, i.e., who lacks courage to attain money in a generally useful manner, acts intelligently in accordance with his goal of enriching himself in an easy way, but cowardly and unreasonably because the better way can never be excluded.

4. A suicide who considers himself too weak to overcome his personal difficulties and therefore (in revenge) rejects everything with one fell swoop in order to escape the feeling of his inferiority, acts intelligently according to his goal of coping with the difficulties of life through a trick, but cowardly, unreasonably, and harmfully to the community.

5. A pervert who excludes the form which furthers the community and pays homage enthusiastically to the shabby remainder, has by this trick escaped the complications of normal love life by safeguarding himself from it in intelligent fashion, but in doing so shows neither common sense nor courage nor social interest.

6. Alcoholics, morphine addicts, etc. have brought their detouring

---

3. The German original, *"die uns alle bindet,"* being in quotation marks, is most likely an adaptation of a phrase from Schiller's poem *"Das Lied von der Glocke,"* reading, *"die das Gleiche . . . bindet."* This occurs in the passage, "Divine Order . . . who joins equals in a voluntary, easy and joyful association . . . !" (Forster, L. [Ed.] *The Penguin book of German verse.* Harmondsworth, Middlesex: Penguin Books, 1957, p. 273.)

before the difficulties of life into an intelligent system, but only by eliminating courage and reason which they render ineffective through stupor.

7. In all forms of pure psychosis (schizophrenia, melancholia, manic-depressive insanity, paranoia) one finds on closer examination an intelligent system, but the exclusion of reason.

Individual Psychology is also in a position to understand feeble-mindedness in the sense that its structure discloses neither intelligence nor reason to any notable extent.

4

Advantages and Disadvantages of the Inferiority Feeling (1933)[1]

From his earlier writings the impression has been gained that for Adler the dynamic force of striving for superiority originated in inferiority feelings and represented the effort to compensate for such feelings. The inferiority feeling would be primary, the striving secondary. But such theory would be parallel in construction to drive-reduction theory, which is today increasingly discredited, and to deficiency motivation (Maslow).

Actually, over the years inferiority feeling and compensation lost their primary importance for Adler. In the three preceding papers, dealing with human dynamics, they are barely mentioned.

When, in 1933, Adler did write about inferiority feeling, he clearly implied that it is to be understood as secondary to the striving. The individual is first described at length as finalistically oriented toward a goal of perfection, security, completion, as striving for overcoming and superiority. It is only against this background that the individual experiences a "minus situation," which is reflected in "the feeling of incompletion, of insecurity, of inferiority." It is noteworthy that even among these secondary "moods," inferiority feeling is given only the last place. —Eds.

1. Original translation of A1933l.

There has always been in the air the tendency to assume the unity of human psychological life, or at least to regard it as if it were a unity (Kant). Even the latest findings of modern psychology (psycho-analysis and Gestalt psychology) did not get far beyond this assumption which rested in theory, although I had brought empirical proof for it in Individual Psychology from the start. Perhaps other researchers became frightened by the presentation of the inviolability of this unity, which I have carried out again and again. I am sure that their methods or their researches, which were often tied only to theory, were inadequate. Also, certain of the general misconceptions stood in the way of a clearer insight, such as that of the split consciousness, the contrast between the "conscious" and the "unconscious."

THE GOAL OF PERFECTION

I myself took the decisive step only with hesitation and armed myself with the greatest skepticism until I was forced to make the following statements, due to the overwhelming proof supporting them, and because of recurring contradictions in the other conceptions:

1. Every individual has from earliest childhood on his own, unique law of movement, which dominates all his functions and expressive movements and gives them direction.

2. The law of movement and its direction originate from the creative life power of the individual, and use, in free choice, one's experiences of one's body and of external effects, within the limits of human capacity.

3. The direction of the psychological movement aims always at an overcoming of difficulties of all kinds, in millions of variations. Thus it has a goal of perfection, security, completion, always in the meaning and opinion of the individual. Meaning and opinion are almost never represented in thoughts or concepts, and are formed, as in creatures without language, usually in a phase of the child's life in which language and concepts are still lacking or deficient.

4. All tasks which are put to the individual are social problems, for which the family is the exercise and training ground.

Movement, the basic law of all life, and consequently also of psychological life, cannot be thought of without goal and direction. The attempt to construct a psychology from drives is a radical mistake because a drive is without direction. Thus I arrived at the finalistic foundation of Individual Psychology which in several points comes into contact with the finalistically oriented modern biology and physics.

Anyone who wants to understand Individual Psychology correctly must orient himself by its clarification of the unitary purposefulness of thinking, feeling, willing, and acting of the unique individual. He then will recognize how the stand an individual takes and the life style, which is like an artistic creation, are the same in all situations of life, unalterable until the end—unless the individual recognizes what is erroneous, incorrect, or abnormal with regard to cooperation, and attempts to correct it. This becomes possible only when he has comprehended his errors conceptually and subjected them to the critique of practical reason, the common sense [2]—in other words, through convincing discussion.

Since psychological movement without direction and goal is unthinkable and could not be carried out, the behavior of the entire great life movement, as well as each part of a movement, is a striving from incompletion to completion. Accordingly, the entire individual life line has the tendency toward overcoming, a striving for superiority. This is due also to reasons of biological evolution, but particularly to oppressive feelings of tension arising from an incompletion.

This striving is communicated to every smallest movement impulse, takes place without words and concepts, and occupies the entire individual creative power of a person. But the goal of overcoming varies in millions of ways and receives its permanent structure from the creative use of innate living material and of environmental influences, among which conscious and unconscious education constitute the greatest part. Once completed in early childhood, the goal and the law of movement of the parts, which depends on the goal, determine the attitude and stand taken by a person.

~~~~~~~~~~~~~~~

2. The English phrase "common sense" is used in the German original.

Individual Psychology measures by the criterion of the never-attained ideal of the fellow man whose law of movement is prescribed by the welfare and perfection of mankind. Accordingly, we observe the individual's distance from the correct, reasonable, generally human solution of a life problem, in order at the same time to raise the question of why he does not bring about a normal solution.

This last question brings us back to a consideration of the earliest psychological development in which the errors in the development of the ability to cooperate and of the social feeling can be recognized. The resulting persistent deficiencies of the life style lead to failure because the problems of life are of a social nature (in society, occupation, love) and inexorably demand social interest[3] for their successful solution. Among the failures we find difficult children, neurotics, psychotics, suicides, criminals, prostitutes, alcoholics, sexual perverts, etc. They are all characterized by lack of social feeling, which also hinders the social preparation in the right thinking, feeling, and acting. Just as this lack of social interest[3] shows itself in the entire life style, it also naturally shows itself in the goal of superiority, which is no longer within the frame of social acceptability but merely promotes a feeling of personal satisfaction without contributing to the welfare of the general community, and is rather likely to disturb it.

INFERIORITY FEELING

As the central motive in this field of forces the feeling of incompletion, of insecurity, of inferiority, is always to be found.[4] The minus situation is at the basis of any psychological form of expression. Guided by the individual goal of completion, it gives the impetus to progression, just as it arises from the helplessness and imperfection of

---

3. Here the German original is actually *soziales Interesse*, not *Gemeinschaftsgefühl*.

4. Here, where incompletion, insecurity, and inferiority are used synonymously, we should like to recall that in *The Neurotic Constitution* Adler recognized his own concept as an extension of Pierre Janet's "feeling of incompletion." "Janet's emphasis of the neurotic's 'sentiment d'incomplètude' . . . is so wholly in harmony with the results offered by me that I am justified in seeing in my work an extension of this most important fundamental fact of the mental life of the neurotic" (A1917a, p. vi).

childhood, and as it has forced all mankind to seek from out of its needs a security-giving culture.

Through its understanding of the uniqueness of each individual, Individual Psychology is sufficiently protected from submitting to the spell of rules and formulas. When it claims that the experience of increased pressure in childhood increases the inferiority feeling and thus disturbs the opportunity to accomplish a far-reaching social interest—as in cases of inferior organs, in pampering and dependency, but also in neglect—this statistical knowledge may be used only to illuminate the field in which the individual case in all its entanglements must be sought.

Positive outcomes. Disregarding such ideal forms as fantasy attributes to a god or a saint, we may derive the following guiding viewpoint, confirmed by experience: The greater the trained social interest acquired in childhood, i.e., the degree of readiness for cooperation, for joining in love, and for fellowmanship, the higher and more valuable the accomplishments to be expected from the mood of the inferiority feeling. Thoughts, feelings, and actions will always be found on the level accorded to the general welfare. Whether or not the man of genius or the everyday fellow man knows this, or even contradicts this view, his accomplishments give him temporarily or permanently a high feeling of value which is identical to the experience of happiness.[5]

In the end all great accomplishments stem from the blessed struggle with the needs of childhood—be they organ inferiorities, pampering, or oppressing circumstances—as long as the child, at the time of his oppression, has already learned the active adaptation to cooperation. Then, and also later on, in the face of all difficulties and torments, only the paths to cooperation will be open in accordance with his inviolable law of movement.[6]

vvvvvvvvvvvvvv

5. Here is one of the few times that Adler speaks of happiness.

6. Elsewhere Adler expressed himself as follows on this point: "To be a human being means to have inferiority feelings. One recognizes one's own power-lessness in the face of nature. One sees death as the irrefutable consequence of existence. But in the mentally healthy person this inferiority feeling acts as a motive for productivity, as a motive for attempting to overcome obstacles, to maintain oneself in life. Only the oversized inferiority feeling, which is to be regarded as the outcome of a failure in upbringing, burdens the character with oversensitivity, leads to egotistical self-considerations and self-reflections, lays the

Negative outcomes. It is understandable that with most persons social interest (see n. 3) does not have this ideal capacity. Probably there is for everyone a test situation which is so heavy and unbearable that his degree of ability to cooperate is no longer sufficient. Also, vulnerability in the face of the various problems of life differs with each person; some answer incorrectly, contrary to social interest, more easily when it is a matter of the interest of others in social life, some when it is a matter of occupation or love. But it is always a failure in a certain situation which gives us the opportunity for appraising the lower degree of the existing social interest. As long as there is no test, we are not in a position to make a definite statement about this; but after the test, the person who has failed it appears totally left to his inferiority feeling.

The psychological tension which takes hold of the individual here leads to those physical and psychological forms of expression which I have described as the inferiority complex (*Minderwertigkeitskomplex,* "Minko" for short, in the language of German students). Stage fright, stuttering, crying, complaining, fear, etc., are his simple implementations which are easily understood and are almost always joined by changes in the physical condition such as palpitations of the heart, becoming pale, blushing, shortage of breath, stomach and intestinal complaints, urge to urinate, sexual excitations, headache, insomnia, fatigue, etc.

But the goal of overcoming has therewith not at all been lost. All these phenomena, by virtue of the social structure of our life, automatically give rise to a feeling of satisfaction which is usually not understood. They appeal to the sympathy and help of others, or produce a feeling of superiority, thus covering up the inferiority feeling, somewhat in the sense of: "What would I have accomplished, if I were not forced to suffer from this disturbance for which not I, but my heredity, my education, the others are responsible."

wwwwwwwwwwwwwwwwwwwwwwwwwwwwwwwwwwwwwwwwwwwwwwwwwwwwwwwwwwwwwwwwwwwwww

foundation for neurosis with all its known symptoms which let life become a torture" (A1928l).

The third sentence is especially noteworthy. It reads in the German original: "*Man sieht den Tod als unabweisliche Konsequenz des Daseins.*" While Adler has been recognized as a forerunner of existential psychology (see Introd., pages 7–9), this is the only instance known to us where he actually uses existentialistic terms, speaking of the realization that death is part of human existence.

What we have characterized above as persons who are failures shows more clearly the search to cover up the inferiority feeling with a fictive superiority complex, which is no more than the exploitation of the social interest of others. The difficult child moves wholly in these paths and enjoys his superiority over persons who have a feeling of responsibility. The nervous person dictates to his environment the rules of its conduct and more or less limits his cooperation. The insane person rids himself of all cooperation and indulges in his grandiose or depressing fantasies. The suicide rejects all cooperation and meets those close to him as a sad victor. The addict secures for himself artificially feelings of pleasure of a self-seeking kind which are supposed to cover up his lack of self-confidence. The criminal feels himself as victor over his victims and the laws of the community—a community which must not be considered in the present or past, but as an ideal community which can never be quite reached, although it is set as a goal. The sexual pervert aims at personal pleasure as the only admissible compensation for his inferiority feeling thereby excluding the bond of happiness between two beings which ultimately is the way to the preservation of the human species.

All failures who are striving for a goal of personal satisfaction which is far from proving useful, are lacking in courage to cooperate. Instead one finds, as the expression and effect of the inferiority feeling and for the purpose of covering it up and assuaging it, anxiety aimed at using the social interest of others. One finds also excitations and vibrations of the psychological and physical apparatus as in the neuroses and psychoses, and tricks and cunning to slink away from the path of social interest and yet to enjoy a shallow triumph over others.

EXAMPLES

A few examples which are somewhat difficult to understand may illustrate the pseudo-triumph over one's own inferiority feeling.

A 15-year-old girl considers herself as unfairly treated since childhood, in comparison with her siblings. She creates her law of movement in accordance with her opinion that what counts in life is warmth and being pampered. She succeeds in having a favored position in school until a new teacher quite unjustly treats her with special disfavor. Now the inferiority feeling which has rested in her since childhood presses toward new satisfaction in the direction of warmth and pampering. Since home and school are closed to her, where else can she come closer to her goal than by way of being pampered by men? She succumbs to a loose way of life, but soon notices that this also does not give her the warmth which alone she craves. What remains for her since no way any longer secures her goal of being pampered? Suicide—from which, however, she remains spared through a kindly discussion with her mother, who forgives the girl even for having thrown her to the floor. Cure occurs through a change in the life goal: Not warmth at any price, but recognition and enhancement of her own feeling of worth through courageous, patient cooperation which even in the event of a defeat must not be interrupted.

An older girl from a religious family has suffered since childhood under the pressure of a generally popular, outstanding younger brother. Her fiancé breaks off their relationship for flimsy reasons. From this time on thoughts arise in her of being able to condemn to hell persons who are disagreeable to her. Now she has secretly far surpassed her brother. Frightened by this enormous superiority which is bestowed upon her, she now seeks to get rid of her sinfulness by freeing the condemned from hell through prayers—a new proof of her superiority. The cure occurs through stronger fitting into the community.

A burglar enters the room of a teacher who is asleep, and robs her of her few belongings. The teacher wakes up, sees the strong young fellow in her room, reproaches him for carrying away the last belongings from a hardworking person, and demands an answer as to why he, such a strong fellow, would not rather look for some honest work. The fellow replies: "My mother brought me up for something better." And then, "Do you know the terrible conditions of physical labor?" Here we have, together with the pampering from his mother, exploitation of the cooperation of others, fear of and escape from his own cooperation, and triumph over a sleeping victim—all processes far removed from social interest and its preparation.

If one has sufficiently sharpened his grasp for the connections within the unity of each individual, one will easily understand how the inferiority feeling presses constantly towards its own resolution. The value and significance of this resolution rest totally in the existence and the degree of social interest which at times more strongly, at times less so, determines the fate, the failure, or the possibility for happiness of a person.

5

The Forms of
Psychological Activity
(1933)[1]

The physicist describes movement in terms of (a) space or direction; and (b) time or speed, which depends on energy. Adler conceived of human life as movement. He described it as taking place in social space and deriving its direction in this space from the degree of developed social interest. This took care of the first part of a full description of movement. The present paper fills in the second part, the time or energy factor, which is herein called "degree of activity."

Such a conception is quite operational. However, the operationalism is modified by "subjective," phenomenological considerations: The individual "experiences all . . . factors . . . according to his individual meaning."

Adler's combination of operationalism and phenomenology results in a pragmatism which is also expressed in this paper, through the Bible quotation: "By their fruits ye shall know them."   —Eds.

Individual Psychology endeavors to obtain an idea of an individual as a whole from his attitude to the problems of life, problems which are

1. Original translation of A1933k, reprinted as A1934g.

always social in nature. In doing so it emphasizes among other important facts particularly the degree of activity with which the individual tackles his problems. Some time ago I explained such facts as the hesitating attitude, self-blockade, detours, narrowed attack, sudden spurts with subsequent sluggishness, and the jumping from one task to another as typical forms of failure [2] when the ability to cooperate is reduced. I also noted that each of these erroneous gaits in their thousandfold variations shows a lesser or greater degree of activity. This varying degree of activity is produced by the personality in earliest childhood with a certain arbitrariness, wherein, however, hereditary and environmental factors play a part, certainly not causally, but in the sense of a probability.

Individual Psychology is also in the position to observe that the degree of activity acquired in childhood remains constant for the rest of life. We have also clearly pointed out that this fact remains, although in many cases the constant degree becomes only conditionally apparent, e.g., when the individual is in favorable or unfavorable situations.

Although it is probably not possible to express the degree of activity in quantitative terms, it is obvious that a child who runs away from his parents, or a boy who starts a fight in the street, must be credited with a higher degree of activity than a child who likes to sit at home and read a book.

I must emphasize that activity should not be confused with courage, although there is no courage without activity. But only the activity of an individual who plays the game, cooperates, and shares in life can be designated as courage. When courage has been observed, one should not forget the numerous variations and mixed cases, as well as those persons in whom courage appears only conditionally, e.g., in an extreme emergency or with the help of others.

Anyone who has become convinced of the constancy of the degree of activity, corresponding entirely to the constancy of the individual law of movement, i.e. the style of life, will give the greatest attention

2. Adler generally uses the term failure (*Fehlschlag*) in the sense of an individual who can be considered a failure in life, such as the neurotic, psychotic, criminal, alcoholic, problem child, suicide, pervert, prostitute. Sometimes, however, the same term is used in the sense of a specific condition of failing.

to observing that individual degree of activity. The appreciation of this problem opens an entirely new and valuable perspective for psychiatric treatment, education, and prophylaxis. For our observation shows that from the smallest traits and expressive movements of childhood we can predict the degree of activity with which this child will some day later face the problems of life.

Although valuable, such a perspective would be practically incomplete unless we connected it with a further observation of Individual Psychology, the constancy of social interest in a given case, which is also proven. Only the combination of both, in which the degree of ability to cooperate gives the direction, permits us to predict if there is the danger of a failure and what kind of failure it would be.

But one must keep in mind that a failure becomes apparent only in the face of a difficult problem; quite generally speaking, on the occasion of an exogenous difficulty under unfavorable conditions. There are a great many such unfavorable conditions. But one may not use an objective measure, and one must be aware of the frequent erroneous overestimation of difficulty. Quite generally, tasks of all kinds appear more difficult to the person who has the greater inferiority feeling.

To this must be added the fact that each individual form of life is incompatible with tasks which contradict the aspired *goal of perfection*. If the life style of an individual is more or less oriented toward the goal of being under all circumstances the first, insurmountable situations will be automatically excluded, and this exclusion will always be affectively toned. If, in another case, the goal of superiority is sought in the depreciation of others, then the life space will correspond to this constant irrefutable demand. If someone always aims only to avoid the disclosure of his presumed worthlessness, then he will arrange his thoughts, feelings, and attitudes so as to leave all problems unsolved, in order thus to have at least the appearance and possibility of a superiority in reserve. If one is a real co-worker, this will become the guiding line of his life and will permeate the approach to all tasks.

In all these cases, with their millions of variations, a uniform kind of activity can always be observed. As a rule, one will be able to perceive the degree of activity also from the extent of the sphere of activity, which is different for each individual. It would be a tempting task for a psychologist to show graphically the extent and form of the individual life space.

ACTIVITY IN VARIOUS KINDS OF FAILURE

In this paper I wish to present only that part of my investigations and findings which refers to the constancy and identity of the degree of activity of failures and their childhood. Here I must start with the traditional conception of types of failure, although I can qualify all failures only as symptoms of a deficient social interest. And I must add that each single case within the typical group shows qualitative and quantitative differences as far as his activity is concerned.

An exact knowledge of the structure of each typical case of failure is a necessary prerequisite for such an investigation. This knowledge serves Individual Psychology to illuminate the field on which we expect to find the individual case. I wish to discriminate and classify the typical failures into problem children, neuroses and psychoses, suicide, crime, alcoholism and drug addiction, sexual perversions, and prostitution.

I made a beginning in the determination of the degree of activity as far back as 1908 in a paper on "The Aggression Drive in Life and Neurosis" [A1908b]. This paper not only led to a basic view of Individual Psychology, but also had a fateful influence on the development of psychoanalysis.

Today I may well say that in problem children the difference in activity already becomes clear and determines correspondingly different measures of education. Wild, unbridled, stubborn, stealing, quarrelsome children are obviously characterized by a greater degree of activity than shy, reticent, timid, and dependent children. The radius of action of the first is visibly greater than that of the second. If we look for the kind of failure which will distinguish the two, it can easily be shown that the weaker degree of activity of the neurosis and psychosis in later life will correspond to the weaker degree of activity in childhood. Of course, within these types of illness, as well as their symptoms, the weaker degree of activity still differs qualitatively and quantitatively; e.g., activity is relatively greater in compulsion neurosis and melancholia, and less in anxiety neurosis and schizophrenia.

A somewhat greater degree of activity characterizes suicides and alcoholics from childhood on, and also underlies the structure of these failures. Their action circle is clearly greater; but their activity develops via the detour of damaging their own person. Pampered in childhood, like almost all failures, they feel their own person so valuable that when they attack themselves they believe they are thereby attacking their nearest and more distant environment.

From the viewpoint of activity, cases of sexual perversion rank from lowest to highest, with masturbation or fetishism possibly at the one pole and lust murder at the other, both extremes characterized since childhood by a corresponding circle of action and by deficient social interest.

Activity shows up most strongly in the criminal, although graded according to the kind of crime to which he is inclined. At the lowest point of the activity scale are possibly the swindler and the pick-pocket, at the highest point the murderer.

ACTIVITY AND OTHER SPHERES OF PERSONALITY

It would be altogether a mistake to try to reduce to innate factors the individual differences in degree of activity, or of social interest which gives the direction to the activity. It would be erroneous not only because there is no possibility of ever isolating the effects of innate forms of expression from the results, but also because the child experiences all innate factors and their effects according to his individual meaning, not according to mathematical or causal laws. The same is true for environmental factors and for the influences of education. From all these impressions which the child experiences he forms, as in an intuition, his style of life which carries within itself as most important structures a specific degree of activity and a specific degree of the direction-giving social interest. As a further structure which characterizes the style of life I have found a prevailing emphasis of parts of the psychomotor sphere.

All this, however, does not relieve us of the task of considering at the same time the other, resonating forms of movement of the psyche. One can easily see that there are persons in whom emphasis or overemphasis of the sphere of thoughts and concepts is in the foreground, so that they express their activity toward life through thoughts. In such cases also, the value of the life style depends on how much social interest they can muster. In the favorable cases, the sphere of feeling and the attitude toward cooperation work together with the thought elaboration so that the proper preparation for the problems of life is assured. In the unfavorable cases, lacking social interest, forms of life result which are cold, talkative, hairsplitting, and may, as I have shown, approach obsession neurosis.

Due to such one-sided accentuation, a fundamental part of the psychological process often appears as if it rested in the "unconscious." In reality, however, the *understanding for the connection with the individual life form* is missing. E.g., a compulsion neurotic may give himself to brooding over words—What is man? Why is he called man?—without comprehending the connection between such brooding and the ever-present arousal of feelings and taking of attitudes.

The misuse of the concept of the unconscious becomes even clearer when we examine persons in whom the affectional comprehension and experience is overemphasized. Here the thought and conceptual aspects seem to have disappeared, as well as the ever-present corresponding attitude. When one transposes the affectional process and attitude into the conceptual sphere, superficial consideration can easily create the impression that one had lifted something from the unconscious into consciousness. If this were true, it would also be the case with any act of education when it is a matter of conceptually illuminating relationships and of making them understandable by explanation and by going back to the reasons for a mistake.

Also, the kind of activity of the individual, his stand toward life in all his uniqueness and in connection with his individual life style, remains almost always not understood by him. At best it will be felt as justified under the pressure of his life style. In the case of others, of a partner or of an opponent, it is exactly the posture, i.e. the individual activity, which may be the visible main axis of life and be evaluated as such. Individual Psychology likewise emphasizes primarily the activity, which may be directed by sufficient social interest, and which, if deviating, can be improved through intelligent comprehension of the erroneous structure of the life form. "By their fruits ye shall know them."

In this total view, the kind of activity which becomes effective in the sense of the right evolution should probably take first place. This demand is firmly founded only when it is connected with a far-reaching, conceptual, intellectual comprehension of the becoming of an individual in his attitude toward the problems of life.

At the same time, in Individual Psychology the feeling sphere comes more fully into its own than in a one-sidedly constructed drive psychology or affect psychology. This follows from the stern demand of Individual Psychology to give the greatest possible expansion to social interest.

Thus Individual Psychology presents itself also as the sharpest opponent of an uncritical, self-flattering heredity psychology. On the other hand, it uncovers unsparingly all errors which stand detrimentally in the way of a *strengthening of social interest* and are indirectly or directly throttling the social interest of the present and the next generation. The honest psychologist cannot shut his eyes against the fact that conditions exist which prevent the entering of the child into the community, prevent his feeling at home, and let him grow up as if in enemy country. The honest psychologist must therefore talk and work also against poorly understood nationalism if it harms the community of all men; against wars of conquest, revenge, and prestige; against the drowning of the people in hopelessness due to widespread unemployment; and against all other disturbances of the spreading of social interest in the family, the school, and the social life.

6

Typology
of Meeting Life Problems
(1935)[1]

"Every man is in certain respects (a) like all other men, (b) like some other men, (c) like no other man."[2] While Adler did develop important general principles (a, above), his main interest was in the description, understanding, and modification of the unique individual (c).

Although he also made further classifications (b), e.g. the influence of birth order position (A1929c, Chapt. 7) and forms of the hesitating attitude of the neurotic (A1914k), these were of lesser importance to him; he did not want them to prejudice the approach to the individual case. After each general or classificatory statement he hastens to warn of the "thousands of variations" in the individual case.

It seems that for this apparent neglect of categories he was often accused of not being sufficiently systematic, against which he protested (A1932h). Possibly in response to this criticism he attempted in his late period two new classifications, described in the present and

wwwwwwwwww

1. Reprinted from A1935e, with omission of the first paragraph and the last paragraph introducing the new *Int. J. Indiv. Psychol.* The title has also been changed to do more justice to the contents of the paper.

2. Kluckhohn, C., & Murray, H. A. "Personality formation: the determinants." In C. Kluckhohn & H. A. Murray (Eds.), *Personality in nature, society, and culture.* 2nd ed. New York: Knopf, 1955, pp. 53–67.

the following paper. The first classification, which is in fact a continuation of the material from the preceding paper, is from a behavioral viewpoint; the second is in cognitive and attitudinal terms.

—Eds.

The raw material with which the Individual Psychologist works is the *relationship* of the individual to the problems of the outside world. The Individual Psychologist has to observe how a particular individual relates himself to the outside world. This outside world includes the individual's own body, his bodily functions, and the functions of his mind.

UNIQUENESS OF THE INDIVIDUAL

He does not relate himself to the outside world in a predetermined manner, as is often assumed. He relates himself always according to his own interpretation of himself and of his present problem. His limits are not only the common human limits, but also the limits which he has set himself. It is neither heredity nor environment which determines his relationship to the outside world. Heredity only endows him with certain abilities. Environment only gives him certain impressions. These abilities and impressions, and the manner in which he "experiences" them—that is to say, the interpretation he makes of these experiences—are the bricks which he uses in his own "creative" way in building up his attitude toward life. It is his individual way of using these bricks—or in other words, it is his attitude toward life—which determines his relationship to the outside world.

He meets problems which are entirely different from those of his forebears. He sees all his problems from a perspective which is his own creation. He sees the environment which trains him with his own self-created perspective, and accordingly changes its effect upon him for better or worse. There is a task in life which no individual can escape. It is to solve a great number of problems. These problems are in no way accidental. I have divided them for clarity into three parts: problems of behavior toward others; problems of occupation; and problems of love. The manner in which an individual behaves toward these three problems and their subdivisions—that is his answer to the problems of life.

Life (and all psychic expressions as part of life) moves ever toward "overcoming," toward perfection, toward superiority, toward success. You cannot train or condition a living being for defeat. But what an individual thinks or feels as success (i.e., as a goal acceptable to him), that is his own matter. In my experience I have found that each individual has a different meaning of, and attitude toward, what constitutes success. Therefore a human being cannot be typified or classified. I believe it is because of the parsimony of language that many scientists have come to mistaken conclusions—believing in types, entities, racial qualities, etc. Individual Psychology recognizes, with other psychologies, that each individual must be studied in the light of his own peculiar development. To present the individual understandably, in words, requires an extensive reviewing of all his facets. . . . Yet, too often, psychologists are tempted away from this recognition, and take the easier but unfruitful roads of classification. That is a temptation to which, in practical work, we must never yield.

TYPOLOGY OF SOCIAL-INTEREST, ACTIVITY

It is for teaching purposes only—to illuminate the broad field—that I designate here four different types in order, temporarily, to classify the attitude and behavior of individuals toward outside problems.

Thus, we find individuals whose approach to reality shows, from early childhood through their entire lives, a more or less dominant or "ruling" attitude. This attitude appears in all their relationships.

A second type—surely the most frequent one—expects everything from others and leans on others. I might call it the "getting" type.

A third type is inclined to feel successful by avoiding the solution of problems. Instead of struggling with a problem, a person of this type merely tries to "side-step" it, in an effort thereby to avoid defeat.

The fourth type struggles, to a greater or lesser degree, for a solution of these problems in a way which is useful to others.

It is necessary to say here that each special type retains his style from childhood to the end of his life, unless he is convinced of the mistake in his creation of his attitude toward reality. As I have said before, this style is the creation of the child himself, who uses inheritance and impressions of the environment as bricks in building his particular avenue for success—success according to his own interpretation.

Individual Psychology goes beyond the views of philosophers like Kant and newer psychologists and psychiatrists who have accepted the idea of the *totality* of the human being. Very early in my work, I found him to be a *unity!* The foremost task of Individual Psychology is to prove this unity in each individual—in his thinking, feeling, acting; in his so-called conscious and unconscious—in every expression of his personality. This unity we call the "life style" of the individual. What is frequently labeled "the ego" is nothing more than the style of the individual.

Individual Psychology has shown that the first three types mentioned above—the "ruling" type, the "getting" type, and the "avoiding" type—are not apt, and are not prepared, to solve the problems of life. These problems are always social problems. Individuals of these three types are lacking in the ability for cooperation and contribution. The clash between such a life style (lacking in social interest) and the outside problems (demanding social interest) results in shock. This shock leads up to the individual's failures—which we know as neurosis, psychosis, etc. Significantly, the failure shows the same style as the individual. As I mentioned before, the life style persists.

In the fourth type (the socially useful type), prepared for cooperation and contribution, we can always find a certain amount of *activity* which is used for the benefit of others. This activity is in agreement with the needs of others; it is useful, normal, rightly imbedded in the stream of evolution of mankind.

The first type also has activity, but not enough social interest. Therefore, if confronted strongly by a situation which he feels to be in the nature of an examination, a test of his social value, a judgment upon his social usefulness, a person of this type acts in an unsocial way. The more active of this type attack others directly: They become delinquents, tyrants, sadists. It is as if they said, with Richard III, "And therefore, since I cannot be a lover, I am determined to prove a villain." To this type also belong suicides, drug addicts, alcoholics—

whose lesser degree of activity causes them to attack others indirectly: They make attacks upon themselves for the purpose of hurting others. The second and third types show even less activity, and not much social interest. This lack appears also in the expression of their shock results, which are neuroses and psychoses.

The principles which guide me when grouping individuals into these four types are (1) the degree of their approach to social integration, and (2) the form of movement which they develop (with greater or lesser activity) to maintain that degree of approach in a manner which they regard as most likely to achieve success (in their own interpretation).

But it is the individual shade of interpretation that matters in the end. And when reconstructing the unity of a personality in his relationships to the outer world, Individual Psychology fundamentally undertakes to delineate the individual form of creative activity— which is the life style.

7

Complex Compulsion as Part of Personality and Neurosis (1935)[1]

The following selection seems sketchy and problematical. We are not even certain how seriously it was intended. This doubt is based on Adler's remark that the Polonius complex "belongs more in the comical area of psychology," and his protestation that such consideration of complexes "is not meant to be a parlor game." We have included this paper, nevertheless, for its systematic significance as discussed in the introduction to the preceding paper, for the sake of rendering a complete picture, and for the stimulation which may be derived from it. —*Eds.*

Individual Psychology is personality research. This means we are focusing on the individual's attitude or relationship to the tasks of life and draw conclusions therefrom as to how he aims at reaching success (superiority) in his sense. Our foremost attention is given to the direction of the individual's expressive movements, his goal. From

---

1. Original translation of A1935j, from a paper read at the Vienna Association for Individual Psychology.

earliest childhood, the individual has fixed a direction which cannot be conceived without a goal-setting.

We have often found how people differ in their secret goals. The goal, although unknown to the individual, directs unobtrusively and unshakably all psychological expressive forms. This is the deepest statement in general one can make about personality research. When one knows the goal, one can comprehend the personality, because one knows its frame of reference to the tasks of life.

Part of the general attitude of a person is the development of psychological complexes. This is for reasons of psychological economy. These complexes can be understood as active organs. These psychological organs, which characterize the individual like a schema, similar to character traits, must always be brought into relation to the tasks presented by the environment. They are derivatives of the directive power of the final goal—simplifications, schematizations. I beg you to remember that schematizations may exist in thousands of variations. They are sometimes less present, so that a doubt is conceivable; they are sometimes extremely strong, in a manneristic fashion. In between there are countless variations of degree of schematization. The perspective grown from such schematization is the basis of what one calls a complex. Perhaps this fact has remained unknown in the discussion of the concept of complex. Since to use the comprehensive concept of complex represents a facilitation, Individual Psychology has been inclined to use it for the explanation of various attitudinal stands.

The complex is certainly not something tangible, but characterizes a number of movements which, in a meaningful manner, strive in the same direction. It is not understood by its bearer, yet used by him. One finds this in everybody. There is no person whose attitudes cannot be resolved into complexes. This is true to some extent within the approximately normal range, to a larger extent within the abnormal. Therefore it is an interesting and valuable occupation to study people with regard to their complexes. This is not meant to be a parlor game, but it offers the psychologist and psychiatrist a suitable, practically valuable prospect because he can gain far-reaching calculations from these complexes.

We owe a particular advance in the use of the concept of complex to the not very original psychologist Jung, whose own complex seems to be that of the fellow traveler.[2] He used the concept under the lively opposition of his teacher Freud, who at the start wanted to have nothing to do with it. Later, however, Freud willingly accepted the concept, and it appears very often in his publications, especially in the form of the Oedipus complex.

Wundt explains "complex" as a connecting unit, a composite concept, a composite formation. Lipps and Meinong bring the concept closer to intended units and relations. Preuss understands by a complex concept the unanalytical mode of thinking of primitive people, the precondition of magic thinking. H. Volkelt finds related phenomena in the concepts of animals. Krueger understands by complex-qualities the diffuse total conditions of consciousness which show a considerable component of motor and visceral elements.

Inferiority and Superiority Complexes

Among the complexes of which one talks, and which are known not only in scientific but also in lay circles, possibly the inferiority complex, which Individual Psychology has used in its descriptions, is the most generally known. It describes the attitudinal stand of a person who thereby expresses that he is not in a position to solve an existing problem. It must not be confused with the inferiority feeling.

2. We must remember that this unfriendly remark about lack of originality was made shortly after the Nazis' rise to power in 1933, when C. G. Jung had accepted honors in the German psychotherapeutic organization under Nazi auspices. Many years earlier, when he still belonged to the Freudian circle, Adler (A1910m) expressed himself rather favorably about Jung's originality, as follows: "Analyses such as those of Jung belong to the most precious contributions of psychoanalysis. Their value rests not only in the confirmation of results that have been doubted, but in the opening and securing of new perspectives."

Adler's "diagnosis" of Jung as a fellow traveler was probably prompted by his collaboration of a sort with the Nazi order (Jung, C. G., "Zur gegenwärtigen Lage der Psychotherapie." *Zbl. Psychother.*, 1934, 7, 1–16)—and would seem to be borne out by Jung's radical realignment by the time of the defeat of Nazi Germany. Then he was found on the side of those supporting the notion of the collective guilt of the German people as a whole. He is quoted in an interview: "All [Germans] are, consciously or unconsciously, actively or passively, participants in the atrocities. . . . The question of collective guilt which occupies the politician so much . . . is for the psychologist a fact" ("Werden die Seelen Frieden finden? Ein Interview." *Weltwoche*, Zurich, May 11, 1945, p. 3).

Adler, by contrast, after World War I had strongly rejected the concept of the collective guilt of a people (A1919a), a rejection with which nearly all psychologists today would agree.

The inferiority complex and its sibling, the superiority complex, are the presentations of the person through which he explains to himself and others that he is not strong enough to solve a given problem in a socially useful way. Needless to mention, in this way no real support is attained. It is well known that this total mood, with all its thought, feeling, and action material, leads to failures. All forms of failure which we know are movement forms of an inferiority complex.

Oedipus Complex

The Oedipus complex is very well known, but one cannot find the proper correspondence of its manifestations with its name. It should mean that a child has some sexual inclinations towards the parent of the other sex, but when we examine the facts, these tell us nothing other than that the name Oedipus is poorly chosen. It only characterizes a pampered child who does not want to give up his mother. This clinging to the mother shows itself in thousands of variations. But the reference to the fundamental sexual drive, as Freud thinks, is to be refuted even when, as a result of the clinging on the part of the mother, actual sexual desires with regard to the mother do appear. According to Freud, the Oedipus complex is supposed to be the foundation of the development of the mental life, but Individual Psychology has shown that it is an artificial error in upbringing.

Redeemer Complex

If one embarks upon complex research, if one has recognized the attitudinal stand of a person as a schema, one can find an infinite number of such schemas. One of the most interesting is the redeemer complex. This characterizes people who in a conspicuous manner, but unknowingly, take an attitude that they must save or redeem somebody. There are thousands of degrees and variations, but it is always clearly the attitudinal stand of a person who finds his superiority, his possibility of success, in solving the inner and outer complications of others. It may very well be that the redeemer complex enters into medical endeavor or the choice of the ministry as a vocation. In the most extreme cases, we will find a bearing as if the person in question were sent by God, as if he could cure all evils of mankind. If somebody believes, for example, that he must redeem an alcoholic, this expresses an abnormal solution of his own problems. Neither through marriage nor devotion can such a thing be accomplished, but only through deep psychological insight and training. Here, too, one sees an escape from normal problems, a seeking for possibilities of success which can satisfy vanity. The afflicted one feels forced to play the redeemer. This complex is frequently found in neuroses and psychoses.

Proof Complex

A further complex is the proof complex. It can be found in many people who want to prove that they also have a right to exist or that they have no faults. They have a terrible fear of committing errors; they consider every action as a test of whether they get recognition from others and are found perfect. They are always on the defensive, trying to justify themselves. In every conversation they want to prove that they are not worthless, although nobody in the environment is interested in their efforts, which, moreover, do not bring them peace. In neurosis the proof complex plays an enormous part and is always mixed with a pointing out of alleviating circumstances, with strong emotions, and with an inclination to retreat.

Polonius Complex

Now I come to a complex which belongs more in the comical area of psychology. This is the Polonius complex. Hamlet to Polonius: "Do you see yonder cloud that's almost in shape of a camel?" Polonius: "By the mass, and 'tis like a camel, indeed." *Something looks like*—thereby a superficial, incidental decision is made which usually means nothing. And yet it turns out that modern psychology is dominated by the Polonius complex. You are told, "This is similar to what one finds among primitive man." "Already primitive man showed such behavior." Not to speak of psychoanalysis, where *everything* "looks like . . ."

But one also finds this complex outside of psychology, where sometimes there may be good reasons for its use. It certainly is contained in the déjà-vu phenomenon where also "something looks like," and in other phenomena which lead to mystical conceptions as, e.g., the impression that something was like this in a former life. The Polonius complex is dangerous in science, as well as otherwise in life, wherever it leads to ridiculous generalizations.

If you remember the interpretation of dream life, you will find the Polonius complex there also. To the dreamer everything "looks like . . ."

I should also like to remind you here of Vaihinger's "as if." [3] For example, in an aboriginal religion an alligator is declared holy, as if it were a deity. Probably there were people even then who did not take the divinity of an alligator seriously. But to make this a fact had great advantages for the tribe, because in this as-if conception all the Poloniuses regarded themselves as brothers. They met in the name of the alligator, and although it was all only an expression of group egotism, it was supposed to alleviate the need of the time. Probably many of these people faltered, but under some circumstances such a religion could be helpful. You see how far the seeking of an alleviation in life, of superiority, of the possibility of success, extends itself in any kind of context which is not understood by the one concerned. It is a phenomenon which Individual Psychology calls the Polonius complex.

You will find people who in their conversation always have a comparison ready; something always "is like . . ." This also lets us understand poetic figures of speech and metaphorical elaborations which serve to bypass the common sense, in most cases in order to arouse feelings and emotions. This is why we find symbols and comparative representations also in the dream. The concern with the Polonius complex is valuable; it throws a sharp light on the unreality of many philosophical and psychological systems.

Exclusion Complex

In Individual Psychology you also will find frequent mention of the exclusion complex. It characterizes many people. One finds it in thousands of variations in people who always want to reduce their sphere of action, who want to remove all problems. The exclusion complex, like the Polonius complex, is used as a crutch by the insecure person. The schematized seeking for exclusion will always be part of

~~~~~~~~~~~~~~

3. Vaihinger, H. *The philosophy of 'as if.'* New York: Harcourt, Brace, 1925.

the person whose goal is to reach personal superiority by an easy way.

Predestination Complex

Another complex which adheres to a great many persons is the predestination complex. It expresses itself as an attitude towards life, as a belief that nothing can happen to one. There are extremes which become immediately apparent. The predestination complex gives the person in question great support and self-assurance. Of course this is gained by a deception because real predestination, e.g., being chosen, as some peoples also believe about themselves, does not exist.

I have noted school children who are so impressed by themselves that they believe they know everything. In a tense situation, they feel they have to answer even when they have no idea about the question at hand. I have experienced some beautiful cases of this kind and am convinced that this attitude can precipitate many a person into a difficult situation. It is the more dangerous when someone in public life believes he can accomplish the most unusual achievements, that nothing can happen to him, that he will prevail somehow. In persons with this complex you can clearly see the pampered life style; they were accustomed to having their mother get them out of difficult situations.

On the other hand, one will find in people who feel themselves quite at home, who are completely rooted in the facts of this earth, a similar state, which presents itself as courage. In this case, the inclination to attempt something beyond human strength will not appear; rather one will note an objective method of approach. These are people who will stop before a task which cannot humanly be accomplished. In these people one will find optimism and self-confidence as traces of the predestination complex, which perhaps seems necessary in view of the uncertainty of the future.

Real possibilities of success exist in both cases, the pampered and the courageous. Of course there are also setbacks. The pampered will overlook them or answer them with a breakdown (possibly schizophrenia, cyclothymia, melancholia, crime); the courageous will remain socially active and respond with quick recovery after the defeat.

I found a beautiful case in a manic paralytic, whom I visited in a sanitarium. He asked me, with tears and begging, to take him home since he was being treated brutally there. Otherwise, he showed insight and great improvement. Once at home, he was quiet and happy. Interrupting a conversation, he turned to me with the words: "You see, that's what always happens in my life; I have success in everything." He was thinking of my agreement to take him home; I thought of the harsh treatment which had left him with several black marks.

Leader Complex

Frequently, one finds in children and adults what one could call a leader complex already in childhood. It is the result of training.[5] Such are people who feel badly in any other role, and who day and night are attempting to be at the head. The second-born and youngest children, but also oldest children who have remained strong, [i.e., have not succumbed to the feeling of being dethroned by younger siblings], are closely related to this complex, e.g., Jacob, Esau, and Joseph in the Bible.[4] In people who lead, one can find that they have developed the leader complex already in childhood. It is the result of training.[5] Such children do not like to be losers in a game, or to be the horse rather than the coachman. All geniuses have this complex, but unfortunately so do others without sufficient ability for leadership, who, due to their training and favorable circumstances, may become leaders and produce risky situations.

Spectator Complex

Perhaps not quite so frequent is the spectator complex. It shows up in people who arrange their life so that they are always spectators

---

4. For Adler's views on birth order see, e.g., A1958a, pp. 144–154.

5. By training, Adler meant essentially a spontaneous self-training. It was that aspect of learning in which Adler was particularly interested since it would best account for the way an individual acquires his unique distinguishing skills. "By watching children we can often see them training for an occupation in adult life. Sometimes, for example, a child wishes to be a teacher; and we can notice how he brings younger children together and plays school with them. . . . A girl who looks forward to being a mother will play with dolls and train herself to a greater interest in babies. . . . They are training themselves in identification and in fulfilling the tasks of a mother" (A1958a, pp. 245–246).

without taking any active steps. Pampered children are often forced into this role. Unfortunately, the spectator complex is so little provided with activity that not much use can be made of it for society. This necessitates a certain method of treatment. It is much more urgent to give encouragement to a person with a spectator complex than to someone who shows activity. One must point out to the spectator how important it is to take part in life.

You will find the spectator complex often showing up in dreams. To sit in a theatre is a frequent dream, because to such persons life appears like a theatre. In their earliest recollections, onlooking often comes to light. They are very often disappointed by life; naturally they will be thrown from the height [from which they usually look]. The inclination to look is often combined with the inclination to be seen (in exhibitionism, but also in exaggerated vanity). These are always visual types [persons given to thinking in visual terms].

"No" Complex

A very frequent complex is the "no" complex. In such cases one must be very careful in upbringing and treatment. There are people who cannot avoid opposition, who find it difficult to agree with anybody, who see something great in disagreeing with others. This can also consist of an inclination to criticize others, often without justification. There are people who have a "no" on their lips even before someone has opened his mouth. They are waiting till they can pronounce the "no." One will occasionally find such people among critics, but also among pessimists. If this inclination is combined with social interest, it is fruitful.

In childhood, this complex is sometimes expressed in a grotesque fashion. E.g., a mother wanted to be conciliatory to her obstreperous child and said: "I brought you some oranges because I know you like them." The child screamed immediately: "I want oranges only when I want them, not when you bring them." The same mother said one time: "Take a cup of milk or coffee, as you please." The child replied: "If you say milk, I drink coffee; if you say coffee, I drink milk." It is a striving not to risk one's feeling of dominance over another by agreeing with him. Here the possibility of success is seen in not being influenced by the other, in not granting him the feeling of superiority.

The "no" complex often plays a devastating part in science. The best advances are obstructed if opposed by people with a "no" complex. Such people are concerned with the satisfaction of self-love and vanity, which would feel wounded by agreement.

All these complexes can connect and cooperate with one another. It is also clear that these schemas can from one aspect be ascertained as inferiority complex, from another as Polonius complex or exclusion complex or as soothing superiority complex. There are enormous possibilities in ascertaining complexes and in this way of better comprehending the personality.

PART II

Theory of the Neuroses

8

The Structure of Neurosis
(1932)[1]

*After a restatement of his general theory, with particular emphasis on
the creative power of the individual, Adler describes in the following
pages the objective factors which tend to predispose an individual for
neurosis, resulting in increased feelings of inadequacy and in underdeveloped social interest. Such predisposition renders the individual
unprepared for meeting his life situations, and he develops his symptoms as alibis. His movement becomes evasive according to one of
four typical forms. These neurotic movement types were one of
Adler's early formulations (A1914k) and he considered them one
of his important systematizations (A1932h).* —Eds.

The subject I have chosen to discuss here, namely, the structure of
neurosis, is one of the most difficult problems in psychology. We
frequently observe fear in people without considering it as a manifestation of neurosis. Frequently, also, there may be found a certain
inelasticity or rigidity of thinking in people who are not neurotic; in
individuals, for instance, who lay great stress on rules and formulae.
But we cannot take this as a characteristic of neurosis. The same
applies to other neurotic symptoms. The symptom of fatigue occurs in

1. A1932i. Reprinted from translation, A1935g.

the neurasthenic as well as in so-called normal people. The symptoms
found in functional neurosis may also be found outside of a neurosis.
Every human being under certain psychic tensions will react according
to his individual make-up. In one suffering from fear we may notice
various reactions such as heart palpitation, breathing difficulties, etc.
Normal human beings may be subject to these symptoms. Contrac-
tions of the throat may be brought on in them by a feeling of
insecurity. Other individuals will, under the stress of fear, react with
stomach symptoms, or intestinal disorders, or bladder irregularities.
There are a great number of individuals in whom fear manifests itself
through the sexual organ. There is a special type in whom fear creates
sexual excitement. Individuals of this type consider such a reaction
normal, and even go so far as to construct theories about it. Let us
remember, then, that in no neurosis is there to be found any
phenomenon which is outside the range of "normal" human psychic
life and its manifestations.

THE SOUL AS PART OF LIFE

In order to bring out the full significance of what follows, I shall
touch briefly here on the fundamental views of Individual Psychology,
especially those relative to its conception of mind and soul. It is quite
clear that in considering this subject we move to a transphenomenal
level.

Watson and his school, who refuse to do this, ignore the existence
and meaning of the soul. There are other schools, also, which take a
purely mechanistic viewpoint on these matters, thus eliminating the
mind and psychic life. In the true sense this is impossible since the
very word "psychology" means science of the soul. Many call
themselves psychologists who in fact are physiologists and, according
to the structure of their scientific training, eliminate the concept of
the soul or think of it in a mechanistic way. The psychologist,
however, takes it for granted that a basic conception of psychic life
includes the various manifestations of the personality. These manifestations are arranged in definite order and direction.

Speculative insight is necessary to understand the context data which may lead beyond the province of experience. But even here, in the sphere outside immediate or tangible experience, there is no evidence which precludes the assumption of psychic life or disproves the existence of it. Let us assume, therefore, that the soul is a part of life.

Life as movement. Now the most important characteristic of life is motion. That does not mean that living things cannot be in a state of immobility, but that the capacity for motion is present as long as life exists, and that all psychic life can be interpreted in terms of movement. Hence, all phenomena which pertain to the psychic life can be seen in space-time relationships. We observe these movements and see them as if in a congealed state—as forms in repose, so to speak. Once we see psychic expression as movement we approach an understanding of our problem; for the chief characteristic of a movement is that it must have direction and, therefore, a goal. Moreover, this direction toward which every psychic movement proceeds could not exist if the entire psychic life did not have a goal, which, as must be stressed at this point, is, in the case of every individual, determinable and capable of formulation, even though the individual himself cannot formulate it. In relation to this we may note that we have in our consciousness a great number of impressions which are not clearly defined concepts and which, under certain circumstances, we can formulate. In this connection, it is sometimes erroneously concluded that if we clothe the nonunderstood in words, we have moved it from the realm of the unconscious to the conscious, which is certainly not the case.

The goal of overcoming. I have said that every movement has a goal. Drives and natural tendencies, such as sexual drives, for instance, have no direction. These abstract concepts cannot, therefore, be well utilized in the understanding of psychic occurrences. The direction which we seem to observe in these drives is merely the direction imparted to them by the movement of the individual-as-a-unity toward his goal. The movement towards a goal shows a unified pattern. It is this goal of the psychic life which makes the whole psychic life a unity. The result is that the aspiration toward this goal is immanent in every part of the psychic movement; therefore, the goal becomes a part of the unity. We must conclude, then, that we understand a part of the psychic life only when we conceive it as a part of a unity which proceeds along the same course towards the same goal with other characteristics of the individual. In the practical application of Individual Psychology this viewpoint is of the greatest importance. Hence it is essential to the understanding of psychic life to explain how the goal originates.

Striving towards a goal, towards an objective, we find everywhere in life. Everything grows "as if" it were striving to overcome all imperfections and achieve perfection. This urge toward perfection we call the goal of overcoming, that is, the striving to overcome.

Language is inadequate to express the full range of interpretations of what overcoming means. The interpretation varies with each individual because the goal of each individual is different. If we say that such a striving is for power or force, or a running away from reality, we have made typical generalizations which do not give a clear insight into a particular, individual case. But we have gained one point. We have illuminated the field under consideration, and must then narrow down the meaning so that we are able to perceive the particular direction of movement of the individual in question. For this we need experience, alertness, and a clósely critical, objective, unbiased examination of each individual case.

The phenomena to which we allude imply the existence of a minus and plus situation simultaneously in the same individual—that is, an inferiority feeling and at the same time a striving to overcome this inferiority. The inferiority feeling can show itself in a thousand ways—for instance, as a striving for superiority. The question then arises as to how the fictitious goal or guiding fiction, which is different in each individual and which he carries within himself from the beginning to the end of life, is established.

The creative power of the individual. We concede that every child is born with potentialities different from those of any other child. Our objection to the teachings of the hereditarians and every other tendency to overstress the significance of constitutional disposition, is that the important thing is not what one is born with, but what use one makes of that equipment. Still we must ask ourselves: "Who uses it?" As to the influence of the environment, who can say that the same environmental influences are apprehended, worked over, digested, and responded to by any two individuals in the same way? To understand this fact we find it necessary to assume the existence of still another force: the creative power of the individual.

We have been impelled to attribute to a child creative power, which casts into movement all the influences upon him and all his potentialities—a movement toward the overcoming of an obstacle. This is felt by the child as an impulse that gives his striving a certain direction. There is no doubt that all phenomena in the psychic life of a child tend toward overcoming his inferior position; and consequently the views of those who believe in the causative influence of heredity on the one hand, or environment on the other, are, as complete explanations of his personality, made untenable by the assumption of this creative power of the child. The drive in the child is without direction until it has been incorporated into the movement toward the goal which he creates in response to his environment. This response is not simply a passive reaction but a manifestation of creative activity on the part of an individual. It is futile to attempt to establish psychology on the basis of drives alone, without taking into consideration the creative power of the child which directs the drive, molds it into form, and supplies it with a meaningful goal.

There are, however, certain factors which affect the child and allure him to mold his life in a certain direction. These factors are not primarily causative agents, but rather alluring, stimulating phenomena. The attitude toward these factors varies very widely in different individuals. No mathematical rule is conceivable that could teach us how to make the proper use of anything which we possess. However, what unprejudiced research is in position to observe is not the disposition or constitution that individuals possess, but only the use they make of what they possess. These factors, as I have indicated, appear as alluring or stimulating opportunities to the individual. It would be erroneous to assume that they act as causes, for, with deepened understanding, we see that a different use is made of the same stimuli by different individuals, and therefore we are justified in assuming merely that it is probable on a statistical basis that they will evoke in an individual certain seemingly typical uses of them. So much we may understand. Any assertion beyond that we may regard as a bit unscientific. In other words, it is the creative factor that comes into play here, and it is this factor which we have to train ourselves to understand better in its working.

INTENSIFIED MINUS SITUATIONS

Organ inferiority. As a result of our experience we understand that children with inferior organs will feel inadequate for the tasks of life and that the minus situation will be felt by a child with inferior organs more intensely than by the average child. This is very significant because our experience confirms the fact that where a situation is felt to be especially insecure, the results are very striking and they show a greater striving for a plus situation. These observations apply to children who are born with inferior sense organs, with inferior brain structure, inferior endocrine glands. The organic weakness does not *necessarily* function as a minus situation, but the child *experiences* the weakness of his organic equipment for average social tasks, and he feels impelled to reorganize it accordingly.

There are innumerable forms of life in which we may observe the striving to overcome the sense of inadequacy rooted in an experience of organ inferiority. Some individuals seek to eliminate problems; some act so as to avoid them. By the avoidance of problems, some feel relieved and so more secure. Others wrestle and struggle with their problems—such as for instance, that of left-handedness—and accommodate themselves more courageously to outside influences.

The outcome depends on the creative power of the individual which expands outwardly according to no rule except this: the determining goal is always success. What constitutes success for him depends upon the individual's own interpretation of his position.

During the first three or four years of life the child forms his life pattern. He has then shaped his concrete goal, determining the way in which he overcomes his problems. From then on one may perceive in his attitude the result of this process of creative goal formation. There are millions of variations of such goals. They differ from each other, metaphorically speaking, in color, shape, rhythm, and intensity.

Pampering. A second group of individuals will show a life pattern very similar to that of children affected by organ inferiority. I have in mind those individuals who have been pampered in childhood. The more deeply I have delved into the problem of neurosis and searched the cases presented, the more clearly have I come to see that in every individual with a neurosis some degree of pampering can be traced. Dependence on another person for the solution of a problem or the carrying out of a task has a determining influence on an individual.

But we must not think too loosely of pampering. When we speak of a pampered child we do not simply mean a child who is loved and caressed, but rather a child whose parents are always hovering over it, who assume all responsibilities for it, who take away from the child the burden of fulfilling any of the tasks and functions it could fulfil. Under such circumstances the child develops like a parasite and emerges as one of innumerable varieties of individuals, ranging from those who are extremely disinclined to accept any suggestion or influence from others, to those who are always seeking assistance. Between these extremes there are, as I have indicated, thousands of differences in type and kind.

I would like to prevent an easily made mistake, however, by stating here that the pampered style of life should not be understood as simply resulting from the attitude of parents or grandparents, but that it also is the *creation of the child himself*. This creation may be arrived at even in cases where there is no question of pampering by other persons. It is the exacting attitude of the child which induces pampering.

Neglect. A third group consists of neglected children; those who are, for instance, illegitimate, undesired, or ugly. The feeling of being neglected is, of course, relative. External circumstances can contribute to it and every pampered child will automatically find himself, later in life, in situations which will make him feel neglected.

INSECURITY FEELING AND LACK OF SOCIAL INTEREST

What we want to get at now is the basic, underlying structure which unites all these types. All three groups face life with a feeling of insecurity. This feeling of insecurity and inadequacy is characteristic of all failures. From the way they attempt to solve their problems we may judge how well individuals in the three categories with which we are dealing are prepared to meet these problems, which are always of a social nature. All problems with which we are confronted are of a social nature. For the purpose of clarification we may classify them as problems of social, occupational, or love relationships. Their solution depends, consequently, upon how well an individual is prepared to make contact with his fellow human beings.

All failures—problem children, criminals, suicides, neurotics, psychotics, alcoholics, sexual perverts, etc.—are products of inadequate preparation in social interest. They are all non-cooperative, solitary beings who run more or less counter to the rest of the world; beings who are more or less asocial if not antisocial.

This viewpoint tends to make of Individual Psychology a psychology of evaluations. What does this signify? The very far-reaching implication is that only the individual who is prepared for social cooperation can solve the social problems which life imposes. By this we mean that there should exist a certain degree of contact feeling—of striving for cooperation—in the law of movement of the individual. Where it is lacking we meet with failures. I have already shown that this inclination for cooperation and social achievement has not been properly developed in children who feel insecure. These insecure ones build a life style which shows a lack of social interest, because an insecure individual is always more concerned with himself than with others. He cannot get away from himself.

We cannot stress too much that in the neurotic there is a lack of interest in others, a lack of social interest. We must not be confused by the fact that some neurotics seem to be benevolent and wish to reform the whole world. This wish to reform the whole world can be merely a response to a keenly felt minus situation. Where the minus situation is strong, the striving to overcome will also be strong. We can perceive this also in the organs of the human body, for where the obstacle to be overcome is great, the tension is also great. The neurotic places the goal of his overcoming high. It is related, just as in the case of a normal individual, to the feeling of personal value. The feeling of personal worth can only be derived from achievement, from the ability to overcome. A lack of social interest prevails in the law of movement of the neurotic and decreases his ability to overcome. This lack is not as great in the neurotic as it is in the criminal. The criminal is more actively aware of his fellow men but opposes them at the same time. The neurotic does not oppose them openly, but his efforts are bent toward testing and utilizing, or exploiting, the social interest of others.

This is characteristic of all neurotics, so that in the structure of a neurosis we find the utilization of the social interest of others and simultaneously the arresting of an individual's cooperative participation by a "but." This "but" is the epitome of all neurotic symptoms. It offers an alibi to the neurotic. The neurotic lives according to the formula "yes—but." All the symptoms which hinder the neurotic from going forward to achievement are found to be covered by this formula. His estimate of his value, therefore, depends upon how much another person contributes to it, and not upon his ability to overcome—not upon his own achievements.

Even in considering neurosis with physical manifestations, we maintain the foregoing viewpoint. In such cases we have to deal with an arrangement of emotions, such as anxiety, insecurity, hypersensitivity, rage, impatience, greediness, etc. These emotions all arise from living outside the scope of cooperation. The tension in which the neurotic lives makes it easy to work himself up into a state of heightened emotion.

This tension makes itself felt at the point of least resistance, and the characteristic effects show up in such places as I have mentioned before, for instance, the stomach, bladder, intestines, heart, etc.

So we come to see that neurosis with physical manifestations can be understood only when we recognize the individual as a unity.

UNPREPAREDNESS IN THE FACE OF LIFE PROBLEMS

When scrutinized, the neurotic will be found to be an individual placed in a test situation who is attempting to solve his problems in the interest of his own personal ambition rather than in the interest of the common welfare. This holds true of all neuroses. All neuroses grow out of the psychic tension of an individual who is not socially well-prepared when he is confronted with a task which demands for its solution more social interest than he is capable of.

The true nature of the so-called endogenic factors in neurosis becomes more clearly marked when the individual finds himself placed in a test situation. Here the individual's interpretation of his own qualities plays a great role. We do not share the opinion that a neurotic is incapable of solving those problems before which he breaks down, but we recognize that he has not yet acquired that amount of social interest necessary for him to make an approximately correct solution of them. He does not possess sufficient contact ability, that is, capacity for making contact with others. There then develops in him that psychic tension which can be found in everyone who feels insecure. This tension affects the whole body and the whole psychic life and always differs in different individuals.

There are individuals—those who are greatly concerned with rules, formulae, and ideas—whom this tension affects intellectually. We can observe this most clearly in compulsion neurosis and in paranoia. With others, another sphere of psychic life is set in motion, namely, the emotional sphere. This is seen for example in anxiety neuroses and phobias.

I want to lay some stress, also, upon the exogenic factor. Both endogenic and exogenic factors play a part in every neurotic symptom. The true bearing of the exogenic factor on the individual can, however, only be understood when we understand the whole individual in the expression of his life style. The therapist has to put himself in the individual's place in order to see that for this particular individual a certain situation seems too difficult.

Recently, a patient came to me who had been previously treated with success up to a certain point by another Individual Psychologist. Before the time of his previous treatment it had been possible for him to be sexually stimulated only when animals were present. It would be interesting to discuss why he chose animals, but I cannot go into that part of his life style here. Anyway, he had, due to a strong inferiority feeling, excluded the normal phase of the love relationship. This exclusion I find is characteristic of all sexual perversion. When he came to me he was planning to get married. He said, "I want to marry, *but* the problem now arises of confessing to my future wife what has gone on before. If I do this, I am sure that she will refuse me." This refusal is just what he was aiming at. He wanted another excuse for evading the solution of the love problem. I said to him, "You should not confess to everybody all the disagreeable happenings in your life for which you are not really to blame. It is unfair and not good taste to speak of certain things. It is only the last remnant of your cowardice which makes you think of talking about it to your fiancée. You must expect that other people are apt to misunderstand what you wish to tell." He perceived this and understood the purpose of his determination to confess to his financée. I hope that his increased understanding has enabled him to rid himself of his fear of the love problem.

NEUROTIC TYPES OF MOVEMENT

If one understands the law of movement of neurotics one will always find that in each patient the mental phase (compulsion neurosis), or the emotional phase (anxiety neurosis), or the motor phase (hysteria), is predominant, although the other psychic processes, too, are always dynamically present. In the treatment of such cases, however, the whole psychic process must be clearly and definitely determined. There are no pure cases. There are only mixed cases in which it can be seen that at one time one aspect, at another time another aspect, of the whole psychic process comes to the foreground.

People who do not sufficiently understand this predominance of one aspect of life over the other frequently talk about the "unconscious." The unconscious, however, is nothing other than that which we have been unable to formulate in clear concepts. These concepts are not hiding away in some unconscious or subconscious recesses of our minds, but are those parts of our consciousness of which we have not fully understood the significance.

If we focus our attention on the goal, direction, and form of an individual's movement, which alone gives us true understanding of him, we find among neurotics several different types of movement.

Distance. There is first the distance complex. This first type of movement characteristic of neuroses shows an attempt to establish distance as a safeguard. There are neurotics, then, in whom the most striking characteristic is that they keep themselves at a significant distance or apartness from the solution of the problem with which they are confronted. This distance may be produced by means of hysteria, fainting, indecision, a tendency to doubt, etc., but all these symptoms mean nothing more than an attempt to stand still in a world that is moving. If an individual cannot decide whether he should do this or do that, one thing is certain, namely, that he does not move. This keeping oneself at a distance can also be seen very clearly in anxiety neuroses. Neuroses with physical manifestations, too, are capable of hindering a person from solving social problems. Thus an individual may be compelled to urinate just when he is about to go to a party. Also, the compulsion neuroses are well designed to effect this distance, and consequently bring about a standstill whenever the neurotic feels himself forced to do something.

Hesitating attitude. The second form of movement manifests itself in a hesitating attitude. The neurotic advances, but advances hesitatingly. An example of this is stuttering. Any problem may be met with a "stuttering approach." This hesitation may lead to a postponement of a solution of one's problems by means of insomnia. The patient with this symptom is so tired that he can solve his task only very hesitatingly. In neurasthenia, the symptom of fatigue is one of the chief characteristics. In agoraphobia it is obvious that the neurotic hesitates to solve his problem without the assistance of another person.

Detour. The third form of movement characteristic of all neurotic symptoms is the detour around the solution of a problem and the refuge in a battlefield of lesser importance. This becomes especially clear in a compulsion neurosis. The patient sets up a counter-compulsion in opposition to the compulsion of social demands. In doing this he only postpones the solution of his problems. An example of this is the washing compulsion.

Narrowed path of approach. The fourth form of movement is the most complicated and the most striking. I might call it the narrowed path of approach. The person does not give himself up fully to the solution of a problem; he takes up only part of it and eliminates other parts, generally those which are most pertinent. This is the case in perversions. Another phase of this same form of movement is one that sometimes leads to great cultural achievements.

CONCLUDING SUMMARY

The goal of overcoming is approached by each individual differently. Proceeding toward a general diagnosis, we may recognize traits of unconcealed despotism purposing to make the other person a slave to the patient, as is the case in anxiety neurosis. Such individuals have learned in their childhood to force others to come to their rescue by frightening them. Another group of individuals use the alibi as the chief form of movement toward the goal of overcoming. Their ambitious tendency becomes obvious when we see them insisting upon their point of view. For instance, they will say: "If I only could sleep, I could be the first or among the first." But they content themselves with having this alibi. Of course, not everyone will present that alibi in such an easily understandable form; therefore we have to take into account the whole of a patient's attitude toward his problems. In a third group we find individuals who create fictitious values within themselves. Such neurotics, for instance, pride themselves on how much they have attained in spite of their neurosis.

I want to stress only one thing more: In psychic processes the single spheres are not as separated as some schools of psychology tend to assume. There is no area where only the emotional or the mental side, either action or volition, can be found to be present. The psychic process comprises the whole of an individual. When we observe a part of it, we should feel forced to search for the rest of it. So, if an individual tells us his first childhood recollections, we may gather from them the mental, emotional, and attitudinal aspects, and only after that may we arrive at an understanding of the unity of his personality. By virtue of our experience we are, with all due precaution, in a position to ascertain the dynamic value of mental, emotional, and attitudinal movements as movements directed toward, or determined by, a goal that, for the individual, has the meaning of securing for him what he regards as his position in life. It is in such a way only that we become capable of understanding these goal-directed movements as the individual's efforts to secure for himself what he interprets, or misinterprets, as success, or as his way of overcoming a minus situation so as to attain a plus situation.

We thus come to the following conception of the structure of neurosis: All neurotic symptoms are safeguards of persons who do not feel adequately equipped or prepared for the problems of life, who carry within themselves only a passive appreciation of social feeling and interest. This appreciation becomes apparent in them only when they take into account and utilize the social interest of others.

As soon as, after long toil and with great experience, one learns to recognize the meaning of this attitude, one becomes more and more convinced that in a neurosis, of whatever description, we have to deal with the pampered type of individual, the type of individual who has not become a cooperative fellowman because in his earliest childhood he was trained to utilize the services of others for the solution of his own problems.

9

The Neurotic's Picture of the World: A Case Study

(1936)[1]

In the preceding section objective situational factors in the development of neurosis were stressed, as well as the behavioral outcomes in the form of movement types. While the cognitive structure of the neurotic was also dealt with, it becomes the main theme of the present paper, illustrated by the discussion of one case.

The neurotic's picture of the world is the construction of the pampered life style. It is essentially an immature picture. "The cure . . . is brought about by . . . the unequivocal acceptance of a mature picture of the world."

Development of the pampered life style, while facilitated by any of the three minus situations of the preceding section, is the creation of the individual. It can be present even where we find neglect rather than actual pampering.　　　　　　　　　　　—Eds.

It is the way in which an individual relates himself to the outside world which interests the Individual Psychologist. The therapist

1. A1936l. Reprinted from translation, A1936h, with one rearrangement.

schooled in Individual Psychology strives to become acquainted with the neurotic personality by looking into the latter's unsuccessful relations to the real world as seen from a social-minded outlook; he endeavors to convince his patient of the coherence of his behavior and to show him his error, to reveal to him his incorrect, fictitious picture of the world and the faulty philosophy upon which he has built his life.

In a somnambulistic sort of way the neurotic person is so much involved in the world he has created during his early childhood that he needs the help provided by discussions under objective Individual Psychological direction in order to enable him to understand himself sufficiently so that he can increase his ability to cooperate. An individual whom we call neurotic is so designated because his behavior shows that he can cooperate only with a meager degree of social interest, and hence with a smaller proportion of "common sense" (sense that can be shared), than those whom we call normal—those whose behavior we are not justified in speaking of as neurotic.

The cure or reorientation is brought about by the destruction of the faulty picture of the world and unequivocal acceptance of a mature picture of the world. The process takes place in ways which we can express only by means of aphoristic terms and phrases such as: growth of social interest, encouragement, giving up trying to *seem* great, development of greater independence of the opinion of other people, etc.

A more mature picture of the world shows us life as presenting a series of problems which constantly demand solution. All the difficulties, great or small, are always found to be related to the three great basic problems of life—work and occupation, friends and social relations, love and marriage. Living is the process of trying to find a solution to these problems. Their correct solution cannot, however, be regarded as a process of acclimatization merely, such as that of a worm acclimatizing himself to an apple, but as a process of meeting the problems according to standards which should be valid for all and for an hypothetical eternity.

There is no question but that the neurotic's faulty picture of the world is constantly being so shaken by reality that he feels himself threatened from many sides. Consequently he narrows down his sphere of activity; he always pedantically presents the same opinions and the same attitudes which he early accepted. Eventually, as a result of the narrowing-down process, he shows an inferiority complex with all its consequences. Then, in order to escape this inferiority complex and because he finally sees himself threatened by the problem of death, he convulsively constructs a superiority complex. This is a compensatory movement.

PAMPERED LIFE STYLE

Extreme discouragement, continuing doubt, hypersensitivity, impatience, exaggerated emotion and phenomena of retreat, and physical and psychic disturbances showing the signs of weakness and need for support are always evidence that a neurotic patient has not yet abandoned his early-acquired pampered life style. These show that a patient endowed with a comparatively small degree of activity, and not possessing sufficient social interest, has pictured to himself a world in which he is *entitled* to be first in everything.

Later, when such a favorable situation does not obtain for him, he is not prepared to render any response other than a more or less spiteful accusation of other people, of life, of his parents. This limitation of his activity to a small circle results in his leaving important questions unanswered, and when he is brought face to face with a problem which he is not prepared to cope with, he suffers a shock and responds with a shock reaction. In such exogenous situations he develops the shock symptoms that correspond to his physical type and to his particular life style, while emphasizing especially those which seem to justify him in evading the imminent problem which carries with it the threat of defeat.

The variety of the symptoms which put in their appearance at such times can, as I have often shown in other articles, be quite fully understood. Of course it must first be realized that certain existing psychic connections have not been made from the viewpoint of the observer but according to the viewpoint and understanding of the patient; thus when dealing with neurotic symptoms we are dealing not with the thing-in-itself, not with *causal* factors, but with idea and attitude, with the faulty world picture of the patient.

In other places I already have brought together enough material to make it clear that a neurosis is the logical consequence of the attitude which can be observed in the pampered life style, and here I do not care to go into a discussion of this point again. The Oedipus complex and its consequences are nothing but the phenomena of the pampered life style.

I only want to point out once more the repeatedly and emphatically demonstrated fact that the pampered life style as a living phenomenon is the creation of the child, though its formation is frequently aided by others, of course. Consequently, this life style can be found occasionally in cases where we cannot speak with any justification of pampering, but where we find, rather, neglect.

One thing, however, seems to me of sufficient importance to mention here. When the child, erring in his pampered life style, has constructed his picture of the world almost as if he were living in a dream, then every one of his later experiences is seen, felt, interpreted, and responded to in the light of this same attitude toward life. It is not the experiences as such, it is not their objective significance which then have an effect on him, but the conception, evaluation, and meaning which he gives to these experiences; he always interprets experiences according to his already existing attitude and life style.

There are said to be some psychiatrists and psychologists who still regard the mere revealing of experiences as "depth psychology." [2] How much deeper the interpretation of Individual Psychology cuts when it shows in all the experiences of a person the same deep life style! Even discovering the resentment which some investigators describe as a sadistic drive is by no means going to the depths of a personality; resentment is commonly found as a reaction, especially in the pampered life style, as soon as the outside world ceases to fulfill the expectations which the faultily created picture of the world of such pampered children seems to promise.

Any sort of problem behavior in children, whether that behavior is concerned with the mouth or any other part of the body, clearly indicates an early revolt of such problem children against the demands of community life, against fitting themselves into a social

wwwwwwwwwww

2. On a previous occasion Adler had set his theory clearly apart from depth psychology. "Individual Psychology is far removed from all the presently declining theories of shallow 'depth psychology' " (A1927c, preface).

life. Thus such children will early appear as a burden to others, and not as a help.

DESPAIR OF ATTAINING SUCCESS

Perhaps I can make these factors clearer by describing the following case. A twenty-one-year-old student of anthropology complains of an inability to concentrate and of loss of memory, and he shows manifestations of extreme fear. We are certain that we will be able to find in his behavior a whole set of additional nervous symptoms.

His mother died of heart disease. Even before her death the patient suffered from severe palpitations of the heart, and they became noticeably worse after her death.

Some people would say at once: "Ah, he identifies with his mother!" Individual Psychology's retort to those who jump to such a hasty conclusion would be: "You come to such a conclusion because you look fixedly in only one direction. And you find what you planned to find. And now, compelled to do so by your pattern of orientation, you keep a sharp lookout to see whether you can find any evidence of a homosexual bent in this patient who wants to take his mother's place in relation to his father."

We would say further that no one is more aware of the important role which identification plays than is the Individual Psychologist. But if what we have here really is an identification with the mother, why should this identification confine itself exclusively or especially to sexuality? Is there nothing else in the personality of the mother—her work in the house, her position in social affairs, the whole make-up of her personality—that might inspire the urge toward identification with her? Might it not be just that very release from duties, that her sickness had vouchsafed the woman, which her son is valuing above all other qualities? However, although the above-mentioned complaints of the patient did actually bring about his release from tasks and duties, we do not wish to be so influenced by our particular viewpoint in connection with that fact as to rush into the error of premature guessing.

Another point, too, presents itself here. We must repudiate all those theories which would consider neurotic symptoms as manufactured to order. Rather, they are the last, automatic end products of deep-seated psychic disturbances. Merely an inclination to identify oneself with one's mother, to imitate her symptoms, never could lead to palpitations of the heart. But that fear, of which the patient complains, could result in palpitations of the heart, can hardly be disputed. Perhaps the Individual Psychologist who is also a trained physician will cautiously adopt the tentative supposition that the patient may have inherited from his mother an organ inferiority of the heart, a conclusion which does not seem too presumptuous in view of the fact that the entire present generation of this particular family shows a relative inferiority of the heart, which seems strikingly evident in the great number of deaths in this family caused by cardiac ailments.

As a further complaint of the patient we discover that he suffers from a weakness of the eye muscles which are concerned with focusing of the eye. This makes him nearsighted and handicaps him in reading.

If we take into consideration that among his symptoms there are the inability to concentrate, failing memory, and inability to read, we are bound to admit that he faces shipwreck in his work as a student.

The picture of fear manifestations is elucidated when we discover that he is about to take an examination for which he does not feel himself prepared. This connection will become convincing to us, and what is far more important, to the patient, when we can show that in accordance with his life style he always responds with fear when success seems endangered, when he feels that his vanity and his pampered life style are being threatened.

Among other things, he mentioned a symptom which is common among neurotics: When walking over a bridge he is afraid of falling or of throwing himself into the depths.

As I have already explained in connection with the interpretation of dreams of falling, the feeling of falling indicates that one feels oneself "above," but is not sure of being able to maintain one's position. In a despondent or warning manner one arouses a mood and a feeling of catastrophe as if it had already occurred. The purpose of the dream is to arouse the feelings appropriate for stimulating one to make greater efforts to avoid a defeat. It is as if one were saying to himself: "Look out, be careful, move cautiously."

The striving for success—the successful solution of problems—is inherent in the structure of life. The thought of suicide, the problem of death always arises as I have shown, when an individual feels that all his paths to success—as he interprets success—are cut off; when he *feels* success is unattainable for him. In the fear of falling or throwing himself into the depths we see an epitomized, symbolical expression of the patient's despair of attaining success.

This patient remembers that all his symptoms reached a culminating point when, shortly before an examination, he listened to a lecture on Napoleon. The description of this unusually victorious man of power and of his debacle perturbed him excessively. In his shock we find the same strength of identification which leads many medical students to a point where they discover in themselves all the symptoms of those diseases with which they have become acquainted in clinical work. This identification with Napoleon is probably much easier for our patient for the reason that he has apparently created for himself a picture of the world in which he, like a Napoleon, stands out above all others.

He describes his father as a worthless person who pays no attention to his family. This description is of the greatest importance in our attempt to understand the patient's picture of the world, because it indicates—though this is completely unknown to the patient; it is not understood by him and has no existence at all in his "subconscious"—that his experience in his earliest childhood situation was too limited to allow him to attain an adequate development of his innate potentiality for social interest. His interest in others probably stopped with his mother.

His mother was an exceedingly kindhearted woman who was entirely absorbed in taking care of her son, who as a child suffered from tuberculosis. She pampered him to the highest degree. One of his grandmothers did the same. One of his mother's friends who objected to this pampering was thoroughly disliked by him. He was an only child.

EXCLUSION TENDENCY

Our patient tells, too, how when he naturally was no longer able to experience life as he did in his early years of pampering, he became obstinate and quick-tempered. This showed, however, only in situations where he felt himself free of all responsibility and where he had the upper hand, as at home. At school, where he could not be the only one, the first, his hostility against the school exhibited itself in continual attempts to disturb. In the presence of strangers he was shy and reserved. It was almost impossible for him to form friendships. This tendency toward exclusion, which from his earliest years had manifested itself whenever he did not feel himself to be master of the situation, was plainly evident in his pattern of life.

I have often pointed out what is most important in connection with this exclusion tendency and its significance. It operates as a process of abstraction, of selection. Because the individual adopts a certain approach, a certain attitude, a certain relation toward the problems of the outside world (the outside world includes one's own body), anything that does not fit in with his early adopted attitude is more or less excluded; or it is wholly or in part stripped of its intellectual content and objective meaning and is interpreted, always in accordance with the individual's view of the world. The same thing happens with regard to the inseparably associated emotional factors and the attitudes growing out of them. We can observe in the whole life style, in every element of behavior—in thoughts, emotions, and actions—simply the direction selected by the individual for his striving.

What is left over, after this process of elimination by the life style, remains as part of the psychic life and operates "unconsciously," as some authors are wont to put it, or as we would say, "not-understood"; the individual with the life style in question withdraws the impressions fashioned by it from his further criticism. The neurotic can maintain his mistaken picture of the world only with the help of such auxiliary forces and devices as he has withdrawn from critical review.

The attitude of our patient accordingly shows how he sought to maintain his neurotic circle of relationships and activity by means of the elimination of other spheres of activity and of other relationships. He narrowed down the radius of his activities in an attempt to protect the fiction of his own uniqueness.

As he advanced into the higher grades and into high school, he came into contact with friendly, sympathetic teachers of a sort he had never had before. There he came to be one of the best and most attentive of pupils. Only mathematics gave him trouble. This is often the case with pampered children who frequently have a feeling of being left alone in the wide field of this cold, impersonal science; experiencing meager success at the beginning, they set for themselves too narrow boundaries. They often take refuge in the belief that they have no talent, and thus eliminate all thought of and impulse toward improvement and success in that field.

Religious instruction had an extraordinarily strong effect on him. He was fascinated by the idea of the omnipotence of God. He passed a number of years in religious devotion and was an habitual church-goer. The sharing in the greatness of God, the consciousness of having a connection with the highest being, fitted harmoniously within his world picture. But his surrender to the highest being began to be too much for him. Then he turned away from religion and avoided going to church.

His teachers predicted a great future for him. Before he went to the university, he was offered and accepted a position as tutor. To have to subject himself to the will of a pampering mother and a spoiled child was too much for him, according to his picture of the world. He stood it hardly two weeks. In a second position he remained five days. Then he gave up tutoring and became a student of anthropology.

But here, too, he was disturbed by his faulty picture of the world. At the university he sat next to a seventeen-year-old girl student. He became overpowered by the fear that this situation might excite him sexually. As the possibility of being examined in the presence of a girl and perhaps failing was intolerable to him, and since in every situation he was able to take only the paths which seemed to him to lead surely to success, he completely eliminated the other sex from his thoughts and reveled in the idea that he was leading a chaste life.

The fact that this chastity was to a certain extent impaired by masturbation did not trouble him. His narrowly limited life admitted of masturbation; indeed masturbation was the sexual expression appropriate to his mistaken life style. In his life style there was lacking a sufficient development of social interest; there was in it no place for the task of love—a task which requires that two persons, devoted to each other and feeling that they are of equal value, consummate a lasting union. His conceited, ambitious life style fashioned and trained the sexual function in a direction which could quite exclude any feeling of defeat, according to his opinion of what constituted defeat.

Since his sexual functioning was not oriented in the direction of social interest, he retained the tendency to exclude normal sexuality and love, and was interested only in the preservation of his own prestige. The consequence was that he could not find the path away from his mistaken way of training and using the sexual function, the path away from masturbation. Let me take this opportunity to stress the point that this lack of social direction in the sexual function plays the chief role in all sexual perversions and in all psychic disturbances of sexuality.

SELF-CONSISTENCY OF THE PICTURE

We should now be in a position to observe with understanding the sphere of his activity, to look at the domain, which with the help of his picture of the world and in correspondence with his opinion about life, he has created for himself. This enables us to predict with reasonable accuracy his entire mode of expression, all his movements, his manner of solving or of excluding problems of life—we say "with reasonable accuracy" because no one can project himself wholly into the situation and life of another; and because we find such a great number of possibilities for evasion.

We might in this case, for example, predict approximately what our patient will reveal to us as his earliest childhood recollection. In all probability he will describe a situation or an event in which his picture of the world will be represented, either verbally or symbolically. His earliest recollection runs as follows: "I looked out of a high window onto a court in which soldiers in uniform were training." Perhaps only Individual Psychology will take seriously the detail that he was looking down from above, and will find that this looking from above shows little activity, and at the same time that it has a connection with his nearsightedness. Children with slight eye defects quite frequently develop a greater interest in the visual world than do those with perfectly normal eyes. Even his early choice of a vocation would not be hard to predict. He wanted, in fact, to be a pilot, an orator, a great political leader, or a locomotive engineer. All of these choices show, either literally or figuratively, the desire to look down from above, to be in the superior, masterful position.

He complains that he is inordinately suggestible. Among people who fail in life and whose failures we designate by such terms as neurosis, psychosis, delinquency, etc., we seldom find any susceptibility to suggestion when it comes to matters in the nature of cooperation and sharing with one's fellow men. When we do encounter suggestibility in the direction of cooperation among problem children of little activity, it is always followed by resentment and secret revolt. Occasionally it also happens during psychotherapeutic treatment that a patient seems to be willing to follow a suggestion; but we know he is not when he does nothing toward improving his behavior.

For the most part we find these complaints about suggestibility exactly where we really find quite the opposite, so that the supposition seems justified that the patient makes statements regarding being susceptible to suggestion in order to protect himself. In general it may be said that suggestibility always appears only where it fits in with the life style. So, apparently, when our patient readily agrees with others, it is because he is afraid that by opposition he might encounter a defeat. His suggestibility is therefore directly connected with his timidity.

This symptom he brings into direct connection with the behavior of the woman friend of his mother already mentioned, who was, and not only for him, the most important person of his immediate environment. When he visited her, he had to dress as nicely as possible, and it was her reproaches which hurt him most. Gradually he came to regard her as his worst enemy, for she was always wounding his vanity.

He frequently visited the grave of his mother, whose close relationship to him had always been the center of his picture of the world, according to which he felt it his right and due to be pampered. While there, he often asked himself what would become of him without her. Then his thoughts would regularly turn to his heart ailment, the existence of which no doctor could affirm. This was a case where the suggestibility of which he complained was not effective in helping him.

He turned to psychiatrists and psychologists for help. One of them asked him whether he felt as if he were being watched on the street. The patient suspected that the physician had in mind the diagnosis of paranoia. He had never before had such a thought. But following this question, he often looked about him while on the street, suspiciously, for fear that someone might be following him.

Another psychiatrist asked him if he ever heard voices. From this question the patient gathered that he was suspected of being schizophrenic. He denied it, but after this remark he always thought he heard noises and ringing in his ears. This symptom was further reinforced when the aforementioned friend of his mother explained, in answer to his apparently disinterested question, that such symptoms were a sign of insanity. One night this ringing in his ears became exceptionally strong. He screamed and cried so loudly that his father had to come and quiet him. Thereupon the roaring in his ears ceased, but it started up again whenever he visited his mother's friend.

Should we deny the fact that he heard a roaring sound in his ears? Or should we, like others, assume that the patient produced it voluntarily? I do not believe that anyone could deliberately produce it; I assume rather that he had a sensitive auditory organ, an organ inferiority which became noticeable in times of emotional stress. It had perhaps occurred even earlier, though the patient before his consultation with the psychiatrist had not given it any special attention or attached any importance to it.

DEFENSE OF VANITY

We see how, for the safeguarding of his picture of the world and for the defense of his vanity, the patient had erected a wall against the demands of actual community life. Without clearly realizing it himself, he was able to exclude or shove aside all disturbing problems of life while he abandoned himself utterly to his feelings and to the observation of his symptoms. These symptoms were the result of the shock which he experienced when, in a difficult situation, he felt himself too weak to arrive at the high goal which he, in his vanity, had set for himself; when he felt too weak to play a pre-eminent role commensurate with that which should be his according to his picture of the world. Thus he was able to avoid the shock of imminent problems and could relegate those problems to the background. Such a procedure of exclusion naturally appeared to him the lesser of two evils.

Individual Psychology finds the striving for success inextricably embedded in the life structure. Now, since this science of human behavior insists that no one can change his life style without changing his world picture, is it not reasonable to suppose: (a) that the striving for success is to be found even in the behavior of this patient, and (b) that the personality of the patient has not yet changed?

He who can identify with this patient will readily find that the latter's present behavior corresponds to his picture of the world, according to which he gives value only to those situations in which he finds satisfaction for his vanity. Of all the possibilities which are conceivable to him in his difficult situation, only two, according to his picture of the world, seem suitable—that of avoiding any defeat at all by constructing a tenable alibi and so saving his vanity in case of defeat; and that of pressing his family into his service. Thus the patient secures the advantage of being able to remain in his ideal situation, i. e., ideal according to his picture of the world. He behaves as if he were saying by such behavior that he could be victorious if only the handicap of his illness were not there, *but* it is. The alibi and prestige-saving device is to be found in the *but*. And he feels that after all this is not his business, but the physician's. He feels that he is free of responsibility.

From this it follows that the personality of the patient has not changed. He still lives according to his old picture of the world. He gives the very answer to the problems of life which we might expect from him when we consider his life style. That response is sure to follow when his exaggerated inferiority feeling becomes active on the occasion of a threatened defeat.

The selection of his particular neurotic symptoms, automatically developed, is thoroughly understandable. At the bottom of them all lies the deep shock resulting from the feeling of not being able to live according to his vain world picture. This shock, because it is long continuing and not merely a passing, temporary shock—due to the fact that the dangerous external situations and the problems which confront him are not temporary and passing, but continuous—

plunged his body and mind into an emotional upheaval. The somatic inferiorities, those of eye, ear, and heart, under the stress of his heightened emotion become evident first. His emotion is associated with his fear of not attaining or of losing his high position, and of wounding his vanity; his anxiety is a manifestation of a strong, apparently hopeless feeling of inferiority. The fear of falling or of throwing himself down indicates in a symbolic way that he is facing the death problem. The seemingly paranoid features were the results of ill-advised hints from the doctors which he fitted into his life style and used successfully for his purposes.

The patient's dream life corresponds entirely to his world picture. His sexual dreams show that he has not yet overcome masturbation; and masturbation indicates his asocial conception of the sexual function. He regards sex as a problem for one person alone. He is troubled by dreams of being followed and of being surrounded by dangers, so that he feels he has to be continually on the watch. In one of these dreams he stands on the summit of a mountain and looks down on the little people below, a picture that corresponds completely to his earliest childhood recollection. Another time he sees himself on a high church steeple, sliding down to land in the country of the communists. Communism is for him a synonym for the worst kind of evil.

He has absolutely gone to pieces in his studies. He dreams his professor is coming up the stairs and wants to speak to him. As the professor draws nearer, he turns aside and says he has made a mistake, and he turns to one of the other students. Feeling forsaken then by his teacher too—a fact that means more to him than his studies—our patient turns his back on science.

He is on the alert for any word which might help him in his retreat, might serve him as an alibi. His attention is directed only toward the problem of avoiding threatening defeats. His mother's friend tells him of a man who at forty suffered a stroke; she adds that the man must have had a suspicion of his future fate, because he had not wanted to marry. At once the thought strikes our patient that he too is going to suffer that same fate.

He has retained one consolation, one support. It is the need for consolation and compensation which moves so many people to fashion a superiority complex out of their inferiority complex. In this case, too, we find that same tendency to try to show at least a seeming success in life. He finds that his forehead has grown tremendously and he is convinced that this indicates that he is qualified to become a political leader. This means of course that his qualifications will be put to the test only in years to come.

PRIVATE MAP VERSUS COMMON VIEW

His life style and his picture of the world are parts of one integral system. He sees everything with the eyes of his vanity. He approaches every situation and problem of life with fearful anticipation as to whether his prestige will be assured, seldom finds this to be the case, and therefore feels compelled to withdraw from the problems of life. His retreat is effected by means of his symptoms, and the symptoms are the results of shock effects. These shock effects he has found useful in obtaining relief from a difficult situation. There is then no incentive for him to give up the shock effects which have served a purpose for him; so he holds on to them.

So long as he does not understand this error, so long as he regards his world as the right, the real one, and the real world unbearable for his vanity, he will remain a neurotic. If he can abandon his dream of a world, a dream which was born of his vanity and which justifies his vanity, then more and more will it be possible for him to begin to feel himself an equal among equals, and less and less will he feel dependent upon the opinions of others. His courage, too, will mount and his reason will gain control over relationships that are not understood.

Coming to understand his own picture of the world—a picture which he built up early in childhood and which has served as his private map, so to speak, for making his way through life—is an essential part of the process of cure. When one is attempting to redirect his life to a more nearly normal way of living, he will need to understand how he has been seeing the world. He will have to re-see the world and alter his old private view in order to bring it more into harmony with a common view of the world—remembering that by common view we mean a view in which others can share. It is not likely that others would share his private opinion, that at all times and in all situations he should by right occupy the position of ascendancy and be the recipient of special privileges.

It can be said of any and all experiences and native potentialities that they do not have a generally valid or an absolute market value, such as commodities may have, but that they have only as much efficacy and value for an individual as his life style permits. An individual's life style is developed as his own unique manner of coping with life's problems, according to the way he feels and sees them in his particular picture of the world. Only one who understands this point may rightly speak of heights and depths in the science of psychology.

IO

Compulsion Neurosis
(1931) [1, 1a]

For Adler mental disorder was the expression of a faulty, immature style of life, as shown in the preceding section. The important matter was to comprehend the individual life style. Not much attention was paid to diagnostic categories; there were no pure cases. Yet one specific type of neurosis was to Adler apparently the prototype of all—compulsion neurosis. He wrote more on this form than on any other.

The present selection is actually one paper plus a later addition, and succeeds two earlier papers on the same subject matter (A1913b, A1918b). The importance Adler attributed to compulsion neurosis is further shown by the fact that he supports his exposition with twelve case descriptions. —Eds.

In the last several decades the medical profession has shown an especial interest in psychological studies. This is largely owing to the fact that the physician has found that psychology provides him with a means for observing and understanding certain developments that

1. A1931f, with exception of the section on "Emphasis on Rational Processes," beginning with the second paragraph, which is from A1936m. Reprinted from translation, A1936i, with some editorial rearrangements and new translations.

1a. Lecture given at the Fifth International Congress of Individual Psychology, Berlin, September 26–29, 1930. Original footnote.

occur commonly in life, but which generally pass undetected. Early preparatory descriptive steps were taken in France, and in Vienna by Krafft-Ebing. It represented a great advance toward clarification when later Westphal decided to include under the term "compulsion neurosis" a certain group of neurotic disturbances. Since then the literature on the subject has grown to vast proportions. In this article I shall indicate the contribution that Individual Psychology has made to the understanding of compulsion neurosis; but to do this I must begin far back.

The efforts of Individual Psychology have always been mainly directed toward grasping the "Why?" of phenomena—*why* (toward what end) a human being behaves in a manner which seems to us extraordinary and pathological. Other psychologists have been more inclined to study the "How?"—*how* certain particular symptoms come into being. Each group, it must be understood, takes both questions—both the Why? (the Whither) and the How? (the Whence)—into consideration, but each always lays the chief stress upon one or the other approach.

In view of our comprehensive general outlook, it is understandable that we should throw into relief the question of why a human being behaves in such a way as not to solve his life problems in the manner *generally expected* in his culture. Accordingly, in 1908, shortly after the completion of my *Studie über Minderwertigkeit von Organen*,[2] I began to develop the finalistic viewpoint of Individual Psychology, and came to the conclusion that we must look upon the psychic life as

wwwwwwwwwww

2. Here Adler added a footnote, as follows: "In this work I tried to show that a child born with weak organs comes to apprehend the weakness and unreliability of his organs; and that, as he builds up his individuality, he has a sense of insecurity, a feeling of being overburdened and under strain, and attempts in a thousand different ways to relieve himself of this strain, to adapt himself to his environment, and to achieve a feeling of personal significance and value."

However, Adler's memory is in error in that the *Studie* (A1907a) mentions neither feelings of inferiority nor a sense of insecurity. He made this error on several other occasions also. Adler expressed himself in this first monograph not in such "subjective" but only in "objective" terms (A1956b, pp. 24 & 44–45). Inferiority and insecurity feelings only appear for the first time three years later (e.g., A1910c and A1910f). A forerunner of such feelings was "a feeling of being slighted," *ein Gefühl des Zurückgesetztseins* (A1909a, p. 536). The latter was pointed out to us in a personal communication by Godelieve Vercruysse on December 6, 1962.

a movement, directed toward the solution of certain almost immutable life tasks. And this activity, it should be added, coexists with a tendency on the part of each individual to arrange factors of the external world in a fashion that, from his standpoint, he feels will best enable him to attain his ideal, his goal. It is evident that the question of the best way of dealing with these inescapable life problems is, to a degree, a matter of arbitrary judgment; it can be considered from different points of view, and solutions can be attempted in various ways. This explains the countless variants in our development and expressive forms.

In 1908 I came upon the idea that every individual really exists in a state of aggression, and, imprudently, I called this attitude the "aggression drive" [A1908b]. But I soon realized that it is not a drive at all, but a partly conscious, partly not understood attitude toward the tasks of life. Thus I arrived at an understanding of *the social component* in personality, the degree of which is always developed according to the individual's *opinion* of the facts and the difficulties of life. The individual's attitude thus reflects not the facts, the thing-in-itself, an existing "reality principle," but what he "thinks" of his ability to fulfill them. Individual psychology thus places the individual into the circle and the relations of social events, an insertion in which everybody remains, however, but on the path toward an ideal development. In this manner Individual Psychology came to note the social content of the life style as I have attempted to describe it in the "scientific meaning of life," and in fact to measure in each movement this ability toward cooperation on the path to superiority.

By way of transition to my special topic, let me mention that in 1918 I delivered an address on compulsion neurosis before the Medical Association in Zurich [A1918b]. In this paper I expressed a view which I believe is discernible today, albeit in modified form, in the theory of every school of psychiatry. I asserted that, under all circumstances, a neurotic symptom is produced whenever a person attempts to evade the problems of life because he feels fundamentally unable to solve them in a manner compatible with his striving for superiority.

HESITATING ATTITUDE

The compulsion neurotic regularly displays signs of anxiety if he fails to develop other symptoms in a given difficult situation. He feels compelled to do something, to perform a compulsive action which he himself feels is absurd—and which he recognizes as being out of joint with social living. Yet he must yield to the compulsion, or else fall victim to anxiety. The compulsion neurotic has a feeling of insecurity, a feeling of not being able to cope. This feeling is always biologically meaningful, never represents a psychological final state, but makes itself effective in the social life.

Anxiety is one of the most concrete forms of the sense of inferiority. It serves a definite purpose, the purpose of protection. For example, a woman patient under treatment for anxiety neurosis had progressed so well that she could go out by herself. One night when she came home she found a stranger standing by the door. She screamed out, "Why don't you go away? Can't you see I'm afraid?" The use of anxiety as a means to power is very important from the social viewpoint.

In the 1918 paper I also pointed out that the compulsion neurotic is apparently at a secondary theater of operations (*sekundärer Kriegsschauplatz*), and exhausts himself *there*, instead of where we expect him, solving his problem of life. Thus we gain the impression that he conducts a battle against windmills, is a veritable Don Quixote, is occupied with matters which do not at all fit into our world, apparently in order to waste time. For time appears to him as the most dangerous foe because it always makes some demand on him, because it induces him toward the solution of tasks to which he feels unequal.

One can always establish that there is actually a lack of preparation for the solution of the life problems and that this lack—whether it really exists or is "believed" only in imagination—prevents him from advancing, so that he lapses into the *hesitating attitude*. It is in this hesitating attitude that the compulsion neurotic turns to the secondary theater of operations, and we must establish that such an evasion can happen only when one is afraid of a defeat. When the compulsion neurotic is on sure ground, he advances; then he is not impeded by obsessive ideas; then he solves his task. Only in a certain sector of his life—occupational life, scientific life, often also love life—one finds particularly strongly developed his inclination to prevent his defeat by proceeding to a secondary theater of operations and eliminating the compulsion of life by a countercompulsion. The countercompulsion gives him a feeling of success—according to his style.

I must also touch upon one other point, which has already been made clear in Individual Psychology, but which often gives rise to mistaken notions. This is the phenomenon of indecision or doubt. Doubt seems often to constitute a special entity in psychology and is frequently so considered. But if we observe this state of mind in its general context and ask ourselves the question, "What part does doubt play in relation to specific achievement in social life?" we will discover that its purpose is to maintain the *status quo*, to prevent change. This is the hesitating attitude of which I have often spoken. Excessive doubt and long-continued indecision represent nothing more than attempts to waste time—to waste time in order to gain time.

I have found that the sense of degradation and humility so common among the mentally sick is simply another device for wasting time.

STRIVING FOR GODLIKENESS AND DEPRECIATION OF OTHERS

I further mentioned that rarely is the striving for superiority so clearly defined as it is in a compulsion neurosis. Many writers on the subject had already noted the patients' belief in the magical efficacy and omnipotence of words and ideas, but, lacking the criteria of Individual Psychology, apparently did not fully understand. Recourse to "primitive, archaic thought," [3] is not an atavism and does not stem from the "collective unconscious," but represents an ever feasible, childish device for achieving a sense of power. It arises from the striving for a unique sort of superiority which I have described as godlikeness. The compulsion neurotic strives after the clearest expression of his godlike quality; but naturally he cannot achieve this end in the realm of social

wwwwwwwwwwww

3. Remember the Polonius complex [see pp. 75–76].—Adler's note.

life since he lacks even the first requisite to success in social life—an interest in others.

We may ignore the opinions to the effect that the compulsion neurotic is distinguished from other individuals by a morbid objectivity. On the contrary, he stands in great need of others; he clearly reveals his feelings of inferiority in the manifestations of his uncertainty and anxiety, and draws another person into his sphere as he advances to an overt inferiority complex. The compulsion neurotic endeavors to overcome this anxiety, and tries to represent himself in the form to which he originally aspired—*as a demigod, who exalts himself above humankind and who depreciates everyone else and puts them in the shade.* He covers over his inferiority complex with a superiority complex and thus appears magnificent enough in his own eyes—for *only* his compulsive idea, so he feels, prevents him from fulfilling his triumphant mission. His fantastic notion of superiority is fully and wholly revealed in his compulsion.

And I found, too, that the so-called sadistic bent in compulsion neurosis is only one of the thousand subtle variations on the theme of seeking ascendancy over others; it is only a manifestation of the desire to dominate, to exalt oneself, by depreciating others. In compulsion neurosis, if it is manifest, it is expressed in a way so that the clear, direct, sadistic intent is covered by the patient's horror of it and his consequent feeling of guilt. But perhaps the absurd struggle of the compulsion neurotic—his effort to raise himself above everyone else in so abrupt and startling a manner—is not without an element of cruelty, since he (like the user of violent profanity) approaches the realm of practical activity with the purpose of depreciating other individuals.

CRITIQUE OF AMBIVALENCE, CONFLICT, AND GUILT

I mentioned further that what some writers on the subject have described as ambivalence, ambiguity, contradictoriness in mental dispositions and feelings, and split personality is simply a matter of contrasting means to the same end, and not a change in the end itself.

This brings us to a question which is of the greatest importance to the whole theory of neurosis. Individual Psychology, since it so strongly emphasizes the unity of the individual's life and endeavors, had to take cognizance of the idea of ambivalence. It explains that the movement of a person who wishes to evade reality—in order to raise himself to godlikeness in his imagination and emotions—must naturally show a point of beginning and an end point. Individual Psychology has always stressed the fact that it regards psychic life as movement, and considers form, expression, function as a kind of frozen movement. Hence, if an individual purposes to raise himself from a lower level to a higher, we should expect to find two seemingly contrasting points in the movement, namely, the point away from which the movement goes and the point toward which it is directed. It is from these points that we are able to learn something of the direction of the movement.

Furthermore, it is also in accordance with the thousandfoldness of the life style that an ideal movement can never be found in it.

Inaccurately considered, the disparities between reality and the ideals of courage, truthfulness, activity, etc., can always be presented as contrasts, when, indeed, we are dealing here with varieties and degrees. It is a pity that we do not have uniform terms and concepts for the variants of a psychic movement. If we did, this error would certainly not have insinuated itself into our thought. Of course, we will also observe the so-called pleasure in suffering which finally gives the neurotic the feeling that he is unique and godlike, and which really is nothing more than the pleasure which a person feels when he has paid the forfeit that exempts him from a greater evil. Such a life style constitutes a palpable failure in life.

We cannot properly speak of a "conflict" in compulsion neurosis, since the patient never deviates from the road of evasion, which he paves with good intentions or feelings of guilt. Conflict means only a standstill. These good intentions, which may appear as feelings of guilt, are absolutely dead; they signify nothing as to any real change in the life of the patient. It means nothing, so far as altered behavior in the patient is concerned, that he makes a great display of his feelings of guilt; he has the assurance that, by acknowledging his guilt and raising trivialities to a rank of importance and dignity, he can appear to be more genteel and more honest than any of his fellows. That these much bewailed trivialities have no "deeper" significance is evident from the fact that, in compulsion neurosis as in melancholia, the patient contents himself with merely expressing a sense of guilt, and would never think of exercising active contrition, shown in the form of improved behavior.

COMPULSION AS SAFEGUARD

The compulsion neurotic early employs and trains an absurd process of reasoning in order to allow himself a sense of great personal importance and worth without achieving anything objectively tangible. A properly conducted inquiry into his past history will reveal certain characteristic traits: a pedantic striving for faultlessness and perfect accuracy; a tendency to side-step difficult tasks by confusing them with unrelated, simple ones; the practice of formalized religious exercises and rituals, with the idea of "tempting God"; the habit of stressing the difficulty of situations in order to make a greater triumph of their solution; a desire to elude rivalries; a pride in a grotesquely exaggerated family tradition. The compulsion neurotic is always a person who reveals the neurotic disposition which I attempted to describe in my book, *Über den nervösen Charakter* [A1912a]. He is a person who feels that he is set apart from other individuals; who thinks only of himself; who is imbued with self-love, and has no interest in the general welfare. He believes that he is incapable of realizing his great potentialities in the social stream of the world, and for this reason he sets himself a high personal goal, above the aspirations of other mortals.

Further, I noted a trait which I called the neurotic tendency to create safeguards, and which is especially prominent in compulsion neurosis. This tendency is not merely a protective device, and certainly cannot be considered a defense against suppressed sexual desires. It is a system of psychic forms of expression, resulting from careful training, and is skillfully contrived to permit the individual actually to attain, in the neurotic manner, his goal of personal superiority. The patient who feels a compulsion to jump out of windows builds up this compulsion into a safeguard; he acquires a sense of superiority by successfully overcoming the urge, and employs the whole situation as an excuse for his failure in life.

I come now to an important fact that seems to have escaped the

writers on this topic. They always seem to consider the compulsion as
if it resided in the obsessions or compulsive ideas. They regard
obsession or obsessional action as if it were wholly divorced from the
normal processes of thought; as if thinking were charged with
compulsion and rises up from time to time, like a demon from a pit,
to overpower and take possession of its victim; as if the compulsion
had an individuality of its own. Freud, with incomparable grace and
ease, invests each of his postulated "instincts" with human attributes.
The compulsion does not reside in the compulsive idea or action; it
originates outside—in the sphere of our normal social life. This is the
source of the patient's neurotic compulsion or urge. He *must* evade
the realities of life, since he feels incompetent to face them and since
his high-flown ambition must elude any sort of palpable failure. He
retreats farther and farther before the bayonets of life from outside,
which he feels are closing in on him—until he finds a secluded cranny
of life where he is put to no real test and can make use of the notions
that give him a feeling of complete superiority. By exerting all his
force he acquires a sense of omnipotence in overcoming some variety
of self-created, imaginary fears. Herein lies the significance of the
safeguarding tendency that I have described. The compulsion, therefore, does not reside in the obsessive symptom, but in the actualities
of life which seem terrifying to the individual concerned. Furthermore, I was able to determine with great certainty that the compulsion
neurotic is characterized from childhood on (as we can see from his
earliest experiences) by sudden successful efforts to pull himself
together.

A short case history will clarify this point. The patient is a man of
forty-five, in good circumstances. You will readily understand that
individuals who strive for [personal] superiority may occasionally
achieve quite estimable results in life. In fact, it is surprisingly
common for the compulsion neurotic to occupy a prominent social
position. He accomplishes something, but he is never satisfied with
what he accomplishes. Such is the case with our 45-year-old patient,
who complains of a continual obsession that he must jump out of a
window. The obsession is most pronounced when he is in an upper
story of a high building. For twenty-five years he has felt this
compulsion. Yet now he stands before me in the flesh. He has never

jumped out; he has always conquered his obsession. He has triumphed over himself. He feels heroic.

To the untrained mind this explanation may at first seem farfetched or artificial. But we know as a familiar fact that we ourselves often take a particular pride in mastering our inclinations and overcoming one or another of our desires. This same sort of pride gives our patient a sense of omnipotence. He feels heroic when he can say to himself: "I have been able to bear up under a whole mountain of woe—wretched Atlas that I am!" Like every neurotic, he does not fix his attention on the really important point, but on a secondary issue. He has an eye to his anxiety, since he needs it as something to overcome; but he does not understand his fantastic struggle for omnipotence or his sense of inferiority which, he feels, compels him to travel on easy byways. He is a fighter of windmills: a hero in his own mind if not to the outside world.

Now let us glance back at the patient's childhood. Individual Psychology has succeeded in making a new science of interpreting childhood recollections; these old memories have begun to talk and tell their tale. Our patient was the youngest child, and his mother's favorite. Like many pampered children he was timid, and his anxiety increased when he entered school. This was revealed on one occasion when a bullying schoolmate singled him out for abuse. But, in the emergency, he mustered up all his energies, attacked the other boy, and knocked him down. Anyone capable of finding the dynamics in childhood recollections cannot help seeing that the patient has followed the same tactics throughout his life. First he is afraid; then he overcomes his fear. This is his method of acquiring a sense of superiority.

SELF-CREATED CAUSALITY

Furthermore, I have found that a personality like that of the compulsion neurotic never comes about as a result of a mechanistic process. According to Freud, the instincts have the power of choice. They can think; they have a consciousness, and know their direction; they have a purposive, creative energy, etc. In short, everything that he finds in the psychic life of the individual is attributed to the instincts. We cannot, however, find the explanation of the origin of compulsion neurosis in instincts or drives, for a drive, as we understand it, is without direction. We are equally unable to lay the blame on heredity, since all the factors entering into the neurosis—character, passions, emotions—are shaped within the framework of human society.

We must consider the great potentialities for mistaken interpretation residing in the human mind if we hope to understand neurotic symptoms. These errors are wholly devoid of causality. No one is forced into neurosis, either by heredity or by instincts, but only enticed, within certain latitudes of probability. The pampered child—and almost all neurotics are pampered children—does not act according to the law of cause and effect when he picks one experience out of thousands and makes it the basis of his subsequent life. We cure the neurotic by freeing him from a false, self-created causality and adapting him to real life.

In trying to understand some given behavior one must turn back to the past life of the patient. For a person's behavior is always based upon the materials of his life experience, and these naturally lie in the past. After his fourth or fifth year every individual possesses an established life style, and, according to his life style, the individual assimilates, applies, and digests the data of all later experiences. He draws from them only such conclusions as fit into his already established apperception schema, attaching importance only to those aspects of any experience which correspond with the picture of the world which he has already formed and with the particular life style which he has developed for coping with that world.

It should be pointed out further that the life style of the compulsion neurotic—this most patent and futile form of striving for godlikeness—naturally accepts everything that suits its purposes, and rejects everything that runs counter to them. I shall illustrate this fact with an example—which probably needs further inquiry and a better foundation, but will serve to clarify a great deal which, even today, is uncritically referred to the province of the unconscious.

The example I shall use is a medical student who, from childhood on, has despaired of his ability to catch up with his brother. This brother has taken life at a canter. The oldest child in the family, and a stepson, he was less pampered and had the courage to make good headway. As a result, the patient continually lived in the obscuring shadow of his overpowering older brother. At present the patient is studying medicine and finds it easy to master the theoretical branches. But now, faced with the necessity of deciding whether to continue his studies, and still looking up to his brother, he suddenly discovers that he is unable to enter the dissecting room, that it is impossible for him to attend an operation, etc.

If we bear in mind the connection between these symptoms and the patient's overestimation of his brother, we can understand his fear, his unwillingness to make a final decision. The patient's dread of attending an operation fits in with his diffident attitude toward his medical studies. He looks into the future, senses a possible defeat, and prepares a means of rescuing his self-esteem. At some later date he will be able to say: If I hadn't felt this mysterious dread, I would have surpassed my brother. He postpones the test which will decide his defeat or victory, and arms himself against an encroachment on his personal ambition. But it seems that his is only the humanly intelligible aim of emulating his brother and not one that expressly strives for godlikeness. His goal is merely a superiority over his brother, and not the absolute superiority to which the compulsion neurotic aspires.

Perhaps Individual Psychology alone is fully cognizant that compulsion neurosis can develop only in cases of considerable estrangement from social interest. At all events, however, we can clearly observe in this patient an automatism which seems peculiar to the human psyche, one which we find in individuals who approximate the normal as well as in those who are designated abnormal. This is the instinctive tendency to single out and stress those experiences which fit into one's life style, and to exclude all those which do not fit in, or to transform them until they do. Each human being evaluates all experiences according to his life style.

EMPHASIS ON RATIONAL PROCESSES

At this point I should like to take up a fundamental issue. Although the problem of compulsion neurosis may be considered as if the chief concern were of an intellectual nature and had to do only with ideas, yet we know that the element of thought cannot be detached from the structure of the whole psychic make-up, which includes feeling as well. Whenever one conceives an idea, one arouses in himself also a series of corresponding feelings and emotions, not only because he realizes that the idea should connote these emotions, but because he actually transports himself into a sphere of thought which is affected and altered by the idea. The various psychic functions, thought and feeling, cannot be divorced from one another. If, for instance, I think of being in a beautiful city, my mental picture gives rise to feelings and emotions such as I might have if I were actually approaching the city, or were already there. This process is especially important as an essential factor in our dream dynamics. When we dream, we awaken feelings and emotions. We do this by conjuring up images with which certain feelings are associated which strongly affect us and move us in a certain definite direction. The same process is at work in a compulsion neurosis. In the thought of absolute superiority we can plainly detect the feeling or emotion of absolute superiority.

The chief disturbance in the psychic life of the compulsion neurotic takes place in the rational processes, in the realm of thought rather than emotion. The unity and indivisibility of the psychic life was earlier and more forcibly stressed by Individual Psychology than by any other psychological school. But I have also stressed the complexity and uniqueness of every individual and the great diversity of life styles. Certain elements, certain aspects of the whole, certain particular psychic movements, are found to be especially emphasized in various individual cases. These particular aspects we may artificially isolate for the purpose of discussion. They may be either chiefly rational or chiefly emotional in character, and may take the form of either active or passive attitudes. Of all the phases of psychic life, the rational is most strongly stressed in individuals who suffer from compulsion neurosis, but it is an ideational life directed in such a way that it runs counter to social interest, and hence to common sense.

This tendency to rationalize and formulate, to pay regard to formal routine and orderly arrangement, is not restricted to the obsessional ideas but reveals itself also in other phases of the patient's life. Often he has a marked feeling for words; he is fond of brooding over ideas; he loves to pick about at maxims and precepts; he acts as if he firmly believed that "in the beginning was the Word." We must grant that persons with these inclinations may achieve fine things, provided that they follow the path of the social good. But, unless turned to the advantage of society, the tendency is futile and results in empty form. This is the case with the phrase-mongering of the compulsion neurotic, and is manifest in his addiction to compulsive prayers, to repetition of ritual-like performances, and to love of formulas; in his overt curses and libels; in his earnest faith in the potency of his anathemas. Certain repetitive actions can easily be understood as expressing an obsessional idea—for instance, the washing compulsion which shouts more loudly than words that everyone but the patient is a dirty swine.

From practice, one gets the impression often that words and thoughts have been set at so high a premium in these compulsion cases because the patient began in childhood to consider the power of linguistic expression as a vital problem in his life. He may have grown up as a self-pampered child in an environment which he felt to be hostile, and in which he was continually put to a disadvantage by others who were more adept than he at turning thoughts, words, and curses to advantageous ends. Words and ideas played an important role in his life. Occasionally the child's own timidity and reticence gives him the impression that:

> *With words 'tis excellent disputing;*
> *Systems to words 'tis easy suiting.*[4]

Here we have another evident point of comparison with schizophrenia which also manifests itself chiefly in a disturbance of the thought processes, and very frequently involves the coining of words, phrases, and maxims, either voiced or silent.

Of course the other elements of the psychic life—other than the one artificially isolated for the purpose of discussion—are not absent, but they seem to follow in the wake of the more dominant element. The dominant element may be, for instance, high-strung emotionalism, anxiety, hypersensitivity. Whatever it is, it corresponds to the individual's lifelong training and shows especially at the time of the shock which the patient suffers when he is confronted by the forthcoming tasks of life for which he is not prepared. Such a shock

4. Goethe, J. W. v. *Faust*. Part 1. Bayard Taylor's translation, lines 1997–1998. —Translator's note.

must inevitably be produced in him as soon as his childish philosophy of life collides with a reality quite different from the one he has trained for, and he feels forced into a retreat. This retreat the patient accomplishes by strengthening his dominant characteristic, which reflects what he has considered as a vital problem ever since his childhood, but which he begins automatically to regard as the very keynote of his existence.

To the best of our knowledge (and the best is none too adequate), we can safely assume that individuals differ considerably in their natural capacities for intellectual and linguistic development. Exactly how much they differ no one can say at the present time, since most of the students of heredity make the mistake of working backwards and trying to deduce the amount of innate capacity from the finished products, or degree of development. We can, however, assume that any superior capacity for language, like any other superior natural endowment, is a definite advantage when properly used; that is, when it is developed, in the stream of evolution and human progress, as a useful contribution to the welfare of humanity as a whole. But if it is imprisoned in a false conception of life, it may be useless or even injurious. This is the case in compulsion neurosis and paranoia.

It is, however, probable (though not inevitable) that the processes of thought and speech will be brought into the foreground through the creative power of the child, and will be more highly developed, if the child experiences his own speech development as a source of inferiority, either in his struggle with his environment or because the environment intentionally or unintentionally impresses this problem on his mind. In such an event, the feeling of inferiority may set in so strongly that the child takes one of two courses. He can go through intensive training to better his results in this respect (either on the useful or the useless side of life), or else give up the battle. Granted possibilities of development in his natural endowment, he may choose either alternative.

In many cases of compulsion neurosis, I have found that continual nagging, scolding, derision, and faultfinding can exert so profound an influence on the child that, whatever his natural capacities, he will make a frantic effort to improve his faculty of self-expression, adopting the same tone that is used toward him, acquiring a nimble tongue or continually searching for words, ignoring affronts or lapsing into the limping sort of wit that stumbles on the proper retort only when it is too late. Or he may invent a standard rejoinder—usually derogatory—which occurs to him on every occasion when his pride and vanity are injured. The compulsion neurotic is generally of the latter type.

One of my patients, who suffered from a washing and tidying mania, had grown up as the youngest, rather helpless, child in a family where shouting and cursing were everyday practices, and she was continually scolded and ridiculed for her faulty pronunciation. Shortly after her marriage, when her husband fell into the same habit of reproving and criticizing her, she began to draw the long bow herself, and freed herself from him and all her other responsibilities by an incessant urge to clean and arrange the house. This was tantamount to her saying, "You fool, now you see what happens when I give in to your critical wishes for order and cleanliness!" If anything was not exactly in keeping with her mania for cleanliness, she immediately gave expression to a formula which was puzzling to those around her who did not understand its purpose. She cried: "Help! Help!"

I once presented these views before a group of physicians that included a good many psychiatrists. In the general discussion which followed my talk, one of the psychiatrists began to attack my statements by picking out individual words and misinterpreting them to suit his purposes. In reply, I innocently tried to make myself clearer with an illustration. "Take yourself, for example," I said, "with your tendency to pick apart words and ideas and attach your own meanings to them. If you were ever so unfortunate as to acquire a neurosis, it would probably be a compulsion neurosis." I was not a little surprised to discover that my words had produced an unforeseen effect. My colleague was speechless; he turned pale, and seemed greatly disturbed. I apologized as best I could, but later on I learned that this psychiatrist had for two years been under unsuccessful treatment for compulsion neurosis.

TWELVE CASES

I have spoken plainly enough on the subject of causality and its slight importance in relation to the understanding of the psychic life, since it governs at best only the physiological processes, not the psychological. And I have described the structure of compulsion neurosis. With all this in mind, we should be able to discover why one particular compulsive symptom and not another appears under a given set of circumstances. A brief account of a few cases will illustrate practically the nature of compulsion neurosis, and show that the application of our principles advances the understanding of it.

1. A common form of compulsion is the impulse *to jump out of windows*. A young singer, who seemed confident that he had a fine voice but felt thrust into the background by his father and his older brother, engaged in an incessant struggle against such an obsession. He believed that it was only his puzzling obsession which prevented him from becoming "the greatest tenor." He was free of it only so long as someone was at his side, and this, of course, was impossible in a theatre or on the concert platform where he would have had to appear if he were to go on with his profession of concert singer. So we can see that his compulsive idea served as a means of putting at a distance the test of his greatness. He was really not sure that the test would result in his favor. He felt that he must surpass his father and brother in some way. Now if he prevents himself from ever coming to the test he can always save his vanity from being hurt. And he can maintain his personal prestige in his own eyes by having arranged a situation in which he can say and believe, "I could have been greater than they if I had not been burdened with this fear. But I was."

By the arrangement of the compulsive idea his real capacity for achievement is prevented from being put to the test. Thus he is safeguarded from any possibility of failure. At the same time, he successfully fought the compulsion; he had never jumped. So he assured himself time and again of the feeling of victory, the sense of heroic triumph.

2. A rarer type of compulsion is to be seen in the case of a girl who could not go out into society because of her impulse *to imitate a cock's crow*. Here we have the masculine protest—an important concept in Individual Psychology—expressed in such a way that the young woman is spared the necessity of proving her superiority in a more difficult way—by useful achievement. She felt that, as a girl, she played a subordinate, inferior part in society. This feeling of hers

certainly has no causal foundation. A great many girls, as well as men, are still possessed of the old superstition that women are inferior beings; and so it is not surprising that an ambitious girl who wants to occupy a leading place should feel that the social system itself compels her to eschew her role as woman in a society where she believes women are valued less than men. Being a woman, she feels, means falling into a low position of no value. She wants a high position of value, and sees it only in the masculine role.

It seems unlikely that this case involves sadistic tendencies. A much more probable explanation is this: The girl sees a kind of godlike superiority in the role of man as compared to the role of woman, in the "masculine principle," and goes a-tilting against windmills. She usurps the role of the male in an easy but useless way, and so spares herself the pains of proving by means of achievements valuable from an objective standpoint her capacity to fill it. This is a common characteristic of the compulsion neurotic; he has a sense of absolute superiority, and at the same time excludes all social ties from his life.

3. Another case concerns a girl whose symptoms set in at a time when she had suffered a defeat in her struggle for superiority. (The neurosis and all the special disturbances always put in their appearance whenever the patient feels that he is challenged to prove his superiority.) She was the younger of two sisters, and felt overshadowed by the older; but she was keenly intelligent and brilliantly endowed for her studies and her chosen work. For a long time she showed no signs of obsessions; but, like all compulsion neurotics, she was engaged in a frantic struggle for absolute superiority. The obsessive symptoms did not appear until she had lost her position through an unfortunate speculation, and a man in whom she was interested gave her clearly to understand that he preferred her sister. Now the patient developed an obsession. Whenever she met a woman carrying a market basket, she was tormented by the thought that *a rusty coin might jump out of her purse* into the basket and poison the woman's family.

She, too, was a fighter against windmills; she strove, futilely, to become a god and save mankind. Her obsession also took other forms. She declared that all books, especially Bibles, were sacrosanct; and if a book or a Bible chanced to fall on the floor, she discarded it and bought a new one. In this harmless way she plainly showed that she was superior to her sister in her esteem for religion and erudition. She was more pious and more ethical, more considerate of others' welfare, and also more respectful toward learning and religion. Thus she found a cheap means of triumphing over her sister, not by way of useful achievement in real life. Her philosophy of life remained the same. She asked herself only the one question: How can I exalt myself above my sister and everyone else?

4. And now another case, from an insane asylum: a man who had suffered since childhood from an inclination to represent himself in quite petty matters as ethical, noble-minded, and superior to all others. His earliest recollections extend back to his first days in kindergarten. He recalls that at some time or other he had made a mistake that escaped the notice of his teacher. For two years he suffered from pangs of conscience, and then, at his father's advice, he went to the teacher and confessed his secret shortcoming. Brought up in a family with a cultural tradition, he felt that his best chances for success lay in the direction of proving himself more noble than others. His life was not without achievement. But every time that he was faced by a real test of his powers, compulsive symptoms set in, and he was unable to meet the test. For this reason he frequently changed his occupation. One day, when he was confronted by such an emergency, he went to church and threw himself on the floor before the altar in the crowded church, and loudly proclaimed that he was "the *greatest sinner* on earth." After this he was committed to an institution, and thus succeeded in evading the test of his worth that goes with living productively.

The desire for a godlike superiority, so plainly revealed in this episode, evinced itself on other occasions as well. One day he appeared stark naked in the dining hall. By this expedient he postponed his dismissal from the institution and put off another imminent test of his powers in a field outside, where he felt uncertain and sensed a possible defeat. He was really a very handsome man, with a fine physique; in that regard he felt superior to others. And so his compulsion—the product of the emergency—revealed itself again as an effort, on the useless side of life, to maintain his exaggerated sense of personal importance by flaunting his superiority over other people.

5. Another patient, who had suffered for many years from a va-

riety of compulsive symptoms, improved notably under treatment. He was the oldest child of a family in which the father occupied a dominant position. The father had hopes that his son would turn out to be a genius, and the boy, extremely devoted to his father, took these high expectations as a matter of course until, when he was five years old, a sister was born. Then the father's affections were diverted to the sister and the boy suddenly began to feel an overpowering urge *to climb up on his father's shoulders*, stand over his head, *and break open his skull*. Later on, he also developed very pedantic traits, and was troubled by gruesome, and sometimes filthy, thoughts whenever he felt slighted. Under such circumstances someone else might have expressed his resentment in a stream of threats and curses.

Compulsive thoughts mean a kind of attack, more than an outburst of profanity and less than a physical assault. Up to the time of his treatment and improvement, the patient was firmly convinced that, even though he failed to meet his father's great expectations, he would certainly have outstripped his father if it had not been for his terrible obsessions. Here we can see how a kind of superiority grows out of the obsession, or out of the aggressive tendency that manifests itself in the obsession. Behind his symptoms the patient sees a star of hope—the hope of quieting his fear of defeat. He looks into a Promised Land, where he sees the possibility of consoling himself with the thought that he could have been superior to his father if only he had not been so unfortunately handicapped by a mysterious ailment which no doctor ever succeeded in controlling. In this manner he saves his self-esteem and guards his vanity from injury. The difficulties in the treatment of a compulsion neurotic are indicated. The therapeutic method of Individual Psychology is not only a science, but an art—the art of invalidating the patient's hollow alibi and teaching him to develop and rely on his actual capacities.

6. Very often the obsession takes the form of an impulse to inflict an injury on someone whenever the patient sees a knife. For example, a woman, who had grown up as an only child and had always been the center of attention, discovered that she was being deceived and slighted by her husband, and she then developed *the urge to take up a knife* and attack either him or her child. This urge reveals about the same frame of mind that moves certain people to blurt out threats such as, "I'd like to kill that man!" In the present case the mood is

expressed in a kind of pantomime, but the feeling is not translated into overt action. Each time it arises the impulse is overcome; and thus the patient experiences a sense of triumph. At the same time she depreciates her husband by showing her lack of regard for him. She takes a cheap and easy short cut to establish a kind of superiority whenever she feels her value threatened.

7. In another case, a much-pampered young woman began to feel this impulse to "do something" with a knife because her husband—a very kindly, well-intentioned man—had the inclination to pick up a book and read instead of amusing himself with her. This was sufficient cause for her to feel the urge to attack him whenever she happened to see a knife. Here again a sense of superiority is plainly revealed—but in such a form that she was content to make a harmless show of her resentment and anger. Her husband was forced by her obsession to concern himself with her.

8. It is only natural that the "runaway" tendency, always evident in neurosis, should clearly reveal itself in individuals who feel too weak to meet the problems of life. In many cases of neurosis, when the problem of sex seems overly difficult, it takes the form of homosexuality. That we often find evidence of compulsion in such cases is easily understandable. As an example, let us take the case of a man who deliberately trained himself, from childhood on, to enchant everyone with his physical attractiveness. Of course, in our culture a girl can do this more easily than a boy; and so the patient early began to practice playing the part of a girl. Once, in a school entertainment, he filled the role of a girl so convincingly that a man in the audience fell in love with him on the spot. The desire to achieve further successes of this kind brought him within the province of homosexuality.

And now the time came for this man to prepare for a profession and to pass the necessary examinations; that is, he was expected to take the normal means—by useful achievement—of acquiring prestige and securing the place of glory that he had always anticipated. But he felt it was much more likely that he would meet with failure in trying to accomplish an objectively useful task than in merely enchanting someone and trying to be charming. It turned out now that whenever he attended a lecture, he suffered from a *sleep compulsion*. This served, of course, as a perfect precaution. It protected him against having to take the coming examination. And in case he did take it, it supplied a perfect alibi for failure. "If I can't help falling asleep," he could say, "no one can expect me to pass the examination." And he really did fail, but with an easier conscience than if he had paid attention in class and failed anyway.

9. Another patient is a married woman who incessantly busied herself with *putting her linen in order,* and in so doing aroused herself to a high pitch of excitement. This ordeal took up the greater part of the day, and clearly indicated a compulsion incident to her striving for a godlike superiority. A servant girl always did the actual work, but under the patient's constant supervision. This woman grew up in a family where there was continual bickering and she had had her full share of slaps and aspersions. She recollected that at one time she said to herself: "Just wait till I grow up and I'll boss other people the way they boss me now." Here we have a clear illustration of what I mean by life style. This motive force, this desire to rule, so common in neurotically disposed children, we see operating time and again in both the greatest and the least of our fellow men. It reduces itself to the thought, "Someday *I'll* be the boss."

It proved that this patient's compulsive symptom served the end of keeping her out of society, where she never felt sure of maintaining a dominant position. She never failed to produce friction and ill-feeling wherever she went, and so consistently offended people that they frankly avoided her. She found herself left alone. By way of compensation, she played God Almighty in her own household, praising or punishing her children as the spirit moved her, and keeping her husband completely under her thumb. Her parents and sisters might take a special pride in their linen, but she outdid them. No one could set a linen closet to rights as well as she. And to have a slave at one's beck and call, to give orders and to see them carried out in an artistic fashion—this she felt to be the very apogee of power. She made herself the reigning queen of the little spot that she had set off for herself, and within her narrow realm no one could make any demands upon her.

10. An especially common form of compulsion is the *washing mania*—the urge to be continually cleaning and scouring. Here we see

an inclination to depreciate others by implying that everyone but the patient is dirty. No one but the patient is allowed to touch anything, and he alone is crowned with a gloriole of purity and superiority. This, too, is only another means of wasting time, thus deferring the solution of some vital problem and evading the necessity of proving one's importance through actual achievements and contributions.

One case of this type concerned a girl who was the younger of two daughters. The older sister had felt neglected after the birth of her younger sister and revolted against the situation which she felt intolerable. All the parents' affections were concentrated on the younger daughter. She was a model child, lauded, loved, and showered with presents. And she came to expect a great deal of life. But her first experiment in living away from the pampering home life, at school, resulted in failure; after that she never completed anything she undertook. She was punished for her laziness, but no one questioned her potential ability; and she accepted the punishment and reproofs rather than risk displaying her inferiority. As a married woman she felt that her position was extremely degrading. Her husband was much older than herself, remarkably dried-up, and in her eyes totally unfit for love and marriage. Her washing compulsion set in when she finally married—after much hesitation. She pronounced her husband unclean, and banished him from bed and board. It is interesting and rather surprising to note that the house of a person obsessed with the idea of cleanliness is often unclean. The reason is that the whole social harmony of the home is destroyed, and the prevailing desire is to find dirt everywhere.

11. The compulsion may also take the form of continual *blushing*. A woman, for example, had suffered since childhood from a lability of the surface blood vessels which manifested itself in frequent blushing. She was downright proud when someone noticed this and remarked about it. Here again we can see the unimportance of causality. At first, her blushing actually gave her pleasure. But when she had her first baby, in a loveless marriage, and an aunt began to irritate her with advice on the proper way to bring up children, this extremely ambitious woman suddenly acquired the notion that her blushing was quite a terrible thing, and that because of it she would have to shun society—as a vanquished hero, but a hero none the less. She made full use of her blushing mania as a source of special privileges within her

home, however. Here she was the mistress; and by reducing her sphere of action to the narrowest possible dimensions, she was able to satisfy her thirst for power.

12. And now one other case, which may not seem to fall within the category of compulsion neurosis. I once knew a housemaid who had an odd habit: whenever she was told to do something, she always repeated the order in the first person. If her mistress asked her to arrange a cupboard, she would say, "*I'll* arrange the cupboard this afternoon." Here we see the rejection of authority. She could act only if she had the sense of acting on her own volition.

This peculiarity of the human mind—the desire to be the leader, to do things on one's own initiative—is recognized in some armies, where the soldier must repeat every command in the first person and actually make himself feel that he is the commander. This tradition is certainly based on a profound knowledge of human nature.[5]

A related case is that of a strikingly beautiful woman who developed the following compulsion: whenever she was faced with a piece of housework that seemed degrading in view of her prestige as a beauty, she always had to give herself the order to do it. This symptom, together with compulsive blushing, appeared when she was reminded by quite insignificant experiences that she was growing older and would eventually lose her beauty.

RECAPITULATION AND CONCLUDING REMARKS

The study of compulsion neurosis reveals the following factors and tendencies:

1. A striving for personal superiority which, from fear of betraying an actual inferiority, is diverted into easy and generally useless channels.

2. This striving for an exclusive superiority is encouraged in childhood by excessive pampering or self-indulgence, and develops into a desire for godlike supremacy which is less mitigated and qualified by a concrete social goal (objective success in the world of reality), by actual useful achievement, than is the case in other forms of neurosis.

---

5. See also p. 180.

3. Compulsion neurosis occurs in the face of actual situations (problems of social living, occupation, or love), where the dread of failure or a blow to vanity leads to a hesitating attitude. This hesitating attitude finds expression in killing time, in seeking out and repeating a single routine or expressive movement or idea which will preclude further contact with the terrifying problems of life. (It is a hesitation that represents a "no" in disguise in response to some difficulty or problem of life.)

4. These means of relief from a difficult situation, once fixed upon, provide the patient with an excuse for failing to reach the pinnacle of existence. Successes in life loom much larger if achieved despite the handicap of a compulsion neurosis; and the kind of superiority obtained by means of obsessions and compulsions also serves to alleviate the patient's strong sense of inferiority, even though it fails to satisfy completely his great vanity. Hence, the form of compulsion —generally plural—is so chosen that the patient can express his striving for tremendous personal superiority (godlikeness) in a fictive guise.

5. The construction of the compulsion neurosis is identical with the structure of the entire life style and personality. The abnormal conduct appears first when the patient faces a problem which demands greater social interest than was developed in his childhood.

6. By reason of his prestige policy, the patient employs a counter-compulsion to meet and evade the compulsion exerted by the social requirements.

During more recent years I have been able to add the following points:

1. The compulsion does not reside in the compulsive actions themselves, but originates in the demands of social living, which the patient feels as a menace and threat to his prestige. He feels compelled to create a safeguard in order to heighten his sense of superiority and to serve as a means of evading failures and preventing a revelation of his inferiority.

2. This energetic quest for personal superiority characterizes the patient from early childhood on, and leads him, in accordance with his training, to a compulsion neurosis, not to other aberrations.

3. An early-developed, unified personality like that of the compulsion neurotic cannot be produced by causal, mechanical means—such

as the operation of instincts, heredity, brain injuries, environment, or the endocrine glands. It is the final product of a particular choice and way of training. The patient is only misdirected and led into a mistaken attitude toward life by such factors as physical inferiority, the influences of environment, or the imitation of examples. Although the error may to a degree be intelligible, we cannot grant the existence of any causal relationship. The development of the child's psyche can never be understood from the point of view of cause and effect; it begins as a groping process of trial and error, plausible perhaps, but never scientifically calculable and predictable. After about his fifth year, the child experiences, apperceives, and assimilates according to a life pattern which by this time he has definitely established and unified.

4. The life style of the compulsion neurotic adopts all the forms of expression that suit its purpose, and rejects the rest.

5. The feelings of guilt or humility, almost always present in compulsion neurosis, are elaborations of the effort to kill time. They show kinship with melancholia, and are so contrived that the patient's environment can easily detect in them the unstable, distorted, pathological element. Like extravagant exercises of penance, they very often serve the purpose of demonstrating the patient's unexampled virtue and magnanimity. But they never lead to any change of conduct or active contrition in the form of improved behavior.

The prognosis of compulsion neurosis is fundamentally the same as that of any other neurosis. There is no doubt that some forms of neurosis begin with an apparent compulsion neurosis, that compulsion neurosis borders on the one side on cyclothymia, and on the other side on schizophrenia, and that it can also resolve itself into one or the other. In rare cases it is not easy to determine whether one is dealing with a compulsion neurosis or depression, or whether one faces the initial stage of a schizophrenia. In the last two cases, of course, a different coloring can be observed. Bonhoeffer has clearly pointed out similarities with cyclothymia, Bumke with schizophrenia. All three groups of symptoms represent variations of a boundlessly increased superiority complex and of varying degrees of the ability to cooperate.

The compulsion symptoms appear when the patient comes in conflict with social responsibilities and tasks which call for more social interest than he has. Then he can maintain the position of superiority which he claims only by falling back into his imaginary and emotional life.

The cure can come about only when there is a reconciliation with the problems of life; that is, through the recognition of the faulty life style and strengthening of social interest, an important share of which are contribution and courage to face life. It occurs only through self-knowledge, in which Individual Psychology with its artistic technique (*künstlerische Technik*)—neither easily learned nor easily understood—furnishes a good guide.

In our introductory comment to this chapter we stated that to Adler compulsion neurosis was apparently the prototype of all neuroses. We did not know at that time that this conjecture had been made explicit by Leonhard Seif, one of the prominent co-workers of Adler during his middle period. According to Seif the dynamics of the compulsion were so essential to all neuroses that "one could call virtually any neurosis a 'compulsion neurosis'" ("Die Zwangsneurose." In E. Wexberg, Ed., Handbuch der Individualpsychologie *[1926]. Vol. 1. Amsterdam: Bonset, 1966. Pp. 507–531).*

In recent years Leon Salzman, in his book The Obsessive Personality *(New York: Science House, 1968), has quite independently arrived at the same conviction. He opens his book with the statement: "The obsessive-compulsive personality type is today's most prevalent neurotic character structure," whereas "Freud used the hysteric as the paradigm. . . . There is now good reason to believe that . . . the obsessional defensive mechanism provides the most widespread technique for enabling man to achieve some illusion of safety and security in an uncertain world" (p. vii).*   —Eds.

PART III

Case Interpretation
and Treatment

All three chapters of the present part on clinical procedure mention "guessing" in connection with arriving at an understanding of a case (pp. 145, 162–63 n., and 197), and Dreikurs points to it specifically in his introduction to Chapter 11. Guessing was an important part of Adler's clinical methodology.

Adler tells us that in interpreting a case, "you have to use your experience, you have to use the Individual Psychology views, and you have to guess" (p. 145). "In medicine and surgery, as in Individual Psychology, you have to guess, but you have to prove it by other signs which agree. If you have guessed and the other signs do not agree, you have to be hard and cruel enough against yourself to look for another explanation" (p. 162).

In stating this, Adler is actually saying that he creates specific hypotheses about a case, based on his general theory and specific information regarding the case, which he then tests against further information about the case, to support or reject the hypothesis. "Guessing" is then one form of the hypothetico-deductive method. Its special characteristic would be that it would enable the investigator to be particularly spontaneous and creative in formulating hypotheses.

When Linus Pauling spoke not long ago in a discussion on scientific creativity, he recommended guessing as a method of hypothesis formation. Pauling showed in his paper on "The Genesis of Ideas" (In R. A. Cleghorn, Ed., Third World Congress of Psychiatry Proceedings. Toronto: Univer. Toronto Press, 1962. Pp. 44–47) that guessing has a place of old standing in the history of the physical sciences, and a technical term—the stochastic hypothesis method. Such guessing is not in the sense of randomness as mathematicians and statisticians have lately used the term stochastic, but in the sense of "to divine the truth by conjecture." "A plausible structure is guessed with the aid of hints . . . as well as knowledge of general principles . . . and the stochastic hypothesis . . . is thereupon either verified or disproved." Pauling advocates the study of the stochastic method, its application to the social sciences in particular, and its use in training researchers in having ideas.

Adler indeed used this method to sharpen his and his students' sensitivity toward discovering the personality structure of an individual in his life space. "I consider it a prime duty to train my students in the art of guessing" (A1963, p. 28).   —Eds.

I I

Two Grade-School Girls [1]

FOREWORD BY RUDOLF DREIKURS [2]

Alfred Adler developed a unique technique for teaching how to understand a case history. Reading aloud a description of a person presented to him by a student, he stopped after each sentence to "interpret" the content.

Adler frankly admitted that he used guessing in this procedure, thereby introducing into science a technique which up to then was considered the most "unscientific" approach to a problem.[3] But Adler demonstrated that we can learn to "guess in the right direction." Adler opened our eyes to the underlying possibilities of small facts which remain insignificant unless we sense their wider implications.

The present article is one of the few yet unpublished papers left by Alfred Adler. It is a true reproduction of one of his famous demonstrations. Instead of adjusting it to a more literary style, we considered it our duty to leave it in its natural simplicity, which will vividly recall to all those who have heard Adler personally, the tone of his voice and the pattern of his speech, and will provide for those who never had a chance to meet him personally a glimpse of his unique and colorful personality.

wwwwwwwwww

1. No date for manuscript. Reprinted from A1941c.
2. Editor of the journal in which this paper originally appeared.
3. Compare above introductory statement.

CASE 1

Here is a case history from one of my students. I must say he is a very well-taught student for he wrote a case history which appears to be a correct picture of a girl seven-and-a-half years of age.

She was in the second grade of public school.

Judging her in regard to her activity, we would say that at seven-and-a-half some children might be in the third grade. So we would not say that this is a very quick child unless there is some reason. I want to mention this because at the very first sentence of a history you have to think—you have to establish the whole situation in which the child can be seen.

We hear now:

She has missed a half year because of illness.

Perhaps she is not slow, but still we would not say she is quick.

Tests in kindergarten have rated her with a relatively high IQ.

You see, the test examinations regarding IQs in kindergarten are not very valuable. Generally I would say the IQ always gives you the result of a development; it does not give you the capacity, or perhaps only if you interpret this IQ, if you know some symptoms with which to interpret this IQ. Therefore, we are not astonished to be informed that the IQ could be changed, probably not for the worse, but for the better.

Now, this child has a good IQ. We are sure she is intelligent.

Her reading age has been rated as from nine to ten years.

Now, we do not believe this to be remarkable. We know only that this child has been trained very well in reading.

Pampering without Fondling

She is the oldest living child in the family.

Now I am glad that I can show you an eldest child in its peculiarity. But:

She had a brother born five years previous to her birth, who died at the age of three.

Therefore she had not been related to this brother at all. She had not known this brother, and so she is an oldest child.

In all these explanations and interpretations you have to use your experience, you have to use the Individual Psychological views, and you have *to guess.* These are the three means I can offer you. But they give a better result than all others.

Now, we can use our experience at this point, when we are informed that an older brother died. How does this involve the family? This boy, three years of age, dies, and two years later another child comes. Now, we are sure that this other child was cared for very kindly, very thoroughly. This is human and obvious. If it were not so, we would be very much surprised. In a family where the first child died the second child is always considered like a revelation, like a redemption. Now, this is such a child in such a position, and we can predict very much on this point. We can understand that this child had been pampered whether it was intentional or not.

The writer of this case history gave me something additional. It must be noted.

During the time that this child was a baby until she was at least one-and-a-half years old, her mother was supposed to have tuberculosis and her doctor ordered her to be with her baby only as much as was absolutely necessary for its care. She was not to fondle or kiss the child. Since the mother was taking complete care of the home, this meant that this child was not fondled or pampered as much as the first child, and less than almost any normal baby.

Now, you see, this seems to contradict our guess that this child had been pampered. But does it contradict it? Not at all! This is an only child, and even if the mother was not always with her and did not kiss or fondle her, this child, born after another child had died, was pampered. This is not a question of the number of kisses or of the extent of fondling; it is the whole atmosphere which has pampered this child, and the child does not question how many kisses she receives. This child feels pampered, no matter what the mother does.

The writer continues:

> How can this be reconciled with every reaction of the typical pampered child which the case shows?

I believe we can reconcile it, but we do not yet know much about her.

> She has a sister who is now five years old.

Now, this poor child was two-and-a-half years old when another child came, and this is a test. We shall see what happened.

Physical Characteristics and Early Problems

> She is at present in perfect physical health, robust, rosy, has a good appetite, sleeps well, has normal height and weight, is very attractive in looks and fortunately not yet self-conscious or conceited about her looks, in spite of the inevitable compliments made constantly to her face by foolish persons about her eyes and her long auburn curls.

That this child has been impressed by this is true without question; that she does not show it is a point which must be considered. But there is also no question that this child, knowing how attractive she is, was pampered the more.

> She was a blue baby when born.

This means that her circulatory apparatus did not function properly.

> But later her heart seemed to be perfectly normal.

However, this does not really mean that this functional condition is now cleared up.

She is definitely right-handed, but very slow in her movements.

This agrees with what we said in the beginning: she is not quick; she is slow. I do not know whether her right-handedness had been tested. If it was tested in the right way, by clasping the hands and crossing in this way the fingers of both hands to see which thumb is on top, then we can say she is really right-handed.

Rather poor coordination, and becomes very clumsy when she tries to hurry such activities as cutting out paper pictures, etc.

Now, she is clumsy, and reading this, I would ask about left-handedness. But it says here she is right-handed. Then she probably is slow, and is not trained.

From early babyhood she presented her parents with problems of various types. During the first months of her infancy she asserted herself by sleeping all day and staying awake vociferously from 2 A.M. to 6 A.M. every night.

This shows that she had been trained to be awake during the night. This can be done with every child.

This habit was not successfully broken until she was almost three months old, in spite of consistency in training.

But this girl had been trained only after the symptom had originated. You see, she should have been trained before; then it would not have happened. It is very interesting that he speaks of training alone, of using efforts and endeavors. This is not enough. These efforts and endeavors must also succeed—this is necessary. And we can be sure that persons who don't succeed are not trained sufficiently.

Her degree of determination was phenomenal. At the early age of about five to eight months she showed many signs of nervousness in spite of being very quietly reared on a regular schedule, and being a very brown and healthy-looking baby.

Now I should like to know what is meant by this "being nervous." I would not call "crying easily" being nervous before I knew more about the case.

For instance, she would get a nervous tremor of the head if strangers with loud voices talked to her too near to her carriage.

Now, she has a certain sensitiveness of the ears, and this would probably make her a very good musician. But we would not call this sensitiveness in the ears nervousness. There are children, and also grown persons, who are terrified by loud noises, and in nearly every city you find meetings to determine how to prevent noises; and there are so many other persons who do not care at all. This is due to the differences in the sensitiveness in the ears, and this child probably has such a sensitiveness. I should be interested to find out if this girl could not be made musical, although I do not believe that she is musical now.

Certain sounds would make her turn white and sick.

Now, this is the same sensitiveness.

Defiance

As she grew older she began to show a constant resistance to all discipline.

Now this is to be expected as she grows older, but we must find out if discipline means what I would consider it means: to make her cooperate. She is an oldest child, in an atmosphere of kindness, pampering, etc., and this child now controls the whole family.

She resists even the mildest restrictions. Any physical restrictions always sent her into a rage.

On this point I want to say she has a certain degree of activity, but we must be very cautious. She has a certain amount of activity at home, but perhaps she does not have it outside the home. We must look.

To be comfortably strapped into a high chair, to have her hand held, to be forbidden to touch anything—all were resisted.

This child wants freedom and does not want others to control her. She wants to control others. This is her goal of superiority. She does not know that she is in the grip of this goal, but we have to know it.

The same technique used successfully by the family with the other two children always resulted in a revolt by this girl.

This is also very interesting. The same mother succeeded with the other children with the same method, but not with this child. We would say first, because she is an oldest child, and besides that, her situation was more intense because an older child had died previously.

Before she could even talk she would do things that were forbidden, apparently for the fun of transgressing. The mother pretended not to see. The girl would grip or pull her dress, point at the forbidden object, shake her head "No, no," then grab or knock it down or tear it.

Now, this is a girl who tyrannized already at the time when she could not yet talk.

The mother made very intelligent and very great efforts to make the child cooperative. But this child had not had it explained to her; she does not know that she wants to control in all circumstances. Only if there is a favorable situation, if everybody submits, does she not show bad signs, because then she has what she wants.

To continue:

When she went to a rhythm class, which she loved, she did excellently.

This is a very promising child, and I am sure that if the activity of this child can be brought into the right direction she will accomplish very worthwhile things. Because she loved this rhythm class she excelled, and you see what it means to love such a class. It means to feel well, and to feel being in a favorable situation.

A very interesting incident occurred later.

One day driving home from the play school, the girl and a small boy friend were in the back seat of the car and her mother was in the front. The girl remarked brightly and happily, "Do you know what I think?" Her mother, thinking herself addressed, replied over her shoulder as she drove, "No, do tell me what," to which the child gave a sudden scream, threw herself on the floor of the car and yelled all the way home. The mother continued to drive as if nothing had happened.

You see, the mother uses a means which is worth while sometimes for a certain length of time—not to pay much attention to such things so that this child does not have the feeling of being looked at too much, of arousing too much interest, too much attention. But that is not what we want. We want to have this child understand what we understand, that she was made controlling in the first month of her life. You see this, even if others believe it is not so. You see the movements, and the movements speak the truth. It is not what somebody believes or what this child thinks about it. Only the movements are important, and these movements mean: ruling. To be sure, this child has accomplished these ruling movements in a mistaken way, but she has accomplished them.

Now the mother said, "We are home now. Are you coming in? Of course, you can't come in while you are making this noise, [because the child had been screaming until now] but you can stay out in the car if you like, and when you get ready you can tell me why you feel the way you do."

Now, if this child did tell, we would see that she does not understand. We know why she feels this way—because she wants to control, and she will utilize everything to control the others.

The child arose from the floor of the car and said, "You answered me when I wasn't talking to you at all. I was talking to Teddy."

You see the majesty. We understand the child. Other things are discussed. For instance:

Servant girls complained they could not stand the cunning with which the girl found their weak points and bore down on them without mercy.

You see she has a whole guard around her like a majesty, and she rules and controls and is very severe with them.

She had and has a genius for finding the Achilles' heel in everyone with whom she comes in contact, and aiming subtle poison into it.

She is a very clever child, and if this cleverness could be used in good things, in a worthwhile way, she could be marvelous.

After one is worn to the breaking point, she senses it and pushes him over the edge. She has put every new nurse and servant through their paces, and leaves each one exhausted. One kind trained nurse, at the end of a day of saintly patience, sank into a chair beside the bed of the girl's mother, and said, "Oh, Mrs. M., what a cross you have to bear in this child."

Now, this is not so. I would rather believe that this is a lovely child, a promising child. But she must have it explained to her; she must understand her style of life, and how it came to be what it is.

The Amiable Younger Sister

Now happens what always happens in a case like this. The second child goes ahead—the second child adapts herself to this situation, and finds a more favorable place. You see, she finds it easier to succeed, to be kind. She sees how her sister is always repulsed, reproached, and disliked, because it is not always easy to be kind and friendly to such a child. She sees how her sister is spanked, sometimes by the father and also by the mother. So this second child, as is usual in such a case, is very amiable and so goes ahead.

But it is also not entirely sure that this second child is wholly on the right way, because perhaps she is learning now always to meet kindness, and favorable and amiable people. This is possible, and I have seen such cases where a second child, when grown up, was always fighting with everybody, ruling the other child who now had become very kind and amiable. The second one had been shocked by the demands of the school and of later life, and became very neurotic. This might not be true of this particular case, but I want to say that it is much more necessary to teach a child to cooperate than, for instance, to conquer the older sister by being kind and amiable.

Now we hear also that the little sister begins to fight the other child and wants her place, and is supported by her own kindness and her better manners. But because we understand the child I can make this brief.

Treatment

The story continues:

In school she does not respond rightly and does not show any responsibility. The teacher had been working in cooperation with the mother. This last week improvement has been shown through a job of honor allotted to her. She takes the attendance slips each morning into the principal's office. She was not told to take them, but when the teacher has filled out the slips she puts them on the desk and the girl picks them up and takes them in to the principal.

You see, she has a more prominent place, and she wants to be prominent. Therefore she does this.

Now in this way, this feeling prominent brings about a certain improvement. And the question arises: Is it really feeling for the job and responsibility, or is it the dramatic role of the important person? Now I believe it is the latter. The writer of this story is more inclined to believe that this child behaves in an infantilistic way. I cannot say so. In a certain way everybody behaves like an infant, because as we have learned, the style of life is born in the early part of an individual's life and recurs always throughout the whole life, so that we are right in saying that the child is father of the man. But I do not see infantilistic trends in the case of this child. These trends would mean, for instance, to lean on the mother and to ask about everything from the mother, and to talk baby talk, and such things. She does not do such things as far as we can see. She wants to rule; and we are not astonished, as we know that she ruled also in infancy.

She had scarlet fever, which developed into many complications —severe glandular trouble with severe pain, and finally double mastoiditis. She was desperately ill and in great pain for a long time.

Now we find out something about the ears. As we said, she has sensitive ears.

Relatives, neighbors, even servants, have preached corporal punishment.

We could have been sure that this was recommended.

Even the writer of this story says at last that the child is gifted.

> *She has a delightful sense of humor; she is a born actress, and an avid and appreciative reader.*

Then he also asks what should be done. Now, if somebody, I do not know who, but if somebody is able to win this child and to convince her of what we have seen now, something could be done. But I do not mean that empty phrases and words should be used. For instance, it would not be enough to tell her, "After your sister was born you were ruling, when a little child." But you should let her tell everything she wants to tell and what she wants to do. For instance, you should ask her, "What do you want to be when you are grown up?" In this way you can start, and you can prove that she is always looking for a ruling role, where she can rule others. Now, what would she say? Perhaps she would say she would like to be a teacher, because small girls always believe that a teacher is such a ruling person. Or she would say she would like to be something similar. And you can explain it. You can ask her, "Why do you want to be a teacher?" She would tell you, and then you could explain to her the things she has said without understanding what they mean.

Then you can ask her about dreams. And then speak to her about the relation of children in the family, how it upsets a child if she wants to keep her place and is confronted with a rival.

And even if this child would refuse the first time, she could not get rid of the influences of this new experience at last, because she would like to prove that you are wrong. Now, how can she prove that you are wrong, that she is not always ruling, that she does not always want to be superior to everybody? How can she prove it? You see, you have the child as if in a trap.[4] Either she agrees with you—then she will change;

wwwwwwwwwww

4. "The therapist's trap" or constructive "double-bind" is, according to Alan W. Watts (*Psychotherapy East and West*. New York: New American Library, 1963, pp. 129–132), a technique common to all psychotherapies. Watts relates: "When a psychiatrist asked a Zen master how he dealt with neurotic people, he replied, 'I trap them!' 'And just how do you trap them?' 'I get them where they can't ask any more questions!'" (p. 29). The description of what constitutes the trap of course varies with the therapist's theory. While the tech-

or she does not agree with you—then she will prove that you are wrong and will behave better. But this is possible only if you have won this child, if she cooperates with you, if she listens to you, and if you are friendly and can convince the child.

Now, this must be done in this case, and it would really be a very worthwhile task. I am sure that you can succeed.

CASE 2

Crying and Temper

I want to give you another case history of a problem child, a girl eight years of age. She cries and loses her temper over the slightest things. This seems to be a little similar to the other case because this girl makes herself very important, always being the center of the stage, even in little things.

The writer says:

> *This gives evidence of a lack of courage and self-confidence.*

I do not know from what reasons this was concluded, but I am sure the writer is correct, because crying and losing the temper always indicate a person who has a feeling of inferiority. And it means using some scheme for being stronger—crying, for instance. I have always called this the "water power." Or such a person uses temper outbursts to conquer another person. You see, it does not mean cooperation and being sure of oneself. It means using tricky methods. This child has an inferiority complex which can be seen in this crying and in the temper outbursts.

> *Although doing very well in school, frets about being late.*

You see, the school plays an important part in the life of the family. Because she is in school the whole family is irritated.

> *She has apparent fear and shows evidence of an overconscientious observance of every school regulation.*

nique of the trap may be common to all therapists, Adler not only used it, but named it as well, although the present occasion is, to our knowledge, the only one where he did so. Otherwise he employed similar metaphors like, "Take the wind right out of the patient's sails" (A1956b, p. 338).

Now you see she makes the school so important that the whole family suffers from it. This is really not the task of the school, but this girl utilizes the school to irritate and control the family. Therefore, this is no cooperation, and we would also not say that this is the right kind of conscientiousness.

She also uses her conscientious behavior for ruling the family directly. This can be done. Some people always show their conscientiousness in order to irritate others. They always try to tell the truth to the others to annoy them. They say, "How pale you are! Are you sick?" etc. They tell the truth for the purpose of irritating others. And so it is with this child.

> *If something she needs is not in its accustomed place, she cries, "I can't find it," before she even begins to look.*

You see how she makes trouble with everything, always. And also her pedantic mood, her pedantic characteristics, show the social relationship between herself and others. To be pedantic means to irritate the others, because you cannot be pedantic without giving others a job; the others have to comply carefully. As for instance, many persons insist, "I want only my quiet." But you cannot give them quiet without taking up a job for them. This desire means ruling others. And so it is in the case of this girl.

The Younger Sister

> *Health history is good, and tonsils were removed last spring.*

This is this American idea that with the tonsils all evils can be removed.

> *She has a sister, five years of age, and a brother, two years of age.*

She is the oldest and was also dethroned when she was three years old.

> *She was a fine baby. Talked and walked at one-and-a-half years. Clothed herself at three. Went to nursery school at three and kindergarten at four-and-a-half. Now she goes to school. The younger sister does not go to school.*

Therefore we can understand why she utilizes the school. She does it in order to arrive at her former favorable position of being the first.

She does not want to be put back; she does not want her place to be made of less importance.

She was always very well, happy, and self-sufficient until about five . . .

Now we will look for the reason; she is eight now, and when she was three this other child came.

. . . when her sister began to attract a good deal of attention.

We do not know why. The sister was two years old at this time. Anyway, this is said. I do not know if it is said as we would say it—that the sister began to attract attention when the mother became pregnant with her third child and that our problem child as a consequence felt neglected and wanted to regain her old favorable place.

Parents made conscious efforts to give her as little cause for jealousy as possible.

You see again these "efforts." But they do not succeed. Why? Because this child had been pampered before. She had not been taught cooperation. If she had been taught cooperation, she would cooperate with her sister. But they wanted only to train her in regard to jealousy and not to change her style of life.

And they also wanted to avoid the sense of loss of importance. But guests praised the baby sister and overlooked her.

That our problem child felt it much more than the parents felt it, is obvious.

Once the kindergarten teacher reported that this girl came in and, finding that she was a little late, burst out in loud cries.

Now, this is too much, to be late and to cry also. One of these would be enough, either being late or crying. But she does not have enough of it if she is only late; she wants to make trouble, she wants to use the water power, to get away with it, to be favored, to be consoled, etc.

Since then she has cried several other times in school because she had been successful in crying when something went wrong or was not clear. Does not seem to have enough courage or assurance to ask teacher to explain.

I do not agree with this idea. I believe much more that she prefers to cry instead of having it explained.

Condition has not improved. Frequently she appears stubborn and sullen, although at times she is very happy and cooperative.

We know what these times are. These are the times when she feels appreciated, when she feels she is in the first place. Then she cooperates.

Treatment

Is extremely fond of reading, swimming, and hiking.

Now, these are active signs; therefore in a certain way we could say this is an active child. And this is an easy case to treat. She is only encouraged in her way by her environment. The environment gives her too much chance to develop in this particular way. But this girl had been a fine baby. She cooperated when she was a baby. She dressed herself alone, and now she can swim at eight years of age, which is mostly a sign of an active child. Children who are not active usually have trouble in learning to swim.

Her continual whining and crying have discouraged the parents, who frequently find themselves scolding her.

You see, this is what I always explained. At last such a child is right in feeling put back, because when she causes worry she is scolded. It is only since her sister came. You see, this is her meaning, and this meaning rules her completely. It is always how we interpret, what our opinion tells us, that decides our behavior. We do not behave according to the truth, not according to the real cause; but only what we mean, what our opinion is of the truth, is important.

They scold her although they realize that this is no cure.

Certainly. But we see that all the efforts which the parents have made would produce different results if the child knew what *she* wants to achieve, namely, to feel superior, to weaken the others. If the girl knew that she uses temper tantrums, crying (the water power), making a fuss in school, in order to suppress others, to get away with everything, to be in the center of the stage, wittingly or not, she would look for other ways, she would not be the same any more, she would be changed. She would change because every time when she would have a temper tantrum or when she would cry (for she would cry also after having the cause explained to her) her crying would be accompanied by the thought, "People probably believe I am crying now in order to be the center of the stage," and this would not fit very well into her striving for superiority.

12

The Case of Mrs. A.
(1931)[1]

FROM THE FOREWORD BY F. G. CROOKSHANK [2]

In January 1931, Dr. Adler visited London and gave a series of lectures. . . . On the occasion of a special meeting, at the rooms of the Medical Society of Individual Psychology, it was felt that a demonstration, by Dr. Adler, of his own methods of reading a "life style" would be of greatest interest. It was therefore arranged, at Dr. Adler's own request, that, at the last moment, case notes made by a practicing physician should be presented to him for his extempore consideration and impromptu interpretation.

To this end, Dr. Hilda Weber was good enough to transcribe, and bring to the meeting, notes taken by her, some time previously, on the case of one "Mrs. A." who had been under her care. The nature of the case was known to no one other than Dr. Weber until the moment when the notes were handed to Dr. Adler on the platform, after the fashion of what undergraduate examinees call an "unseen!" It is perhaps right to say that Dr. Weber, when these notes were first taken down, was not personally interested in Individual Psychology, while it is certain that no alteration was made in them for the purposes of the meeting. . . .

In preparing for publication the verbatim notes taken by Miss

1. Reprinted from A1931e.
2. Editor of the series in which this paper originally appeared.

Margaret Watson of Dr. Adler's demonstration, Dr. Adler's own words have been allowed to stand practically as uttered. Only the absolute minimum of alteration necessary to secure understanding was made, for it was felt, not only that all suspicion of editing should be avoided, but that any attempt at stylistic or syntactical emendation would destroy at once the charm and the essential lucidity of the spoken word. For, as a matter of fact, in so much that Dr. Adler has said and written *in his own way* his meaning has thus been better conveyed than it otherwise could have been. Few writers and speakers have suffered more at the hands of translators and editors.

If we try to understand what Dr. Adler thinks and means, whether he is addressing us in his native tongue, or in our own, we succeed more perfectly than if we undertake a verbal or grammatical analysis. We come thus best to appreciate the stark significance of some of his aphorisms and judgments, even when they seem to some of his critics most simple and commonplace, or even banal. . . .

GENERAL INTRODUCTORY STATEMENTS

I have first to thank you all for your attention and for your eagerness to look into the workroom of Individual Psychology. My purpose is to approach it in this way: As you are partly trained and accustomed as doctors, I asked to receive an analysis of a sick, neurotic or psychotic person, knowing nothing about it. So you see this really is a clinic and you know what you have to do. You have to use general diagnosis and special diagnosis and so on. So you see we are in the general field of medicine. We do not act in any other way. We know that in general medicine we have to use all our means, all our tools, because otherwise we would not feel justified in going on to therapy.

Now in this case we have to deal with mental conditions and we must have an idea, a conception of mind. We are looking for mind as for a part of life. I do not believe we can go further. We do not know more, but we are satisfied, because we see that in other sciences also they cannot explain more. What are electricity, gravitation, and so on? Probably for a long time, or forever, nobody can contribute any more to our knowledge of mind than that it is a faculty of life, a part of life. Therefore, if life can be understood, we shall find that mind also wants to grow up and develop towards an ideal final goal.

This means that we have to consider at least two points. One is the point from which the symptom expression takes its rise. We shall find that wherever we can lay our finger on a complaint there will be a lack, the *feeling of a minus*. The second point is that mind always wants to overcome this minus, and strive for an ideal final form. We say that wherever there is life there is a striving for an ideal final form.

I cannot explain today all the finer features and characteristics of this growing up. It is enough if I remind you that in Individual Psychology we are looking for the situation in which a person feels confronted, and does not feel able to overcome a certain problem or difficulty. Therefore, we have to look for the direction in which such a person is striving.

In this direction we meet with a million varieties, and these varieties can be measured to a certain degree if we have an idea of what *cooperation* means, and *social interest*. Very often we are able to calculate how far away from a right degree of cooperation we find this kind of patient striving. Therefore it is necessary—and each good analysis has to bring it about—to find on which point a person proves not to be prepared rightly for the solution of social problems, not to be prepared rightly because he cannot afford what is expected of him—the right degree of courage, of self-confidence, of social adjustment, the right type of cooperation, and so on. These things must be understood because you will see how the patient cannot pay, how he declares himself not to be able to solve his problem, and how he shows what I call the *hesitating attitude*, the stopping attitude. He begins to evade and wants to secure himself against a solution of the necessary problem.

On this point you will find him in the state of mind I have described as the *inferiority complex*, and, because of that, he is always striving to go ahead, to feel superior, to feel that he has overcome his difficulties in the present situation. You must look for this point where the patient feels satisfied on account of feeling superior. Now he cannot feel superior in regard to the solution of his present problem in a useful way and therefore his superiority is proved in the line of uselessness. In his own imagination he has reached his goal of superiority and perhaps satisfied himself, but it cannot be valued as a goal of usefulness.

This is the first description we would expect in each case history, in each analysis of a mental case; it belongs to the *general diagnosis*. Again belonging to the general diagnosis, we have to find some explanation of why this person has not been prepared. This is difficult to understand and to recognize. We have to delve back into the past of this person, to find out in what circumstances he has grown up, how he has behaved towards his family, and to ask questions resembling very much the questions we ask in general medicine. We ask: "What were your parents like?" The patients do not know that in their answers they express their whole attitude—if they felt pampered and the center of attention, or if they resented one or the other of their parents—but *we* see it. And especially on this point always give "empty" questions! You will then be sure that you do not insinuate and give a hint to the patient to speak as you want him to speak.

At this point you will see the origin of the lack of preparation for the present situation, which is like a test examination. Why the patient has not been prepared for it must be seen and explained in the case history.

That is the general diagnosis, but you must not believe that when you have done this you have understood the patient. Now begins the *special diagnosis*. In the special diagnosis you must learn by testing. It is the same kind of testing as you need, for example, in internal medicine. You must note what the patient says but, as in general medicine, you must not trust yourself. You must prove it, and not believe—if you find, for example, a certain frequency of the palpitations of the heart—that it necessarily means a particular cause. In medicine and surgery, as in Individual Psychology, you have *to guess*, but you have to prove it by other signs which agree. If you have guessed and the other signs do not agree, you have to be hard and cruel enough against yourself to look for another explanation.[3]

~~~~~~~~~~~~~~~~~

3. Elsewhere Adler defended the technique of guessing as follows: "It is a mistake to point, often with derogation, to the ability of guessing which we are practicing and have well trained with the greatest care. Some consider it even 'un-

What I want to do today is to take an analysis such as we might have in a clinic, for example. The doctor makes an analysis of a patient he has not seen before and tries to explain. We, perhaps, may work in this way, for then the whole audience is forced, willingly or unwillingly, to think it over.

Individual Psychology expects you to prove every rule. You must reject each rule and try to understand, and at last you will feel justified in your general views.[4] Of course, you cannot help being influenced in your inquiries by those general views, but it is the same as in other sciences and especially in medicine. You must get rid of your understanding, for instance, of period, of constitution, of the work of the endocrine glands, and so on. But it is very worth while, because you have a hint, and you can go on what you find in this way. It is really the result of your thinking, and shows whether you are thinking rightly or not, if you are experienced or not, and so on. It is the same with Individual Psychology and, therefore, so far as I can see, Individual Psychology agrees wholly with the fundamental views of medicine.

THE CASE OF MRS. A.

Marital Situation

Now here is the case of Mrs. A. What we can see is that she is a married woman—perhaps a widow—we do not know more. You must fix each word and turn it over in your mind so that you may get everything that is in it.

---

scientific.' As if new results had ever been achieved in any other way than by guessing!" (A1929b, p. viii).

Why would Adler speak at all of the necessity of achieving "new results"? Because for him the problem of diagnosis was not to isolate a generally-known pathogenic factor, but to discover in each case the uniqueness of the patient's personality structure, including his hidden goal, his style of life which is his creation. Adler needed a clear formulation of this to be able to explain to the patient his mistake in such a way that he would understand it.

4. This statement would seem to be the clinical counterpart to the statistical requirement of "disproving the null hypothesis" familiar from quantitative research. "You must reject each rule" would correspond to the term null hypothesis; "at last you will feel justified in your general views" would correspond to its disproval.

The patient A., who forms the subject of this paper, was thirty-one years old at the time she came for treatment.

Thirty-one years old and a married woman! Now we know circumstances in which a woman, thirty-one years old, and married, might find herself. There could be a problem of marriage, of children, perhaps also a problem of income in these times. We are very careful. We would not presuppose anything, but we feel sure that—unless we are surprised later—there is something wrong in one of these ways. Now we go ahead.

She had been married eight years . . .

That carries us further—she had married at twenty-three years of age.

. . . and had two children, both boys, aged eight and four years respectively.

Now she had a child very soon. Eight years married and the child eight years old! What you think about that is your own affair. Perhaps we have to correct a recollection. You see the sharp eye of Individual Psychology!

Her husband was a lift man in a store.

Then they are probably in poor circumstances.

An ambitious man, he suffered considerable humiliation from the fact that, unlike his brother, he was prevented, he felt, from obtaining a better type of employment because during the war his right arm had been disabled.

If we can trust this description that he is an ambitious man and does not feel happy in his employment, this must reflect in his married life. He cannot satisfy his ambition outside the family. Perhaps he tries to satisfy it inside; tries to rule his wife and children and to "boss" them. We are not sure and we must be careful enough not to believe it and to be convinced, but we have a view. Perhaps we shall find something in this way. An ambitious husband!

His wife, however, had little sympathy with his trouble . . .

Now if we are right that this man wants to prove himself superior in his family life and his wife does not agree and give in, if she has little sympathy with his style of life, there must probably be some dissension in the family. This man wants to rule; his wife does not agree and does not give him a chance. Therefore, there must be trouble in the family.

Fear of Death and Cleanliness Compulsion

> . . . *being far too occupied with the compulsive thoughts and fears of death from which she suffered.*

Compulsive thoughts and fear of death! It does not look like a compulsion neurosis; it looks more like an anxiety neurosis. Now on this point I should like to give you a rule out of our experience which can be used. I like to ask: What happens in these cases? What are the results if a married woman is suffering from fears of death and perhaps from other fears? What would it mean? She is occupied too much with it, as we can see, and so many of her necessary tasks would not be fulfilled. We see that she is much more occupied with her own person. She is not interested, as we have heard, in the troubles of the man.

We are, therefore, in agreement on these points, but we are not far ahead. We can understand that such a person cannot cooperate rightly if she is interested in the fear of death and other fears, and we understand that there must be many dissensions in this family.

> *These fears, indeed, occupied her mind to such an extent that she found difficulty at the time she came for treatment in thinking of anything else.*

At this point we are justified in answering our question as to what happens: She cannot think of anything else. Now I want to tell you that this is what you will always find and, if in any cases it appears not to be so for a time, you will find confirmation later in the description. This shows that it is worth while, and encourages us because we know we are not right off the mark but have predicted what will be later.

We read that she is thinking only of her fears.

> *Thus a careful housewife—she had previously been governed by an almost obsessional hatred of dirt and love of tidiness . . .*

This gives another picture—a compulsion neurosis in regard to cleanliness, probably a wash-compulsion neurosis. If she was afraid of dirt she must make it clean always. She must wash and clean everything and herself. In the same way she is suffering from fear of death. There must be a mixed neurosis. This is really very rare. In our general experience the wash-compulsion neurotics do not suffer from fear of death. They may combine the two ideas and say: "If I do not wash this desk, or these shoes and so on, my husband will die," or whatever it may be. But that is not the fear of death as we find it in many anxiety neuroses. As I explained in a lecture in this room on "Obsessions and Compulsion in the Compulsion Neuroses," there is always an underlying idea. Here the idea is that of cleaning away the dirt.

Now we understand more on this point. We see that this woman is occupied in another place than that in which she is expected to be. She does not cooperate; she is interested only in her own sufferings, making everything clean, and perhaps the wash-compulsion. Therefore, we can judge: This is a type that can solve the social problems of life; but she is not prepared in cooperation, but much more prepared in thinking of herself. We know out of our general experience that we find such a style of life mostly in children suffering from imperfect organs, and in the great majority of pampered, petted, and dependent children. More rarely we find it in neglected children, because probably a child wholly neglected would die. The great majority of these neurotic children have been pampered, made dependent, and given such an idea of themselves that they are more interested in themselves than in others.

This woman is striving for a high ideal—to be cleaner than all the others. You can understand that she does not agree with our life; she wants it to be much cleaner. Now cleanliness is a very nice characteristic and we like it very much. But if a person focuses life on cleanliness she is not able to live our life, and there must be another place for such a person; because if you have really inquired into cases of wash-compulsion neurosis, you will be convinced that it is not possible to arrive at such an ideal of cleanliness as these people want to arrive at. You will always find some dirt and dust. You cannot carry on life by pointing to one part only—cleanliness, for instance—because it disturbs the harmony of life.

So far as I can see there is only one part of our emotions and life that can never be overstrained and that is social interest. If there is social interest you cannot overstrain it in such a degree that the harmony of life can be disturbed; but all other things can do so. If you point to health and think only of it, you ruin your life; if you think only of money, you ruin your life, in spite of the fact that, as we know, it is unfortunately necessary to think of it. If you turn to family life and exclude all the other relations, you ruin your life. It seems an unwritten law that we cannot turn only to one point without risking many damages!

Now we will see more.

> . . . *hatred of dirt and love of tidiness, both with regard to her home and to her own person—she now began to show neglect in both these particulars.*

This also is not usual, for we mostly receive such persons, with their care for cleanliness and avoidance of dirt, in this frame of mind. But this woman has broken down, so she gives up. We do not know how she appears now in this state of mind, but it is very probable that she did not succeed in her imagination with this compulsion neurosis and, therefore, she has made one step forward, coming—if I have read and understood rightly—to a state in which she begins to neglect herself and to be dirty.

Now here is an interesting point. I have never seen persons so dirty as those suffering from a wash-compulsion neurosis. If you enter the home of such a person there is a terrible fume. You find papers lying about, and dirt everywhere. The hands and the whole body are dirty, all the clothes are dirty, and they do not touch anything. I do not know if it is so here, but this is the usual condition among people with a wash-compulsion neurosis, and it is funny that all these persons experience some adventures that others never experience. Always, where there is dirt, they are mixed in it. Probably it is because they are always looking around for dirt and are not so clever as others in avoiding it. I have had a very queer experience with such persons who are always soiled where other people can avoid it. It is like a fate hanging over such people, that they must always find their way to dirt.

We do not know what the breakdown means in this case—perhaps a step nearer to psychosis. That happens sometimes in persons suffering from compulsion neurosis.

Her fear of death referred to above was related to a definite knife phobia . . .

You can call a knife phobia also a compulsion idea, a very frequent one which persons suffer from if they see a knife. They feel that they could kill a person. But they never do. They stop at the idea. The meaning behind such an idea is hidden; we must find out its whole coherence and what it means. Now I have explained what it means. It is nearly the same as a person wanting to curse, "I could kill you," and such things.

Uncooperativeness and Hostility

We spoke before of dissensions. The husband is ambitious. She, as we know from our general diagnosis of neurotic persons, is ambitious. She wants to rule, to be the head. She wants to be the cleanest person, and we can understand how she avoids her husband, his personal approach, his sexual approach, because of his lack of cleanliness. She calls everything dirty. She can call a kiss dirt. We cannot commend her. We must find how far she is going to look for this dirt. She has two children and we must believe that this had not been at her own wish. Here we see the lack of cooperation. If you look a little nearer you may be sure this is a frigid woman. Do you see why? She is always thinking of herself, and the sexual functions among men and women can be right only if they are fulfilled as a task for two persons. If a person is interested only in self the sexual feelings are not right. Thus you have frigidity. More rarely you may have vaginismus, but it is mostly frigidity, and you can be sure that this is a woman who does not cooperate. This can be seen in the form of her sexual urge, which is sexuality. We must remember the difference—sexuality is a form and sexual urge is a movement. Therefore we can be sure and can predict—though we must not allow ourself to do so, but should wait and be patient—that she resents sexual intercourse.

We next read that this knife phobia was

. . . connected with tendencies both suicidal and homicidal.

In the discussion of suicide, I have explained that this is always a sign of a person who is not trained in cooperation. He is always looking after himself, and when he is confronted with a social problem for which he is not prepared, he has such a feeling of his own worth and value that he is sure that, in killing himself, he hurts another person. If you have seen such cases in this connection, you have understood them. Therefore we can say in a certain way that suicide is always an accusation and a revenge, an attacking attitude. Sometimes it is an attack of revenge. Therefore, we must look for the person against whom this phobia is directed. There is no question that it is her husband. It may be guessed very surely—the husband with whom, as we have seen, she must be in dissension. He wants to rule and she is interested only in her own person, and therefore if there is revenge or attack or aggression against somebody, it must be against the husband. You can guess it, but please wait to see if we can prove it.

Her aggressive thoughts and feelings towards other people were shown in other ways.

We see "other people." We do not know who they are, but it contradicts in a certain way our view that the husband is meant.

She experienced at times an impulsive wish to hit her husband . . .

That is what I said before. It is as in general medicine. If you have guessed before, you may find a proof. If you have rapidly diagnosed pneumonia, for instance, you may find signs later that will prove it and which you can predict; when we find such proofs we feel that we are on terra firma.

. . . her husband or . . .

We know what must follow—her husband or the children. There are no other persons she could accuse. She would not like children. If you asked her: "Do you like children?" she would say "Yes; my children are my all!" In Individual Psychology we learn from experience that if we want to understand a person we have to close our ears. We have only to look. In this way we can see as in a pantomime. Perhaps there are other persons. Perhaps there is a mother-in-law. It is possible. We would not be astonished. But, so far as we know the situation, we expect the children to follow.

> . . . *her husband or anybody else who happened to have annoyed her.*

Who are the persons who can have annoyed her? We can see that this woman is very sensitive, and if we look for what sensitiveness means in general diagnosis we find that it means a feeling of being in a hostile country and being attacked from all sides. That is the style of life of the person who does not cooperate and feel at home, who is always experiencing and sensing enmity in the environment; and, therefore, we can understand that she reacts in such a strong manner with emotion.

If I felt that I was in a hostile country and always expected attacks, expected to be annoyed and humiliated, I would behave in the same way. I also would be sensitive. This is a very interesting point. We cannot explain these persons only by looking to their emotion; we must look to their mistaken meaning of life and to their bringing up. She really believes she lives in a hostile country and is expecting always to be attacked and humiliated. She is thinking only of herself and her own salvation, her own superiority in overcoming the difficulties of life. These emotional persons must be understood from this point of view. If I believe an abyss is before me, whether there is an abyss or not, it is all the same; I am suffering from my meaning, not from reality. If I believe that there is a lion in the next room, it is all the same to me whether there is one or not. I shall behave in the same way. Therefore, we must look for the meaning of this person. It is "I must be safe"—a selfish meaning.

Now we read:

> *These characteristics had of late extended in two directions. On the one hand she experienced at times a strong desire to hit any casual stranger she happened to pass in the street.*

Is it not as I have described? She is living in a hostile country, where everybody is an enemy. To want to hit any stranger she meets in the street means to be impossible, to compromise herself. It means: "I must be watched; someone must take care of me." She forces other persons—or one other person—to take care of her. Whether she says it in words or not she speaks by her attitude in life and forces other persons to take care of her if she behaves in this way. But we must also look for the impression the husband has of it. His wife wants to hit every stranger in the street and he is living with her in social relations. Therefore, whatever she does affects him. He must do something. What can he do in such a case? We suppose this husband is not a fool or feeble-minded and we can predict what he has to do. He has to take care of her as far as possible, watch her and accompany her and so on. She is giving him the rules for his behavior in so doing. You see, this ambitious woman, with an ambitious husband, has conquered. He must do what she wants and commands. She behaves in such a way that other persons must feel responsible. She exploits him and is the commander and, therefore, we can understand that on this point she rules.

Wanting to Enslave Her Husband

Now let us see more:

> *On the other hand she entertained homicidal feelings toward her younger son, a child of four . . .*

This we have not seen before, but we have guessed it—that the attacks would be against the children. Here we have the second child specially pointed out, and it gives us a chance to guess that she wanted to avoid this child, that it was an unwanted child; and it finds expression in this way, that she is afraid she will kill him, that she does not treat him rightly, and so on. These feelings are sometimes so intense that the husband must watch her. The husband now becomes a slave, and probably this woman had nothing more in her meaning and imagination long ago but to make him a prisoner and slave. She would have been satisfied if her husband had submitted in a general way, as sometimes husbands do submit. But we have heard that this husband was ambitious; he wanted her to submit, wanted to subjugate her. He has lost and she has conquered. She could not conquer in a usual way, convincing him, or perhaps taking part in all his interests; therefore she came to a point that we can understand. She is right; she acts intelligently. If her goal is to be conqueror, to subjugate her husband, she has acted absolutely rightly. She has accomplished a creative work, a masterpiece of art, and we have to admire this woman!

Now I want to tell you something of how I go on with such cases. I explain it in short words. I say: "I admire you; you have done a masterpiece of art. You have conquered." I put it pleasantly.

Now we want to establish a coherence. This woman is looking for a fear that she will kill somebody. We have to look for the whole coherence. She is leaning on one point and is not looking for the others. Other psychologists will say she is surprised, but she is not surprised. I see it clearly. She does not want to see it, because if she did, her remainder of social interest would rise up and contradict it. No person who is not feeble-minded or crazy would agree that he wanted to rule other persons in such a way and, therefore, she is not permitted to look. But we must make her look and, therefore, I prefer to have such a nice talk and to praise her for her cleverness: "You have done rightly."

Then there is the question whether, even before, she had no other meaning or goal in her mind but to rule everybody. On this point we have to find out whether in childhood also she was "bossing" and wanted to command everybody. If we can prove it as the next backward step in our understanding, what shall we say of all the skepticism, all the criticisms that we do not know anything about this woman and how she was as a child? If we can show that as a child she was "bossing," in what other science can you be so sure that you can postulate something which happened twenty-five or twenty-eight years before? If you ask her for her earliest recollections, I am sure she will tell you something in which you will find a "bossing" attitude, because we are soon to grasp the whole style of life of this woman. She is a "bossing" woman, but she could not conquer in a normal way. She had no chance—poverty, an ambitious husband, two children very soon, not cooperative, as we have seen. She had to be defeated in a normal way and she is looking for her conquest in another way that we could not agree with or call a useful or social way.

Sometimes the idea of killing the boy was so intense that she feared that she might carry the intention into execution.

The more she was afraid she would execute it, the more her husband must watch her.

She stated that these symptoms had been in existence for one-and-a-half years.

If this is right we should be interested to find out what happened one-and-a-half years ago, when this child was two-and-a-half years old. I should understand it better if it had happened before the second child came, but if it be true that the symptoms originated one-and-a-half years ago we must know in what situation the woman was at that time and what has affected her. We shall find that she had to offer cooperation and could not, that she was afraid she would be subjugated, and resisted, and wanted to conquer. But we must know.

More careful examination, however, seemed to show that definite neurotic traits had been in existence many years, and had been accentuated since marriage. She herself indeed volunteered the information that she "had not been the girl she was since she had been married."

"Since marriage!" This is very interesting, because from our general experience we know there are three situations which are like test examinations to show whether a person is socially interested or not: the social problem—how to behave to others; the occupation problem —how to be useful in work; the marriage problem—how to converse with a person of the other sex. These are the test examinations for how far a person is prepared for social relations. If her symptoms have been worse since marriage it is a sign that she was not prepared for marriage because she was too much interested in her own person.

The Example of Her Parents

Now what of the family history? Many family histories I have read do not say very much. We Individual Psychologists are used to hearing of some situations and facts that involve the child in a way we can understand, but we would reject all decriptions in which we are referred to heredity only, such as that an aunt was crazy or a grandmother a drunkard. These do not say anything. It does not contribute to our understanding. We are very interested in imperfect organs, if we are to grasp a case, because we find very often children out of a family tree where persons have suffered in some organs, and we may suspect that they suffer from some lack of validity in those organs; but mostly we do not get much information from these decriptions.

The family history showed signs of neurosis on both sides.

This is worth while, because we can see that the family history of the child had been a bad one. Neurotic means that the parents were fighting for things, to boss, to rule, to subjugate others, to utilize and to exploit others, and so on, and therefore the children in such an atmosphere are really endangered. On this point, however, I have to say that although they are endangered, we are not sure that they must really suffer. They can overcome these dangers and get success and advantage out of them. But a certain probability gives us the right to expect that the danger is that the whole make-up and style of life will be in some way selfish.

At the same time it must be remembered that the informant on this matter was the patient, whose attitude to her parents, at least, was not without personal bias.

We want to see what her attitude was and this probably means that it was a hostile attitude to the parents; she has struggled against them.

For example she felt aggrieved that both her father and mother were only children—for, as she pointed out, this meant that she had no uncles or aunts and could not receive presents as did other children.

This is a woman who is always expecting to be presented and here she betrays a good deal of her style of life. She is the type that wants to receive, not to give. We understand that this type is in danger and must have difficulties in life, especially if she meets an ambitious man.

The father was a laborer. The mother was a hard-working woman who did everything to keep the home together. She avoided responsibility, however, in one important particular. If her children needed correction, she preferred to leave that matter to her husband.

This means that she did not feel strong enough, and utilized her husband for punishments, as happens very often in families. It is a bad thing for the children, because they begin to disesteem and ridicule the mother and to make a joke of her, because they see her express herself as a weak person who cannot do the right thing.

This fact was unfortunate—since the latter was very sadistic.

I do not think "sadistic" here is to be interpreted as meaning that he had sexual satisfaction when he slapped the children, but that he was rough and ruling and bossing, and subjugated the children. Now we can understand that she has put her goal in the subjugation of others. I have known many cases where the child who has been beaten hard has gone round with the idea: "When I am grown up I will do the same with others—rule them and boss them." The father in his roughness has given this child a goal. What does superiority mean? What does it mean to be the most powerful person in the world? This poor girl, as a child who is always suppressed and maltreated, could have no other idea than that it is much better to be above and not down, to maltreat others and not to be maltreated. Now we see her from this standpoint and on this level.

When he learnt from his wife that his children had misbehaved in any way—especially with reference to anything that touched his purse—for instance, if they wore out the soles of their boots quickly —he would beat them almost unmercifully.

This is a point where we can learn something in regard to corporal punishment.

The consequence was that the children lived in dread of their father, at the same time that for obvious reasons they did not confide in their mother.

Where should they learn cooperation if neither with the father nor the mother? Some little degree of cooperation there must have been in this girl's mind, because she could get married. She may have learned it from other children, comrades perhaps, but not from father or mother.

Nevertheless she maintained that he was a good father, except on Saturday nights, when he frequently came home drunk.

This would mean that she preferred the father. I am impressed, when I read this, with the idea that she was the oldest child. Mostly the oldest child, whether boy or girl, turns towards the father. When another child comes, relations with the mother are interrupted and the throne is vacant, which gives the father his chance. But this is only a guess and we have to prove it.

He would then strike his wife as well as his children and openly threaten to cut their throats.

She imitates the father in her compulsion idea: to kill somebody with the knife—child, or husband. Did I not say that the father gave her the chance to put her goal of superiority in this way?

Notice that the father cursed only; he did not cut the throats of his children. Therefore I believe I am right in thinking that when she says she could kill somebody it is just a curse, an idea—"I could kill you!"

This latter point is possibly of interest in view of a similar symptom exhibited by A. Indeed in many respects her neurotic symptom formation tended towards an imitation of her father's characteristics.

The writer, who is a doctor, goes on to say:

She was apt in the same way to hit her own children without adequate provocation.

With this we do not agree. She has a provocation. She wants to be superior, as the father wanted to be superior. That is a provocation— she was provoked: "If I want to boss I shall use my children, because they are the weaker ones and cannot hit back."

Though it is true she afterwards regretted her cruelty . . .

This reminds me that we very often hear something said about regretting, feeling of guilt, and so on. Now we Individual Psychologists are skeptical in this matter. We do not judge this regret and feeling of guilt very highly. We say it is absolutely empty and useless. After a child is beaten hard, the regret does not matter. It is too much. Either one of these two things would be enough—the regret or the hit—but both! I would resent it very much if somebody hit me and then regretted it. I have seen that this feeling of guilt is a trick so that we shall not see this cruel attitude in bossing others. It means: "I am a noble woman and I regret it." I believe modern society should be warned not to take very seriously this regret. We find it among problem children very often. They commit some act, cry, and ask pardon very much, and then do it again. Why? Because, if they did not regret, but only continued doing it, they would be put out. Nobody could bear it always. They make a sort of hinterland where others will not interfere with them; they have a feeling that they are being smart children or people. So there is this woman, she is cruel and regrets it, but what does that matter? The facts are all the same.

> . . . *this feeling had little or no power to prevent similar out-bursts on a subsequent occasion.*

We expected that, because it is a trick. Where you find the feeling of guilt it is in cases of melancholia and it is always a trick. It doesn't work. You see we guessed rightly.

Other Childhood and Youth Situations

> A. *was the second child and girl of a family of eight—four girls being followed by four boys.*

In regard to second children, we know they are generally—though there are no rules, and we speak only of majorities—much more striving. It is like a race, and they want always to overcome the first child. The reason why I said I believed she was a first child was that she turned to the father, but there are circumstances in which the second child may do so, especially if she has been pampered and a third child comes and she is in a situation which draws her towards him.

We find second children striving to be first; there is a very good picture of this in the Bible picture of Jacob and Esau. It is very interesting, too, to see from statistics in America that, among juvenile delinquents, second children are in a majority. An inquiry into children of one and two years and younger has been started by Individual Psychologists, and there is a big field, which can be used for some understanding of their whole style of life. There will be something good or something wrong about second children. It is like a race; they try to overcome the first. Perhaps it was so in this case, but we do not want to say more.

As a child, she said, she had been on the whole happy-go-lucky, cheerful, and healthy . . .

If so, she had been in the center of the stage and favored. She was perhaps the favorite.

. . . very different from her oldest sister, whom she described as being silent and reserved, characteristics which A. interpreted as selfishness.

Now, surely, it is selfish to be reserved because it means to think of one's self. We can see that she had been lucky in her striving, and the older girl had the aspect of a defeated child and was overcome. We find this feature in her whole make-up—how to overcome. She is able to succeed in her goal to be mother and father and to boss, in an easy way, because the older sister has given way and been conquered.

The parents seemed to have held a somewhat similar opinion, and treated their oldest child with special severity.

Now the parents help her in her race, by suppressing the oldest child.

She was frequently in trouble, and the severe beatings which she received from her father filled A. with terror.

She had been scared because the oldest child had been beaten so severely.

The rest of the family A. regarded with considerable affection, with the exception, significantly enough, of her oldest brother.

That is, the first boy, who when he came was probably worshipped and appreciated in a way she did not like; and therefore we can conclude—though we must really prove it—that her position in the family was endangered by this boy.

As with her sister, so with him, she considered that he was selfish and inconsiderate, "so different from the rest of us, except, of course, T." (the oldest sister).

That she agreed with the other children means that she could rule them; they did not make difficulties. This boy and the oldest sister made difficulties and therefore she did not agree with them.

Personal History: *As already mentioned A. had been a healthy child and prided herself on her robust health. From the age of fourteen to seventeen inclusive, however, she had some degree of goiter from which she subsequently recovered.*

We see here a certain organic imperfection, as we find very often among neurotic patients. How far this influenced her we could learn only from the first child, of whom we have not many remarks.

Though she had no return of the trouble, yet, from time to time in the course of treatment she had considerable difficulty in times of stress in getting her breath—a symptom which caused her considerable anxiety.

This probably was not due to pressure of the thyroid, or it would have been recognized and treated. It probably was a psychological problem; she could not breathe when she became emotional under the treatment, or it may have appeared when she was wishing to pose, or felt she was unjustly treated. All this may have affected her breathing, but it could have been seen clearly if the thyroid was causing pressure.

Her school attainments were quite good and she had at that time no difficulty in making friends.

Do not forget that such persons, selfish from the beginning and striving to be in a favorable situation, do not lack all degrees of cooperation. Therefore, we are not astonished that she, who probably succeeded in the beginning and wanted to be ahead and lead the school, found it easier to make friends. Probably they were friends who were willing to submit to her, but that is a point we could find out in an interview.

She left school at the age of fourteen, but continued to live at home for some months, going from there to daily work, which she enjoyed.

In that case she probably fell on a good place, where she could express her opinion and perhaps also rule others.

But as soon as she entered domestic service away from home, new troubles began.

Now domestic service means to submit, and this woman cannot submit. She cannot submit in any way that can be accepted as cooperation. She must be ruling and here we have a new proof. She is not prepared for a situation in which others are ruling. We find many girls who have to do domestic work and cannot submit. For instance, I remember a governess who, when the woman who employed her asked her to clean the cage of the parrot, said: "You should ask what I want to do this afternoon, and I will say that I would like to clean the cage of the parrot." Thus it appeared to be her own idea; she was commanding. You meet the same thing in the exercises of the army, where the soldier, after he is commanded, must repeat the command in such a way as if it were his own. "I shall go on this parade." You see the wisdom of that rule in the army.[5]

Within a week of her arrival she was attacked by such bad carbuncles on her back that the doctor ordered her home again.

I do not go so far as to say that those carbuncles were the result of her dislike, but it is a fact that if a person does not feel well in a certain place, something may happen. My daughter, who is a psychiatrist and has made researches into accidents, found that half of them occur among persons who do not like the job in which they are working.[6] When people are run over, fall down from certain places and hurt themselves, or touch something, it is as though they would say: "It is because my father forced me to go to this job, and I wanted another job." Half of all the accidents! Therefore, I am quite sure that

---

5. See also p. 135.

6. Adler, Alexandra. "Unfallshäufung und ihre persönliche Bedingtheit," *Arch. Gewerbepathol. Gewerbehyg.*, 1931, 2, 361–380.

things like carbuncles can occur if a person does not like a certain situation. I would not go further.

This she did with considerable trepidation because she knew that her eldest sister, who had once similarly returned, owing to illness, had had a very bad reception.

She had learned how not to behave!

For a time, however, everything went well. But soon her father became openly dissatisfied at having to keep his daughter "eating her head off" as he put it. Matters came to a climax when, one morning as A. entered the kitchen to have breakfast, her father, without a word of warning, rushed at her with a shovel, obviously intending to hit her over the head.

It was in the morning, so he was not drunk!

She rushed from the house in terror and hid from the family for the rest of the day. It is possibly of significance, in view of her later fear of coffins, undertakers, and all matters relating to the subject of death, that she spent most of this time in the churchyard.

Now a new idea appears. In a certain way we can see that the illness and the neurotic symptoms of this woman are an accusation against the father whether she knows it or not. We are studying the natural history, the biology, of behavior. Now if we find one bone—such as this neurotic symptom represents—we can relate it to the father. The father is guilty and it is an accusation against him. She might put it in these words; "My father has tortured me so much that it is because of his treatment that I am as I am." Now the father had not been right, but does it follow that the daughter also must not be right? Is it really like cause and effect? Is she forced to be sick and to make mistakes because the father has made a mistake? The importance of this question is very great because that is what this woman, if we read her aright, is really saying—that because the father has made a mistake, she also must do so. But there is no causality in mind; only the causality *she* has effected. She has made something into a reason which must not be a reason, and I have seen other children who have been tortured by their parents go through this compulsion neurosis. It is not like the causality we find among dead things; and even among dead things causality is now beginning to be doubted.

In the evening, however, she was found by her mother, who persuaded her to return home. Her father treated the incident as a joke, and laughed at her for "being such a silly." His daughter, however, did not treat the matter so lightly and vowed that she would never return home to live again, a resolution which she kept for a long time.

Another resolution she had made, as I said before: "I must never be in a situation where another person can rule me." In the childish fashion which we always find in neurotic patients, she knows only contradiction and antithesis: to rule or to be ruled. This is very interesting that among all the failures in life, and not only among neurotic persons, you will find that they know only contradiction. They call it sometimes "ambivalence" or "polarity" but always they are forming judgments of contradiction—down, above; good, bad; normal, not normal; and so on. In children and neurotic persons, and in the old Greek philosophy, you find always this looking for contradiction.

She has concluded, in this way, never to be ruled.

After this affair she went once more into domestic service and appears to have worked hard and diligently. She showed, however, a preference for rough work. Her dislike for doing "fiddly work," such as dusting, she distinctly stated to be due to her dread that she would break ornaments and so on.

What is in her mind is that she is a girl of strong health, who values strength and does not like housekeeping. When we remember her contradiction towards the oldest boy, because a boy had been preferred, she probably did not want to be a woman at all. She disliked doing such things, being occupied with dusting and such little matters. This would explain why she was not prepared to be a married woman. This would be what I have called the *masculine protest*. In such a case, if you force a person to do things she does not like, she tries to exaggerate. There is a certain anger and rage and exaggeration.

This fact is of interest as being the possible forerunner of her later openly destructive wishes and feelings. . . .

Premarital Difficulties

At the age of eighteen she was engaged to a young man whom she appears to have dominated.

We find the writer of this case history has been on the same track as we have, and she describes this domineering symptom when she points out that she dominated this man.

In course of time, however, she came to dislike him for what she considered his "stingy ways" and, after two or three years, dramatically broke off the engagement by throwing the ring in his face.

That is not what we expect from a girl; we expect milder processes!

She related, however, with pride, that he still maintained a somewhat dog-like devotion to her, and even at the time she came for treatment still continued to ask after her. In spite of this manifestation of devotion she never showed any regret with reference to her behavior in the whole matter.

In this case she does not regret because there is no reason for her to do so.

During the war she entered a munitions factory in a provincial town, and it was then she met the man who is now her husband.

We now remember this man. He is a cripple, and sometimes you find among men and women who want to dominate that they are very fond of cripples and people who are weak in some way—sometimes alcoholics whom they want to save, and people of a lower social status than their own. I would warn people—girls especially, but also the men—against choosing in this way, because no person in love or marriage can safely be looked down on. They will revolt, as this man revolted.

He was quartered in hospital at the time, invalided home from the war. He fulfilled her ideal of a possible husband in two most important respects—he was tall and he was not an alcoholic.

We can understand that the father had been strong with his drunkenness, and the reason many persons, especially girls, are afraid of alcoholics is that they cannot rule them. Alcoholics and creeping things, like mice and insects, they fear sometimes. You find very often that this fright is because they cannot rule them and can be surprised by them. We can understand why she would resent an alcoholic, but why she preferred a tall man we do not know. It may have been the remains of her admiration of the father, or she may have been tall, or have thought it was more worth while to rule a tall man than a short one. This could be found out only by asking her.

It is also possible that his injuries appealed to her love of power —her wish to assume the dominant role was a notable trait in her character.

The writer has taken the line which I explained. We would underline this and say her style of life was characterized by a very domineering and bossing attitude.

For a time all went well. But when her fiancé went to London, he then, for reasons best known to himself, wrote letters well calculated to rouse her jealousy.

If we understand that she wanted to rule him, to be alone with him and the center of his attention, we know that jealousy is very near at hand. She has to look to it that she is not dethroned as she was when the other children came in the family, and when the boy came.

Unhappy and suspicious, A. followed him to London, obtained work as a waitress in a restaurant, and did all in her power to hold her fiancé.

You see how she is striving to keep him.

With this the attitude of the two lovers towards each other seems to have undergone a change. Not only did the woman assume the more active part in their relations . . .

We note this in proof of her meaning—she took the active part!

. . . but the man, from being attentive and kindly, now became careless and inconsiderate.

We saw in the beginning that she had forced him to be careful. At this point we read he had become careless.

They made appointments for which he either came late or did not keep at all. A. became suspicious, tearful, and "quite different from her former bright self."

She was afraid of losing her former ruling position.

Matters came to a head when he failed for a second time to keep an appointment with her—she having in the meanwhile waited for him for hours in the cold and fog of a November night.

This is a hard thing, and there is no question the man also was not adapted for such a marriage. Any girl would be right to look upon such negligence as an injury. This girl could find no other way than the creation of a compulsion idea with which she could again conquer him.

When she learned from him next day that he had not kept his appointment because he had gone out with some friends, she angrily told him she did not wish to see him again.

She would feel defeated. Perhaps we should be glad to get rid of such a partner, but this person does not want to be defeated. She wants to keep him.

Her attempt to break off the engagement, however, did not take place—a fact for which she felt thankful when, three weeks later, she discovered that she was pregnant.

Here is a good chance to speak of relations before marriage. It may seem in some cases to be an advantage, but I have found that it is a disadvantage and as doctors we should advise to wait. It always causes trouble.

Marital Difficulties

She felt desperate at this finding and entertained now for the first time definite suicidal feelings. Her fiancé endeavored to comfort her and promised to marry her as soon as possible—which he did three or four weeks after. The question of her residence for the next few months now arose. She dreaded to return home because her father had said that he would have nothing to do with any of his daughters if they got into trouble. Though his threat proved to be unfounded, and she was allowed by her parents to return home, she felt very unhappy during this time.

Really, she felt defeated.

Her misery was accentuated by the birth of a son; for both she and her husband had hoped for a daughter.

This is something we should not expect. We should expect that if a child was coming they would hope for a son. Why they wanted a daughter could be explained only by these two persons. But perhaps if they had had a daughter, she would have been disappointed.

It may be pointed out in passing that A.'s desire for a daughter and subsequent disappointment were connected with her later hostility towards her sons.

As we cannot verify her statements without asking her, we must assume she had disliked the men in her environment, her father, then her brother. Probably, too, she was looking for the antithesis man-woman, because these neurotic people look on men and women as *opposite* sexes. You know the widespread notion—the opposite sex. If you exaggerate this you will get an opposition against the opposite sex, which is very often to be found, both in men and women, and especially among neurotic persons.

After this event she then returned to London to live in two rooms with her husband. Matters, however, went badly from the first. It is true that to begin with she got on well with her neighbors, but soon feelings of inferiority began to assert themselves. These seem to have been connected with a certain jealousy of her husband, who was popular and well-liked generally. She interpreted passing words and looks of those around her as criticisms directed against herself.

She looked on the neighbors, probably, as subjects she could rule, and therefore good relations never existed.

As a conscious reaction formation against the sensation that she was despised, she not only avoided making friendships, "keeping herself to herself" as she described it, but she also used to sing hymns in a loud voice to show her neighbors firstly, that she was not afraid, and secondly, that she at any rate had been well brought up. Unfortunately her criticisms of her neighbors were not without justification, quarrels and drunken brawls not being infrequent. In addition she and her husband found constant cause for disagreement. The methods she employed to gain his sympathy were characteristic. Thus after a quarrel she would retire to bed and threaten to kill herself and the child unless matters improved.

You see how she wanted to use force!

So matters continued, going from bad to worse until A.'s neurotic symptoms became so manifest that her husband took her to see a doctor. The diagnosis of nervous dyspepsia was made, and the recommendation given that all her teeth should be extracted.

I presume this was meant as a punishment; not as medical treatment!

After some hesitation she decided to take this advice, and with this end in view went to hospital accompanied by a friend. The latter was then considerably annoyed when A., after an hysterical outburst in front of the doctor and nurses, refused to have her mouth touched.

This suggests that she really understood the situation better!

Not unnaturally this same friend refused to accompany her a second time to hospital. On the second occasion, therefore, A. went alone, when it is noteworthy that, though nervous, she was able to have three or four teeth extracted without trouble. On the next occasion, however, matters did not go so smoothly. She had an hysterical outburst following the extraction of twelve teeth, due, she maintained, to the fact that she saw and felt the whole operation although under an anesthetic. The fantastic nature of these "memories" was obvious. In accord also with her sadistic tendencies it is hardly surprising that these "remembrances," to which she had not infrequently referred, made a deep impression on her.

Now, imagine this woman: thirty years of age! They extracted, as far as I can count, sixteen teeth! I think a woman who had no "sadistic tendencies" would not look on this fact in a humorous spirit! It makes a deep impression. If you know what it means to a woman or a man to lose the first teeth, you will appreciate that this woman has lost sixteen. And she is jealous of her husband! She explained how she had suffered. I hope I am explaining it rightly, but this may have another explanation. This woman likes to explain how much she has suffered. Probably she had some dreams, as happens in narcosis, and she tells these things to impress others how she has suffered.

I do not think we should speak of sadistic tendencies in the way that has become common in our time, because we should use it only when the person has a sexual gratification. If we call all forms of attack "sadism" everything disappears in darkness.

The Final Exogenous Situation

Shortly after this her second child was born.

We see that it was a time of distress, when she was fighting hard for her superior position.

The fact that he was a boy caused her great disappointment— she had been quite certain that the infant would be a girl. The impotence of her wishes in the face of reality severely wounded her vanity—and from now on her neurotic tendency became more and more evident. The resentment she felt toward her infant was the obvious prelude to her later consciously felt wish to kill the child.

You will remember that in speaking of the first symptoms and when they occurred, I said I could have understood it if it had been when the second child came, because her importance would weaken and become less since she now has to share with two children, and she wants herself to be the center, not the children. She will feel resentment more strongly, and a desire to kill.

At the same time her pursuit by a drunken neighbor, who with a knife in his hand threatened to take her life, gave her a reason for an exacerbation of her symptoms. It also gave her a reasonable ex-

cuse for refusing to stay in the house where they were living although it was impossible to obtain any other room at the moment in the neighborhood.

Now really this house had not been very well fitted for a bossing woman. The neighbors did not like her. In this case you can find also that a paranoiac symptom appears and you can see that in a certain way the manner in which this woman behaves is in the neighborhood of paranoia—as if the others would pursue her and be interested in her and look at her. But even a compulsion neurosis reaches further and touches some symptoms which are generally described under another title. There are mixtures in this way.

In addition—by this means she was able to leave her husband for a time, she and her children finding a temporary home with her mother-in-law, her husband remaining alone in London. The arrangement, however, did not prove happy.

The mother-in-law probably also did not submit!

This position was partly due to the critical attitude of the mother-in-law towards her daughter-in-law, and partly to the fact that A. felt hostile towards her mother-in-law from the start, owing to the unfavorable comparisons which her husband was accustomed to draw between her and his mother.

The usual fact!

By mutual consent, therefore, the arrangement was terminated and A. and her children went to stay with her parents. From there she was recalled to London, owing to the fact that her husband had had a "nervous breakdown" in her absence and wanted her to nurse him.

We do not know the husband. Perhaps he also wanted to dominate somebody.

It seems improbable that it was only a coincidence that at the same time he had been able to find rooms for the family.

Probably he worked with nervous symptoms and wanted to impress her in this way by a "nervous breakdown."

Shortly after her return to London she was overcome by the obsessive thoughts and feelings which gradually came to occupy her attention more and more—to the exclusion of almost all else. She dated this phase of her illness back to a terrifying dream of angels surrounding a coffin.

This is the thought of death, but you see what it means. It affects the husband. *He* has to take care of her; so she has a dream of angels surrounding a coffin.

Of significance is her constant association of this dream with a picture of her old home, at which she frequently gazed when pregnant with her first child.

We understand that at this time she played with the idea of suicide. She looked round and the picture was there, and the other members of the family would be impressed. She would get the idea: "What would make me master of the game would be if the others were afraid that I would commit suicide."

.   .   .   .   .

The rest of the case-paper deals with treatment, which is not part of my lecture. I have simply wanted to show you the *coherence of a life style.*

13

Technique of Treatment
(1932)[1]

For Adler, diagnosis and treatment were so closely related that even in the present paper, given under the title of "Technique of Treatment," we find along with specific technical treatment suggestions, discussion of general principles and diagnostic methods. Included are birth-order position, early recollections, dreams, and a number of diagnostic questions, all aimed at understanding the individual in relation to his social environment.

How diagnosis and treatment become intertwined is illustrated by Adler's reaction to the information that a patient was disorderly as a child: "One sees the shadow of another person who picked up after him. . . . You can explain to him, 'You were disorderly, you passed on your obligation to others. It is still the same today. You are afraid to go ahead alone, by yourself.'"

Treatment is essentially to get the patient to recognize the mistake *in his life style, the striving for a socially useless goal of superiority, as the therapist has understood it, and thereby to increase the patient's ability to cooperate. This is a process of cognitive reorganization, of belated maturation.* —Eds.

1. Original translation of an unpublished manuscript, A1932l, headed: "Physicians' meeting, July 6, 1932. Dr. [Rudolf] Dreikurs, chairman; M[artha] Holub, secretary."

I feel today like St. Augustine who once said, "If you don't ask me, I know it; when you ask me, I don't know it." [2] This happens to every one of us when he is asked to speak about technique. For years I have been occupied writing about it—I hesitate, not because I don't know it; it has become automatic with me. But a description founders in that here nothing can be formulated into rules. Here the artistic side of Individual Psychology shows itself most clearly.

When I speak today about certain aspects of treatment, please keep in mind that in another case these can be quite different.

MINIMIZING THE SIGNIFICANCE OF THE SYMPTOMS

One of the chief aspects is: You must strive to debase the great significance which the neurotic attributes to his symptoms. This must be done in a friendly manner. There may be patients who do not tolerate this at all. How far you can go in minimizing the symptoms, when you must be more strict, etc., calculating reason cannot tell. Here an impression must be decisive. It is an artistic task from which the patient benefits when you succeed in coming closer to him in spite of his negative life style. I should like to become more systematic and to describe how you can do this.

It starts with the first appearance of the patient. You must be as unprepossessed as possible toward the patient; avoid everything which could make him believe that you are sacrificing yourself for him. As tempting as it may appear to tell him, "It is the greatest task of my life to make you well," this would be wrong with regard to what you want to achieve: to attribute the task to the patient. It is advisable to keep in mind the aspect of letting him understand this with each movement. This ability can very often help you to overcome great difficulties.[3]

2. Adler is apparently paraphrasing the following quotation from St. Augustine: "When I am here, I do not fast on Saturday; when at Rome, I do fast on Saturday" (*Epistle 36, to Casulanus*).

3. At one point Adler stated the crucial role of the patient in the process of psychotherapy in the following words: "The most important therapeutic aid of

One of the greatest difficulties is the treatment of melancholia. The patient endeavors to explain his complaints, he cries, he describes his symptoms as if they were something that had never happened before. You must not shock him. But when you have listened to him you will understand that this is a waste of time, and you can propose to him in a friendly way: "Now that we have seen what impeded you, we really want to get to work." This might be indicated, for example, when a patient spreads out his symptoms before you as safeguards, because he is afraid if he gives them up it will turn out that he is not as valuable as he would like to appear. "Now we do not want to talk any more about what prevents you from being the first, but how you have come to want to reach the goal, as if on command." Then you will observe how the patient wants to turn away from this. You must endeavor to bring the problem of cooperation closer to him. Many patients come from our competitors, and attempt to explain all symptoms sexually.

It is advisable to point clearly toward cooperation. The fact of cooperation is easily understood, although in most cases it turns out to be inadequate. If a person cooperates, he will never become a neurotic. This you must inculcate in the person during treatment. In some cases I have had success by saying, "Now I am not going to listen to you any more, now you are disturbing our cooperation." I would not always do it in this way. Sometimes I say, "Now we are clear regarding this point, now we must go to work."

THE FIRST INTERVIEWS

When the patient comes for the first time it would be a great mistake to assign him to a definite place. All patients want to sit on the "bench of repentance." It is good if you disturb the seating order, have a series of chairs, let the patient choose. Then he must show himself actively. You can draw conclusions from minor facts, such as that one sits closer, the other further away. One moves toward the

~~~~~~

the physician is always the patient himself. In harmonious cooperation with the physician, the sources of error of the incorrect upbringing must be recognized and the patient be brought to pull himself out of the swamp by his own boot straps (. . . *sich beim eigenen Schopf aus dem Sumpfe herauszuziehen*)" (A1928l).

desk; that is favorable. Another moves away; that is unfavorable. You can use this later on as evidence.

Of course, everyone complains quite differently. They speak in an abstract manner, they say nothing precisely. You pretend that you understand and wait till you can gather something concrete from their complaints. "Are you perhaps afraid?" The patient becomes relaxed and complains about anxiety or compulsions. A number of patients talk a lot even if they do not suffer from hypomania. We shall not make the mistake of many others who might say, "Make it shorter." You must suffer this. I have had patients who talked for three hours incessantly. Sometimes you can get a word in. There are patients who after an hour don't want to stop talking. In this event you can say during a breathing spell, "You have told me so much that I must think it over." A certain tactfulness toward the patient is indicated, so that he doesn't have the feeling of standing there like a defendant. We shall presume as part of human nature that no one tolerates subordination. Never yet has anyone subordinated himself without protest.

Then you ask, "Since when have you had your complaints?" In psychotherapy this is even more justified than in organic pathology. We want to find out what the situation was which appeared difficult to him. You must focus on this point: How did it come about that he failed in a certain situation? This must derive from his childhood. Therefore you go back into his childhood. It is not necessary to say, "Tell me something about your childhood." Instead you can ask about the parents. "How were your parents? Well, or nervous?" We don't think of heredity but of the atmosphere of the relationship of the parents to the patient. In many cases it is best to say, "Tell me something about your father." No individual escapes explaining his father's relationship to him, for when he says, "He was kind," we remember there is no character trait without a relationship to others. When the patient says, "My father was kind," this means "he was kind to *me*." When he says his mother was critical, the idea which penetrates is that he attempted to keep at a distance from his mother. One must say it again and again to naive researchers: Everything develops within the frame of the possible in the sense of a psychology of use, not in the sense of a psychology of possession.

An important question is, "How many children were there?" We place much emphasis on finding out which position the patient had in the sibling order. Further: "Who was the favorite of your father? Of your mother?" Among our patients we find remarkably often that they were the favorite of the father or the mother, sometimes of both. This does not appear to be favorable. Altogether, pampering is the worst. When you have reached this far, you are possibly at the starting point of the weakness in the structure of this personality.

"In your childhood were you a bad or a good child?" This is actually not so important for us, yet the reply shows us whether he was active or passive at an early age. Then other questions: what kind of friends he had, whether he was enlightened early regarding his sexual role—although this latter question is sometimes so much in the dark that the patient can hardly answer it correctly. The psychoanalysts would say it is in the unconscious. This is not true. He has never formulated it into words. It lies in him all the more, however, because his reason could not make any attack against it. You must keep this in mind with regard to many of our statements, namely, that we are dealing here with processes of consciousness which have not been formulated into concepts. If one finds such a process and transposes it into words, he will believe that he pulled something from the unconscious into consciousness. But there is no difference.

THE PAMPERED CHILD CONCEPT

Now we come to the point which is so important for us: the psychopathology of the pampered child. I have become more and more convinced that in nervous persons we are always dealing with pampered children. This concept tells us more than the usual usage of the term. It is a view of life in which the individual assumes that the other person is there for him. This view is based on experience; such a person must at one time have had this experience. Also dependent on experience, on the influence of other measures, is the possibility of making the child into a co-worker at an early age. It depends on how the child assimilates impressions. This is the creative power of the child. The child's response is never causally determined, although he who confuses statistical probability with causality believes that everything develops causally.

If you also consider the facts of organ inferiority, you have already gotten very far.

The neurosis of which the patient complains is the admission of his weakness. He declares himself bankrupt. The proof of pampering is accomplished best if you can show that the patient never participated, that he was never capable of such an accomplishment. For example, if he was disorderly, one sees the shadow of another person who picked up after him. This small phenomenon is already extremely significant. You can explain to him, "You were disorderly, you passed on your obligation to others. It is still the same today. You are afraid to go ahead alone, by yourself." There are a great number of other phenomena. It may also happen that a pampered child is very orderly and finicky. This is not difficult to understand if one considers that pampering can sometimes be bought by orderliness.

An important question is friendship. It cannot be overlooked that a person is irritated by this question. One does not like to admit that one has had no friends. The hesitating attitude can be seen from the reply. It is not an easy question for anyone to be asked whether he made friends easily. Children often give incorrect answers; with adults the answers are usually more precise. If the answers turn out as we expect, that it was difficult to make friends, then we have the confirmation that these are persons who did not become good partners. How great the deficiency is we cannot find out from this. But we can gather it from further facts, e.g., if he only made contact with girls or children who subjugated themselves to him. Here one can see how the desire to dominate has emerged from pampering.

Anxiety interests us the most. One finds it always in pampered children. There could be lesser degrees of pampering, where children have become accustomed to being alone early in life. But it will turn out that they scream at night, or walk around, which shows that they tolerate their seclusion poorly.

There are still other character traits which interest us very much, such as nail biting. This shows a child who revolted against accepting culture. In pampered children you will find all the phenomena which psychoanalysis characterizes as sexual discharges, e.g. constipation. This also holds for urination.

Thus we understand also that children who have been pampered cannot stand the denial of a wish. There are always thousands of variations, and you must find out intuitively the degree to which such an attitude emerged. By comparison with the present situation you gain new confirmations showing how significant the early childhood years are.

When you are finished with anxiety phenomena, it is advisable to ask whether there were difficulties at night, such as bed wetting, to confirm the fact that so many children regard the night as something that should not be. This is still not the discovery of the total context. But we see that such children attempt to bring about a condition in which pampering would not be interrupted.

EARLY RECOLLECTIONS AND DREAMS

When you have come to this point, say, "Think far back into your childhood." You know the great significance of this suggestion. We have made the exploration of earliest childhood recollections into a valuable technique. I should not like to leave any patient without questioning him on this point. The information regarding memory is significant. Memory is an activity. It is based on the life style, which here steps in by selecting from old impressions a single one. This leads us to the question, why this single one? In it the entire life style resonates. We must remember how one can represent psychological processes to oneself clearly, namely, by looking not only at the thought processes but also at the willing and acting. There are processes which are not conceptualized, which are connected with feelings and actions. One cannot assume that infants have no consciousness. One must complement what one hears. *Here we are in the field of guessing,* but we have already received enough hints. We are not without aids, we can draw on other fragments. But what we have guessed must be supported by other findings. If this is not possible, then we were wrong.

The more one is occupied with earliest childhood recollections, the more attractive the matter becomes. One hits upon relationships which show human nature in a shattering light. Even the greatest errors can be surpassed. E.g., a manic-depressive who experienced depressions at short intervals had this earliest recollection: he had a tantrum, was angry, when his mother died. This is the thought: How could my mother do such a thing to me, to die and leave me alone. A pampered child—what a thought of sovereignty! In his further life it was also always like this; he had differences with his father who was not able to fulfill all the patient's wishes.

One childhood recollection is sometimes not clear enough. You must draw on further recollections. You can then see much more clearly; you find what they have in common. You find certain degrees of the we-function, or its lack. This is enough work for several days. You can give the patient suggestions to add further material for the purpose of cooperation. It is an advantage if you tell the patient who says that he cannot think of anything that this is a lack of cooperation. It could happen that this fast diagnosis would be an error. You must go further in the technique; you must be able to predict what the patient will do in a certain situation.

A further aid is the dream life. Here also there is much greater clarity in Individual Psychology than in other schools. In the dream nothing happens that doesn't occur during the waking state. The patient feels attracted toward acting contrary to the common sense. He intoxicates himself in the dream to do what his life style proposes. It is an attempt at self-deception. If the patient would really attack the problem, he could not do without logic. The dream analogy deceives him. The same also holds true for poetic analogies.

UNVEILING THE FICTIVE SUPERIORITY

The life style dominates. The person is cast all of one piece. This you must find again in all its parts. In this self-consistent casting, the striving for fictive superiority is contained. There is no nervous patient who does not attempt to veil through his symptoms the fact that he is worried over his fictive superiority. We know this from experience. The neurosis is altogether a veiling maneuver. Behind the illness is the pathological ambitious striving of the patient to regard himself as something extraordinary. Imagine the situation, and you will immediately arrive at the technique of treatment.

The symptoms are a big heap of rubbish on which the patient builds in order to hide himself. The fictive superiority of the patient dates from the time he was pampered. He cannot free himself from this. The power which he exercises over others is that he expects them to look after him. This dates from the time when the fictive superiority was not structured conceptually. Therefore we must talk about it, so that it can be comprehended through logic.

You get the patient "in the flower of his sins." When the question arises, "Where were you when the world was divided up?"[4] he will point to his rubbish heap, which prevented him from accomplishment. While we see clearly what he is doing, he is unknowingly busy erecting his obstacles; like a seasoned criminal, he is seeking to secure an alibi. Yet far be it from me to blur the great difference between the neurotic and the criminal. [The neurotic's alibis run about as follows:] "I cannot sleep"—otherwise I would be the greatest. "I must wash my hands all day long"—therefore I cannot reach the high goal. While he regards one point, we must look at the other. He looks at his obstacles; we must look at his attempt to protect his fictive superiority and rescue his ambition. It always ends in, "What couldn't I have accomplished if I were not impeded by the symptoms." Our task is to make conceptual what was in him unconceptualized, for the sense of his immense value is intuitive.

EXTENDING THE ABILITY TO COOPERATE

Individual Psychology stresses enormously that the psychological development of a person can reach a normal condition only when he can achieve the necessary degree of ability to cooperate. This you must realize for yourselves. Furthermore, we emphasize that all problems of life demand a certain degree of the ability to cooperate. On the one hand you see the endogenous factors, the exogenous factors, the situation in which the complaints have arisen. On the other hand, the patient must declare himself bankrupt;

mmmmmmmmmm

4. This line, frequently cited by Adler, is from Schiller's poem, *"Die Teilung der Erde."* Jove offers the earth to man, and each grabs his share—the peasant, the nobleman, the abbot, the merchant, the king. After the partition is all over the poet arrives and finds that everything is gone. When Jove asks, "Where were you when the world was divided up?" the poet replies, "I was with you. My eye was fixed on you, my ear on the harmony of your heaven. Pardon the spirit who, intoxicated by your light, lost sight of the earth." To this Jove offers the consolation, "What to do? I have given the earth away. But you may any time live with me in my heaven."

this is demanded by his goal of superiority. Even when he represents the inferiority complex in the crassest way, this does not signify the admission of his worthlessness, but is a hint at something apparently pathological. The admission of inability happens rarely. Rather you hear of puzzling phenomena such as sleeplessness.

In the face of exogenous factors, when he does not have the necessary ability to cooperate, every patient will get into psychological tension. Here his entire body begins to vibrate. In the inferior parts this becomes more clearly visible. They are not necessarily organically inferior. A symptom may also show up otherwise, proof that the symptom must be suitable to hide the inability. In different persons psychological tensions will take different paths, such as that of thinking (confusions, hypomania, obsessions). The feeling of fictive superiority is not touched by the neurotic process. Here also we have the alibi. The tension may also take hold of the sphere of feelings (anxiety, sadness). This symptom proves itself particularly suitable for intellectuals. There are also people in whom the motor system becomes irritated (hysteria). In normal persons such impulses would in no situation provoke an action leading to a failure such as suicide, homosexuality, or crime. The normal person aims to arrive through his actions at a solution of the problem despite his deficiency. These are the cases where the lack of the ability to cooperate is not too great.

Part of the technique of treatment is in any case information on these aspects, and extension of the ability to cooperate. This is the core of Individual Psychology treatment. In the cooperation between physician and patient I have greatly stressed how the patient must be brought closer to the problem, so that he is slowly brought into this path of cooperation until it appears to him a matter of course. The result is the extended ability to cooperate.[5] This puts him in a better position.

〰〰〰〰〰〰〰〰

5. The following is a further description by Adler of the aim of psychotherapy: "The patient must be guided away from himself, toward productivity for others; he must be educated toward social interest; he must be led from his seclusion from the world, back to existence (*zurück in das Dasein*); he must be brought to the only correct insight, that he is as important for the community as anyone else; he must get to feel at home on this earth" (A1928l).

FURTHER PRACTICAL SUGGESTIONS

Of course a thousand questions arise; for example, whether one's personal development would not be harmed if one thinks too much of others, or how one goes about making friends.

In the course of time one gathers a collection of slogans. "You are in the same position as everybody else. If something appears difficult to you . . . [here a crucial word is missing] It is always this way with new tasks." It is necessary to have a series of dramatic illustrations at one's disposal. These are more effective than sober expositions. I am thinking here of Shaw's *Androcles and the Lion:* it is good to create the impression that the matter proceeds like child's play. It is all right if occasionally one adds friendly irony; but one must not go too far. You must give the patient the impression that you take him seriously.

It is important never to be perplexed, to accept everything in a friendly manner, and to establish the connection [with the life style].

Regarding the problem of the fee: One should not primarily make a business of Individual Psychology. One would also not succeed with this; that would be a striking contradiction. On the other hand, one should expect that the Individual Psychology physician must be able to cover his livelihood by his work. Therefore it is necessary that one clarifies this question soon. [If the patient finds it difficult to pay] it is better not to make the concession that he pay some time later. Rather send him to the clinic. It is not good to treat a larger number of patients free, because the patients believe they note a difference in treatment [between themselves and the paying patients], and furthermore it is not pleasant for them to meet people who are well-dressed. Better send them to the clinic.

As to duration, you may say right at the beginning, "It will take eight to ten weeks." In doubtful cases: "I don't know. Let us begin. In a month I shall ask you whether you are convinced that we are on the right track. If not, we shall break off." I have very often proposed this in difficult cases.

[The following fragments are from the last three lines of the typescript, which are mutilated.] . . . requires trained sagacity and ingenuity, a jovial attitude . . . blessed with cheerfulness and good humor . . . also extreme patience and forbearance.

PART IV

Various Topics

14

The Differences between Individual Psychology and Psychoanalysis (1931)[1,2]

Remarks by Adler pointing out his differences from psychoanalysis are interspersed throughout his writings. The following paper, however, is the only occasion where he attempted to bring some of these remarks together—except for the papers read twenty years earlier (A1911a and A1911b) at the famous meetings which ended in his separation from Freud. But these papers were never translated in their entirety, although large sections have appeared in English (A1956b, pp. 56–69); and both Individual Psychology and psychoanalysis underwent considerable development between 1911 and 1931.

The present paper is also the only one in this collection where Adler discusses at somewhat greater length his theory of dream interpretation. We have not included his last paper on the subject (A1936f) because a similar treatment is readily available (A1958a, Chapter 5). —Eds.

᠁᠁᠁᠁᠁

1. Original translation of A1931o, with some rearrangements.

2. The further footnotes here are supplementations from an unpublished English manuscript by Adler, entitled "Individual Psychology and Psychoanalysis" (A1930m), which despite the same title differs from the present paper. Footnotes 6 and 11 are exceptions in that they are citations from a later paper (A1935i).

In discussions on psychoanalysis one finds of late with increasing frequency such comments as that Individual Psychology stands on the same ground as psychoanalysis, or that it does not reach its depth. I would object. Does not the deeper foundation of all psychological facts asserted by Freud—e.g., the censorship of the unconscious, the Oedipus complex, narcissism, the death wish, the superego—rest altogether on the striving from below to above?

INTERPRETATION OF PSYCHOANALYTIC TERMS

Censorship

Who creates and guides the censorship? According to which viewpoints does the censorship work? Is it not a striving for significance and superiority, to get away from a feeling of inferiority and to hold on to a feeling of totality, of equality?

I should like to say that we cannot possibly be satisfied by assuming that the censorship plays a role biologically. If such a thing exists, it could have meaning only if it veiled and changed some unconscious impulses for some purpose. For what purpose? We shall hardly be able to find any other purpose than one which serves to hold and enhance the feeling of one's own value. This would mean that the deeper basis for such a concept would again be found in the observations of Individual Psychology, in the striving to get away from a feeling of inferiority to some kind of superiority.[3]

But this would also mean that in the work of a man who has explained the concept of a censorship, the idea is active which has been stated by Individual Psychology, namely, the upward striving. This would mean that in the unconscious of Freud the Individual Psychology conception is confirmed. If this conception does not become conscious, one would have to assume in Freud, according to

3. "The growth of the mind, intelligence, feelings, adaptation, all must be considered in the growth of the ego, for the ego to begin to create. . . . The censor is the ego, the style of life, and creative power of each child and adult" (A1930m).

his own view, the existence of a censorship which veils this deeper foundation. This censorship also would be guided by the striving from below to above.

Oedipus Complex

Since one often comes across the claim that psychoanalysis goes deeper, we may indicate that the Individual Psychology conception also points the way for the thinking of the psychoanalyst in the instance of the Oedipus complex, i.e., the idea that the child would like to possess the opposite-sexed parent libidinally.[4]

The view has changed of late—girls do not have an Oedipus complex—because with growing experience the Oedipus complex could not be retained as the fixed pole.

One thing is certain, that this thesis also could not be conceived without at the same time thinking that the son strives for the laurels, the possibilities, the strength of his father. Whether one conceives this as sexual libido or sees it in broader terms, it is certain that this view could not be held if the thinker were not unconsciously influenced by the idea that the boy wants to grow beyond himself, wants to attain a superiority over his father.

We see how strongly the fact of the striving for significance influences all our thoughts, as well as the thoughts of other schools. I do not think one could ask for more from a theory. In this conception also the deeper dynamics of Individual Psychology can be seen.

Narcissism

Freud announced his concept of narcissism during a period in which Individual Psychology sharply pointed out the egocentric aspect of the neurotic. It is a question of terminology. If I understand by narcissism only sexual self-love, then narcissism is no more than one of a thousand variations of self-love. When sexual self-love appears, it is merely one of the many manifestations of a person

~~~~~~~~~~~~~~

4. "The Oedipus story means many different things. Socrates used it to warn people not to abandon crippled children, as was the custom in those days, since you do not know what may happen later. It was a revolt against this cruelty against cripples and a call to worship the life of children. 'If you do not trust yourself and the gods and do not worship the life of each human ‚being, you will be in trouble' " (A1930m).

thinking only of himself. This, however, takes place not only within his developing sexuality, but in all relationships of his life. We then find the picture of a child or adult turned in upon himself, a life style which can come about only when one was previously able to exclude all other persons from one's experience.

Since the natural progression of development is not like this, we cannot regard a phenomenon such as narcissism an innate component or phase of development. We regard it as a secondary phase which occurs when a person has excluded social relationships that are self-understood and naturally given, or when he has never found them. In this event, nothing is left for experience but the experiencing of one's own personality, the solution of all life problems with exclusive regard to one's own person.

If one expands the concept of the narcissist enormously, as in psychoanalysis, it shows nothing but the type of egocentric person whom we have described extensively. We shall have to observe that this exclusion of others signifies a lack of social interest. This lack must have arisen because the person does not have the self-confidence and has not learned how to do justice to the tasks with which he is confronted within the frame in which he is placed, the human context.

Thereby we say that in the conception of the narcissist the most important part has been overlooked: the permanent exclusion of others, the narrowing of the sphere of action. From this we justly conclude that such a person is one who does not consider himself strong, that narcissism signifies a feeling of weakness which originated from a feeling of inferiority. At the same time this feeling seeks compensation through seemingly making the situation easier. That this attitude comes into conflict with the social questions of life is obvious. Thus we find here a lack of social interest corresponding to a stronger feeling of inferiority, when a child sees himself as if in enemy country and believes he cannot accomplish anything any more, or only if he refers all events almost compulsively to himself and excludes every obligation.

Death Wish

The death wish, which later played a great role in psychoanalysis, is similar to narcissism in every way. It is nothing but the further exclusion of all relationships to life. It also is the expression of a feeling of weakness.

This death wish runs parallel to the idea of pessimism. Psychoanalysis is pessimistic. The death wish is perhaps an unrecognized confession of weakness in the face of reality, as well as a lack of interest in others, of cooperation. We find in it a lack of social feeling; it is a last resource for the weak in heart. An author who arrives at the view that the death wish is the general condition thereby confesses to being weak in heart. He experiences the world full of unrest and difficulties and capitulates before it. Here too it is the expression of an inferiority feeling presented in scientific form.

Castration Complex

Some psychoanalysts have themselves pointed out that the castration complex has developed from the "masculine protest." In our culture the error is inherent to regard feminine form and behavior as inferior, as a diminished form of life. In *The Neurotic Constitution* cases are described of patients who express their feeling of being diminished by talking of loss of penis [A1917a, p. 306].

Ego Ideal and Superego

The ego ideal is a late conception of psychoanalysis. It is mighty similar to social interest. The ego ideal means nothing other than the ideal represented by social interest: the striving towards a goal of fellowmanship. Thus we find hidden in the ego ideal the finalistic view of Individual Psychology.

Regarding the superego, we would say that it is a later conception of what we have come to know as the fictive goal of superiority. It is only a new and unattractive word, modeled after "superman." If it were named thus, everybody could recognize the imprint of the striving for godlikeness. It is not called so because [superman is Nietzsche's term and] Individual Psychology has erroneously been placed near Nietzsche.[4a] In the superego we find nothing other than the Individual Psychology goal of superiority.

BASIC DIFFERENCE

With these discussions I have not yet touched on much of what is

4a. For a discussion of the original significance of Nietzsche for Adler, see Ansbacher, H. L. "Adler's 'Striving for Power,' in Relation to Nietzsche," *J. Indiv. Psychol.*, 1972, 28, 12–24.

important. I could talk about the different significance which we attribute to childhood recollections. We do not distinguish a type of child who has the Oedipus complex, but a child who is pampered. We also know other types, children with inferior organs, and those who never have had the experience of fellowmanship. Here the frame is much wider than in the psychoanalytic view. Also, the views on the dream are fundamentally different.

Now I should like to show the decisive basic difference between psychoanalysis and Individual Psychology. It is not that Freud has taken up drive psychology, which was first created by Individual Psychology and was then left behind as incorrect [5] when I brought the striving for significance to the foreground. This is not the basic difference. The difference is that Freud starts with the assumption that by nature man only wants to satisfy his drives—the pleasure principle—and must, therefore, from the viewpoint of culture be regarded as completely bad.

Concept of Human Nature

The Freudian view is that man, by nature bad, covers this unconscious badness through censorship merely to get along better in life.[6] Individual Psychology, on the other hand, states that the

~~~~~~~~~~~~~~~~

5. Here Adler undoubtedly means the concept of the aggression drive (A1908b) about which he says: "The aggression drive had been meant as an attitude towards life and its external demands. I understood from much experience and evidence that this attitude towards life comprises all movements and forms, including all symptoms. Freud and his pupils took up this idea of aggression but, following the older understanding of the term, explained aggression and the resulting attitude toward the external life as a bad, hostile and sadistic tendency which is inherited. In this way he started his psychology as a 'drive psychology' " (A1930m).

6. Later on Adler warned of the detrimental practical effects which a psychological system may exert which proclaims that man is by nature bad. "What shape will such influence take when we hear, as the implication of a psychological system: 'Why should I love my neighbor? Does he love me?'; or, when we are told that the fundamental drive of human psychic life is an omnipotent drive for destruction which can be but externally mitigated either by the shrewd insight as to how easily that drive may bring injury to one's self, or by the moral teachings of the parents, so often lacking?

"We should understand what happens when, into the already so predisposed philosophy of life of persons in positions of leadership, there creeps stealthily the development of man, by virtue of his inadequate physique, is subject to the redeeming influence of social interest, so that all his drives can be guided in the direction of the generally useful. The indestructible destiny of the human species is social interest. In Individual Psychology this is the truth;[7] in psychoanalysis it is a trick.

Individual Psychology, accordingly, maintains that, due to his physique, i.e., physical condition, a biological factor, man is inclined toward social interest, toward the good. We find neurotics, psychotics, suicides, etc., only when social interest is throttled. In this case the child becomes egotistic, loses interest in others, and presses his biologically founded striving for significance toward the useless side to reach his goal of *personal* superiority.

If one has clearly comprehended this difference, one will not be able to think that these two theories have anything more in common than a few words. That much any theory has in common with any dictionary. It is not admissible to rely on such things.

Basic Drives and Heredity

It seems to me that in the entire problem of basic drives and heredity there prevails great confusion. Let us assume that in the life of a person nothing develops for which the possibility has not been present from the start. Then we see how this undeniable fact can be abused. Anything which shows later in life is already present in the embryo as a possibility. But this does not imply that what we see in

conclusion that humanity is radically bad by nature and can only be brought to reasonable behavior by external suppression. . . .

"Let us bear in mind that we are dealing here with the practical effects of scientific systems. These effects are not merely alterable surface layers easily detachable from the context of the whole system. The unity of the personality of their authors, and the seeming logic of their systems, however patched up they may be, mislead individuals of a similar trend of mind to regard as normal their own social deviations, once they have been sanctioned by a scientific system" (A1935i, p. 5).

7. "Freud tried to explain that eating is a sadistic act and to suck the breast of the mother is the first sadistic act. Individual Psychology, always looking for contributions to the style of life, has found that sucking of the breast of the mother is cooperation. The mother's breast must be sucked—nature creates such a cooperation between child and mother. . . . To make a child clean is cooperation between child and mother. Freud assumes a drive of the child to make himself dirty, and to enjoy it" (A1930m).

later life before us was already present in the embryo in this very form. Each possibility can materialize in different ways.

If we want to illuminate a conception of the striving for significance in this light, we must say: Of course, it can come about only if it is founded in the original disposition. But what we see, such as the character, cannot be thought of outside society, because the striving for significance, seen as character, must be regarded as a social function which can show itself only within a social frame.

We shall not forget that the child experiences in his first days his physical weakness in the face of the cultural demands, and that this acts as a sting to the child, especially when he begins to make comparisons. Whatever the opportunities may be to develop a striving for power, the sting always leads to wanting to be more. Since the factor of evolution is incessantly effective—and the striving for significance is its psychological expression—the striving can degenerate into a striving for personal power.

Here social interest steps in as a regulator. The striving for power is only the distorted aspect of the striving for perfection. The child is urged daily to get beyond his difficulties to a point where he finds security, where he can expect satisfaction of his needs. *But goal setting must precede this.* Thus we must understand the striving for significance as a function rooted in biology, although not in the form in which we see it later on as striving for superiority. If this were the case, then of course one would arrive at the conclusion that man, so often greedy for egotistical power, is evil by nature. What we do find is always that the personal striving for power comes about through an error from earliest childhood when the mind of the child is not sufficiently mature to draw correct conclusions.

We see that after the fourth or fifth year of life a *prototype* forms itself, an original form of life, *a psychological constitution*, which will act independently, draw independent conclusions, develop in a thousand variations according to the individual's original peculiarity. From our viewpoint we can trace to what extent and why this orginal development of the child deviates from our comprehension of a social being. One cannot talk of an original drive of egotistical power striving, because power striving is a realization in the face of a social context, a phenomenon of social relations.

Pleasure Principle and Social Interest

I have never yet heard of an attempt to establish a relationship between the pleasure principle and social interest. The pleasure principle, according to Freud, is connected with the drive life. Social interest is the compensatory factor for the physical inferiority feeling of man. One cannot conceive of man in his weakness in any other way than being supported through society. One could say that this creature cannot live in isolation, that he is viable only through the aid of society. We can regard society as the most important compensatory factor for human weakness.

The experience of social interest has nothing to do with pleasure [in the sense of lust]. It is pleasurable for the social person only because he is embedded in society; it is unpleasurable for one who experiences society as a chain to which he is tied, and who desires only personal satisfaction. E.g., for the murderer it is pleasurable to act against social interest; for the neurotic it is pleasurable to lean on others.

It is the goal, the style of life, which will force pleasure or displeasure. In this connection I must comment that the fellow man strives in his goal not for pleasure but for happiness.

Since we Individual Psychologists emphasize so very much *the unity of psychological life* ("as in a kind of elephantiasis," Pfaundler), it is beyond any question that the feeling of pleasure must run parallel to the goal. Nietzsche said approximately: "Pleasure sets in when it is in accord with a person's gait [in the sense of his characteristic way of walking through life]." Therefore the pleasure principle cannot be used as a regulative concept. Only the striving for the ideal end form can be used in this way.

For some time I have tried to discover a biological analogy here. I do not know if it is more than a simile, but there is in the organic realm a similar process. The possibility, e.g., that a chicken's egg always develops into a chicken, rests in the germ cell. Here is an organic process which has a finalistic tendency, which, in turn, is latent in the original germ cell. Obviously a finalistic tendency is also admixed to the original psychological process and will seek to penetrate somehow. Thus I arrived at the concept of the *striving for totality* which can only mean the seeking of a situation in which all forces, drives, feelings, conscious and unconscious impulses, etc., strive in a self-consistent fashion toward overcoming the difficulties of life. This search, this movement takes on a form. Thus I may speak of an ideal end form.

DREAM INTERPRETATION

With Freud the dream was at first a wish fulfillment—to bring infantile sexual impulses to a release and gratification. In consequence he had to comprehend sexually everything that happens in dreams, and there arose the view of the sexual symbols.

Freud assumes the dreamer wants to look backward. I have pointed out that the dreamer looks forward; he intends the solution of a task. This is the basic difference here. I do not believe that Freud has taken over this viewpoint, that the dream attempts to bring a present problem to a solution.

In due course new aspects were added to our view—e.g., what is the purpose of the dream?—and, what occupied me most—why do people dream if they do not understand their dreams? The answer which Freud gave is quite unfounded: Man is supposed to dream in order not to wake up, to be occupied with the fulfillment of his infantile impulses and not to disturb the sleep. I often find that patients wake up when they dream.

Why does a person dream? I did not find an adequate solution until the thought came: It is the intention of the dreamer not to understand his dreams. He *wants* to withdraw the dream from understanding. This must mean that something happens in the dream which he cannot justify with reason. The intention of the dream is to deceive the dreamer. The person attempts in a certain situation to deceive himself. I have also understood why one does not understand the dream. Its purpose is only to create a *mood*. This emotion must not be clarified; it must exist and act as an emotion, created from the individuality of the dreamer. This apparently corresponds to the desire to solve a problem by an emotional episode and in accordance with his life style, since he is not confident of solving his problem in accordance with the common sense.

Examination of the dream devices shows them to represent the right arsenal for self-deception.

1. *Selection of certain pictures.* The explanation is not to be found

in the pictures but in their selection; i.e., the dreamer is guided by a tendency in the selection of his thoughts. We know the force which selects: it is the individuality of a person, his unity, his goal; and so we find in this one aspect already that here the individuality reigns and not the common sense. The person attempts to solve the problem by selecting a picture which produces an emotion suitable to his life style. What happens through the emotion is what he would have done anyway on account of his individuality. The dreamer wants only to strengthen himself, to justify himself. Thus I could understand that the dream represents the bridge from the present problem to the individuality.

2. *Similes and symbols.* Other dream devices for the purpose of auto-intoxication are similes and symbols. Here also the most important questions are: Why these similes in particular? Why a simile at all? In the psychological structure of the simile the inclination toward self-deception is also contained. It would be very interesting to uncover the psychological structure of the poetic simile; here also there is a deception, a deception in the broader sense of doing justice to an intention through a detour, in this case for the purpose of poetic transfiguration. All symbols have the purpose of filling the person in question with a mood through which he does what he would do on the basis of his individuality alone.

3. *Simplification.* There are a number of further devices, such as the simplification in the dream. This is the significant device of self-deception, to narrow down a problem so much that nothing is left but a small "harmless" remainder. Then the dreamer does not experience the problem as a whole, but only as a small part; he has a better possibility of going the way he wants to go than if he were to look all around.

These devices are not unique for the dream. If a person wants to deceive himself during waking life, he uses the same devices. He works with the selection of certain memories and pictures, he uses similes and symbols, and also simplification.

Thus our result is completely different from that of psychoanalysis, which considers, "The dream is the royal road to the unconscious." This signifies a contrast to waking thought. We say this contrast does not exist. The unconscious is no contrast to the conscious. If, in analyzing it, one tears the conscious from its context, one can also discover differences within it. But he who learns to interpret the conscious appreciates that it may be as little understood as the unconscious, i.e., remain as unconscious as the latter. A contrast does not exist here. Therefore Freud's view that neurosis arises from the conflict between the conscious and the unconscious was not tenable.

CONCLUSION

One cannot understand the psychological structure of a person through the drive life because the drive is "without direction" (see also Hermann Schwarz). The main problem of psychology is not to comprehend the causal factors as in physiology, but the direction-giving, pulling forces and goals which guide all other psychological movements. Thus Individual Psychology arrived at its finalistic conception.

The necessity for ego formation is founded in the evolutionary tendency of the original germ cell (of men and other living creatures). The cell with its evolutionary tendency represents the ego. Outside of this ego there is nothing—no "id" and no "drive" and no "libido"— that would furnish material for taking a stand towards the problems of life. Wanting to develop the ego from the drives—to crown it all, from the sadistic and masochistic drives—means to attribute to these drives the figure of the ego. It means to place knowledge and cunning into the censorship and into the development of the superego and the ego ideal; likewise, to put direction into all three against persons, persons who appear only after birth; to put a striving for significance into the Oedipus complex, into the ego ideal, into the castration complex; to put a goal into the alterable sexual tendencies, etc. In short, the drive here becomes a demon in ready form.[8]

The problem of the wholeness of the personality, which represents the essential contribution of Individual Psychology to modern medicine, appears in psychoanalysis as unessential. How this wholeness penetrates every psychological part-phenomenon and colors it individually is omitted from the considerations of psychoanalysis which,

8. "The drive in the conception of Freud . . . is sly and has a brain and mind, attitudes, feelings and understandings. The drive is an ego and personality. It knows what to do if suppressed; it works from the unconscious but resists like a person" (A1930m).

as if it were hypnotized, looks in each part for the sexual-libidinal structure.

Although it would take us too far afield to prove in this paper, Freud's psychology is *taken from the psychopathology of the pampered child, and describes it in sexual dialect.*

In all points one finds the sad results of overlooking the whole as that which gives form to, and is the basic melody of, the penetrating motive which compels all parts, forces, and drives—including sexuality—toward a self-consistent stand. Consequently, the misunderstanding of a contrast between conscious and unconscious; consequently also, the enthusiastic acceptance of ambivalence—both in contrast to the unity of the personality.

In treatment also psychoanalysis shows itself as inadequate. This is not to deny that there are patients who have been cured. We are attacking the basic principles—transference and the weak expedient of sublimation.

Transference in psychoanalysis has two faces. In the first there is nothing more than the unalterable wholeness of the personality, including its stand toward the therapist. This aspect, then, belongs to the Individual Psychology personality theory. The second face is the continuous underscoring of sexual connections whether they exist or not. As always in life, such underscoring brings about a sexual atmosphere, and this leads to approach or rejection.

As to sublimation, which is supposed to be all that remains for dealing constructively with the bad drives, how can it be carried out without first raising the social interest, without having awakened the courage for fellowmanship and achievement? *Sapienti sat.* (A word to the wise is enough.)

To point to cured or improved cases is not sufficient proof for the goodness of a method. Uncured cases would be more suitable. For despite all formulas the physician is forced to bring to bear his ability to take the common sense into account. Also, the patient can free his own common sense in the course of discussions, perhaps often without the physician noticing it. Common sense—that means thinking which corresponds to the *human community.*

Despite the many scientific contrasts between Freud and myself, I have always been willing to recognize that he has clarified much through his endeavors; especially, he has severely shaken the position of positivistically (*materialistisch*) oriented neurology and opened a wide door to psychology as an auxiliary science to medicine.[9] This is his chief merit, next to his detective art of guessing through common sense. That he did not get any further is due to the limits of his personality and the limits of the personalities of his disciples.[10,11]

In a future history of psychology and psychopathology Freud's doctrine will figure as the admirable attempt to describe, in the strongest expressions of sexual terminology, the psychological life of the pampered child as a generally valid psychology.

wwwwwwwwwww

9. "I remember very well when as a young student and medical man I was very worried about and discontented with the state of psychiatry and tried to discover other ways, and found Freud was courageous enough, actually to go another way and to explore the importance of psychological reasons for physical disturbances and for neuroses" (A1930m).

10. "Freud was wholly confined in a mechanistic conception and used a mechanistic principle for the explanation of mind and psyche. We cannot deny that he attempted to make psychoanalysis into a self-consistent system. He tried to find an underlying, unifying concept which could explain the different immediate experiences, and serve as the focus for all the differences. But this concept cannot apply to all the facts. . . . Thus he always had to make additions and find new factors, e.g., the Oedipus complex" (A1930m).

11. "A psychological system has an inseparable connection with the life philosophy of its formulator. As soon as he offers his system to the world, it appeals to individuals, both laymen and scientists, with a similar trend of mind and provides them with a scientific foundation for an attitude towards life which they had achieved previously" (A1935i, p. 4).

15

The Sexual Function[1]

Generally when Adler discussed the problem of sex, it was with regard to the individual's attitude toward his sexual urges, toward his sexual role in life, and toward members of the other sex. The present paper is an exception in that Adler also deals with the sex function as such, and makes a distinction between a primary, immature, autoerotic phase of the sexual function, and a secondary, mature, social phase, where it becomes a task for two persons of different sexes. —Eds.

Because of the confusing, unverifiable and misleading interpretations of the sexual function, we have to return to the fundamental physiological and psychological facts. There is no reason to accept views such as the farfetched one of the omnipotent sexual libido.

The real reasons for such a distorted theory as that which makes sexual libido the ruling power of human mind and psyche, as it appears in the ideas of Freud and in some variations of Jung, are: (a) the novelty; (b) the great number of troubles of the great number of

1. No date for manuscript. Reprinted from A1945b, with a few modifications. We did especially substitute autoeroticism for self-satisfaction since this generally means self-complacency.

persons with neurotic trends; (c) the open or obscure feeling of the unsatisfied wishes that are in the main structure of the mind and psyche of persons for whom wish fulfillment is the main problem of life.

Indeed, it is the great desire of mankind to find a unique ruling power behind all appearances and experiences of life. This desire affects individuals and masses. Individual Psychology in a much broader and deeper sense accepts, instead, the fact of life in its solvable and unsolvable aspects. One of the first of these aspects is that all strivings, thoughts, feelings, characteristics, expressions, and symptoms aim toward a successful solution of social tasks.

The great number of failures in regard to sexuality, love, and marriage can be traced back, as can all other failures, to a lack of preparation. Individual Psychology does not recognize perception of a sexual object. Sexuality, love, and marriage are tasks of two equal persons, tasks of forming a unit, and can be rightly solved only if persons are trained for sufficient social interest.

Individual Psychology objects to the idea held by other schools of thought that individual wishes or the bad results of their suppression can be regarded as the main problem of life. Such a concept betrays the self-centered nature of a person, as it is often seen in pampered children. It is not much more constructive to stick to the heritage of our ancestors, who in some ways had not reached the present, and still not sufficient, degree of social interest. I wonder if scholars easily can overlook the fact that these authors turn their glances back to ancestors, satisfied in indulging in some inherited possessions without making efforts to use these possessions for new contributions to the welfare of mankind, for an increase of social interest.

SOCIAL ADAPTATION OF HUMAN FUNCTIONS

So far as we can see, a human being is human and rightly called so because he possesses by inheritance all the possibilities needed for coping with social problems. For this purpose he has to develop himself bodily and mentally as far as possible. But the main question which arises now is: For what? For what goal has the individual to strive and to develop his inherited human possibilities? Individuals and mankind as a whole use these possibilities, gifts of our ancestors, for increasing these gifts in a world changed by human beings for the benefit of the whole human family. This has been done, of course, only so far as the level of social interest allowed. In addition, we have to understand that all problems of life can be solved adequately only by a sufficient degree of social interest.

So all the functions of man—brought into the world by the newborn child as possibilities for development in a social environment—must be adapted in relation to the demands of the outside world. Eating, looking, hearing, making sounds, and moving become more and more adapted to the achievement of this goal.

In regard to human functions, we can say they all are, in the beginning of life, in a state of confusion, automatic, and only slowly directed toward interplay with others and with the environment. After some time the creative power of the child accepts the challenge of the outside world, takes up experiences and works them out in a way which seems to be, for him, successful for taking part in the surrounding social life. His eating becomes proper, his looking, hearing, touching, and moving prove his willingness to cooperate more or less. His thinking and talking contain more and more common value and common sense. His functions of excretion are, or should be, in agreement with the social form of his environment. Thumb sucking, nail biting, etc., as unsocial actions and sources of infections, stop if the child accepts the social rules-of-the-game of his environment. If the child will not conform, it is always because he has not found the way toward social culture and is striving for a *personal* goal of superiority.

THE PRIMARY SEXUAL PHASE

There is no question, also, that the sexual function is derived by inheritance and shows itself, in the beginning, in a higher degree of the tickling sensation. Expanding, along with all the others, this function leads to turgescence, erections, and concomitant feelings through automatic impulses. Touching and the resulting pleasurable tickling feeling lead to early repetition of the act, the more so if the child, as a whole, likes to go his own way and is more inclined toward wish fulfillment than toward cooperating, as this characterizes the pampered child.

In that way the right cooperation is deferred until a much later time. The child is therefore compelled to stick to the primary phase of the sexual function. Till he is at the right age to make the sexual function a task for two persons of different sexes—in the secondary, social phase of the sexual function—nothing is left but autoeroticism in its many different forms.

In the primary phase, the usual course is masturbation. The social spirit of mankind has been and always will be opposed to masturbation—opposed because mankind, in its hidden sphere of thinking and knowing, wants the second phase of sexuality to be developed. The discrepancy between the slow development of the complete sexual function, the thorough opposition toward permitting children to perform the secondary phase, the dangers in an early complete function, and the need to defer this second phase to bodily and mentally developed boys and girls, bring children of younger age into a situation that is unsolvable. Not only parents and teachers and dangerous, stupid books and remarks increase the conflicts in the mind of the child, but his social interest gained in the first three years also counteracts autoeroticism. Physicians and clergymen agree more and more that the primary phase cannot be avoided entirely, that it is a natural development and should not be treated harshly, and that it does not harm the child bodily or mentally.

During this primary phase one can see the power of the social interest. Remorse and diversions are frequent and willingly accepted. There is also a diminution of the frequency. But the pampered and greedy child, not able to resist any temptation, is in a worse state and often uses autoeroticism for other purposes—to abuse the attention of the parents, to entice other children, or as an alibi for defeats in school or later life.

PERVERSIONS AND DEFICIENCIES [2]

In their distress, children often turn to other varieties of masturbation, such as indulging in erotic fantasies, using erotic pictures and other means of incitation, sometimes another child. In the latter case the way opens for so-called homosexuality, which is only one of the many

2. More on sexual perversions is to be found in A1938a, Chapter 11.

varieties of masturbation, often found among egocentric, vain persons who stick to the primary, autoerotic phase of the sexual function.

Certain types, who show sexual stimulation when irritated or fearful (as others respond with heart palpitations or intestinal or bladder troubles), indulge in sadistic or masochistic day and night dreams. This type may later become a complete failure in his sexual function by developing the perversion of sadism or masochism.

All the other perversions—fetishism, sodomy, necrophilia, etc. —are varieties of the primary phase of the sexual function. They probably always betray the misconception and the style of life of a pampered or neglected child who has not grown up to the sufficient degree of social interest which would enable him to cooperate fully with others. This is also true for persons who are promiscuous, masturbators, or exclusive frequenters of prostitutes.

The neurotic symptoms of sexual deficiency betray also the primary phase of sexuality; such symptoms include neurotic impotence, neurotic frigidity or vaginismus, and ejaculatio praecox. These neurotic symptoms are always found in persons who have not overcome the primary phase of the sexual function because of a lack of social interest.

SECONDARY PHASE

Love, as a task of two equal persons of different sexes, calls for bodily and mental attraction, exclusiveness, and a total and final surrender. The right solution of this task of two persons is the blessing of socially adjusted persons who have proved their right attitude in having friends, being prepared for a useful job, and showing mutual devotion.

16

Physical Manifestations
of Psychic Disturbances
(1934)[1]

Whereas the original monograph of Adler on organ inferiority (A1907a) dealt with the influence of the organic on psychological processes, the present paper points out that each organ is capable of expressing feelings and emotions: The individual expresses himself through his organs. This is what Adler called the organ dialect. Those organs which lend themselves most readily to such expression are perhaps weaker, are places of least resistance.

In this paper Adler's organismic position is most clearly expressed. "You must not forget that the organism is a unit, and that through a shock in one place the entire organism is set to vibrate." —Eds.

Some day it will probably be proved that there is no organ inferiority which does not respond to psychic influences and does not speak their language, a language which corresponds to the problem confronting the individual. This is important in regard to symptom selection, particularly in regard to what we still call hysteria, or functional

1. A1934h. Reprinted from translation, A1944b, with modifications from the original.

neurosis. It also justifies one of the basic tenets of Individual Psychology: When a transitory or permanent defect becomes apparent in an organ, this organ must be scrupulously examined, so that it may be determined in what way it is characteristic of the individual himself. Sometimes one organ, sometimes another, is more influenced by outside impressions. In this paper I will deal chiefly with those psychological influences which transmit the excitation to the body through the arousal of feelings and emotions.

Psychic influences are being accepted more and more today. Even from the standpoint of general medicine it is no longer denied that the uniqueness of the individual causes variations in every illness. The doctors of yesterday realized that a child who was always subject to infectious diseases was a hypersensitive child. But only recently has it been discovered that in less sensitive children also, organs such as the endocrine glands can become involved.

It is important to observe whether these general phenomena induce transitory or lasting changes. For instance, people usually respond to shock with heart symptoms, but what is important is the duration of this change in the functioning of the heart. Only occasionally is it lasting, as in certain neurotic cases. But we know very definitely that an inferior heart, or a heart that has been injured through illness, is more susceptible to such influences, and that they can open the door to subsequent lasting and serious illnesses. You must not forget that the organism is a unit, and that through a shock in one place the entire organism is set to vibrate. We know too little to lay down any rules, but it is fairly certain that through such a shock an organ may be damaged.

Not much is known as to how a psychic impression reaches the organs, but without doubt its effect is a general one. The organism has a strong tendency to preserve its equilibrium. There is plenty of evidence that disturbances can be caused by affects. Here the uniqueness of the individual must be considered and must first be explored. Individual Psychology finds this not too difficult. We usually succeed during the first interview.

I may point out how frequently we are dealing with people who expect others to step in for them, who seek help, alleviation. This disposition can almost always be traced back to their training in early life. In a world such as ours it is such individuals who appear to be the most heavily burdened, for to them the world is a place of enmity, a place in which difficulties cannot be overcome, but must be avoided. If we wish to see this in relation to organic disturbances, I hardly know of any organ which cannot be used as an example.

Menstruation

For instance, most gynecologists agree that many disturbances during menstruation can be attributed to emotional reasons. The patient herself understands little about her feeling of irritation, her frame of mind. She does not comprehend why she should feel so oppressed by such an insignificant event. She is reconciled to the fact that something happens once a month, but she does not realize that her whole disposition exerts the greatest influence upon this relatively minor occurrence.

We must realize that many girls quite instinctively oppose menstruation by adopting a defensive attitude. They are not helped if we merely tell them this. We all know from experience in other walks of life that good suggestions are not necessarily accepted. What we must do is to study the patient so as to find out why she is not prepared to face her difficulties, and then explain this lack of preparedness to her. Wherever there are menstrual troubles we will find a certain disposition, one which occasions a defensive attitude and leads to some kind of occlusion. We must consider that perhaps this instinctive defensive attitude of a girl would not be of such significance if her uniqueness would not have to be taken into account. The peculiar idiosyncrasy of a particular girl can give us an important key as to why the customary defensive attitude was intensified. Perhaps the girl has learned of, or experienced, the difficulties in which a girl can become involved during and after puberty. This is a point which must be given serious consideration; it is the exogenic situation which releases the trigger, which affects the whole disposition.

Pseudopregnancy

This also belongs here. Today we still know very little of how pseudopregnancy is caused. But I once had a case which was most revealing. The patient had had sexual relations with a man for many years and he had told her he would marry her if she should ever become pregnant. Her abdomen began to swell just as in pregnancy and continued to do so for six or seven months. It was then that I saw the woman and became suspicious; I advised her to consult a gynecologist. An hour later she returned; her abdomen had shrunk to its normal size. The gynecologist had found that she was not pregnant at all. Under heavy manipulations the flatus had been expelled through mouth and anus. It had been a case of meteorism [flatulent distention of the abdomen] the non-conscious creation of the woman herself, possible only in the case of a person desirous of taking on this symptom.

Air Swallowing

I have found that many men and women are able to develop meteorism. They swallow air. This is a fact which is too often neglected in internal medicine. There may be various other accompanying manifestations, and the gulping down of wind can cause symptoms of anxiety neurosis. This I have frequently observed. It is plain that a person with a tendency to anxiety symptoms can be seized by a state of giddiness arising from inflation of the stomach. Other symptoms, as well, can be caused by this. It should be understood that the swallowing of air takes place when the patient does not feel able to face a certain situation, when the inferiority feeling is intensified and a sense of oppressiveness arises. If we study these individuals, quite apart from their symptoms, we always find that from their earliest childhood they have been well aware of the social significance of anxiety, i.e., of how other people can be inpressed by a display of anxiety.

Endocrine Glands

In recent years I have had plenty of opportunity for studying the influences of the feelings and emotions upon the endocrine glands. It has been very clear to me that the endocrine glands can be affected by the emotions, and it seems to me that the sex glands, also, can be put in a passive state by emotional influence. Here again we must not fail to take the individual's opinion into account.

Take for instance the case of a youngster who feels he is unmanly and, accordingly, does not live a life conducive to the development of the sex glands. He eliminates certain activities which the normal glandular development demands. Some boys are kept in an environment in which only girls are found as a rule; they are made to sit quietly at home, interest themselves in dolls and cooking, and are prevented from behaving actively. This can result in their having feminine appearance in later years. I have seen such youngsters become more masculine looking once they have been brought into proper contact with other boys.

The New York anthropologist Boas has pointed out that sports have made the American girl approach closer to the masculine type. There can be no question that, apart from whether the individual takes the sexual role seriously or not, the sex glands and thereby the physical structure are influenced by athletics. We also find that the sex glands of individuals who have an unusually strong leaning toward the other sex develop an increased activity and efficiency if this attitude persists.

When we consider how effective such influences can be we realize the nature of what we call "functional inadequacies." For instance, the retrogression of the woman during the climacteric is by no means an unvarying occurrence, but is also conditioned by the woman's mood—she may regard the climacteric as a danger or an illness. We physicians are particularly obligated to remove damaging beliefs.

Thyroid Gland

A most important role is played by the thyroid, particularly in the case of Graves' disease [Basedow's disease, exophthalmic goiter]. I once had an opportunity to examine a number of such patients in Zondek's clinic in Berlin. Zondek claims that Graves' disease cannot be investigated without the individuality of the patient being taken into consideration. Now this is not always easy. For instance, there was one patient, a mechanic of 26, who had suffered from Graves' disease for two years. The symptoms were distinct; the basic metabolism was increased 30 per cent. I found that the patient had been the only boy in the family and was most hypersensitive. He said to me: "When a person's ill, he's put under observation because human beings are always suspicious." He spoke reproachfully, in a tone which suggested that he was very sensitive and found it difficult to make contact with other people. I could see that he was very impatient and probably prone to outbursts of emotion. He would tell me no dreams, but his earliest recollection showed that he greatly disliked any change of situation. Nothing would have induced him to leave the place in which he was working.

These details told little about the exogenic factor, the situation which had provoked the illness. I asked him if anything had happened which might have contributed to his trouble; whether he had been upset by anything. But he made little response. Finally he mentioned a love affair. Six months before he fell ill, the woman had gone off with another man, but he assured me that this break had been a very trifling matter. "On the whole I was rather glad," he said. "She did not suit me." Knowing that nervous persons want to keep their hold on another person and feel deeply injured if a third person is preferred, one will regard this break as the exogenic factor, especially since it occurred at the same time as the first symptoms of trembling set in.

Other Organs

Let us now discuss what little we know about the influence of the psyche on the organs. It is obvious that the psychic force must pass through the sphere of consciousness; there must be a transformation of the absorbed influences, followed by irritation of the vegetative system. Through the latter the irritation is transmitted further in very diverse ways, in accordance with the uniqueness of the individual and the uniqueness of the organs. His organs begin to respond.

The irritation always excites the whole organism; however we are able to observe the excitation only in those parts of the organism which manifest it more clearly. Many glands can be affected, including the liver, which like other organs responds differently in each individual case. There are some persons who, while one might expect the irritation to induce anger, respond with attacks of pain in the liver area. It has been demonstrated that the irritation also causes a change in the bile outflow, and that it can affect the pancreas and the Islands of Langerhans. Certain people respond to the irritation by hyperglycemia and glycosuria, and it is obviously the physician's duty to put such patients in a frame of mind which does not expose them to disturbances of this nature.

When the vascular system is affected by the psyche, the skin is often affected too. It is recognized that skin diseases may be provoked by psychological influences. Of course this does not apply rigorously to all patients with skin troubles.

The Brain

Psychosis and epilepsy are still more complicated problems, and no sensible psychiatrist can fail to realize that here, too, a part is played by the exogenic situation. (The same applies to melancholia and schizophrenia.) To touch on but a single aspect of the problem, we can state that in psychogenic epilepsy a part of the brain responds to the irritation. It is possible that there are also certain organic changes. E.g., old cases of schizophrenia show changes of the brain substance. This can in part be regarded as a variation of the brain structure which characterizes the uniqueness of the individual from the start. Perhaps edema can affect the brain. Neurotic manifestations can be conditioned through the tissues' being influenced by the retention of water, as demonstrated in cases of sudden withdrawal of morphine (Alexandra Adler).[2] This aspect is significant for the study of other similar processes, and is not in contradiction to the views of Individual Psychology.

Scoliosis and Flatfoot

Structural changes, resulting from psychic irritation, are seen particularly clearly in cases of scoliosis and flatfoot. Such cases as I have seen were predisposed to these troubles; they had not always had them, but began to be troubled at some definite time—usually when the patient lost his poise and self-confidence on being confronted by a particular situation.

We have known now for twenty-five years that pains in the spine are more complicated than appears at first glance. There are pains which become localized on the anterior wall of the chest and begin when the patient is in a depressed state. This we find, for instance, among melancholics, but also among nonmelancholics when they feel unfairly treated.

I do not believe that the simple explanation of the nerves being

2. Adler, Alexandra. "Die Störung des Wasserhaushaltes während der Morphiumentziehung und deren therapeutische Beeinflussung durch Euphyllin." *Klin. Wschr.*, 1930, 9, 2011–2015.

pinched is correct; it is too naive an idea. Also, I have little faith in the idea of radiating pains, say according to the theory of Head's segments. Long before people began talking about "orthostatic albuminuria" I drew attention to the fact of how often curvatures of the spine are connected with manifestations in the kidneys. It is possible that the whole segment is irritated during embryonic development. All curvatures indicate very clearly that a congenital defect exists, which is characterized by the naevus (birthmark) at the top of the curvature or in the segment. I have had astonishing experiences in regard to this and have been able to predict where the naevus lay.

Cases of flatfoot are very similar; the sufferers of such pain are often depressed individuals. There can be but one explanation of this, namely, that depression can cause a loss of muscle tone. You can see this on the entire person; whether he is flatfooted or not, he shows by his bearing what goes on inside him; he speaks with his muscular apparatus. We must learn to understand the organ dialect.

Predisposition, Illness, Accident

If a person is endogenously predisposed for an illness, is he bound to contract it? Say, for instance, that he is predisposed to schizophrenia (we have partial knowledge of the physical make-up of a schizophrenic), does that mean that he is really bound to contract schizophrenia? The answer is: As long as the physical peculiarity of the patient would be brought under conditions in which he maintained his equilibrium, he would not have to fall ill. We can influence him so that psychological influences will not have this decisive effect upon him.

On the other hand, it seems that even if an organ is subject to psychological influences over a long period of time, it can be lastingly harmed only if it is already inferior. Here again we are faced with the question: Where does the inferiority of the organ begin? Perhaps one must think more of injury through the whole system which manifests itself in "the place of least resistance" (*locus minoris resistentiae*).

There are many examples which show injury in the physical sphere. Accidents belong here. E.g., a man was run over by a car on the day on which, through his malicious disposition, he had been trying to force his attentions on a girl in his office. She mobilized friends to consult what should be done with him. Such coincidences being possible—which to us are not mere coincidences—one can imagine that in the difficulties which always surround man, those persons will be more likely to be injured who are psychologically not strengthened. We see the same also in epidemics.

Physiognomy

I wish to mention one other phenomenon—the external formation of the human body, the physiognomy. Although we cannot say how much, there is some value in physiognomy, because it is shaped by movement; it is movement which has become form. We recognize this transition all too little. We judge by external appearances, often most rashly, but without always realizing that moods affect the physical substance, making the features appear pleasant or unpleasant. Any one who has observed the appearance of a melancholic during his melancholic phase and afterwards will be amazed. Similarly in everyone the mood leaves its aftereffects in the expression.

We are returning to our fundamental view, to the foundation of all proper functions: the proper embeddedness in the evolution of mankind. Only in this way can we understand how we assume that one man is sympathetic, another not; that this takes place automatically; that we understand this better only when we succeed in formulating this process into concepts. This is a thought which fits only in an evolutionary view. From this vantage point we shall understand what is to be regarded as erroneous and as approximately correct.

A widespread error exists regarding the concept of society. To understand it correctly we must realize how strongly it is interlinked to the evolution of mankind as something to strive for. The physiognomy is bound up, far more than we have ever realized before, with the degree of harmony existing between the individual and the society for which to strive.

17

Sleeplessness
(1929)[1,2]

This short, unpretentious piece could well serve as an epitome of Adler's approach. Effortlessly it takes an everyday problem as its vehicle and shows the dynamics of neurotic symptoms and how these are common to the normal as well as to the melancholic—the latter term being perhaps the most technical in the whole talk. In the same way he proceeds to indicate the treatment; by a trick, as it were, he gently and simply places the patient into a "trap" from which he must choose between two alternatives, both of which are in the "useful" direction. It is also characteristic that the reader may go along with the repetitions of informal discourse and then of a sudden come upon a nugget, a most significant thought expressed aphoristically, as in the sentence: "We may find differences in the blood of someone suffering from agoraphobia, but not the reasons for it."   —Eds.

Sleeplessness may be the consequence of an organic illness, as, for instance, patients are sometimes sleepless in the early stages of

1. Reprinted from A1944a, with some modifications and one addition from the English manuscript (A1929l), marked "Clinic—November 21, 1929."
2. Footnote by the editor of A1944a: "We feel justified in publishing these rather informal remarks, as they remind us of the informal and personal way in which Adler spoke to us, his students.—R. D[reikurs]."

typhoid fever; it may occur in disorders of the glands and in some cases of nephritis. It also plays a big part in the beginning of some cases of insanity.

In those cases of insanity which begin with sleeplessness, when the patient has decided to become schizophrenic or melancholic, a great tension has to work and create an insanity as an artistic creation. In the severe illnesses and melancholia and insanity, probably the emotions which rule the whole picture also rule the endocrine glands, and probably certain blood changes will be found.

In the literature we find the contention that such secretions are the cause of insanity; we maintain that they are the consequences of it. The glands are affected by the irritation of the vegetative system, and we shall probably also find such disturbances of secretions in some neuroses as well. We may find differences in the blood of someone suffering from agoraphobia, but not the reasons for it.

If we can exclude an organic reason, insomnia can be explained psychologically. Then we must look into the whole personality, and we will find that sleeplessness fits in perfectly with the whole personality.

If you want to find out how it fits in with the whole personality, you can ask the person who suffers from sleeplessness: "What would you be able to do if you could sleep?" Then he will tell what he is afraid to do; e.g., if he could sleep he could work better and could take his examination. He is so afraid of his problem that he is tense, and this mental tension will not let him relax and, thus, he cannot sleep.

Sleep is not a passive state, and it is not true that we are passive when we sleep. So far as our understanding goes, sleep is an activity; we have to make ourselves sleep. We are trained from the very beginning to accomplish this, and therefore it happens easily.

There are always some reasons if we fail to accomplish it; and especially emotions and tensions are able to disturb sleep. If a person is afraid of something, he may not sleep. Some patients, especially women, cannot sleep because they think of their housekeeping, whether it is in the best order. You can see that, because what do they do when they do not sleep? They think of their housework, of the party tomorrow, whether they will be criticized, or whether everything will be as it should be. In this way they cannot sleep. And once they cannot sleep due to the tension, they discover in many cases that it has its advantages.

PURPOSES SERVED

A man who had been suffering from a compulsion neurosis insisted that he could not sleep since his early childhood. The most he slept was one or two hours. This is probably not true, as many people are wrong in their belief that they have not slept. Some admit that they do not know whether they have slept or not, but many patients are satisfied if they can impress themselves and others that they have not slept, because then they always have an argument and alibi. They can claim attention because they themselves are impressed with their inability to sleep.

Some people sleep and still hear and see everything. They are easily awakened and therefore notice everything that goes on—the striking of the clock, the passing by of a person, or whatever it may be. They really are not refreshed in the morning and, therefore, this way of spending the night is a variety of sleeplessness. There are many ways in which people can find an excuse very much like not being able to sleep.

Hitting at Another Person

You will find that every person who does not sleep has a certain purpose in which he is supported by not sleeping. This boy [referring to a presented case] fights with his family. He does not earn money, because in this way he hurts them, as they need his income. When he cannot sleep, they know what it means and begin to tremble; and this is his purpose. You can see therefore how he uses his sleeplessness.

You will always find another person involved. The sleeplessness is an effective way of hitting at this other person, who usually is near by. Married men and women hit at their wives and husbands.

Bolstering Ambition

Sometimes sleeplessness is a tool of competition—at least it can be used for this purpose. "I know I do my job well and everybody is satisfied with my work; but what could I not accomplish if I could have more sleep!" Therefore, you find sleeplessness among very ambitious persons.

I was proud when I discovered that sleeplessness was a symptom of ambition. Then I found out that this was known two thousand years ago. Reading Horace, I found the following words: "Ah, these people, too, cannot sleep at night. They are the people who try so hard to have reality agree with their own plans, and do not want to adjust their own plans to reality." Horace knew the meaning of sleeplessness, and probably everybody knew it at that time, and it has only been forgotten. It has been rediscovered, as probably much other knowledge has been forgotten and must be discovered again. Horace also remarked about the people whom he mentioned before: "They do not suffer from sleeplessness alone, but also from headache." That is very true and you find these two often together. The results of such a high ambition are sleepless nights and headaches. We can understand that. If somebody must use the night for conscious thinking, if he is not satisfied to use only the day for this purpose, then it can be assumed that he is a very ambitious person. It is only a variation of a type who studies during the night; that is also a sign of ambition, only in such a case it is not difficult to understand the connection.

But you can probe whether our assumption is right by asking the patient in a subtle manner: "What do you think about when you do not sleep during the night?" Then you will get another proof. The patient thinks always either of his business or his duties, and repeats what happened the day before. As he may go over his accounts and books in the evening, so he does during the night to see whether he acted the right way. Many persons behave in this manner. Their ambition does not let them forget the slightest mistake they may have made the day before.

Supporting Melancholia

The illness in which sleeplessness plays the most important role is melancholia. If a melancholic person is not sly enough to hide what he is thinking during the night, you can easily find how he is striving to worsen his temper and is always looking for bad things and collecting them, like a bee. This inclination is very important to remember for the treatment. We must show the patient that he tries continuously to pick out bad things. In that way he arouses feelings and emotions which constitute melancholia.

Melancholic depression means really to look for bad possibilities and not for anything which is promising and hopeful. This looking for discomforting thoughts occurs also during the night, and so we understand why the melancholic patient does not sleep. In an ambitious way he collects. He could not continue this collecting if he were to fall asleep. Therefore, with the emotion which he creates, he disturbs his sleep.

TREATMENT

His activity during the night can be used in the treatment of the sufferer from sleeplessness. When such a person complains about his sleeplessness, he usually maintains that he is lost because without sleep he cannot go on any longer. If you tell him that it does not matter, that you yourself do not sleep more, and that others you know do not sleep much more either, the patient will become angry. But if you are kind and do not ridicule him, you can make an impression on him. Tell him, "You can use the time in which you cannot sleep to help in our treatment. You can collect all the thoughts you have during this time and remember them and tell me tomorrow, and then we can make use of your sleeplessness."

It will be a new experience for him to use his sleeplessness in a constructive way. Sometimes he cannot maintain his sleeplessness if it can be used for a good cause. He can remain sleepless only if he regards it as a disturbance. In either case, if he remembers his thoughts or if he now falls asleep, he may be able to recognize the purpose of sleep or sleeplessness. He may even understand that his sleeplessness has not played the role which he believed it did.[3]

I never give a patient a medical prescription for sleeplessness; but I have seen many patients who came to me taking medicines they received from others. And it is difficult to stop them. To have a medicine is the same thing as not to sleep. It means, "I am sleepless and can only sleep taking drugs." He could sleep if he would take

~~~~~~~~~~~~~~~
3. This is again the technique of the trap, or the constructive double-bind mentioned earlier (see p. 153).—Ed.'s note.

sugar water and believe in it. Sometimes it is possible to prove that. But I never try to fool a patient.

It is very interesting to observe how many people disturb their sleep by using certain rules. One of the best methods to disturb the sleep is to count to a thousand and then back. It takes two hours, and in these two hours the person has not slept. Yet he believes it is a means *against* sleeplessness, while it actually *creates* it. When after these two hours he finds himself still sleepless, he says: "Even such a powerful means could not help in my case; I must be terribly sick." To go from one doctor to the other is also a very good method to increase sleeplessness and to get attention on the side. Some people insist that they cannot sleep until one o'clock; or they cannot sleep without playing cards until two o'clock. These are all excuses.

SUMMARY

Many persons go through life with a sleep disturbance. It is like claiming a privilege: A person who cannot sleep must be considered in a special way. Everybody can see that he could accomplish much more if he only could sleep. Therefore, he has a certain privilege and cannot be measured with the same gauge as others. We are not sure he really could accomplish more. In the therapy we make him understand that it is not entirely true that he would accomplish more if he would sleep. Amount of sleep and accomplishment are not related and cannot be measured by each other. But many connect the two. They insist that they can sleep only if they do not drink black coffee, or if they drink liquor. With this assumption, combining two things which have nothing to do with each other, they regulate sleep as they need it. They arrange their sleeplessness when they are not sure of success, when they need an alibi for an expected failure. Sleeplessness occurs only in a situation in which a person is confronted with a problem for which he is not prepared, and is used in that situation to arouse the needed feelings and emotions.

18

The Death Problem in Neurosis
(1936)[1]

For Adler the problem of death is how one of the basic facts of
life, the inevitability of death, one's own and that of others, is "used"
by the individual in accordance with his life style. In the mentally
healthy person this "irrefutable consequence of existence" (p. 54 n.)
will not detract from active adaptation to the problems of life. The
neurotic, who is characterized by not facing these problems courageously, may wish for death or seek it, in order to avoid loss of
prestige; he may be obsessed with the fear of death, as a way to solve
a certain problem; or he may "arrange" compulsions involving
death, deriving "unconscious" satisfaction from struggling with
them.   —Eds.

Little is known about the way in which the experience of death affects
the child at an early age. Certainly no single answer can be found.
According to our findings it is certain that the completion of the style
of life at about the third year makes a decisive difference. Before this
time, the impression or retention of such an experience hardly seems
different from the impression made by the disappearance of a more or

1. Original translation of A1936j, with minor editorial rearrangements.

less familiar person or object, a very frequent event in the life of the child. Such an impression may bring about the child's adjusting to the fact of disappearance according to his own opinion. He will probably learn to reckon with the fact that persons and things can disappear.

LIFE STYLE AND ATTITUDE TOWARD DEATH

The situation is different when, after approximately the third year, the child has taken an attitude to the problems of the environment through the main lines of his style of life. Then the experience of death or the sight of a dead person will be measured, perceived, assimilated, digested, and responded to according to these main lines; the degree to which the child is able to cope with accomplished facts will manifest itself. The same is true for adults.

In such a situation the "pampered style of life" with its "all-or-nothing" complex, with its self-reference, with its suffering in the face of unfulfilled wishes, and with its aroused feelings, will show up more clearly, in a thousand variations. This can be easily determined.

Incidentally, regarding this pampered style of life, I have always emphasized that it is the child's own creation and that it is in fact found almost more frequently in neglected children or in those who feel themselves neglected.

In the event of death, the child's degree of attachment to the deceased person plays a main part. The death of an unloved person, or of one disturbing the attachment of the child to another person, may produce no sad feelings; occasionally it may even produce satisfaction. One must certainly also consider whether the child believes the disappearance to be permanent or for a limited time only, and how great he considers the misfortune which has befallen the deceased and the environment.

How little death may affect a child with the pampered life style is shown by the case of a six-year-old boy. While pampered, he was at the same time accustomed to the fact—one of the thousand nuances—that the governess who took care of him withdrew persons and things. When he was told of the death of his father, he turned to his governess and asked: "May I go and play now?" I met him thirty years later after he had suffered financial ruin. He was as untouched by this as he had been by the death of his father.

Again, the generality of the fact of dying shows different effects, certainly always in relation to one's own person. Everyone reacts to the fact that life is limited, and he does so in accordance with his entire attitude toward life, in which all psychological and automatic forms of expression participate. Suicide and disguised forms of it, such as insanity and addiction, are more or less active reactions against what the individual presumes to be barriers in the face of which he is no longer able to continue following the laws of life.

PRESERVATION OF LIFE, OVERCOMING, AND SOCIAL TASKS

There will be no disagreement with the Individual Psychology view that three main lines can be identified in the structure of life which prevails with evolutionary force: one line aims at making human life permanent, another at the successful overcoming of external difficulties, and the third at taking a stand towards the tasks of social life.

All three tendencies are parts of one indivisible whole, the function of life. The threat to one, the blockade of one, in the feeling of a living person—due to an erroneous direction, erroneous final goal, or erroneous style of life—threatens the whole, appears as a danger to life. The resulting shock effects are overcome in the most favorable cases. But otherwise, through the threatening danger of a decisive defeat, they become fixated as alleviating alibis (neurosis), or in the case of greater activity are carried further through active failure (delinquency, etc.) to a devious path which seemingly promises success. The shock manifests itself always in the expression of the inability to solve a necessary social problem which is at hand (inferiority complex). The ensuing involvement of the body and the soul results in the retreat from the problem, or the ascent to it, or, in the case of deficient social interest, in active failure.

This phase of shock is always in the direction of the fear of death, because the line to the successful solution to the problem at hand seems to be cut for the time being. However, the successful solution of the problem is part and parcel of the possibility to live.

PURPOSE OF THE DEATH WISH

A five-year-old boy was slapped in the face by his aunt. Crying loudly, he exclaimed: "How can I continue living after you have humiliated me so?" In later years he developed a melancholia in which death and suicide were continually on his mind.

Neurotics, as I have shown, all have the pampered style of life, and have in their childhood developed little social interest as well as little activity. In their overemotionality, whenever they believe they are confronted with a defeat which threatens their vanity, their prestige, they suffer such a severe shock that they feel it as death. Going one step further, they see in death (suicide, or toying with a death wish) the only hope of avoiding an imminent loss of prestige.

Freud showed this death wish in the dreams of his patients long ago, but misunderstood it in accordance with his view of sexual libido and the innate drive to destruction. In spite of my pointing this out, he has so far overlooked the fact that one who is from childhood a potential neurotic thinks too much of himself ("Why should I love my neighbor?"). Because his picture of the world is alienated (*entfremdet*) from reality, the potential neurotic lives as in enemy country; he is oversensitive, impatient, and overemotional. Overestimating his own person, he invariably arrives at the artificial error of upbringing which may be called the "passive" resentment, as I have shown in *"Aggressionstrieb in der Neurose"* [A1908b] and in *The Neurotic Constitution* [A1917a]. The inadequate development of his social interest and of his activity turns him into the expecting type (see also Kräpelin) who presupposes the social interest of others and exploits it, in contrast to the delinquent who considers others as opponents and prey.

The shock which evokes physical and mental irritations, i.e., the symptoms, is always occasioned by an "exogenous fact," a task which is to be solved socially. The potential neurotic believes that he cannot cope with it and that it threatens to destroy his exaggerated desire for prestige. Now the rescue from a final loss of prestige occurs as it did in his childhood if a success was denied. The entire interest of the neurotic is turned to the shock results, the symptoms. The actual task which threatened loss of prestige is almost forgotten. The patient declares that he is unable to solve his task "on account of the symptoms, and only on account of them." He expects its solution by others, or at least to be excused from all demands, or sometimes only to be granted "extenuating circumstances." He has his alleviating alibi and feels his prestige preserved. His line of success, embedded into the life process, can remain uninterrupted by his paying the price. The important principle of life, the striving toward the successful solution of a problem, is no longer threatened. The problem of death moves into the distance—Freud would say: repressed in the unconscious—but may also remain more or less clearly in focus, depending on the style of life of the person.

The suffering of the patient is real, usually exaggerated as a protection against loss of prestige. A general abuse in the psychiatric literature is the concept that the patient fled into the neurosis as if he were in love with his symptoms, as if he did not want to give up his symptoms. Quite the contrary, he would like to give them up if thereby he would not risk the seemingly greater evil: the danger of death through loss of prestige.

Foolish beginners in the understanding of Individual Psychology conclude that we want to make the neurotic responsible for his suffering. This misunderstanding is probably due to lack of knowledge or the inadequacy of our language. Because we make the symptoms comprehensible, they conclude that the patient could also comprehend them. But he is only responsible *after* he has comprehended them. The same holds for the critics.

The comprehension of the above problem opens a broad perspective. Actual death also means the end of the striving towards successful solution of the problems of life, and the many efforts to reduce the significance of physical death are well known. Spiritual death, especially as the neurotic sees it, is of no less frightening power.

PURPOSE OF OBSESSIVE FEAR OF DEATH

Here is an example from clinical practice. A thirty-year-old teacher who had been married for six months lost her position in the economic turmoil of the recent years. Her husband, too, became unemployed. Thus she decided much against her will to take a job as a clerk. Every day she rode to work in the subway. One day in the office she was taken by the thought that if she did not get up from her chair immediately, she would have to die. Colleagues brought her home, where she recovered from her fright. But now the same terrible thought of sudden death overcame her every time she used the subway, so that a continuation of her work was altogether out of the question.

The general insight into this case was not difficult. Individual Psychology, more than other schools, emphasizes the kind of movement and considers it, like the movement of talking, one of the forms of expression of the individual which can be interpreted. Conceptual and verbalized material is also permeated by tendencies which are not understood, as I have shown. The same holds true for all other forms of movement which show themselves in connection with the environment.

The field of investigation of Individual Psychology is the relationship, carried out in actions, of a peculiarly stylized individual to problems of the environment. Other schools are more interested in content and separate functions, such as perception, memory, thinking, feeling, instincts, libido, drives, reflexes, wholes, etc. We are grateful for any extension of our knowledge in this direction, but are far from assuming that the puzzle of a unique personality can be understood even from recognized content. Therefore we are concerned with the relationship of the unique individual to the problems of life, which can almost be measured. If one does not recognize these differences among schools to be differences in the material investigated, one may easily be inclined to reject any school but one's own as "unscientific," as "not deep enough," etc.

If we overlook for the time being the thought content of the patient which makes death appear to her as threatening, we find a movement which, according to our premise, must be regarded as successful for the patient. She moves from a place which is felt as a defeat, to another place which in some way promises protection from this feared defeat. If we now fill in the content, any sitting down, and what is obviously connected with it, namely the work, must have appeared to her as humiliating, as a complete defeat. From this alone, much can be said regarding the patient's style of life and her view of the world. She must be very vain and conceited, probably has an exaggerated self-esteem, and must show a deficit in social interest and a lack of activity—a special nuance of the pampered style of life. Only strong counter-arguments could refute these conclusions.

But as much as we may be convinced of these conclusions, we have the duty to convince the patient and to teach students. Therefore, we must gather confirmations from her biography, even at the risk of having to correct ourselves.

She was the second sister among three children. The third child was a boy. I have shown that the second-born easily works out his success possibility in the direction of outdistancing the first child. This was true here also. The patient stated that her sister never could get anywhere with their sullen father, but that she, herself, always could, usually through crying. This relationship to another, which could be called "water power," is the weapon of the weak, of the less active individual, and promises success by softening the other. By the same means she also succeeded in claiming each of her sister's advantages for herself. When on the occasion of a final examination her sister received a ring from her mother, the patient continued to beg and cry until she was given one just like it. The younger brother was a strong rival. He was the favorite of the father, who paid little attention to his wife and daughters. Furthermore, the parents' marriage was far from happy, which had always shaken the patient's view of the reliability of men. When asked whether she was happy in her marriage, she began to cry vehemently and declared she was the happiest wife. When asked why she cried, she answered that she was always afraid it could not remain that way. Thus we see that all defeats shake her vehemently, the possible as well as the real. Obviously, her final goal was to strengthen her superiority and security by habitually presenting the picture of an easily disturbed person who counts on the softness and indulgence of her environment—of course without understanding the context. Thus, like all neurotics, she belongs to the above-described type, who takes little interest in others, rather considers them objects of exploitation, and who shows little activity.

Between herself and her job, which she considered humiliating, she has inserted the death problem as a security measure. That is, it inserted itself when the patient considered herself deprived of all possibility of success. In this connection, her dreams are of interest, in which pictures of deceased persons always appear. Anyone who knows the Individual Psychology theory of dreams will not be surprised by this. He could even have guessed at the contents of her dreams. Her style of life had to select in such a way as not to let the thought of death disappear. Thus she strengthened her frightening conception of death by carrying on a strengthening training in her dreams. Her attitude in the neurosis can be expressed simply and briefly as if she wanted to say: "Better to die than to keep this job." In the last analysis this does not mean to die, but to give up the job.

All she knew were incoherent details. What she did not know was the context which was composed of her form of life, her picture of the world, and the external factors. Some call this not-understood context the unconscious. But in that case it is also in the unconscious of all those who do not understand this context.

PURPOSE OF COMPULSIONS ABOUT DEATH

The death problem which appears in the neurosis admits further complications, quite frequently and in many nuances. I shall discuss this in the following case.[2] A fifty-year-old man complained about the compulsive symptom to jump out of the window as soon as he was on an upper floor. This symptom had frightened him since puberty, especially since his work, in which he was very successful, forced him to visit people on upper floors.

The first thought which occurred to me was that, after all, this man is alive in front of me. This means that apparently he had overcome the "death wish" successfully, and still manages to overcome it. It seemed to me like one of the many games that children play, often secretly, not to step on the crack between the stones, etc. Also, a similarity with certain superstitious tendencies could not be denied. He appeared as the victor over a heavy oppression.

His biography revealed that he was the youngest in a large family, the pampered favorite of his mother, and that he had all the traits which I have described as characteristics of a pampered child. But by now he had largely overcome them. Again he stood in front of me as the conqueror.

My view found a beautiful confirmation in the meaning of his

2. This appears to be the same case as that on pp. 120–21.

earliest childhood recollection, as interpretations of earliest recollections appear to me as one of the most valuable contributions of Individual Psychology. He said that he was afraid when he arrived at school on the very first day. There he met a boy who looked as if he wanted to jump at him. He almost fainted. But then he collected all his strength, threw himself at the boy, and emerged as victor from this terrible situation.

This case shows how the fear of death, born in shock, can be used as a motive for feeling like a victor through conquering this fear. If the patient had known this connection, the heroism would have appeared to him as a childish game. But, as it was, his occupation gave him frequent opportunity to prove his worth in a fictitious manner. He was looking at the shock results, the symptoms of his neurosis, whereas I looked at the consequences. If he had [knowingly] enjoyed fooling death, he would soon have tired of the cherished game, and this would have placed the whole value of his chasing after success in question. But his vain, self-satisfied style of life had the upper hand and dictated what he should look at and what not to look at.

19

Suicide
(1937)[1]

Early in his career Adler (1910b, trans. 1967c) gave a bold interpretation of the dynamics of suicide as an "act of revenge," "to force [one's relatives] to appreciate what they have lost." Thus he in fact defined suicide as a form of communication, a view held quite generally today. The following paper is his final formulation of this thesis, describing the suicidal individual as one who "hurts others by dreaming himself into injuries or by administering them to himself."—Eds.

The frequent fact of suicide is surrounded by mystery for the average observer. When he is not personally touched by the suicide of someone near to him, he usually resorts to a superficial explanation which occasionally makes the suicide comprehensible, but usually leaves it incomprehensible. The members of the suicide's intimate and wider circles also usually find the occurrence strange and inexplicable. This does not seem very significant, since, in general, an understanding of human nature and thinking directed toward prophylaxis cannot be taken for granted.

Attempts at explanation often begin with the frequency of suicide among mentally disordered individuals, especially depressed persons, to all of whom suicide appears as a way out of their distress even if

1. A1937h. Reprinted from translation, A1958d.

by their words they seem to reject it. Thus the approximately normal person is inclined to regard suicide as an entirely pathological phenomenon.

SITUATIONAL FACTORS

Even so, there are certain situations from which the normal person regards suicide as the only way out. These are situations which are too distressing and unalterable, such as torment without any prospect for relief, inhumanly cruel attacks, fear of discovery of disgraceful or criminal actions, suffering of incurable and extremely painful diseases, etc. Surprisingly enough, the number of suicides actually committed for such reasons is not great.

Among the so-called causes for suicide, disregarding the cases of the psychologically ill, loss of money and unpayable debts take the first place. This gives us much to think about. Disappointed and unhappy love follow in frequency. Further frequent causes are permanent unemployment, for which the individual may or may not be responsible, and justified or unjustified reproaches.

Another cause is suicide epidemics which, puzzling as this may be, do occasionally happen. Harakiri, although on the decline, still exists among the Japanese. Among women and girls, suicide or attempted suicide takes place relatively frequently at the time of menstruation. Lastly, suicides increase strikingly after the age of fifty. All these facts ought to be explicable through Individual Psychology.

It is not surprising that qualified and unqualified circles often endeavor to work for the reduction of suicides. So far as we can see, such attempts have not succeeded in reducing the suicide rate. This is because individuals who turn to associations for the prevention of suicide would only be those who still regard the future with a certain amount of hope. In our time, the number of suicides is unchanged, possibly even increasing.

THE INTERPERSONAL FACTOR

The frequency of suicide is a serious accusation against the none-too-great social interest of mankind. In view of this, a comprehensive exploration of this puzzling phenomenon is urgently needed.

Among inner, endogenous causes, Individual Psychology considers only the style of life which is established out of heredity and environmental influences by the individual's own creative power with his incomplete, humanly limited insight. In addition, one must determine the external, exogenous cause which reveals the inadequate preparation of the individual in question for the urgent situation before him. When the self-consistent life style thus clashes with the external situation, the extent to which the individual stands the test of living with others in society becomes apparent.

Observations of Individual Psychology have shown that every step of an individual is directed toward the successful solution of a presently imminent task in accordance with the total conception of his self-consistency. What the individual considers success is always a matter of his subjective opinion. Our experience has also shown that all tasks which the individual may have to meet require, without exception, adequate social interest for their correct solution. Each individual is so joined to society that he can make no movement, think no thought, and express no feeling without testifying to the degree of his connectedness with society, to his social interest. From this it follows that suicide is a solution only for one who in the face of an urgent problem has arrived at the end of his limited social interest.

This coming to the end of their limited social interest shows itself in all failures, be they active or passive, in their greater development of the inferiority complex. That the suicide departs from the line of social interest is quite obvious. All forms of working together, of living together, and of fellowship are lacking. Further, it must certainly be admitted that this departure occurs in an active way. The activity has a particular curve, however, in that it runs apart from social life and against it, and that it harms the individual himself, not without giving pain and sorrow to others.

The suicide generally gives little or no (conscious) thought to the shock which he causes others. But this difficulty in the way of a further understanding can be resolved. Could it not be that he would have to eliminate others from his thoughts before he could commit suicide? In some cases his social interest might well be great enough for that. Moreover one finds quite frequently, by contrast, that in his last letter or words the suicide hints at asking forgiveness for the sorrow he has afflicted. The movement and the direction of the suicide cannot avoid the fact of sorrow to another. And perhaps there are many on the brink of suicide who, through greater social interest, are deterred from afflicting this sorrow to another.

The "other" is probably never lacking. Usually it is the one who suffers most by the suicide.

PREDISPOSING FACTORS

Individual Psychology continuously seeks to understand the unity and self-consistency of the individual. We are prepared for failures and try to prevent them, always in the conviction that the origin of a misconception of life and its organization can be traced back into early childhood. Therefore we must try to find the type of child which can be regarded as the potential suicide type. Studies of the past life and the childhood of suicides and of those who have attempted it always bring to light those traits which we have found in similar forms in all those failures who combine lesser social interest with a relatively large degree of activity. Suicidal persons have always been problem children, spoiled at least by one side of the family, very complacent, and oversensitive. Very often they showed hurt feelings to an unusual degree. In case of a loss or defeat, they were always poor losers. While they seldom made a direct attack against others, they always showed a life style which attempted to influence others through increased complaining, sadness, and suffering. A tendency to collapse under psychological pain when confronted with difficult life situations often stood out, in addition to increased ambition, vanity, and consciousness of their value for others. Fantasies of sickness or death, in which the pain of others reaches its highest degree, went parallel with this firm belief in their high values for others, a belief which they usually acquired from the pampering situation of their childhood. I have found similar traits in the early history of cases of depression, whose type borders on that of the suicide, and also of alcoholics and drug addicts.

Among the early childhood expressions of the suicide one also finds the deepest grieving over often negligible matters, strong wishes to become sick or to die when a humiliation is experienced, tantrums with willful self-injury, and an attitude toward others as if it were their duty to fulfill his every wish. Occasionally inclinations toward self-accusation come to the fore which elicit the sympathy of others, deeds of exaggerated foolhardiness which are performed to frighten others, and at times stubborn hunger strikes which intimidate the parents. Sometimes one finds ruses in the nature of a direct or indirect attack against others, acts of aggression followed by suicide, or only fantasies, wishes, and dreams which aim at a direct attack while suicide follows later.

Examples of suicide in the family have an attraction for those of similar tendency, as do the example of friends and well-known persons and special places associated with suicide.

SUMMARY

Reduced to the simplest form, the life style of the potential suicide is characterized by the fact that he hurts others by dreaming himself into injuries or by administering them to himself. One will seldom go wrong in determining against whom the attack is aimed when one has found who is actually affected most by it. We find in the suicide the type who thinks too much of himself, too little of others, and who is unable sufficiently to play, function, live, and die with others. Rather, with an exaggerated consciousness of his own worth, he expects with great tension results which are always favorable for him.

The idea of suicide, like all other mistaken solutions, of course always breaks out in the face of an urgent confronting exogenous problem for which the individual in question has an insufficient social interest. His greater or lesser activity then determines the direction and development of the symptoms. The symptoms can be done away with through an understanding of the context.

The psychiatrist will do well to keep his diagnosis of a potential suicide to himself, but to take all precautions. He must not tell it to others, but must see to it that something is done for the patient to enable him to find a better, more independent, socially oriented attitude toward life.

20

The Structure and Prevention
of Delinquency
(1935)[1]

Adler expressed himself twice before on delinquency and its prevention under similar titles, in a shorter paper (A1930g) and a larger book chapter (A1931b, Chapter 9). The latter makes several excellent points and contains a number of case histories. While there is understandably a good deal of overlap between the thoughts expressed earlier and the present paper, the new formulation shows the following developments: The concept of the pampered life style is introduced with the assertion that "in criminals we invariably find evidence of the pampered life style." The relatively high degree of activity in criminals from childhood on is brought into clear focus. The criminal personality structure is shown to consist of the first two factors plus underdeveloped social interest and a conviction of superiority. In the last section, Adler speaks at far greater length as the social reformer than he did on the two previous occasions.—Eds.

The title of this article may be understood in two ways. In one sense it refers to measures aimed at preventing the commission of any criminal action; in another, it refers to the reduction in number of criminal acts. The two aspects of the problem, however, are inseparable. We can successfully tackle the problem of reducing the number of crimes only when we understand what is fundamentally responsible for the commission of any crime.

In our present culture, there are certain conditions of the social system in which, during the course of his development, an individual meets difficulties with which he cannot cope because he has not been properly prepared to meet them. Therefore, one may speak of burdens under which the individual goes to pieces. As Individual Psychologists we speak of burdens for the bearing of which the social interest of the individual has not been sufficiently developed.

Although it will never be attained, one can imagine an ideal state in which man would be able to cope with every burden to which he might be subjected. I shall not dwell on those burdens. We understand, however, that a number of our social institutions act as a pressure on many individuals who have not been prepared in childhood to meet them.

Indications are that crime is not diminishing; at certain times and under certain circumstances, it is even increasing, as statistics show. Some people have assumed that the increase in the cost of living was the cause of increasing crime; others, that the decrease in the cost of living was responsible for it. Even when a country is prosperous, criminal tendencies appear which were not present at other times. When times were comparatively good for almost everyone in the United States, when there was no crisis, the increase of crime was laid to prohibition, or to the fact that people became rich easily.

The problem of reducing crime is extraordinarily complicated. One can approach the problem with various assumptions without being able to say that any one of them is decisive. In this article, however, we are concerned with those fundamental problems recognized by Individual Psychology, the solution of which leads to preparing mankind, better than it has been prepared in the past, to withstand the trials which will come to it inevitably.

We are concerned with the strengthening of that interest in others which is the one thing that will enable man to withstand his trials. Those who have seen the results of Individual Psychology will understand what I mean when I say that the important element is the cultivation of the inborn potentiality for social feeling to the point where the individual shows in his behavior a sufficiency of active social interest. In that way the whole attitude of the individual regarding the tasks of life is directed toward common usefulness.

INSUFFICIENT DEVELOPMENT OF SOCIAL INTEREST

What we really understand by crime is an intentional injury of others for one's own advantage. Obviously then, the problem concerns human beings in whom social interest is not sufficiently developed. From many years of experience, we know how this state of things comes about. We understand how it was that social interest—this gift of evolution—did not develop sufficiently in those individuals.

We are prepared to explain the determining factors which enable us to educate the child for assuming his future problems and for attempting to solve them in accordance with the common welfare. A child so trained will feel himself to be part of a whole, a member of the whole human race, a member who lives with, works with, and plays with other members, and who regards first the small tasks of his childhood and later the greater tasks of his maturity in only one way—by asking himself this question, "What can I contribute?" An individual so trained in childhood will never show criminal tendencies, even when the pressure of external circumstances becomes as severe as it is today when so many are failing.

Even though I assume that my readers understand a great deal about Individual Psychology, I must say something here about the potentiality for social interest which we, from our viewpoint, regard as inborn, as a gift of evolution. There is no denying the fact that owing to communal life, which has existed since the emergence of man, one of the chief problems has always been the way in which the individual relates himself to others, the way each individual contributes to the advancement of the community. In this process of the individual's relating himself to the community, many mistakes have been made for which mankind has paid. Certain it is, and wise men have always said so, that the happiness of mankind lies in working together, in living as if each individual had set himself the task of contributing to the common welfare.

The development of the inborn potentiality for cooperation occurs after the child is born. It occurs first in the relationship of the child and mother. The mother is the first other person whom the child experiences. This relationship has its foundation in nature. The child and mother are dependent on each other; this relationship not only arises out of nature, but is favored by it. When other schools of psychology maintain that the child comes into the world a complete egoist with a "drive for destruction" and no other intention than to foster himself cannibalistically on his mother, they overlook in the relationship the role of the mother which also requires the cooperation of the child. The mother with her milk-filled breasts and all the other altered functions of her body (not to mention the new emotional development of her love for her child) needs the child just as the child needs her. They are dependent on each other by nature. The potentialities for social interest take on life, become tangible first in the relationship between mother and child. Here is the first opportunity for the cultivation of the inborn social potentiality.

But even here, at the very beginning, many mistakes can be made, for the work of man is frail. For instance, the mother is often satisfied with a restricted social development for the child, and does not concern herself with the fact that he must go from her care into a much wider circle of human contacts. In such a case the mother concentrates the child's social potentialities upon herself. She does not help the child to extend his interest to others than herself. Even the father may be excluded if he does not make a special effort to enter this "closed circle." Other children, strangers, etc., are, of course, excluded also. It should, however, be the mother's task to keep the child from seeing in her the only person with whom he can make contact.

Among other developments, there may be that of a child becoming spoiled if he suffers from a feeling of privation and senses that only in the mother can he find the possibility of satisfying his wants. This is especially true, for example, of children born with organ inferiorities who consequently face life as if under a burden which causes them suffering. In such a case, the child learns to expect everything from the mother, and, becoming conscious of a feeling of deprivation, apprehending his burden, he forces the mother to occupy herself exclusively with him.

PAMPERED LIFE STYLE

It cannot be said that the bad training given by the mother is the element which is responsible for producing the pampered life style. The child stumbles into this mistaken way by himself when the mother is the only person with whom he makes contact. This attitude could not occur unless the child claimed for himself all the advantages to be had in such a relationship. In other words, the child, under the circumstances indicated, will always think of himself, will see his only possibility of success in expecting everything from his mother, in contributing nothing, in always taking and never giving. That will be the extent of his social feeling; it will go no further. Consequently the child's picture of the world will be one in which he expects everything from others.

Such a child can not do otherwise in the obscure processes of his thinking than to regard others as objects. If I expect everything from others without giving anything to them, then others are, for me, necessarily nothing more than objects.[2] With this viewpoint it is impossible to develop the feeling of equality with others. I cannot keep the interest of others in mind if others are only outsiders who have to look after me and who have been made available to me for exploitation.

We assert that in criminals we invariably find evidence of the pampered life style. Delinquents who have committed one or more crimes picture the world as a place where everyone else exists for their exploitation, where they have the right forcibly to take possession of the goods, health, or life of others and to set their own interest above the interest of others. In such cases we can always find a certain attitude which can be traced through the life history of the delinquent back to childhood. Delinquents are always individuals whose social interest suffered shipwreck in childhood, whose social interest did not attain full maturity. They begin very early to take forcibly anything which seems to them to belong to them.

Always, however, the intelligence of delinquents must be taken into

2. Adler undoubtedly had in mind the psychoanalytic usage of the term "object," as in libidinal or love object.

consideration. If that is missing then we cannot call them criminals. We cannot employ the concept of crime in relation to a feeble-minded individual who commits an offense. That term applies to the deed planned intentionally and maliciously for the purpose of enriching the perpetrator.

Once again, let us emphasize that this coincides with the pampered life style which, under every circumstance, attempts to force satisfaction of the individual's wishes. It is the pampered life style which will insist on "wish fulfillment."

Trials are harder for those of pampered life style to withstand, because they feel their own wishes more strongly than others do theirs, and they consider themselves entirely justified in these personal desires, so that they seek to solve their problems in such a way as always to maintain their personal prestige.

All Freudian research and its findings are related to the pampered life style without acknowledgment of that fact in the circles where they are accepted with so much enthusiasm. The popularity of this school, and the resentment implicit in its theories, points to a readiness in those of pampered life style to accept it because they feel anything that stems from the pampered life style to be justified and right.

ACTIVE ATTITUDE

There is something else to be said: This state of affairs will assume a variety of colors depending upon whether the child takes an active or passive attitude toward life. Even in a passive way, he can expect everything from others; but if he shows more activity he will proceed actively to take from others whatever he wants that is not given to him voluntarily.

Right here is the beginning of delinquency! It seems to me a most important result of Individual Psychological findings that they have made possible the determination of the psychic structure of a child who is a potential delinquent and is in danger of heading for a career of crime.

Criminals whom I have studied, whether in life or literature, have all been of this type. They were always children who, through pampering or self-pampering, came to an early halt in the development of their social interest and displayed a great amount of activity.

Let us stress here that the criminal's mistaken picture of the world can be traced in his earliest childhood recollections. One hears, for example, things like the following: "I was helping with the wash when I saw a piece of money on the table, so I took it. This was when I was six years old"; or, "When I was five, a freight car burned at our railway station. A lot of children's balls were thrown out and I grabbed as many as I could hold"; or again, "My mother was careless about leaving money lying about, so each week I took some of it."

Such lack of social interest bound up with activity will be found again and again in the early recollections of delinquents. That in these early recollections, the pampered life style, combined with great activity, is clearly expressed, I hold to be one of the most significant findings of Individual Psychology.

Rioting, injury of others, lack of consideration for others, running away, all kinds of attacks on others appear early in these people; it is evident that interest in, and for, others is missing in them.

DIFFICULT SITUATION

These are facts that one dare not forget in studying delinquency. I am not overlooking the fact that with the commonly inadequate development of social feeling the inclination to crime is more prevalent than the actual commission of crime, which requires also an external "cause" to be found in the difficult situation that confronts the criminal. The criminal sees in the commission of his crime the only possible relief from the burden of his difficult situation. His crime seems to him his only possibility of success. The difficult situation is never missing from any crime. It is like a test of the criminal's social interest.

The situation, however, which appears to the criminal to be sufficiently difficult to make him commit the crime can appear quite insignificant to the non-criminal. For instance, a man who has no money and wants to take a girl out may become a burglar. Such mistaken behavior shows an extraordinary degree of arrogance, of diseased ambition which becomes extremely acute when the criminal sees others in possession of anything he covets.

CONVICTION OF SUPERIORITY

The criminal is under the conviction that he will triumph by his crime, that he will not be caught. This firm conviction, too, has its roots in early childhood. I have never seen a young delinquent who had not already committed several offenses without being caught. So delinquents get this impression: "I can injure others without being caught at it." From experience they acquire a certainty about it.

Here we must consider another factor. There is no crime committed without a previous plan. Everything has been thought out in advance by the criminal, and his careful plan gives the criminal the certainty that he is superior to the police, the law, and his victim. His premise is this conviction of his own superiority. He finds some grounds for this attitude in the fact that almost forty per cent of criminals are not apprehended and that most criminals have committed various greater or lesser offenses before capture.

To this fact can be attributed in part the great difficulty of reforming criminals. Only through transforming his picture of the world from one in which he exploits others to one in which he sees others as fellow human beings can an individual be turned from the criminal path. With our present methods of dealing with crime we exert too little effort to increase his social interest. This statement is not intended as criticism or blame. Crime is the most serious of all the psychic mistakes. If we seriously wish to bring the criminal to a more useful way of life, then the best educators must be employed. We must employ those who understand thoroughly the point upon which success hinges, that is, the increase of social interest in the criminal.

As a rule, the criminal has the impression that had he only been cleverer he would not have been caught. This impression exists even among criminals who stand in the shadow of the gallows. I remember a murderer who said again and again, "If only I had not forgotten my glasses, then I would never have been caught." It is very difficult to approach the criminal while he labors under this conviction, especially as even in prison he receives advice and instruction from other criminals as to how his crime might have been more perfectly executed. So long as this problem is unsolved it will be difficult to approach criminals. So long as the criminal is convinced that had he only proceeded differently in this or that small way he would not be in prison, he will reject with disdain any other explanation of his dilemma.

The characteristic of all ambitious persons is that they prepare an alibi whenever threatened with a defeat that might injure their prestige. "Prestige diplomacy" is the essence of this characteristic of ambitious people. We are not surprised that at St. Helena Napoleon said, "If I had only gone to Spain first and then to Russia, the whole world would now be at my feet." These alibis are both a comfort and a challenge to be cleverer next time. Thus the criminal preserves his feeling of worth and his psychic balance. For him, his failure was due to a trifle only.

The difficulty is to make clear to the criminal that it is a mistake to seek his triumph by defrauding others, and to make him understand that his happiness and good fortune consist in contributing as much as possible to society. He should be shown his mistaken style of life from childhood on.

SELF-DECEPTION AND LACK OF COMMON SENSE

In order to commit any crime, the criminal has to goad himself to it. This, however, is a bright spot in the consideration of the human psyche since it may be taken as evidence that even the criminal has social interest. The real trouble is that he has not enough of it. For the purpose of committing his crime he must overcome, both mentally and emotionally, whatever amount of social interest he possesses. He must exhaust his social interest before he can proceed on his criminal way.

There is a wonderful picture of this in Dostoevsky's Raskolnikov. Raskolnikov lies in his bed for two months considering whether or not he dare commit a murder. He tries to kill his social interest by picturing to himself how much good he could do with the money of his victim. But he was not successful in that way—he still had too much social interest—and at the end of two months he exclaims, "Am I Napoleon or am I a louse?" Now he is armed—he behaves like Napoleon and murders the old woman. What has happened? He has selected a comparison—a kind of metaphor—which has no connection with reality. He is, of course, neither Napoleon nor a louse, but he sets up these alternatives because he doesn't want to give up the crime which is his goal. Now there comes an impulse which facilitates for him the carrying out of the deed. He has exhausted his social interest. But it comes back to him after the deed is done because the metaphor he used to stimulate its accomplishment no longer serves him. This same thing happens in all crimes.

The criminal who forgot his glasses said, "Why set so much store on the boy I killed? There are a million other boys." Here he shows his need of an idea which is incompatible with common sense. This man, who murdered his brother, used a distorted concept to facilitate his crime, and in reference to it again exclaimed, "It was either him or me. The earth was not big enough for both of us!" It is natural that similar ideas should play a part in lesser crimes. For example, take the remark of a criminal who had stolen a sum of money. He said, "That man had plenty of money anyhow; why should he have left that money lying around?" Or again, "The man had fine clothes and I had none; so I had to kill him."

It is evident that this method of thinking does not show feeble-mindedness, for we all make use of such help when we resort to poetic expression in order to carry through our purposes. We do the same thing when, for instance, we emphasize the qualities we like or dislike in other people—when we want to represent someone as bad or even when we attempt to make friendly contact. Such poetic expressions, such devices, are attempts to support our purposes. Let us say, for example, that someone wants very much to go to the country; he begins by seeing pictures of the mountains, and before long he finds himself there even though he should stay in town.

This ability to incite themselves to do something good or something bad is given to all human beings. The ability to develop feelings from thoughts and pictures gives an impetus to achievements and attitudes which, though they would no doubt be accomplished anyhow, would be accomplished much less easily under the inhibitions imposed by common sense.

In the very fact that the criminal considers others so little that he regards them only as victims, one can see his mistaken picture of the world—his pampered life style. He, who is lacking in social interest, will be subject to fantastic inclinations, because, having only a "private intelligence," he lacks that common sense which binds the human race together. Social interest endows its possessor with a degree of reason which keeps him from deceiving himself. If he does not deceive himself he will not wish to deceive others.

That quality which has so rightly been termed "common sense" is the highest development which reason can claim. Its values are constant and incontrovertible. That reason, common sense, and intelligence have been undervalued by so many indicates perhaps a lack of social interest in those who undervalue them.

A PLAN FOR PREVENTION

We have now come to the point where we can speak of the prevention of crime. We know how it comes about that social interest remains undeveloped, just as muscular power may remain undeveloped. We know that the security of mankind and the attainment of its highest destiny require that the child be made into a fellowman, a co-worker, one who feels himself to be part of the whole, one who feels at home on the crust of this earth. The fellowman, the cooperator, unlike the individual who just lets himself be carried along, is given to a great deal of activity, but it is activity which is socially useful. This fellowman develops so that without thinking much about it, almost automatically, he moves along the way which leads to the common welfare. Moving in this direction, he develops a large number of his many latent potentialities. The chief task of education lies in developing such fellowmen.

Social interest is not inborn in human beings; only the potentiality of developing it is inborn. The inborn potentiality requires cultivation. The sense of touch also is inborn, but to develop it to a point where it is useful is the business of the creative power of the child under the guidance of his life style. When one finds such a degree of development of the sense of touch as is reached in the cases of Helen Keller and Laura Bridgman, one can be sure that this development came about through intensive training. A prominent neuropathologist, Frederick Tilney,[3] who examined both these women, found that

~~~~~~~~~~~~~~~~

3. Tilney, F. "A comparative sensory analysis of Helen Keller and Laura Bridgman." *Arch. Neurol. Psychiat.*, 1929, 21, 1227–1269.

inherently their sense of touch did not differ from the normal, but that through training they enabled themselves to accomplish much more than is normal. Sight can be the same in two individuals, but just what each does with it depends upon the training he gives it, and may vary greatly. This important finding of Individual Psychology will sooner or later modify the inheritance psychologies so that they will be more in accord with our understanding.

It should be possible to develop social interest to a degree where it suffices the individual in withstanding trials of all sorts, not in order to suppress wishes but in order to turn them into the channels of general usefulness.

FUNCTION OF SCHOOL AND TEACHERS

Now it seems, at first sight, that on the mother should devolve the task of developing in the child the inborn potentiality of social interest. But we must acknowledge that making the majority of parents into good educators would be an endless and hopeless undertaking. So we must turn to the school. It is possible for the school to assume the task of developing the inborn potentiality for social interest in the pupils, and for the teacher to correct any lack in the training for social interest. If this were done it would become the task of the school to so educate children that when they leave school they would be in possession of sufficient social interest to meet the tasks of life.

I should have no objection if our legislators made it a law that no child could leave school until it was certain that he could take a useful place in society, that his interest in others was sufficiently developed to enable him to meet the tasks of life.

I must point out, too, that children who do develop in the direction of social interest and strive for the general welfare are the very ones who achieve most in their studies. And in turn, school achievement is a kind of preparation for later social usefulness. But how can a pupil attend to his studies if being useful is foreign to him?

To be sure, this training would impose a new responsibility upon the teacher; but after all, the teacher is the person who should be most concerned with these matters. The wisdom of the teacher should go so far as to make the child understand why he should be interested in learning the various things taught in school, and also to understand which of his schoolmates is a fellow worker, which a malingerer, and which asocial.

The teacher who is master of this art is, as we have often found, soon capable of instructing other teachers in these methods. He soon discovers that the essential thing necessary to help a child is to see that he walks the way of common usefulness, that he does not feel himself in an enemy country, and that he seeks his happiness in being, living, working with others.

Only in this way will the children of coming generations be in a position to solve the problems of life and make contact with their fellowmen. Only in this way can we hope that individuals will find true vocational worth, and that the problem of love will be solved so that happy marriage based on the equality of the sexes will be possible and choice of partners may be made by women without any reflection on them. To make the child a cooperator, to make him a help instead of a burden, could soon become the common tradition of education.

As soon as teachers come to understand the advantages of a position where they would take their places among the leaders of mankind, as soon as they see that they would have in their hands the power to guide future generations, many will join this great work. The teacher as an individual would find that these amplifications of his work and his position would make it easier for him. It is certainly easier to teach social-minded, well-balanced, useful children than to drag along a number of maladjusted, negligent ones.

If anyone still doubts that the delinquent lacks sufficient social interest and is, therefore, unable to solve the problems of life, I would like to refer to two points. The first is that fifty per cent of the delinquents who are arrested are untrained and unskilled, which means that even as children they did not cooperate and that it was impossible to bring them to that degree of development of social interest necessary to business or professional life.

A second fact that gives cause for reflection is that fifty per cent of criminals suffer from venereal diseases, which is evidence that they are unable to solve the problem of love in a normal way or to consider it a task for two equal partners. Venereal diseases are often the result of considering sex as something which concerns only one person, whereas it is a task for two which can only be truly accomplished when each partner has sufficient interest in the welfare of the other. These two points are a strong verification of my conception of the problem of delinquency.

IMPLEMENTING THE PLAN

In conclusion, I should like to say that mankind would profit enormously by travelling the road proposed by Individual Psychology. I am not worried about the economic cost which would be involved in my program for the prevention of delinquency. The cost of the present system of detection, punishment, and maintenance of criminals is far greater than the cost of beginning with children and educating them to social feeling and interest in others, to be, in short, useful contributing members of society. The poorest community could afford to do this even at present. Nor would it take a very long time before a sufficient number of teachers were educated to the task. In Vienna we already have a great number of teachers equipped for this work.

It should be added that even the closest scrutiny cannot find the proposed educational measure injurious to the religious or political requirements of any nation. I can imagine no form of government in which the increase of social interest, such as we propose, would be harmful; in fact, all great movements include it in their programs.

If the question presents itself here as to whether Individual Psychology alone, and not other schools who believe they can accomplish the same results, should participate in this work, I must answer: We Individual Psychologists are broad-minded enough to hope that they too will have the opportunity of showing what they can do to educate teachers for this work.

I see no reason why this exceptionally fruitful idea should not become reality. I have found, however, that being right is not enough, that sometimes to be right is a disadvantage. However much you and I are filled with this idea, which is so important to life that the future welfare of mankind depends upon it, I do not think we will accomplish at once what seems so obviously necessary to us. But that should not hinder us from constantly hoping and thinking of it, nor from working toward it, nor from regarding such problems as the prevention of delinquency from this standpoint.

We have worked at the problem from this standpoint for a long time, and I believe we have had good results. The solution we offer is not only theory; it is a practical solution for the problem of crime.

But when we say that the problem can be solved, we do not mean that it will be solved immediately. Any new theory meets with the same incredulity and resistance that this one is meeting. It has always been so when anyone found a new way which differed from the customary trend. It was so in the development of industrial technique. The first steam boat and the first train were looked upon as enemies of man. Even scientists declared that anyone who used them must be mad. Yet it has since been demonstrated that man can endure far greater speed. Those who fear that children trained in our way will surely develop headaches[4] are raising objections similar to those raised against the steam boats and the trains.

We must not keep to ourselves the findings that we have thoroughly tested and found sound; we must not bury them. We are under the obligation to disseminate them and challenge the world by subjecting them to further proof. It can be foreseen that as a result of this increased understanding of Individual Psychology the one-sided view held by the hereditarians, the environmental theory, the endocrine gland theory, and the Freudian sexual theory of crime would be subject to a severe test of their values.[5]

A deeper understanding of Individual Psychology would also be of great assistance in the diagnosis of feeble-mindedness, which at present is very uncertain, especially in borderline cases.

wwwwwwwwwww

4. A reference to a psychoanalytic explanation of headaches as resulting from the repression of certain impulses.

5. When Adler proposed this plan that teachers be trained in the development of social interest, and thus as leaders in social reform, at the National Committee on Prisons and Prison Labor, New York, 1930, he concluded: "I recommend to you the adoption and promulgation of the following proposition: With a view to discovering the most successful methods of dealing with the problem of crime, and of giving every single school of thought the opportunity of showing what it can achieve, we Individual Psychologists propose the establishment of various clinics in which the methods of Individual Psychology, of psychoanalysis, of the specialists in endocrinology and pathology, of the behaviorists, and of the believers in heredity may severally be tried" (A1932e, p. 59).

If our work had only this one result, that someone reading this would test how far these ideas are correct, how far it is necessary to go to prove our theories, then I should be satisfied. In view of the general inertia of mankind, we must comfort ourselves in knowing that at least we have done what we were convinced we had to do.

PART V

Religion
and Mental Health

2 1

Religion and Individual Psychology
(1933)[1]

The following essay appeared originally in a volume by a Lutheran minister, Ernst Jahn, and Adler.[2] The volume consisted of an essay by Jahn entitled "The Psychotherapy of Christianity," Adler's reply to it, and some closing statements by Jahn. This is probably the only instance of such a collaboration between one of the founders of modern personality theory and psychotherapy, and a member of the clergy. It reflects Adler's continued endeavor to bring psychology to bear upon everyday life, which would include the integration of psychology with other disciplines having the same concern. The first collaborator with Adler on a book was an educator, Carl Furtmüller, author of the biographical essay presented in Part VI.

We were fortunate in getting the Reverend Jahn to write a new introduction to Adler's essay on religion, relating the background of the original collaboration and the frame within which Adler replied.

While Adler took a very positive attitude toward the socially relevant aspects of religion, he could not be called a religious man in the theistic sense. His position would best be identified as that of a humanist.   —Eds.

1. Original translation of A1933c, with rearrangements to bring the various topics together as much as feasible.

2. Jahn, E., & Adler, A. *Religion und Individualpsychologie: eine prinzipielle Auseinandersetzung über Menschenführung.* Vienna: Passer, 1933.

NEW PREFACE BY ERNST JAHN

Twenty-nine years have passed since my study, "The Psychotherapy of Christianity," was published jointly in a book with Alfred Adler. During all these years I have been active as the pastor of the St. Luke Congregation in Berlin-Steglitz, and from 1947 to 1961 I taught pedagogy and psychology at the Berlin Theological Faculty.

Already in my student years Ernst Troeltsch, the well-remembered theologian, philosopher, and sociologist, had made me aware of the importance of psychology in pastoral work. The prevailing elementaristic psychology of Wilhelm Wundt could bring about psychotechnics, but could never explain the inner organization of the mental life. The psychology of empathy, created by Eduard Spranger, sought to grasp mental activity intuitively. The pragmatic psychology of William James impressed me greatly, especially his psychology of religion.

Then came the revolutionary development of the study of the mind, the psychoanalysis of Sigmund Freud. In its attempt to grasp the soul in its hidden drives and instincts, it seemed almost like a physical science of the mental life. In 1927, I took a stand toward this view in a monograph, *The Ways and Limits of Psychoanalysis.*[3] What I considered particularly destructive was Freud's assertion of religion being a neurosis, an illusion, at best an "oceanic feeling."

I saw ever more definitely that in many people self-centeredness and striving for importance confused the setting of their goals. And this brought me to the Individual Psychology of Alfred Adler. In studying his works, especially *The Neurotic Constitution*, I found clarity of observation, limitation to empirical data, and the rejection of all speculation. Adler had created an excellent basis for diagnosis which clarified many phenomena for me.

Let me speak of my own practice. We are continually confronted with marital crises. One of the partners is after power; the other finds himself in the position of being dominated and rebels against the

3. Jahn, E. *Wege und Grenzen der Psychoanalyse.* Schwerin: Bahn, 1927.

power striving of the first. In this way the conflict arises. Disturbed family situations are particularly destructive for the children. One child is the model child, the other is the black sheep. Sometimes they change places. The mother loves the one with a veritably destructive strength, and soon she complains that the child is rebelling, complains with a certain hatefulness. And this is a love which was drowned in the will to power, which had brought the child, so mightily loved, unconsciously to rebellion.

The children then carry these impressions into adulthood. They become isolates, or querulous individuals whose undeveloped social interest brings them into a constant opposition, or people who always feel hurt while they are themselves hurting the feelings of others. People who are tormented by their drive for importance and their inferiority feelings no longer have the strength to get together with others. Probably many tragedies of our time are due to the disturbance of social feeling. Moved by this thought, I published a book, *The Will to Power and the Feeling of Inferiority,*[4] and this led to my meeting with Adler.

Adler's appearance has always remained unforgettable. He was a man wholly taken up by his idea, without a trace of pathos, and yet filled with an enormous thirst for knowledge. At his suggestion, we undertook to present the theological and medical-individual-psychological aspects of therapy, respectively, in a book together.

The perspective of the psychotherapist and the view of the minister are not entirely comparable. Psychology is, as a rule, convinced that man can free himself from his conflicts, or that the psychotherapeutic treatment can do so. According to the religious view, redemption is brought about only by the gift of grace or the gift of salvation. Luther said that the beginning of sin is pride, disregard of God, and the love of self. The greatest achievement of Individual Psychology is a similar understanding that men break down because of their demonic self-love. Adler's therapy is to bring the patient with love into society. For him the brotherhood of man is a goal of almost religious enthusiasm. While we agree with him fully with regard to the human community, we maintain that beyond this there is also an other-

4. Jahn, E. *Machtwille und Minderwertigkeitsgefühl: eine kritische Analyse der Individualpsychologie.* Berlin: Warneck, 1931.

worldly community, the community of God, the *unio mystica*. For Adler, the meaning of life is the experience of fellowmanship and the courage for it. There are, however, human problems which can be solved neither by fellowmanship nor by courage. Furthermore, while Christianity unreservedly endorses the call for encouragement, it holds that there can be no courage for life without faith in God. And it is God who gives life its ultimate meaning. For Adler, God is a human idea; for Christians, God is revealed.

There is another significant difference. Adler speaks of error in the life style. He is right in his interpretation that incomprehensible human behavior is often grounded in mistaken upbringing and hence in a lack of social interest. But one cannot equate error and guilt. The error in the life style is not always purely intellectual and therefore capable of being cured by insight. The error may just as well be caused by inadequate control of the drives; and then it is guilty.

We must point out these differences in the understanding and guidance of man, for it is precisely the recognition of the differences which leads to a deepening of our own views.

The purpose of our joint study of 1933 was, however, not the separation of the two viewpoints, but the comparison, the deepening, and the achieving of understanding for one another's viewpoints. This task seems to me today, after 29 years, to have become even more urgent and serious.

The overpowering goal of Adler is his conception of the brotherhood of man. For the theologian the earth is God's creation and man is God's creature. From this view the brotherhood of man is the eternal ideal of mankind.

Berlin-Steglitz
June 13, 1962

FUNDAMENTAL EXPOSITIONS OF INDIVIDUAL PSYCHOLOGY

The present paper by Jahn can neither be denied understanding for the depth of Individual Psychology, nor be reproached for any vacillation in the idea of God and in the will for religious education. The truth-seeking intention of the author agrees with both positions. It also will not be possible to bypass the moral seriousness of the author with empty phrases such as to maintain, perhaps, that his expositions are predetermined by the illusion of a theistic religion and therefore narrowed down. Rather one can recognize that his educational as well as religious views have resulted from a deep relationship with mankind and a striving to be a co-worker in its welfare with the goal of completion and perfection.

Among the fundamental findings of Individual Psychology which touch upon the above topic the following may be mentioned.

The Idea of God as Goal of Perfection

The striving of each actively moving individual is towards overcoming, not towards power, as Jahn, Künkel, and others present the view of Individual Psychology. Striving for power—better, for personal power—represents only one of a thousand types, all of which seek perfection, a security-giving plus situation.

One concretization of the idea of perfection, the highest image of greatness and superiority, which has always been very natural for man's thinking and feeling, is the contemplation of a deity. To strive towards God, to be in Him, to follow His call, to be one with Him—from this goal of striving (not of a drive), there follow attitude, thinking, and feeling. God could be recognized, could reveal Himself, only within a thought process which moves toward the quality of height, toward the guiding idea of greatness and omnipotence, only within feelings which experience greatness, omnipotence, omniscience as redemption from oppressing tensions, from inferiority feelings.

Man as an ever-striving being could not be like God. God, who is eternally complete, who directs the stars, who is the master of fates, who elevates man from his lowliness to Himself, who speaks from the cosmos to every single human soul, is to date the most brilliant manifestation of the goal of perfection. In God's nature, religious mankind perceives the way to height. In His call it hears again the innate voice of life which must have its direction towards the goal of perfection, towards overcoming the feeling of lowliness and transitoriness of the existence here below. The human soul, as a part of the movement of life, is endowed with the ability to participate in an evaluating fashion in uplift, elevation, perfection, and completion as a measure of experience.

The idea of God and its immense significance for mankind can be understood and appreciated from the viewpoint of Individual Psychology as concretization and interpretation of the human recognition of greatness and perfection, and as commitment of the individual as well as of society to a goal which rests in man's future and which in the present heightens the driving force by enhancing the feelings and emotions.

Individual Conceptions of God

The more thoroughly one examines a personality and the more precise the characterization one attains, the more one arrives at the conviction that the uniqueness of the individual in thinking, feeling, talking, and acting manifests itself again and again, that we are always dealing with individual nuances and variations. It is partly due to the abstractness and limitations of language that the reader and listener must discover what lies between the words they read and hear in order to gain a true understanding of and proper contact with the author of those words, as with a partner. When two persons act the same, it is not the same; but also when two persons think, feel, or want the same thing, differences exist. Therefore we cannot do entirely without guessing if we want to understand another person correctly. As soon as a person takes a stand [on an issue] or forms his view of the world, the individuality of his style of life will stand out strongly. This is especially true when he is left entirely to the make-believe world of his feelings.

It is no different in religion, which is transmitted to us by word of mouth and in writing. The nuances diverge as soon as it is a matter of concretization of the goal of perfection. Even if we disregard the original religions in which animal figures symbolized the goal of superiority, we still cannot overlook how differently the supreme power is reflected in human minds depending upon tradition, way of life, and even climate, cosmic, and telluric influences.

One could readily assume that the monotheistic religions corresponded more and more to the world view of civilized man who obviously was able to think and feel the expression of highest strength in the master of the world events. But here too we shall have to concede that each individual, in a thousandfold variation, forms an image of the functioning and shape of the supreme being which differs by nuances from that of the next man.

The ideal, ultimate union can hardly be attained, whether one forbids the making of an image or attempts to bring about identity with an image. No wonder that in the millionfold diversity of concretization the scale ranges all the way from personification to its opposite, especially when man no longer sees himself as the center of world events and is satisfied with a more meager concretization, with the recognition of causally acting forces of nature as the image of highest strength. Individual Psychology, which has not till now attempted to extend its investigations and insights into this area, would by the essence of its view be forced to regard such an unpremised, mechanistic view as an illusion inasmuch as it is without goal and direction, just like drive psychology, which is cut from the same cloth. While the materialistic view lacks the goal, which signifies life, the religious view, far ahead in this respect, on the other hand lacks the causal foundation. For God cannot be proven scientifically: He is a gift of faith.

God as Reflection of Man's Concerns

Individual Psychology would have to proceed differently. It would consider unessential the question of whether man is the center of the world. Its intention would be to make him the center. In this way man attains a task and a goal which, although unattainable, would point the way. This is the path man has always taken. Once put into the world, with his bodily and psychological disposition, he must strive incessantly toward self-preservation and ascendency. In this manner he found God, who points the way, who is the harmonious complementation in the goal for the confined, contradictory, groping, and erring movements on the path of life. The striving to attain something of the strengthening grace and the gracious strength of the divine goal always flows from the insecurity, the constant inferiority feeling of needy mankind.

When we look dispassionately we find that the difference in form over the course of time is not essential. Whether one calls the highest effective goal deity, or socialism, or, as we do, the pure idea of social interest, or as others call it in obvious connection with social interest, ego ideal, it always reflects the same ruling, perfection-promising, grace-giving goal of overcoming.

Religious arguments should find little fault with this view, except when disordered thinking, such as that of Pfister or David, becomes concerned with it without critical consideration. Perhaps it will even meet with enthusiastic recognition by all those who struggle and have struggled for greater clarity in questions of the idea of God and have, perhaps implicitly, harbored impressions of a similar nature.

We do not want to be outdone by anyone in being critical of Individual Psychology, and thus a remarkable doubt follows here. How could it really have been the strongest endeavor of mankind to create an image of omnipotence, of unlimited greatness, which would not include that which always has been and always will be mankind's hourly concern—the concern for the preservation of itself and of the individual, the compulsion toward the ascendance of the whole and the parts? Did not a very large share in the process of concretizing the supreme power have to be taken up by the strongest concerns and motives of mankind—the care of the young, preservation of the species and its advancement—in order to attain the upper hand over the difficulties of life, in order to enjoy life undisturbedly?

It may have taken an unthinkably long time and certainly a great number of tentative trials to recognize a satisfactory image, to experience the revelation of this supreme being to whom leads the way of hope and belief in protection and security for the species and for the individual. It certainly was a nonverbal, nonconceptual recognition in religious fervor in which the sacred uniting of man with the goal-setting God took place, as it still takes place today in every religious soul.

Sanctification of Human Relations

The strong possibilities of a concretization of a final goal of perfection and the irresistible attraction to it are firmly anchored in the nature of man, in the structure of his psychological apparatus. So, too, are the possibilities of psychological joining with others. The sanctification of these possibilities strengthened them and their development by setting the entire thinking and feeling apparatus into continuous movement. Included in this progressive strengthening were the ties between mother and child, marriage, and the family, all to the advantage of the care of the young. At the same time—and originating from the same need—life and the love of one's neighbor were sanctified. Probably the strongest and most significant step towards the preservation and perfection of mankind was taken when man accomplished his unification with God as the goal of redemption from all evil.

Should, or could, mankind have waited until it rose through scientific illumination to the active recognition of the unavoidable necessity for brotherly love and the common weal, and thereby also to the active recognition of the correct relationship of mother and child, the social lawfulness in the cooperation of the sexes, and the interest in others' labor? Such spiritual and psychological clarification, which leads to the most profound recognition of interconnectedness, which closes all doors to error and proves that virtue is teachable, has not as yet become realized by many. Religious faith is alive and will continue to live until it is replaced by this most profound insight and the religious feeling which stems from it. It will not be enough only to taste from this insight; mankind will have to devour and digest it completely.

The fact that an increasingly large part of mankind resists religion does not arise from its essential nature. This resistance rather originates from the contradictions which have resulted between the work of the power apparatus of the religions and their essential nature, and probably also from the not infrequent abuses of religion.

Individual Psychology has recognized the amount of social interest which dwells in each human being, and traces it as an inviolable part of human nature to innate dispositions which await development. The mightiest promoter of social interest is the mother, who even after the birth of the child is functionally tied to it and its welfare. She and the father sense, and should also understand, that the child is a part of themselves, a claim to their earthly immortality.

The community, which Individual Psychology invokes, is a goal, an ideal, always unattainable, but always beckoning and pointing the way. This community, the power of the logic of men's living together, blesses those who follow it and punishes the unwilling and erring. Its growing influence in the life of peoples creates institutions to act continuously as a goal, to strengthen the weak, to support the falling, and to heal the erring. Mankind, which has undertaken to be and to become the center of earthly and the cosmic events, can bring its task closer to a solution only if the bodily and psychological welfare of all is taken as an unalterable factor in the accounting of life. Even here abuse occurs readily, be it by opponents or adherents of Individual Psychology.

Individual Psychology and other Social Movements

Movements which independently have made society the guiding goal of their striving are responsible for showing whether the good of all is assured in their conduct, or only in their words and feelings. Often this is a matter of becoming effective in the distant future, in which case the decision is sometimes not easy since no one can claim to know the absolute truth. I would acknowledge as valuable any movement which guarantees in its final goal the welfare of all.

This is my personal view and belief to which I would not pledge anyone else. From this follows the attitude of Individual Psychology towards all religions and all political parties. The very foundation of my scientific work resists the norms formulated in the rigid laws of all other movements which are beyond science, and cannot possibly accept such laws. While tolerant of every movement which unmistakably includes the goal of the well-being of all, Individual Psychology must resist being shut off from scientific research by methods of thought which do not spring from its view of life, or which even contradict it, and must resist absorbing tendencies which stand less constantly for the goal of an ideal community, or even run counter to it. It is not my office, nor have I ever conceitedly taken it upon myself, to praise or criticize movements which, like Individual Psychology, have the well-being of all of mankind in view. And I cannot suppress my feeling of awe and admiration for the great accomplishments of such movements. But Individual Psychology must use only purely scientific methods, must remain a pure science and reach the people in this unalterable form, in the hope of being fruitful also to other scientific movements and currents which stand closer to practical life.

Individual Psychology does not deny that the religions with their powers, their church institutions, their influence on school and education, have a strong advantage. It will be satisfied in the practical application of its science to protect and further the sacred good of all-embracing humaneness where the religions have lost their influence. A conflict with church or political movements could only arise where, on the basis of the scientific insight of Individual Psychology, this good appears threatened or not sufficiently protected.

I myself am less inclined to take a hand in religious or political movements, since I have confidence in the strength and effectiveness of Individual Psychology, although I have always been convinced that I would have to reckon with a long time before this would be felt. Meanwhile I am satisfied to see how its views keep on gaining ground in the ministry, the schools, criminology, education, and psychiatry— as even in the political parties the idea of the community continues to gain, although often inadequately. I consider it the given task of Individual Psychology to maintain a central position and to make its results available to all. Whoever wants to contribute to the common weal must keep his social feeling, even in a controversy. Jahn has gone this way, and I shall follow him.

TAKING ISSUE

After these fundamental expositions I am now in the position to take issue with the presentations of Jahn. According to pure and practical reason it must be obvious to all but a few insignificant exceptions that Individual Psychology and religion have things in common, often in thinking, in feeling, in willing, but always with regard to the goal of perfection of mankind. Therefore I can limit myself to take issue with those presentations where I feel obligated to establish the correct rendition of our views. Jahn is not to be blamed in the least for having missed my own findings, which I may well call those of Individual Psychology.

Perhaps it is sometimes only the limitation of language which forces me to give expression to my differing opinion. At other times it is perhaps a consideration by Jahn which does not correspond to our honestly defended conception of the inseparability of psychological processes from the total life style of the individual. Now and then I meet presentations which originate from secondary sources. I shall attempt to go into some of these observations.

The network of Individual Psychology as a form of regarding

psychological expressions in characterology and personality research, pathological phenomena, psychological failures of all kinds, relationships between body and soul, and mass movements is presently so firm that it is undisturbed by any inconsistency.

It is different with the interpretation of the individual forms of expression, their understanding within a clarified self-consistent context, and with treatment. In these respects artistic ability is a prerequisite. This can be attained only through self-knowledge, quick repartee, persuasiveness, conviction, and sufficient ability to guess, to identify, and to cooperate. Although all these abilities overlap, their development is different in everyone who practices Individual Psychology. We find the same difference in the ability to describe the process and in the unresolved remnant of preconceived opinions in every psychologist. This leads to differences also, and occasionally to contradictions, in presentation.

Perhaps the work is too difficult for some who want to work in Individual Psychology, and even more so for some critical observers. Such persons are likely to betray their tendency to ease the work by useless weak attempts to smuggle into Individual Psychology justified or unjustified thoughts from other areas. Then the naive reader may at times gain the impression of contradiction, lack of clarity, and entanglement with other thought currents. From his differing viewpoint on religion, politics, world philosophy, or psychology, he may exercise criticisms which in his opinion apply to Individual Psychology. But criticism must be based on a comprehension of Individual Psychology as a whole, as that discipline which I described initially.

The manner in which Jahn does justice to Individual Psychology must be appreciated. But occasionally he has not gone to the source and has taken exception to remarks which are not part of the essence of Individual Psychology, to say the least.

Emphasis on Actions rather than Feelings

The emphasis of the present discussion is, perhaps to the surprise of many, on the understanding of the role of feelings in the self-consistency of psychological life. Individual Psychology, which not only presupposes and proclaims "wholeness" but in each case endeavors to demonstrate it, stands and falls with the assertion that the feelings, too, are oriented towards a unitary goal, like all other psychological processes and in unison with them.

Whether, in a religious vein, I call my goal scientifically, or more or less intuitively, God and look up to Him; or whether, in an exclusively scientific way, I strive after a goal of ideal perfection of mankind—my feelings will always be determined by my final goal. And it is certainly correct to assume that where there is less closeness to God, the love of one's neighbor, or *agape*, may be less than where there is a strong permeation of social feeling. Naturally, it may be the other way around.

Individual Psychology is not interested in the verbal expression of feelings, but only in the intensity of a person's movement. Therefore it will not be able to evaluate the representatives of various religions by the way they express their feelings, but only by their movements as whole individuals, i.e., by their fruits. These fruits must, of course, be recognized *sub specie aeternitatis* (under the aspect of eternity).

Jahn believes that Individual Psychology sees the soul in its relationships to life and the community. This statement must be supplemented. It is true that I see the soul as well as the whole person as a part of the community, a part of the cosmos. But I see the person also as striving—once he knows the right way—for an ideal community, a striving movement coming to him as an earth-born creature through intuitive or scientific knowledge.

When the minister misses in Individual Psychology the investigation of religious and ethical feelings, he overlooks the fact that these are included in the broad discussions about social feeling.

Jahn distinguishes historically and factually four kinds of guidance: religious, idealistic, educational, and psychotherapeutic. We should attribute unqualified goal consciousness only to the first. Goal consciousness can be attributed to the other three only if they subordinate all their efforts, in scientifically irreproachable fashion, to the goal which Individual Psychology has posited as for the present the most correct solution of the problem of human guidance: education toward the ideal community.

Once the goal of perfection, albeit in a never-to-be-reached ideal community, has been established for all types of human guidance, then these would actually differ only in their means, perhaps also in their way of looking at things. Whereas Jahn claims that it is faith that urges man toward community, in Individual Psychology guidance it is the deeply felt conviction that the only right way of solving human problems is that which would benefit an ideal community.

Salvation through Social Interest

The problem of salvation and grace also develops smoothly within Individual Psychology guidance. We attempt in the case of the problem child, the neurotic, the delinquent, etc., to understand his life style as constructed erroneously in early childhood, and to call attention to his mistake as one which is only human. If one succeeds in doing so and has the necessary tact, art, and fellow-feeling not to put him to shame for his mistake, the subject will experience a clear transformation of his life style without rebellion of his feelings, not to mention contrition. The latter is what Künkel, for example, tries to insinuate into Individual Psychology, and wants to bestow mercilessly on his patients.

Individual Psychology, which postulates the equality of all human life—not to be interpreted as equality of achievement—has at its disposal sufficient consolation, encouragement, and redeeming power to correct a mistake, to give consolation in its comradely work performance, to educate, and to teach. But one can only teach when one has acquired the knowledge of the whole, of the mistaken life style of a person.

Just as from the religious viewpoint it goes without saying, as we have shown, that a man must know himself to be before God in order to become a member of society in the highest sense, so in Individual Psychology the erring human being stands before the common sense and what is recognized as the "right" ideal of an ultimate society, the measure of all purified action.

Strangely enough, there are psychologists who do not think much of the common sense. This is so, apparently, because it contradicts their "private intelligence." For the benefit of doubters I should like to mention that the common sense grows with the development of human understanding, and that it represents the highest attainable measure in every period for the judgment of human reason and for the control of human action.

Since failure in life is due to error, it is also understandable that occasionally, in rare cases, a person may free himself from his error if, in spite of it, he has remained strong in the spirit of the ideal community. In religion this may happen, as Jahn points out, from the contact of the self with God. In Individual Psychology, during its mild barrage of questions, the erring person experiences grace, redemption, and forgiveness by becoming a part of the whole.[5]

The problem of guidance as it presents itself to the physician, the minister, and the teacher is to point out to a person who is inadequately prepared for the tasks of mankind, who is shaken by a social task which faces him, the error in his method of living, and to make a better preparation possible for him. It seems to me that also in religious guidance there is no other way than that of "persuasion." To this end Individual Psychology, as far as I can see, has prepared the best means, the best insights.

I shall pass over many of Jahn's valuable discussions on Christian guidance. In part I have already answered these from the viewpoint of Individual Psychology.

The drama of the human soul which is redeemed through the grace of Christ from sin to freedom may very well apply to the person who is on the way to the ideal human community. Understandably, "God-reference" will appear to many to be more forceful, concrete, and endowed with stronger emotional reference. But it is not quite correct to say with regard to the intelligible viewpoint that the view of theological anthropology is completely different from that of psychological anthropology. This is especially not correct when for the purpose of comparison one projects the first onto the plain of common sense.

Künkel,[6] as usual in his thinking, goes the reverse way and believes,

〰〰〰〰〰〰〰

5. The German for "barrage of questions" is *Fragefeuer* (fire of questions) by which Adler played on the German word for purgatory, *Fegefeuer* (literally translated, cleansing fire).

6. Fritz Künkel, M.D., founded the Berlin Association for Individual Psychology in 1924 and was especially successful in bringing Adler's psychology before Protestant ministers. In 1932 Künkel and Adler separated over theoretical differences, Künkel eventually including some of Jung's ideas in his We-Psychology (Orgler, Hertha, *Alfred Adler: the man and his work*, 3rd ed., London: Sidgewick & Jackson, 1963, p. 189). His We-Psychology is presented in *Character, growth, education* (Philadelphia: Lippincott, 1938) and *How character develops* (New York: Scribner's, 1940). According to Jahn, Künkel had introduced the concepts of revelation and grace into Individual Psychology (Jahn & Adler, *op. cit.*, p. 28).

in doing so, to have found something new. Allers [7] does the same, when he does not undertake to make "psychological anthropology" a part of the Christian ministry, which would be the task of Individual Psychology with regard to any great movement, but tries to make it more palatable to the ministry by using ministerial terminology. Künkel says (as quoted by Jahn): "From the viewpoint of the patient, conversion is a matter of grace; from the viewpoint of science, it is a miracle." The psychotherapist may be not a little flattered to be the bringer of a miracle. But when one has correctly recognized the unity of the individual, and also the mistake in the construction of the erring personality, and furthermore has been able to persuade the erring individual to a better style of life, one will not find it possible to call this a miracle, since it is obviously an understandable human accomplishment.

Likewise Liertz, whom Jahn gives as a reference, overlooks what enters into the case of improvement when he introduces the *exercitia spiritualis* into psychotherapy and strongly emphasizes the influence of the will on the emotional life, ascetic exercises, and the significance of self-control. As training, these may occasionally lead to an advance, but only if one succeeds in developing the urge toward cooperation, being a fellow man, social interest. That is, such training can become effective only on the ground of social interest, if it is already there. Otherwise the attempt to influence the feelings remains sounding brass and tinkling cymbal. Whether such complicated methods are necessary, once social interest is assured, remains the question.

When the religious psychotherapy of Hilty tries to establish that the awakening of the strength for idealism is possible only through faith, we would have to add that faith in science and its progress can also lend such strength.

wwwwwwwwwww

7. Rudolf Allers, M.D., Ph.D., LL.D., belonged for a time to the inner circle of Adler's collaborators. Invited in 1937 to take over the chair of philosophical psychology at the Catholic University of America, he taught there from 1938 to 1948, when he was appointed professor of philosophy at Georgetown University. He is author of numerous articles and of several books, among which are *The successful error: a critical study of Freudian psychoanalysis* (New York: Sheed & Ward, 1940) and most recently *Existentialism and psychiatry* (Springfield, Ill.: Thomas, 1961).—Personal communication from Dr. Allers. March 31, 1962.

The Dialectics of Individual Psychology

Dialectical theology stresses that development implies conflict and crisis, and redemption comes from grace

Individual Psychology maintains that the life style as prototype, as psychological constitution, is already completed and becomes visible after three to four years, and preserves itself throughout life, unless the individual becomes convinced of the error in it. This conviction develops out of his far-reaching understanding of the connection of all partial forms of expression with the whole, and his recognition that in earliest childhood he constructed incorrectly. Suffering on this account, almost synonymous with a guilt feeling, would create moods in the individual which promise no recovery so long as they merely continue as such. "Conscience pangs are indecent," said Nietzsche, pointing to this fact.[7a] Looking back sadly to the errors of early childhood—mistaken opinions, misunderstood organ inferiorities and their often unsuccessful psychological compensations, the mistaken conclusions drawn from wrong upbringing, such as pampering which plays the leading role in the unsuccessful life plan—is actually a hindrance to encouraging a new life and must be replaced by a general human understanding.

"Since I have recognized the mistaken meaning of my life, I am worse off than before," one often hears patients say—as long as they do not feel themselves as part of the whole. One may call it conflict when a person outfitted with an erroneous life plan founders on the social necessities of our life; call it crisis when he is in the process of change; call it grace when he finds the new way. But one should avoid that at the fringes of these concepts (James) moods creep in and become reality, which stem from belligerent relationships, from sad disease processes, and from the morality of a subject (*Untertans-moral*) when there is mention of grace outside religion.[7b]

Dialectics in the sense of thesis, antithesis, and synthesis is, of course, found in our view as in the other social sciences. It becomes

7a. This quotation is from *Twilight of the Idols*, "Maxims and Arrows," No. 10.

7b. Adler probably meant here Nietzsche's term "slave morality" (Sklaven-moral), the morality of "the ruled, the slaves and dependents of every degree" (Nietzsche, *Beyond Good and Evil*, Sect. 260).

apparent most often when we are dealing with persons who expect to be spoiled by others (thesis). When they do not receive such treatment, they fall into hate and resentment (antithesis), until they find their way through to contribution, to general humaneness (synthesis). The *"flectere si nequeo superos, Acheronta movebo"* ("if I am unable to bend the gods, I shall move Acheron," a river in Hades below) must find its synthesis in social interest.

In organic life as well, the urge toward synthesis shows itself, in the new equilibrium of the whole organism achieved by its reacting to organ inferiorities with organic overcompensations.

Incidentally, this equilibrium which life seeks is not death, or psychologically seen, the death instinct, but a harmony of the body which strives toward evolution. It is not the second law of thermodynamics, the turning into nothing, which often plays a role in people. This would be but a premature anticipation of a condition which perhaps may happen in millions of years, which presently, however, is certainly to be regarded as an error, as a disease symptom.

Incongruity of Life Style with Social Demands, rather than Inner Conflict

Individual Psychology is indeed more than a psychology of inferiority feelings, as Jahn points out. But I cannot agree that it attempts to describe man in conflict with himself. What it describes is always the same ego in its course of movement, which experiences the incongruity of its life style with the social demands. Here the ego tries erroneously to maintain its life style instead of developing it higher so as to accord with these demands, that is, instead of developing in the direction of a stronger social interest.

In this way—contrary to Jahn's view—defiance, personal ambition, the feeling of defeat, and flight from the community cannot be explained as psychological attitudes resulting from a lack of conquest of one's own ego. Rather, these attitudes are parts of the life style and are resources, guiding lines, or means used by an individual, with little inclination towards the community, in meeting problems of life which require more social interest than he is able to muster. They are means which can finally save at least the semblance of a personal superiority for the individual, on the useless side of life.

For example, a thirty-four-year-old unmarried man complains about inferiority feelings when meeting intelligent men and attractive girls.

He grew up in a family atmosphere which lacked any warmth and where every member tried to outdo the other in an unmannerly way. In school he experienced his triumph, was always the best pupil and popular with his teachers and classmates, although he did not succeed in making real friends with them.

When later he took a job, in which he was always trying to distinguish himself, he met with haughtiness and coldness in his superiors, as employees and workers often do. He could maintain himself there only because he did his work with redoubled zeal and the greatest effort. But he was continuously tired and in bad humor, and transferred his defiant and querulous feelings to his brothers and sisters. Since childhood he expected, due to his almost unequivocal experiences in life, only coldness and criticism from others. Even in school he could gain respect only with extreme ambition, and saw himself always as if before an examination. The recollections of his past showed him life only as a life of struggle and fear of humiliation.

The meaning of life for him seemed to be that he was always facing an examination, the poor result of which he tried to prevent by retreating. Throughout his life he had acted like a student who tries to get out of an examination. His ambition to win warmth, recognition, and praise was well protected in this way. His ambitious ego, always seeking recognition and warmth, remained unchanged. He made a wide detour around defeats, both assumed and real. But he could continue along this way of the person who thinks more of himself than others, only by the retreat described above. A change and improvement in his life style was possible only when he recognized the error of his method of life, which was made clear to him through his domestic life, and when he made room for a stronger interest in others. He had not been fighting with himself; rather, his ego came up against problems which it could not solve in a satisfactory manner.

What is called the "crisis of psychology" is probably more a crisis of the psychologists. And the "contradictory character" of man, as the deepest of Christian insights, first becomes evident, in our view, when the erring individual, on the road to initial improvement of his social interest, no longer can defend his error as strongly as before. The apparent contradiction in the neurotic does not lead to change in the neurotic attitude. As long as there is a contradiction, only one thing is certain: no change will set in.

Subordinate Role of Drives and of the Unconscious

Jahn raises the often-voiced question of whether the intellect has indeed the power to brake the drive and to ennoble it. Individual Psychology makes a sharp distinction between "private intelligence" and "reason." One cannot deny that the stubborn child has intelligence when he always acts in opposition to prove his superiority and to occupy his mother with himself. His mischief will always be intelligent enough to lead him to his goal. The girl who, protesting against her feminine role for mistaken reasons, has made it her goal to behave like a boy, whom she regards as superior, acts quite intelligently in accordance with her goal when she turns her feelings of love away from men. Even the insane person, who has completely turned away from life and its demands because he expects defeat in all directions, acts intelligently when he secludes himself from the world and seeks at least in his fantasy the enjoyment of a fictive superiority.

Reason, on the other hand, common sense, is the integration with the social demands of our life and the resulting insight in their social relatedness.

As to "drive," it is a theoretical construct which is not improved by attributing to it partial drives or by pledging it to sexual libido. It then ekes out its existence by secretly having been infused with a goal, ability to choose, cunning, malice, and especially demoniacal egotism. But all these are attributes which obviously show social references as we know them from the ego, and which belong only to the ego.

If one proceeds critically enough one will find that the "drive" is without direction of its own, and receives a direction only from the goal, i.e., from the life style of the ego. In other words, everything that has been imputed to the drive (in order to be taken out again subsequently) will be recognized as erroneous only through reasonable insight into the whole context of the ego. One will be able to improve it only by changing the whole, the life style.

This consideration of the whole applies also to the process which the Utopian Fourier, then Nietzsche, and, later, Freud have called sublimation. An individual will only be able to better detrimental inclinations when he has already become more of a fellow man. Thus the intellect has not the strength to direct the drive differently, but the altered goal, the altered life style has.

If this is the work of reason, one must not forget that its budding cannot take place in isolation. Feelings and emotions are always connected with it; but in different people these are at different distances from their focus. And there is always a change of attitude; in the most favorable case this is toward cooperation, toward active social connectedness. In our judgment it is always the attitude which is decisive. It teaches us whether the insight into the whole has really taken place. To speak of intellectualism in Individual Psychology means to misunderstand both. For us every form of expression is permeated by the law of movement of the whole.

I should like to express myself briefly on the question of the unconscious, because Jahn occasionally seems to use Freud's conception of the unconscious to cast doubt on the power of scientific persuasion in guidance. There is much less room for an independent unconscious as part of the ego when one views the psychological structure as a whole. Still, we also can characterize the goal of psychological movement as unconscious—better, as unrecognized, and recognizable only from its context.

This is true also of the individual's life style and the opinion which underlies his actions, namely the opinion of his capability and of the manner in which he should perform the tasks of life in accordance with his law of movement. Here the individual lacks understanding and words. Freud takes the characteristic of consciousness to be the verbal and conceptual formulation of a psychological phenomenon. In addition, he regards the disturbance or holding back of conceptual expression, the looking away from the accompanying feelings and emotions, the obstructed insight into the connection between attitude and final goal, as repression into the unconscious. Those who agree with him are forced to make all kinds of interpretations in order to paraphrase our views. According to Individual Psychology, all the above-mentioned processes are intended by the life style, which tries to retain its form, direction, and movement.

The assumption of a censorship became necessary for Freud to explain the repression of perverse drives and its consequences. Jahn is quite right when he raises the question of the sources of this censorship; only this censorship does not alter the strength of the repressed drives. In the psychoanalytic view it is a means of coercion to keep down attacks dangerous to the culture. At best this leads to an adaptation to the demands of the environment, of the presently conventional morals, from fear of counterattacks, and forces, according to Freud, the neurosis. If one dispenses with Freud's anthropomorphic view of the nature of censorship, nothing remains but a relatively slight social interest which, when tested by a social problem, brings about no other result but the mistaken solution of this problem, namely, developing the neurosis.

Arvid Runestam comes from the Freudian line. According to him the neurosis originates when the uninhibited, luxuriating drive life represses the religious strivings. Not the severe but the lax morality creates neurosis; in the neurosis ethics defends itself against the drive.[8] This is pretty much the last refuge of the Freudian conception.

As to connecting psychoanalysis with the Christian doctrine of sin and conscience, I could do this only in the case of a person who persists in his sinfulness while at the same time having continuous conscience pangs.

Explorations in the unconscious resulted in the aggression drive of Individual Psychology, which to us means striving for perfection; in psychoanalysis, which throws the baby out with the bath water, aggression means sadism and masochism. The ego ideal and the censor, the latter created by the former under the pressure of reality, are, if not show pieces of cunning, slyness, and cringing, parts torn from the early acquired social feeling as Individual Psychology understands it.

Not only words determine the conscious. One cannot deny consciousness to infants and animals. There is also consciousness in our feelings even if they are without words, in our musical experience, and especially in our actions. But what we seldom find in these is an

---

8. Arvid Runestam, a Swedish bishop, presented this view of neurosis in his *Psychoanalyse und Christentum* (Gütersloh: Bertelsmann, 1928: English translation reprint: *Psychoanalysis and Christianity*. Rock Island, Ill.: Augustana Press, 1958). The view is today shared by O. H. Mowrer (*The crisis in psychiatry and religion*, Princeton, N. J.: Van Nostrand, 1961, pp. 83–91 & 125–29) who points out that it has also been expressed by A. T. Boisen (*The exploration of the inner world*, New York: Harper, 1936) and by W. Stekel (*Technique of analytical psychotherapy*, New York: Liveright, 1950).

understanding of the context which, once it is clad in words and uncovered without contradiction before the common sense, gives us the right to be convinced and to convince. This incontrovertible clarification of the errors in a life style, certainly no easy task, persuades and produces the new life style, which is actively adapted, not entirely to the existing reality, but to the growing, becoming reality. In this view, there is no longer room for doubting that intelligence is capable of diverting drives of the unconscious to another goal. Do we not often see how even the illusion of a conviction is capable of diverting drives to false goals?

The Creative Power of the Child

The assumption of an evil principle, active in each individual, plays only too well into the hands of those elements who have set their goal on the domination and subjugation of others. By nature, man is neither good nor evil. All his traits show themselves as socially oriented and thus betray their origin in the relationship to his environment. They are not innate but acquired "in the stream of the world."

What happens to be innate is never immediately visible, but always, beginning with the first day of birth, intermingled with the mutual relation of mother and child. We include here the quality of the organs and their correlation with the external necessities, which is always experienced as a feeling of tension between organ quality and external demand. The child, without finding words or concepts for it, uses the innate component for active equalization as a building stone. The child, not a calculating machine, proceeds by trying out the situation, by tentative estimates, until he finds an approximately satisfactory way. Always streaming toward a goal of enhancement and perfection, he also finds this goal in a more earthly, more concrete form. Should I add that this is always within the frame of the humanly comprehensible and possible? Not what a child brings with him, but what he makes of it, is decisive for his life style.

Likewise, the influences from without, the milieu, can be considered only as building stones, received and used by the child freely for the same goal of superiority. Individual Psychology is a psychology of use and differs sharply from instinct, drive, or hereditary psychologies, which are essentially psychologies of possession.

What is decisive is the divining factor in the creative power of the child, his creative intuition. Possibly this also has hereditary elements at its basis. But the cultivation and development of these is left to a high degree to education in the broadest sense. This means not only bringing favorable influences to bear, but also having to keep a sharp watch to see how the child uses them, in order to intervene further, if necessary.

The connection we find so often between organ inferiorities or environmental influences and failures shows primarily how easily the creative power of the child can be led to incorrect ways if a correct educational method does not provide a counterbalance.

Since each child represents a finely-shaded problem, it is not surprising that generally well-regarded educational measures sometimes prove inadequate. This holds for all forms of education, religious as well as secular, or those scientifically tested. If the life style of a real fellow man, interested in the common weal, is not achieved in early childhood, for which there is probably no uniform prescription, one will always witness the inadequate ability of such a person to participate properly in the tasks of mankind, both small and large.

Certain educational measures, such as those of incompetent authority, severity, and pampering, as well as hereditary organ inferiorities, are very often observed in connection with failures. This is related to our presently inadequate influence in helping to develop fellowship in time, in spite of adverse circumstances. But this can be understood only in a statistically given probability, not as a causally comprehensible law of direct relationship. The reason is that the factor of the creative intuition of the child, incalculable and not operating in causal lawfulness, is inserted between experience and its elaboration.

Herbart's view of the dependency of character formation on the train of thought may seem "intellectualistic" and therefore inadequate. From our view of the unity of the individual, a complete understanding and clearing of the conflicting forces is unthinkable without a simultaneous change of the entire life style. The same holds for Kerschensteiner's fourfold division of the character concept into will power, clarity of judgment, sensitiveness, and emotionality. If one has mastered the art of education, the ministry, or treatment, he can start at any visible point of psychological life and be successful. To be sure, he can do this only with the help of the subject, who is always supplementing and structuring the instruction he receives so that his cooperation counts as well and must be carefully checked. Thus one may believe he is treating an isolated symptom, such as will power; but if he has seen correctly, his treatment will carry over to the whole.

Strengthening Social Interest, rather than Inhibiting Bad Impulses

I believe that Individual Psychology, by its clear formulation of the concept of "community" (*Gemeinschaft*), has given a clearer meaning to older findings. It is not a matter of words or concepts. Whether one sees the human ideal as "moral self-assertion" or as "self-denial," social (community) interest comes to life only when it proves itself valuable *sub specie aeternitatis* for the welfare of mankind. We can speak of self-assertion or self-denial only in situations in which social interest is taxed particularly severely. To use and alter a well-known saying: social interest must happen like breathing. Since Individual Psychology does not think only of family community and school community, as Jahn emphasizes, but rather wants to have these two understood as training for life in the community of mankind, it must pay particular attention to family and school life in order to prevent and correct failures.

Also, in the question of sublimation I must go one step further than Jahn. Freud believes that we are moved by social reprehensible pleasure-bringing drive components, by which he means sex drives which are sadistic and attached to certain parts of the body. The possibility of sublimating these, in our sense of using them for the benefit of the community, can be carried through honestly only when the subject's social interest grows. If one should succeed in bringing about a sublimation, as Fourier, Nietzsche, and also Freud proposed, while contradicting or even counteracting our formulation regarding the necessary increase of social interest—then the egg was smarter than the chicken: the patient increased his social interest against the will and intention of the therapist.

Jahn says that Individual Psychology has in fact recognized that the establishment and elimination of inhibitions are among the cardinal tasks of guidance. This would presuppose that an individual "by his very nature" must fight against bad impulses. This I cannot wholly affirm. We find inhibitions, or lack of them, only in individuals who do not have enough social interest. Although the ideal amount of social interest is hardly ever found, there would be no necessity to speak of overly strong or weak inhibitions unless there was an evident lack of social interest. If one succeeds in strengthening the latter, inhibitions in either direction are no longer a matter of concern.

I do not have much hope that the establishment of inhibitions by threats, punishment, etc., without the strengthening of social interest, could contribute to the change of a personality, unless the subject discovered the significance of social interest by himself through his own understanding—the egg being smarter than the hen. In this, one can help him better through Individual Psychology instruction.

Likewise, pathological inhibitions, which run counter to cooperation, can hardly be removed otherwise than by teaching the one so afflicted to forget himself, his vanity, his fear that his glory might be hurt, and to devote himself entirely to the task from which he is shying away. Not the inhibitions, but the lack of connectedness with the whole must be treated. Jahn understands this, too, when he agrees with Individual Psychology in teaching the patient to make his peace with mankind.

Jahn speaks of the "necessity of rules to prevent an overgrowth of man's drive nature, making the individual an absolute," and believes that such prevention is not guaranteed through the striving for an ideal community, especially not in the adolescent who is not yet free, not fully mature. My reply is: I see presently no possibility of carrying out an immediate maturation of mankind. But I see it as the task of the mature individual to protect society from damage through the immature and to do everything toward their maturation. The person who strives for the ideal condition needs no further rules, any more than he does for breathing. He will never be a fully finished person; he will always be seeking. But he will always weigh his course carefully by means of his intelligence and that of others.

Jahn seems to me to be too much entangled in the bonds of drive psychology. One must ask oneself from where the drives receive their direction. As we understand it, the drive has no direction; it is the drive psychologist who anthropomorphizes the drive into a ready demon which possesses intelligence, selectivity, direction, a life of its own. In short, he represents a complete self, equipped with cunning and tricks. The displacement of the self into the drive is carried to a fantastic degree.

Individual Psychology sees these things much more clearly; I would say much more deeply, if this term had not already been claimed prematurely and unessentially by a psychology which seeks superficial and strict rules. The drive, in so far as we can disregard its abstract nature, is a part of the self-consistent personality, like character, thinking, feeling, volition, doubt, emotion, or action. The drive thus depends on the law of movement of the individual. The drive receives its direction from the totality and can be changed only simultaneously with the self-consistent personality. The change takes place on the way to a better understanding of the meaning of life.

The Unethical Nature of Neurotic Guilt Feelings

The neurosis, or rather the neurotic symptom, appears always in the face of a social problem, never in a favorable situation, as our experience has shown. In the face of the exogenous factor the inferiority complex shows itself as in an examination of one who is poorly prepared. As far as I can see, this finding of ours is rather generally accepted. The problem at hand is not solved, but leads to an enormous psychological tension on account of the threatening defeat because the erring individual does not muster what the life problems require: social interest and cooperation. The shock he experiences as soon as he feels socially unprepared transforms body and soul into disastrous vibrations. But the confusion which ensues, the reflex (according to Pavlov), the disturbed equilibrium, are not yet a neurosis. They are human reactions, differing only according to constitution, bodily and psychological structure.

Now the question arises: What will follow? What position does the unity of the individual take toward this often deep-reaching change, in order nevertheless to rescue the self-esteem, to carry out the striving for superiority? In our view, socially poorly-prepared persons will not in this situation strive for a solution of the problem at hand, for which more social interest is required than they possess. Rather they find relief by coming to terms with the disturbance which has arisen, remain with it and use it as justification for declining a solution because they fear defeat more than they expect success. Thus they secure distance from the solution of a feared problem by consolidating the disturbance which has arisen in a shock-like manner. They make a detour towards the side which appears easier to them. In doing this, it is not that they "make" the symptoms, as it appears to most psychiatrists and psychologists, but rather that they do not feel a real inclination to give up a solution which they feel is easier.

In this way they not only have a clear conscience, but are not disturbed in their striving toward apparent personal superiority, since they consider their lack of cooperation justified by pointing out their suffering. They feel that their personal superiority is impeded only by their suffering.

This feeling of personal superiority and the claim to it, blocked only by illness, is in many cases increased because the sufferer attributes the blame to himself. He gladly adds a guilt feeling, conscience pangs, an ethical uplift to his other neurotic symptoms, thus rendering himself still less suited for the community because he remains with these as with his other symptoms instead of getting to work, which would obviously be more important.

Take the following case. A man, an only child, was very spoiled by his parents who always impressed upon him what a wonder child he was and what a high position he would hold some day. As one might expect, from lack of proper development of social interest he foundered on the three problems of life which involve the community, occupation, and love. Since he could not be the first, as he expected from childhood, without useful effort—useful to others—he withdrew more and more into his family and eliminated from his life friendship, vocation, and women. The shock when he came up against these problems was unusually strong. He lost all interest in reality and gave himself up to various dreams in which he excelled over all others.

Physically healthy, he was as a pampered child especially subject to the sex drive. But his sexual demand endangered his desired seclusion from the environment in which his exaggerated idea of greatness seemed certain of defeat. Urged by the sex drive outward, but blocked off from the outer world by the fear of being without personal triumph, he found in the confusion of his feelings only one woman whom he could command. This was his mother, of whose pampering he could be certain.

Now his guilt feeling set in, especially since his father was in his way. Proof of an Oedipus complex, the reader may say. In reality it is the wish of a pampered child to realize immediately the fulfillment of his wishes without regard for the community.

The impossibility to fulfill his desire brought him to the point where he hated his mother. He heaped all kinds of reproaches on her, developed a weakly aggressive attitude toward her, and arrived at the obsession that he might kill her whenever he saw a knife. I said "weakly," because in his ever unrealized idea not even the strength of an open insult can be found, as for example, if he had cursed her, saying, "I could kill you." Sexuality, which obliged him to participate in the community, appeared to him the worst evil, as shown by his present goal of superiority, which was to retreat in order to escape any danger to his vanity.

Thus he developed a further guilt feeling by assuming that he had ruined himself for life by excessive masturbation. (Excessive masturbation also corresponds to the tendency of the pampered child to let no enjoyment escape him.) Is it so difficult to understand that his cumulated guilt feeling only forced him further to cut himself off from the environment? Is it not clear that he felt high above those who had gone through something similar but without carrying the armor of ethics?

Conscience pangs and guilt feelings are signs of reluctant and twisted ethics. Otherwise they would justly be the occasion for a strengthening of social interest. As it is, they are only suited to serve as a strengthening of the neurotic symptoms. This becomes most obvious in depression. In view of these facts, one should not in these cases use such big words as conscience, guilt feelings, or ethical struggles.

When Jahn says the ego gains (during catharsis) an insight into itself which was formerly hidden from it, this really includes the way in which the insight of change has to proceed. Insight without the arousal of affects (and a corresponding attitude) is according to our findings not possible. Even if the insight does not go so deep as to eliminate the erring way, it will nevertheless always remain effective as an accompaniment of the mistake. The important thing is in which direction the counsellee has developed his life style more strongly, where his greater interest lies, whether in thinking, feeling, or willing. All these functions are connected and parallel, conforming with his law of movement, only that sometimes one, and sometimes another, is more strongly emphasized in the focus of the individual as well as, unfortunately, in the focus of the counselor. In the counsellee one will find change in accordance with his life style, sometimes more clearly in thinking, sometimes in feeling or action. I prefer the change in action. It gives more evidence of the change than all other functions.

In favor of this view I would abandon strained, hair-splitting thought attempts and outbursts of feelings. This also includes the notion that "the individual becomes frightened by his own abysmalness."

It is in the nature of all religions to emphasize the feeling process over all other expressive movements. But in our form of advancing the individual it is better to forego the contrition of the erring, in the conviction that it will at least delay the proper action, if not prevent it. The stronger emphasis on understanding in our form of treatment, on comprehending mistakes which are today still generally human, prevents the counsellee from becoming frightened.

The view of contrition as something desirable seems to me to date from the once quite general idea that man's improvement depends exclusively on his suffering, on his punishment. But today we are attempting to mitigate this idea even in our laws. Could it be that these two diverse viewpoints reflect the difference between the rigorous Prussian tradition and the more friendly way of life of the Viennese? In any event, we can draw conclusions regarding the "increase in worth" of the reborn personality not through his emotional overflow, but only through his conduct.

Contrition and despair represent a very difficult way to purify man. To these and other rather unfriendly terms Jahn adds a new one, "fall and death of the ego." I know the depth and impact of metaphorical expression too well to underestimate their effect. But I also know that, outside of art, metaphorical expression can be a dangerous means to deceive oneself and others regarding reality. I later found this view was also generally accepted in linguistic circles. I am not affected by careless people accusing me of having presented poets as liars. Where it is proper to inflame feelings, the poetic phrase is well in place. Probably also in religion. But it must remain prohibited in science, in the awakening of understanding. In this sense I have also pointed to the danger of the metaphorical expression, because it is a means to take the critical common sense by surprise—and to remain with the old way of living as under the effect of intoxication. The dream with its poetic similes is also a means of this sort.

One should also make a sharp distinction between inferiority feeling and inferiority complex. The inferiority feeling never leaves a person. It becomes an inferiority complex only if its bearer proves his inadequacy to solve a life problem of a social structure from lack of adequate social interest. What becomes evident is always a failure, be it neurosis or crime.

The inferiority complex appears in the face of an exogenous burden which is too heavy, in persons who in their form of life have always shown a strong inferiority feeling. Due to their unfavorable start in childhood their interest in their own person grows so strong that it becomes more or less impossible for an interest in others to develop. Thus "asocial conduct" is inseparably connected with serious inferiority feeling and shows itself sooner or later in the form of crime or in another form occasioned by an outer releasing cause, always in the form demanded by the life style of the individual. I cannot discuss here in detail this important fact, how the form of the error fits the life style. In the volumes of the *Internationale Zeitschrift für Individualpsychologie* (Leipzig: Hirzel) I have illuminated this connection in detail. As far as the criminal is concerned, one will always be able to observe in his life style a degree of activity which can be traced back to childhood.

Self-Boundedness, an Artifact of Education

Self-boundedness (*Ichgebundenheit*) is the central point of attack of Individual Psychology, as Jahn has seen correctly. The self-bound individual always forgets that his self would be safeguarded the better and more automatically, the more he would prepare himself for the welfare of mankind, and that in this respect no limits are set for him. The numerous quotations from the Bible are confirmations for which to be grateful. They are the deep insight of sublime leaders of man into the foundations of human welfare, and express in an imposing way much of what Individual Psychology attempts to make available to thought through modest scientific work.

What I was able to say earlier about finding God is confirmed in the writings of Emil Brunner. Brunner declares that through his call

God ties man to Him, the creator, and thereby ties man at the same time to man. We find, similarly, that the goal of perfection can be thought of only in community with the welfare of all mankind.

According to Jahn, he who loves God must love man, and love of man springs from love of God. I believe I am in accord with Jahn when I supplement this sentence to the effect that here again it is a question of the proper understanding of this love. Without having attained this understanding, the goal of God, religion, can be abused, as Individual Psychology can be.[9]

We agree completely with Jahn's sentence that the danger of self-love rests in its penetration to most subtle religious-ethical motives. Obviously, in this event only the exact knowledge of an abuse can bring change, as well as the realization of the necessity that social interest must be increased.

On the other hand, I must considerably expand Jahn's assertion that for psychological research self-boundedness is a psychological datum. According to Luther, self-boundedness is guilt. Individual Psychology maintains that the self, not the self-boundedness, in its striving for ideal perfection is capable of development, however, only if this striving takes the direction of the common weal. Viewing the present state of culture I find that this striving must be developed much more strongly. There is too little knowledge or true scientific understanding of this striving for it to be sufficiently alive. Individual Psychology does not want to judge, but to be of scientific help. It is not its place to administer praise and criticism. Therefore I do not speak of guilt but only of error, originating in childhood and continuing especially because this erroneous conduct is not even formulated into words or concepts and for this reason remains removed from the attack of awakening reasoning. I would rather attribute guilt to those who have recognized this fact, or had the opportunity to recognize it and yet have not contributed sufficiently toward change.

wwwwwwwwww

9. Such abuse of religion has recently been explicated by G. W. Allport (*Personality and social encounter*. Boston: Beacon Press, 1960). In the many obvious cases where a religious attitude is found with otherwise undesirable attitudes, he finds that the master-motive is self-interest, while religion plays only an instrumental role. He calls this *extrinsic* religion (p. 264). It is contrasted with *intrinsic* religion which "marks the life that has interiorized . . . the commandment to love one's neighbor. A person of this sort is more intent on serving his religion than on making it serve him" (p. 257).

Self-boundedness is an artifact thrust upon the child during his education and by the present state of our social structure. The creative power of the child is misled towards self-boundedness. Teachers, ministers, and physicians must be freed from their own self-boundedness and, together with all those who want to work honestly for the common welfare, must prevent these seductions of the child. Until that time, it will always be the single case only which will find its way to the physician, and not before the error of the child has led to considerable damage to all.

The point of attack for such a movement would have to be first of all the school. For the time being, parallel movements of guidance through all qualified persons such as parents, physicians, ministers, and especially trained aides should be considered as indispensable help. The beginning would have to be made in kindergarten. The goal should be that no child could leave school without the assurance of being a real fellow man.

I would also like to elaborate on two further statements by Jahn. He says that states of anxiety by which a person is tortured are, according to our interpretation, aftereffects of anxiety-laden inhibitions which once were imposed on the soul of the child. In the realm of psychological strivings and movements Individual Psychology avoids all laws but the law of movement of the individual. As I have shown, anxiety is the justified or unjustified anticipation or hallucination of a danger. If the individual is tied to his individually conceived goal of superiority—whatever it may contain—there is in the broadest sense only one danger: that he becomes diverted from his goal, i.e., experiences what is for him a defeat.

A deviant goal will show itself to be pathological in all its partial manifestations. An actual life-danger will fill almost everyone with the feeling of fear, but pathological fear of a defeat indicates self-boundedness, arrogance, and discouragement, a goal of personal superiority.

The most frequent seduction toward such a goal, I have found, is the pampering of children within the family, which at the same time excludes the child's cooperation and leaves it undeveloped. Besides, the impact of inadequate education strikes those children who through bodily defects are easily driven to think more about themselves than of others. My own presentations (*Study of Organ*

Inferiority) and others, often parallel with those of Kretschmer, give a picture of the importance of these facts. [Further, hated children are particularly susceptible to goals of personal superiority.] But complete lack of social interest in the environment, or wholly hated children, are seldom found. This is a bright spot in the social structure of our society, perhaps because a wholly hated child could hardly remain alive for any length of time.

The pathological anxiety which we find in patients is always the fear of loss of the goal of superiority, of loss of self-esteem. Although the structure of the anxiety is individually different in each case, it can perhaps always be traced to an excessive longing to be pampered and to a lack in ability to cooperate, which expresses itself in wanting to take and not wanting to give.

Education for Ideal Cooperation, rather than Love

The striving for perfection is toward the solution of life problems in the interest of the evolution of the individual as well as of mankind; it is supported by the weakness of the child and his ever-present inferiority feeling. Individual Psychology postulates that this striving is the psychological archetype of the human line of movement, and reckons with a millionfold variation of it. A large part of this line of movement can be regarded as the striving for personal power, a movement-form which lacks the proper degree of social interest in varying degrees, must therefore be designated as erroneous, and carries in itself the sign of later inadequacy in the event of an emerging social problem.

The only salvation from the continuously driving inferiority feeling is the knowledge and the feeling of being valuable which originates from the contribution to the common welfare. This feeling of being valuable cannot be replaced by anything else. Similarly, in the general human striving to hold on to fleeting time, not to disappear completely from the community of men, it is the contribution to the general welfare (children, work) which holds promise for the claim of immortality.

The spirit of our ancestors who have contributed to the welfare of mankind continues to live on among us.

When Jahn says courage is only where there is confidence, one is tempted to say in reverse that confidence is only where there is courage. It seems that in this way we do not get any further. Individual Psychology with its goal of the common weal believes that everyone who has once recognized this goal as the effective pre-supposition for the development of mankind will seek to gain his own development, his worth, his happiness only according to this pre-supposition. He will regard all difficulties of life, whether they originate within himself or outside his person, as his task, to be solved by him. He will, so to speak, feel at home on this poor earth crust, "in his father's house." Thus he will regard not only the comforts but also the discomforts of this life, which come to him and to others, as belonging to him, and will cooperate in their solution. He will be a courageous fellow man, a co-worker, without asking for any other recompense than that which he bears within himself. But his work, his contribution to the common weal is immortal, his spirit will never perish.

Anyone capable through his creative power of constructing with artistic perfection a useless, mistaken life style, previously hardly understood, is also capable of changing himself and of producing a generally useful form of life. Being one with the world and man, understanding the relationship to human society, to occupation, and to love, then shows him the way which leads him higher. That is why Individual Psychology does not demand fitting into the community "along with" encouragement, but maintains that courage is one of the many sides of community.

I should like to join with Jahn in correcting the misinterpretation of certain meddlesome critics that Individual Psychology wants to educate the child for our present-day community or for any one of the present-day communities. This would mean the end to a higher development of human society. Individual Psychology educates for a real community for which one must work and strive. Among the present-day community efforts it will give recognition only to those which lie in the direction of an ideal community, which although never attainable will still be effective as a goal.

Unquestionably doubts in various directions are possible regarding the value of the present-day efforts for community. I would recognize as valuable any of these efforts provided it strives honestly for the common weal. Thus we would accept as worthwhile only the kind of "education community" which offers preparation for being the fellow man of the future.

To see it clearly: The relaxation of the tensed soul does not happen through the healing power of love. The healing process is much more difficult. Else it would be enough to surround every problem child, the neurotic, the alcoholic, the sexual pervert, with love in order to cure him.

Also, the word "love" has far too many meanings, meaning for many sexual libido, for others pampering, for some humaneness. Individual Psychology wants to train fellow men; it must therefore prove its fellowmanship in its dealing with the erring. Only in this spirit can the erring individual be won for cooperation; only in this way is it possible to give him a clear understanding of his mistaken style of life. The healing process must begin with winning the erring human child for cooperation. But the cure occurs as the very own work of the subject treated, after he has gained adequate understanding.

Once again: Individual Psychology as science must not use religious dogmas; it must leave Christian guidance to those qualified for it. But it cannot banish God from the world. And it must also reckon with the man-earth relationship. Individual Psychology considers itself qualified for this relationship. It will always welcome the chance to make its experiences available to the minister as well as to all educators of mankind. The qualms of Jahn in this respect obviously arose through false information.

I have always felt certain that the neurotic condition is not the unavoidable result of environment and development, and that development is not determined by fate. And I have shown that in psychological life there is no strict causality, but that everything which looks like a causal event in the existence of the individual—such as organ inferiorities or educational and environmental factors—is made into a cause by the creative power of the child. The child uses all experiences of hereditary and educational influences in free artistic creation for the construction of a self-consistent form of life. Only this form of life gives to all expressive movements their meaning and direction. That is why to educate means not only to bring favorable influences to bear, but also to keep a sharp watch to see how the child uses them, in order to intervene further, if necessary. If beginning with the first day the child has been brought to cooperate, then his creative urge will not desert this way. It will be otherwise under different circumstances.

The difficulty in our society to find the right way has been repeatedly emphasized by me. The deviation, the child's mistake in the construction of his life style, can be measured only by his distance from social interest, which must be learned or trained. All character traits have most fundamentally a social meaning. Man is not born good or evil, but he can be trained in either direction. Whose fault is greater? That of the erring community or that of the erring child? When I have repeatedly pointed to the frequent connection between organ inferiority, pampering, and neglect with failures, I have at the same time always warned that one should not see more in this than statistical probabilities, in the broadest sense, and should keep aware of individual differences, including the frequent avoidance of failures in all these cases. These observations of mine are meant to serve as illumination of the field in which the individual case in his uniqueness is to be found—or missed. The free decision is left to the erring individual as soon as one succeeds in winning him for cooperation in correcting the mistake.

Jahn is right when he says one should not limit oneself to telling the disturber of the community that the cause of his hatred for the community is his self-boundedness. He would understand this as little as many critics of Individual Psychology. One will have to convince him of this through subtle consideration of his development and his life style. But we are also convinced that the criminal is not cured by telling him that this self-boundedness is his fault and that therefore he is responsible for his self-boundedness. The responsibility of the erring individual begins, as we see it, at the moment in which he recognizes his lacking community sense and its faulty effects.

CLOSING WORDS

May I finally say that I regard it as no mean commendation when Jahn emphasizes that Individual Psychology has rediscovered many a lost position of Christian guidance. I have always endeavored to show that Individual Psychology is the heir to all great movements whose aim is the welfare of mankind. Although its scientific foundation obligates it to a certain intransigence, Individual Psychology according to its whole nature is eager to receive stimulation from all fields of knowledge and experience, and to return the stimulation. In this sense it has always been a liaison work. It is connected with all great movements through the common urge which guides the development of every science and technology, the urge toward a higher development of mankind and the welfare of all.[9a]

wwwwwwwwwwww

9a. The same thought is expressed most succinctly in a letter by Adler, written in English, dated April 3, 1933, in reply to a letter by the Reverend Edgar B. Rohr-bach, with whom he subsequently became very friendly. Adler's letter reads:

"Dear unknown friend, I am glad to know one man in the church who has so thoroughly understood how Individual Psychology struggles hard to interpret in a scientific way the highest ideals in the right development of mankind. What I had been working out had been only a contribution in *understanding* what mankind had known in the main parts long ago and what has created all the great streams in mankind, the high good of mankind in the current of evolution. Yours sincerely, Adler" (*J. Indiv. Psychol.*, 1966, 22, 234).

PART VI

Alfred Adler:
A Biographical Essay
by Carl Furtmüller

EDITORIAL INTRODUCTION

Adler was fully convinced that in the study of man, man's potentialities must be imaginatively explored to provide a plan for his *becoming*. He would have approved of Allport's (1955) book by this title. Adler was not the cold, detached scientist who held to what Dewey called a "spectator theory of knowledge" (Feuer, 1960, p. 125), which in positivistic fashion is interested in establishing only what *is*. Not the being, but the urge toward becoming was for Adler the species-specific fact of human nature. And he insisted that the science of psychology should be committed to making a great contribution toward steering this becoming, the individual and societal evolution, in a direction which promised the welfare of all. Thus he was in his scientific endeavors the warm participant, fully aware of the psychologist's responsibility regarding the future of mankind and its betterment.

No wonder there was an affinity between Adler and those who were committed to other areas which traditionally had the same concerns, the areas of religion and the progressive political parties, in addition to education.

Even before his interests had turned toward psychology, while writing as a physician, Adler was oriented toward action for social betterment. In one of his first publications, entitled "The Penetration of Social Forces into Medicine" (A1902), he pointed out that the discovery of bacteria as a cause of disease and the discovery of the conditions under which bacteria thrive brought the science of medicine face to face with social misery. Consequently the development of prophylactic public health efforts beyond measures of sanitation coincided with trends toward improvement of social conditions in general. Adler distinguished four such trends: (a) "Higher standards of living of the disowned classes, shorter hours, Sunday rest, expansion of hospital facilities, sickness insurance, old-age care, accident insurance, homes for children, increase and improvement of the public schools, etc." (b) Relief of the poor. (c) "Rise of the working class. Its increasing intelligence, progressing organization, and realization of common interests are leading this class to demands which, raised in the fight for civil rights and against expropriation, naturally prove to be eminently hygienic demands." (d) A fourth social trend would be the union of the medical profession. "Only when this joins with the other trends would security and clear-sighted action in medicine begin. Only then would mankind advance . . . from the period of timid, difficult, often hopeless therapy, toward the period of confident prophylaxis; from the period of weakness . . . to the period of purposeful action." This paper appeared on page one, number one, of a new journal devoted to the interests of the physicians of Austria. Its policy statement included, "to strengthen the solidarity feeling among physicians and, through first-class organizations, form them into an army whose wishes cannot simply be ignored" (Grün, 1902).

In Adler's time and place, those politically most interested in human betterment and progress gathered under the name of socialism. Eventually, one-third and more of the people of Vienna voted the Social-Democratic ticket, and since World War I the freely elected city governments of Vienna have been socialistic. Beginning with his youth, Adler's sympathies were with the socialists.

But as one whose endeavor was also that of a scientist, although a committed scientist, Adler saw himself eventually obliged to draw a clear line between Individual Psychology and religion as well as between Individual Psychology and socialism. While he welcomed the use that both could make of his psychology, he fought against it becoming identified with either. This led to a break with some of the socialists in his circle and with others who were strongly religiously oriented (Bottome, 1957, pp. 169–174).

In the preceding essay on "Religion and Individual Psychology" (pp. 274–308), Adler presented his stand toward religion. But he never did the same with regard to socialism. One of the merits of the present biography is that it includes at least a brief discussion of Adler's relationship to socialism by his closest friend, himself a socialist. We learn that Adler was attracted by Marx's sociological rather than his economic views and that he always retained a certain aloofness from party matters, although immediately after World War I he held for a short while a minor political office. According to all accounts he was a member of the Social-Democratic party until the 1920's, when it gradually lost importance for him.

Adler's Socialism and its Meaning

Since the question of Adler's socialism has come up again and again in the literature, we are taking the present occasion to go further into the matter.

Objective evidence of Adler's socialism, supplementing Furtmüller's account, can be seen in Adler's occasional contribution of psychological articles to socialist periodicals and newspapers (e.g., A1905a, A1908c, A1923b, A1924a, A1925c), in his use of Marxist terms, in his interest in Marxism, and in some outright statements. In 1909 he read a paper before the Vienna Psychoanalytic Society on "The Psychology of Marxism" (Jones, 1957, p. 336). This paper has not been found, but its content is preserved in the careful and adequate minutes kept by Otto Rank.[1] According to these minutes, Adler expressed his admiration for Marx's psychological insight, crediting him with the first mass analysis, and showing how Marx's ideas could be interpreted in terms of drives.

At a later time, Adler (A1918e, p. 598) expressed himself similarly with regard to his high opinion of Marx's psychological discoveries, although he now traced the basis for the conceptual kinship through goals and social interest. "Only in socialism did social sense (*Gemeinsinn*), as the demand for unhindered human living together, remain the final goal and purpose. All the ingenious socialistic Utopians who sought or found systems, as well as all great reformers of mankind, instinctively placed mutual advancement

---

1. We are greatly indebted to Ernst Federn for making these minutes, in German, available to us. They have now been published in English (A1909d).

above the struggle for power. And Karl Marx discovered in the dark workings of psychological life the common struggle of the proletariat against class rule. He elevated this struggle forever into the consciousness of its bearers and showed the way toward the final realization of social interest."

What socialism actually meant to him is well reflected in the following lines by Adler (A1907b, p. 33) which are very much in the style and vocabulary of the socialists of that time. The meaning was a striving for and belief in a better future for all. The lines, rendered here for the first time in English, are found at the beginning of a paper on organic defects of children, addressed to parents. "In our children rests the future of the people! All the production of peoples, all urging forward, the destruction of old barriers and prejudices, usually happen for the sake of the progeny and are meant first of all to help them. While today the struggle for the freedom of the mind rages, while we are shaking the pillars of superstition and serfdom, tomorrow our children will sun themselves in the mild light of freedom and drink from the fountains of pure knowledge, unconcerned about the threats of a decaying manner of thinking. Whereas today the old and rotten collapses, having lost its right of existence, some day the church of true humaneness will arise more proud and daring than our thoughts can comprehend, before which any falsehood and deceit will evaporate. For our children! They shall enjoy that to which we yearningly aspire: air, light, nourishment, which today are still kept from the people—our children shall fully partake of them! We are fighting for healthy housing, adequate wages, for the dignity of labor, for solid knowledge, that these may some day be assured for our children. Our sweat is their peace; their health is our struggle."

Separation from Socialism

Adler, then, was clearly attracted to socialism by its humanistic side. He was also completely identified with the democratic tradition that was an important part of socialism in Germany and Austria (Lichtheim, 1961, p. 264).

When communism ascended to power in Russia, Adler (A1918e, p. 600) immediately took his stand against it, on account of its use of power rather than democratic principles. Referring to the Bolshevists, he wrote: "This party . . . pursues goals which are also ours. But the intoxication of power has seduced them. . . . We see former friends, old brave fellow travelers, in dizzy heights. Seduced by the power drive, they arouse everywhere the demand for power. . . . If there are means to call them back, it can only be the remembrance of the miracle of social feelings, a miracle which we must perform and which will never succeed through the use of power. For us the way and the tactics result from our highest goal: the cultivation and strengthening of social feelings."

We do not know whom specifically Adler may have meant by "former friends . . . in dizzy heights." But we do know that A. A. Joffe, a close associate of Leon Trotsky in prewar days in Vienna, and his wife were good friends of the Adler family (personal communication from Mrs. Adler, April 21, 1961), and that he was also a patient of Adler (Trotsky, 1960, p. 220). After the Russian revolution Joffe headed the first Soviet peace delegation at Brest-Litovsk and later was Soviet ambassador to Japan (Trotsky, 1960, pp. 363 and 535).

While the radical Marxist wing became guilty of endorsing the excesses of the Bolshevists in Russia, the moderate Social-Democratic majority had for years settled down to an optimistic determinism. The understanding was that the elemental forces in the social process would spontaneously work out all right, without the necessity of individuals exerting themselves for such an outcome (Bauer, 1952, pp. 13–20; Lichtheim, 1961, pp. 235–238). This had started at the turn of the century under the name of "scientific socialism," when scientific meant adherence to a strictly deterministic view. This determinism, incidentally, has often been made responsible for the fatalistic inactivity with which the Social-Democratic parties, strong and powerful though they were, faced the threat of fascism (Bauer, 1952, p. 16n; Lichtheim, 1961, pp. 243 & 267).

Adler was, of course, in agreement with the democratic orientation and the optimism. And at the beginning of his writings he also found no fault with the determinism; this was the unquestioningly accepted orientation in science. But gradually he recognized the necessity for postulating the relative autonomy of the self, the "creative power of the individual."

Determinism had first become an issue in Adler's controversy with

Freud, of whom, in 1911, he asked the question: "Is the driving factor in the neurosis the repression, or is it . . . the deviating, irritated psyche, in the examination of which repression can also be found?" (A1956b, p. 61).

Determinism also became an issue with regard to the socialists. Since their determinism was one of optimism, Adler countered it by insisting that man makes mistakes. How could this be so if man were completely determined? Adler (A1927a, p. 19) accepted "as one of the basic facts for the understanding of human nature that we must take the immanent rules of the game of a group . . . as an absolute truth," and continued, "An important part of these basic facts is noted in the materialistic view of history which Marx and Engels have created. According to this theory it is the economic foundation, the technical form, in which a people gains its livelihood, which determines the 'ideological superstructure,' the thinking and behavior of man. To this extent there is agreement with our view of the effective 'logic of man's living together,' of the 'absolute truth.'"

"But," Adler went on, "we learn from history, especially from our insight into the individual life . . . that the human psyche is likely to respond with errors to the impulsions of the economic foundations, errors from which it escapes but slowly. Our path to the 'absolute truth' leads via numerous errors." This was his restrained answer to determinism.

This quotation is from *Menschenkenntnis*,[2] the book based on lecture series before lay audiences at the *Volksheim*, the Vienna adult education institution, which audiences can be assumed to have included a good many Social-Democrats. As if to point quite definitely to what he meant by this passage, single comment though it is, Adler (A1927a, p. iii) stated in the preface: "The main purpose of this book will have to be sought in understanding the shortcomings of our efforts and accomplishments in terms of society through the erroneous behavior of the individual; in recognizing these mistakes; and in bringing about a better adaptation into the social context." Thus Adler confronted the notion of the social determinism of the individual, through which society would carry the full blame for

2. New translations from the German edition (A1927a) are used here, rather than quotations from the English edition, *Understanding Human Nature* (A1927b), to do more justice to certain important nuances.

the shortcomings of the individual, with the proposition that it is the errors of individuals which determine the shortcomings of society. Thereby he placed responsibility with the individual in addition to the social determinants.

Elsewhere Adler expressed this difference from environmental determinism as follows: "More important than disposition, objective experience and milieu is *their subjective evaluation*; and furthermore, this evaluation stands in a certain, although often strange, relation to the realities. In mass psychology it is difficult to discover this fundamental fact because the 'ideological superstructure over the economic foundation' (Marx and Engels) and its effects force an equalization of individual differences" (A1924j, p. 4). In the English translation (A1925a, p. 6) this crucial second sentence is not included.

The fatalistic determinism of the moderate socialists, on the one hand, and the endorsement of the use of violence by the radical socialists, on the other hand, were undoubtedly involved when, during the 1920's, Adler gradually separated himself from the socialists in order to preserve the integrity of his theoretical and practical endeavors as a psychologist. Still he remained in sympathy with the humanistic socialist goals and occasionally wrote for the socialist daily newspaper, the *Arbeiter-Zeitung*, as late as 1925. He also continued to attribute great importance to all environmental factors. But these, like heredity, were not seen as the molders of the individual; rather they were considered building material from which the individual creatively constructs his own unique style of life.

Polemics by Opponents

From the start there was a tendency among Adler's opponents to discredit and dispose of his theories by pointing to his socialism. He only once replied to these aspersions. On that occasion Adler (A1928k, p. 24 n.) acknowledged his "well-known socialist world philosophy," commenting that Freud wrote about it with "polemical intention."

This polemical intention has persisted and can still be seen today. One recent example is in the *Minutes of the Vienna Psychoanalytic Society*. The editors, Herman Nunberg and Ernst Federn (1962), make a commendable effort to be fair and objective on this issue.

Thus, while they mention that Adler was a socialist, they point out that Freud counted socialists among his close friends and "was as familiar as Adler with the socialistic ideas of his time" (pp. 352–353 n.). Elsewhere Ernst Federn (1962, p. 31) also states that his father, Paul Federn, who remained a faithful Freudian all his life, "was a reformer and an active socialist."

And yet, Nunberg and Federn (1962, p. xxxiii) repeat what has frequently been said about Adler, namely, that "in later life, his scientific views became greatly influenced by his political beliefs." Thereby the false impression is created that in later life he had compromised his scientific integrity through his political beliefs.

In fact, however, from his childhood on Adler had been interested in helping man in overcoming his difficulties. This was at the basis of his vocational choice to become a physician, which choice he made while still a small boy (Bottome, 1957, pp. 32–33). Together with this interest was the belief in the possibility of improving the human condition. In his early manhood Adler found in socialism an expression of the same interests and beliefs, as reflected in his paper (A1907b) quoted above (see p. 314). Thirty years later, Adler still maintained his basic conviction of the possibility of human progress, as shown in the first selection of the present volume (A1937g). There is no question but that these two writings are of the same spirit. But whereas he expressed this conviction in the earlier paper in the language of contemporary socialistic writings, in the second paper he was able to formulate it in the concepts of his mature psychological theory. Careful logical analysis of the assumptions and methods of this theory has shown it to be a highly developed humanistic, organismic, and operationally or interactionally oriented psychology, opposed to mechanistic and reductionistic thinking (Ansbacher, 1965).

We may say then that Adler tended to show his socialism in some of his earlier writings. But contrary to Nunberg and Federn, this tendency disappeared rather than increased as he reached a full clarification of his own theory of human nature.

The custom among Adler's opponents of stressing his one-time socialism started with a rationalization by Freud in support of his conviction that he alone proceeded scientifically in his theory construction, while his opponents did not. Freud did not consider the possibility that his was only one possible approach to psychology; that it was a theory only, which, as any other theory, could be questioned; and that it could be anything but the ultimate truth. Thus he wrote in 1913: "Naturally everything that tries to get away from our truths will find approbation among the general public. . . . That will change a great deal in our personal fate, but nothing in that of Science. We possess the truth; I am as sure of it as fifteen years ago" (Jones, 1955, p. 148).

Freud could not admit that Jung and Adler could have refuted essential parts of his theories on scientific grounds, that is, also had "truth" on their side. Thus Freud (1914, p. 352) looked for at least some further, supportive explanations as in the following: "The importance of theological tradition in the former history of so many Swiss is no less significant for their attitude to psychoanalysis than is the socialistic element in that of Adler for the line of development taken by his psychology."

Theory and Life Style

Freud was, of course, right here. A person's approach to psychology will be consistent with his own personal basic assumptions, his philosophy of life, his life style. This is very much in accord with the organismic principle of the individual's self-consistency. But obviously Freud did not consider that his own psychology also would be consistent with his outlook on life. Freud was not sensitive to the problem of reflexivity or self-reference in psychology, i.e., that a psychologist's universal propositions must be applicable to himself (Oliver and Landfield, 1962).

Freud's outlook on life can be described as aristocratic and pessimistic. According to Jones (1953) Freud's boyhood ideals were Hannibal and Napoleon's General Massena (p. 5); and he devoured Thiers' story of Napoleon's power, searching himself for "power over men" (p. 30). Riesman (1955, pp. 229–232) has shown that Freud held views "remarkably similar to those of the great theorist of autocracy, Thomas Hobbes. . . . Like Hobbes, he was afraid of anarchy. . . . The lower classes of human society . . . servants, nurses, porters, and so forth . . . are viewed as dubious rather undifferentiated beings, scarcely credited with personality. . . . Freud tended to view differences as implying relations of super- and subordination" (pp. 229–232).

As empirical evidence in support of the contention of Freud's autocratic world view, his attitude toward Mussolini may be cited. This was essentially positive. When the father of an Italian patient asked Freud to present Mussolini with one of his books, Freud inscribed the volume: "From an old man who greets in the Ruler the Hero of Culture" (Jones, 1957, p. 180; Lehrman, 1963). In sharp contrast, Adler said about Mussolini: "The whipped, starving, unloved slum child becomes a bank robber. . . . The bandit sees himself a romantic hero. . . . And Mussolini becomes dictator through violence, and rules through violence. . . . The more intense the inferiority, the more violent the superiority. This is the equation. Mussolini's life shouts it. . . . It accounts for the threat to the peace of the world . . . and the forcible suppression of all individualistic movements which oppose Fascism or advocate liberalism and democracy and personal liberty or in any way vary from the dictator's formula" (A1926z).

Freud's lack of faith in the average man is confirmed by Fromm (1959, p. 94), and it is in refuting the more optimistic views of man —of Marxist socialism and of religion—that Freud made some of his most pessimistic statements about the nature of man. Against Marx's contention that there is no primary evil component in man which needs to be repressed, and that work, under the proper conditions, is man's most species-specific form of living, his great joy in asserting himself through being creative and constructive, Freud argued "that every culture is based on compulsory labor and instinctual renunciation" (Jones, 1957, p. 344). And against religion Freud (1920, p. 56) found that "what appears in a minority of human individuals as an untiring impulsion towards further perfection can easily be understood as a result of the instinctual repression upon which is based all that is most precious in human civilization."

While it is always interesting to trace the relationship between a man's world philosophy and his scientific theories, for it may help to clarify the theories, it is decidedly unfair to imply that the latter can be reduced to or explained away through the former. Once a theory has come into existence, it must be examined for its own merits if the discussion is to remain on an objective basis. If the personal views of the author are introduced, the argument becomes one *ad hominem,* that is, directed to passions or prejudices rather than to logic.

Such a diversion away from the logic of the issue is exactly what the opponents of Adler are in fact doing when they associate his name in a cliché-like manner with the label of socialism, without associating Freud's name with aristocracy or autocracy. This is what Adler objected to as "polemical intention."

Common Ground between Adler and Marx

Although Adler moved away from the Marxism of his time, his concept of man strikingly approached that of the young Marx. This is all the more interesting since Adler could not have known of this relationship; the relevant early writings of Marx were not published until 1932 and remained little known for a decade or so after their publication (Tucker, 1961, p. 167).

Adler's position was one of man's interaction with objective factors rather than determinism. This had also been Marx's very argument when he first offered his historical materialism as the alternative to a mechanistic materialism which he attacked. "For the early Marx— and in a measure for the mature Marx too—nature and man are complex realities whose interaction is studied in society. This is precisely the reverse of Engels' habit of deducing historical 'laws' from the operation of a nature conceived as an independent reality external to man" (Lichtheim, 1961, p. 251). Accordingly, Marx stated in the third of his famous theses on Feuerbach: "The materialistic doctrine that men are products of circumstances and upbringing . . . forgets that it is men that change circumstances" (Marx & Engels, 1959, p. 244). Adler expressed the same concept, quoting the sentence from Pestalozzi: "The environment molds man, but man molds the environment" (see p. 28).

Actually the passage which Adler quoted from the Swiss educator, who lived from 1746 to 1827, reads: "That much I saw soon, the circumstances make man, but I saw just as soon, man makes the circumstances, he has the power within himself to steer these in a variety of ways according to his will" (Pestalozzi, 1938, p. 57, lines 28–31). Marx and Engels (1953, p. 35), writing in 1846, used the same words: "The circumstances make men just as men make the circumstances."

The renewed interest which Marx is receiving in the Western world today derives largely from this attempt to replace mechanistic materialism with interactionism, or better, organismic thinking. This is also why the original Marx has today been counted among the existentialists. "In modern parlance the Marx of 1844-5 was an 'existentialist' in revolt against Hegel's all-embracing pan-logism; he was not a positivist," according to Lichtheim (1961, p. 236). And Fromm (1961, p. 5) finds likewise: "Marx's philosophy constitutes a spiritual existentialism in secular language and, because of this spiritual quality, is opposed to the materialistic practice and thinly disguised materialistic philosophy of our age." By the same token Adler is today also recognized by some as belonging among the existentialists (see pp. 7-9).

From this similarity in basic approach follow a number of important parallelisms in Adler's and Marx's concepts of man. Dreikurs (1960), one of the leading Adlerian psychiatrists, lists as basic assumptions in Adlerian psychology: (a) the social embeddedness of man, (b) self-determination and creativity, (c) subjectivity of perception, (d) teleo-analytic interpretation of behavior, and (e) the holistic approach. Each of these can be matched with statements from Marx's early writings, as shown in the following. The Marx quotations are taken from Fromm (1961), except for one quotation from Lichtheim (1961).

1. *Social embeddedness of man.* "The essence of man is no abstraction inherent in each separate individual. . . . It is the ensemble of social relations" (p. 228). "Every self-alienation of man, from himself and from nature, appears in the relation which he postulates between other men and himself and nature" (p. 105). "It is above all necessary to avoid postulating 'society' once again as an abstraction confronting the individual. The individual *is* the *social being*. . . . Individual human life and species-life are not *different things*" (p. 130).

2. *Self-determination and creativity.* "Free, conscious activity is the species-character of human beings" (p. 101). Men are "the authors and actors of their history" (p. 13). "The materialist doctrine con-

cerning the changing of circumstances and education forgets that circumstances are changed by men" (p. 22).

3. *Subjectivity of perception*. "The chief defect of all materialism up to now . . . is that the object, reality, what we apprehend through our senses, is understood only in the form of the object or contemplation; but not as sensuous human activity, as practice; not subjectively" (p. 11). According to Lichtheim (1961, p. 306), "For Marx as for Kant, the world of experience was not simply 'given,' but mediated by the human mind."

4. *Teleological nature of behavior*. "At the end of every labor process, we get a result that already existed in the imagination of the laborer at its commencement. He not only effects a change of form in the material on which he works, but he also realizes a purpose of his own that gives the law to his *modus operandi*" (p. 41).

5. *Holism*. "Naturalism or humanism is distinguished from both idealism and materialism, and at the same time constitutes their unifying truth" (p. 181). This is very much like the position of holism. For Smuts (1926, p. 117), the father of the term holism, it designates an ontology opposed to materialism and spiritualism or idealism "to express the view that the ultimate reality . . . is neither matter nor spirit but wholes."

The intrinsic similarity between Marx's original view of human nature and Adler's view is reflected in important similarities between present-day theory of educational and child psychology and psychotherapy in Russia and the iron-curtain countries, on the one hand, and Individual Psychology, on the other hand (Ansbacher, 1961b, 1962c). Yet, ironically, under Stalin, Adler was vigorously rejected in the *Great Soviet Encyclopedia*.[2a] He is described as "reactionary . . . a student of Freud," holding "a completely unscientific theory . . . utilized for . . . imperialistic ideology" (Schwartz, 1951).

Summarizing the Relationship

We may sum up this discussion of the relationship of Adler to socialism as follows. Adler was, from his early youth, concerned with human progress and betterment. Thus he became attracted to

---

2a. In the 1970 edition the entry on Adler is new, longer, and adequate and fair. Similarities with Gestalt psychology, K. Jaspers, E. Fromm, and K. Horney are pointed out, and recent literature is mentioned. (*J. Indiv. Psychol.*, 1970, 26, 183–185).

socialism, the influence of which is reflected in some of his early writings. As his own theories matured, socialism became less important to him. He immediately denounced the excesses of the radical Marxist wing in Russia and increasingly disagreed with the materialistic determinism of the moderate wing in Central Europe. Actually, however, Adler's mature concept of man turned out to be strikingly similar to that of the young Marx, a relationship which Adler could not have known since the relevant writings of Marx had not been published.

Carl Furtmüller (1880–1951)[3]

Carl Furtmüller, educator and socialist, was Adler's most intimate and faithful friend, according to Phyllis Bottome (1957, p. 17). He was the logical person for her to interview for her biography of Adler, which she did at length. She calls the friendship with Furtmüller "in some ways the deepest and certainly the most lifelong friendship in Adler's life . . . two minds following one common aim: the educational betterment of mankind."

Furtmüller was born in Vienna on August 2, 1880. In 1898 he entered the University to study philosophy, and received his doctorate in 1902. Even then he must have shown an unusually active interest and competence in civic betterment, for at the age of twenty, as a student and secretary of a social science club, he was, together with many prominent citizens, a member of the founding committee of the *Volksheim* (*Fünfzig Jahre Volksheim*, 1951). The *Volksheim* was a consolidation of numerous adult education efforts which were then in existence. At around the same time he also joined the Social-Democratic movement.

From 1901 to 1903 he was a student teacher at a *Gymnasium* in Vienna, and from 1904 to 1909 a teacher at the *Gymnasium* in Kaaden, now Kadan, some 200 miles from Vienna near the northern border of Bohemia, now a part of Czechoslovakia.

wwwwwwwwww

3. Primarily based on a personal communication from Mrs. Leah C. Furtmüller, December 16, 1962, and an appreciation by Dr. Hans Fischl (1950); but also on an unpublished biography by Dr. F. Wernigg, director of the Vienna municipal library, written on the occasion of the 75th anniversary of Furtmüller's birth and made available to us through the courtesy of Dr. W. K. Wilbur; and on the history of the Austrian School Reform by Dr. E. Papanek (1962).

In 1904 he married Aline Klatschko; they had two children. Aline's parents were revolutionary political thinkers, emigrants from Russia. It is likely that Furtmüller came into contact with Adler through the Klatschkos, since Mrs. Adler was also a Russian-born liberal and the two families were probably in close contact.

The Klatschkos were known for their open house on Sunday evenings which they kept for young socialist intellectuals, a tradition which was continued by the Furtmüllers. Ernst Federn, the son of Paul Federn, writes about the Furtmüllers' Sunday Evenings: "This was a cherished social event among socialist intellectuals in Vienna. . . . I remember these meetings, and Carl Furtmüller, who was a man of caustic wit and great intelligence. Aline Furtmüller was a close friend of my mother, but the split between Adler and Freud severed the relationship. We children did not carry on this feud. On the contrary, we were very close until the Nazis separated us." [4]

This report is independently confirmed by Leah Furtmüller, the widow of Furtmüller's second marriage, who lives in Vienna. "Even now, years later, old friends of the Furtmüllers talk to me about the Furtmüllers' Sundays. The intellectual elite of the socialists interested in education came regularly. Young people were warmly welcomed. There were not only all kinds of discussions, but also much music, singing, readings, private theatricals. Every Sunday for years, I think until the Nazis came to Vienna in 1938, these Sundays were kept up. [While they were still in Vienna] the Adlers came often (one of the children played duets with Aline on the piano); the Kramers (Dr. J. was a contributor to *Heilen und Bilden*), the Gassners, and Hans Fischl, were always there." [5]

But to go back to Furtmüller's earlier years, he returned from Kaaden to Vienna in 1909, where he taught as professor at a *Realschule* until 1919. During the war years, 1914–1918, he was absent on military service.

In 1909, also, Adler introduced Furtmüller to Freud's circle. In Furtmüller's own words: "It was Adler who first awoke my interest in Freud's psychology. I began to read the literature and, every time I came to Vienna (from Kaaden), I had long talks with Adler on this subject. Although he spoke with great admiration about Freud's

---

4. Personal communication, July 4, 1962.
5. Personal communication, December 16, 1962.

genius and his daring in searching for the roots of psychological conflicts, I could not fail to notice that Adler from the beginning saw these roots elsewhere than Freud. His early papers, especially his *Study of Organ Inferiority*, make this clear. In 1909, when I came back to Vienna after an absence of several years, Adler introduced me into the Freud circle. The weekly meetings of this group are among the most fruitful intellectual experiences I have ever had. The center of interest was always to see how Freud and Adler would interpret in their different ways the factual material presented by the members of the group. Unfortunately Freud later reacted with growing irritability to these differences in basic conception. It was in 1911 that Adler formally separated from Freud. I left the Freud circle with Adler." [6]

Subsequently, Furtmüller became Adler's most active and prominent co-worker until, beginning with his government appointment in 1919, his new duties took up more and more of his time. He was co-editor with Adler of the volume *Heilen und Bilden* (Adler and Furtmüller, A1914a), and of the *Zeitschrift für Individualpsychologie*, which was founded in 1914.

After the war, in 1919, Furtmüller, long concerned with the need for school reform, was called to the Reform Division of the Ministry of Education of the new Austrian Republic by Otto Glöckel who headed the Ministry. In this Division the foundations for the School Reform, including a unified grammar school education, were prepared, and Furtmüller had a decisive share in all the work. When in 1922 Glöckel had become acting second president of the Vienna Board of Education (the Mayor being first president ex officio), Furtmüller was appointed Superintendent of Secondary Education there. In addition to the regular duties of this office, he devoted himself until 1927 to a broadly based experiment with the secondary-school curriculum. Despite great difficulties his effort is said to have succeeded beyond expectation (Fischl, 1950). Beyond this, Furtmüller wrote on educational, psychological, and social subjects; lectured on problems of education and psychology to psychologists, educators, parents, and teachers; and gave courses in French at the Pedagogical Institute.

∿∿∿∿∿∿∿∿∿∿∿∿

6. Letter from Carl Furtmüller to Mrs. Eleanor L. Pirk, April 8, 1946.

With the seizure of power by the Austrian fascists in 1934, Furtmüller was dismissed. After Austria was taken over by Hitler, Furtmüller and his wife were forced to emigrate. They first went to France, then to Spain where they were imprisoned for three months. They finally reached the United States in January, 1941. Here they came under the care of the American Friends Service Committee, spending some time at its workshop in Haverford, Pennsylvania. At the end of that year Aline Furtmüller died.

The following year Furtmüller married Leah T. Cadbury, descendant of an old Quaker family, who survives him in Vienna today and is active in the work of the American Friends Service Committee there.

During the war years in America, Furtmüller first worked as a stock boy in a men's clothing factory in Philadelphia. He then taught Latin for a year in the Baltimore Friends School. From April 1944 to August 1945 he worked for the Voice of America in New York, eventually as editor at the German desk.

Finally, in 1947 he was able to return to Vienna, and became in 1948 director of the Pedagogical Institute. But his heart was not in good condition, and he died on January 1, 1951, a few months after his seventieth birthday.

In one of his publications Furtmüller (1930) described the modern classroom procedure as a cooperative enterprise, with the teacher as a member of the group rather than the traditional exalted figure. He explained that this new conception would require the teacher to develop self-confidence, clearness of purpose, and at the same time a willingness to keep in the background. All three attributes seem to have been characteristic of Furtmüller himself. He was essentially a modest man, despite his keen intelligence and wit, activity and determination. The reader of his biography of Adler will not fail to note the way Furtmüller keeps his own person completely in the background, so that we would not know anything about him or his relationship to Individual Psychology, were it not for the accounts of others and his own publications.

About the Present Biography

History. The present biography was written by Furtmüller toward the end of 1946, while he was still in New York waiting for his permit to return to Austria with his wife. The suggestion for writing the biography came from Mrs. Raissa Adler and Mrs. Danica Deutsch. Furtmüller wrote the biography in English, which he had corrected by his wife. When they returned to Vienna, it had reached its present form, more or less; he found no time to do further work on it. After her husband's death, Mrs. Furtmüller did the final editing with the assistance of Dr. Hans Fischl, Furtmüller's intimate, lifelong friend and co-worker in the days of the School Reform. In 1953 the manuscript was sent to Adler's daughter, Dr. Alexandra Adler, in New York, with the view to getting it published.[7]

Dr. Alexandra Adler handed the biography over to the present editors several years ago, and it was not until now that the opportunity for its publication presented itself.

Limitations. The special features and interests of this biography have been pointed out above. Its limitations are those of emphasis as to subject matter and time span. Furtmüller, the educator in Vienna, wrote as he knew Adler personally.

Thus Adler's work as a psychiatrist and theorist of personality receives less emphasis than his work in education and child guidance. Yet, in the light of subsequent history, it is Adler the theorist and psychiatrist who stands out. The renewal in interest, the "rediscovery" of Adler which we were able to point out in the introduction to the present volume, is due to his theories of personality and psychotherapy, which have so well stood the test of time that they are increasingly becoming vindicated.

The second and related limitation is that the last ten years of Adler's life, which took him more and more away from Vienna, are quite telescoped so as to appear relatively insignificant. Furtmüller devotes proportionately over twice as much space to the first twenty years of Adler's creative career (1907–1927), as to the last ten years (1927–1937). Yet these last ten years actually represent the crowning period of a world-wide personal impact as well as the final theoretical refinements of a truly holistic-organismic and humanistic theory of human nature. All the selections in the present volume are from this period.

To establish a balance here, the reader is referred to the biographies

---

7. Personal communication by Mrs. Leah C. Furtmüller, December 15, 1962.

by Hertha Orgler (1963), student of Adler's who likes to be known as his "standard-bearer," and by the English novelist Phyllis Bottome (1957). While these give more detail regarding the last ten years, they are less informative about Adler's earlier Viennese period than is Furtmüller's essay—thus the three works supplement one another.[8, 8a]

Finally, due to the circumstances under which it was written, Furtmüller drew almost entirely out of his memory facts which, for a biography, should have been verified. We have checked these facts wherever possible against other accounts, and were amazed at how accurate his memory was. The occasional minor discrepancies have been noted in the footnotes.

Yet, as Mrs. Furtmüller observes, the purely biographical details are only incidental to the elucidation of Adler's character and development. "What we have here from Carl Furtmüller is a portrayal—as three places in his manuscript show, a portrayal-in-process, not completed (see pp. 334, 361, and 375, where incomplete material is omitted). Which nicely offers to the interested student the stimulating challenge: How to finish it?"[9]

About the footnotes. In the footnotes we supplemented some of Furtmüller's accounts as seemed indicated, presented corroborations for others, and noted occasional minor discrepancies with other sources. We also added the references.

8. There are also two biographies in German. One, the first biography of Adler, is by the writer and novelist Manes Sperber (1926), who has been living in France for the last several decades. An essay of only 33 pages, it focuses on Adler's basic concepts and is written with the enthusiasm of a young man. The other is by Paul Rom (1966), educator and editor of the *Individual Psychology News Letter*. It not only synthesizes the previous accounts of Adler, but also affords very enjoyable reading.

The most recent and best-documented biography, containing new data and broad conceptualizations, is by the existential psychiatrist and scholar Henri F. Ellenberger (1970). It constitutes a chapter of 86 large pages in his work on the history of dynamic psychiatry.

8a. In the year of the 100th anniversary of Alfred Adler, Manes Sperber (1970) published a biographical–critical work on him, "a brilliant essay," in the words of one reviewer, yet "grey-toned," from the perspective of a lonely man. The book is in German.

9. Personal communication, February 15, 1963.

EARLY YEARS

Background

On February 7th, 1870, Alfred Adler was born in Penzing, then a town, now a part of the 13th District of the City of Vienna, as the son of a Jewish grain merchant. The family, at least during Alfred's childhood, lived in easy middle-class circumstances. He was the third child in a family of five boys and two girls, the oldest child a boy, the second a girl. One of the brothers died in early childhood. A psychological analysis of the family situation and its influence on Alfred's personal development cannot be an object of this study; it is doubtful, besides, if sufficient reliable material on which to base such research could be made available. It seems, however, that relations between Alfred and his father were especially trustful and close, and unusually informal, particularly for a small-town family in nineteenth-century Europe, and that he did not feel quite so close to his mother. The situation between him and his oldest brother was rather strained during childhood and boyhood. It may be that this fact was not without influence on the forming of some of Adler's theories.

Adler's parents changed their residence several times but always stayed in one of the western or northern suburbs of Vienna. This was of decisive importance for the growth of Alfred's personality. There were some parts of Vienna where Jews lived in a voluntary ghetto situation, others where Jews were a distinct minority group. In the suburbs where the Adlers lived, the few Jewish children, submerged in the overwhelming majority of gentiles, lived as comrades with the other children without becoming much aware of any difference. During the eighties and nineties a strong movement of anti-Semitism spread in Vienna, some partisans being as rude in words as Nazis later were in acts. It is interesting that the Adler children, neither in their relations with their playmates nor in elementary school or *Gymnasium*, seem to have been molested because of their being Jews. The anti-Semitism in Vienna in this epoch had some traits of Vienna's *Gemütlichkeit*. The Jews were attacked as a group, but even the anti-Semites made exception for Jews they knew personally.

While Jewish children in the ghetto or majority-group situations became distinctly Jewish in the coloring of their language, in nuances of behavior and gesture, Alfred grew up just a boy of the Vienna outskirts. For his whole life his spoken German was that of the typical highly-educated Viennese. When he wanted to, he spoke the pure vernacular itself with complete mastery. But Adler was not the only Jew who was so typically Viennese. Many of Vienna's most popular songs, some of which have gone around the world, have been written by Jews in the most natural and lively Vienna vernacular.

But it was not a matter of language alone. Adler's early experiences made him unable to feel the difference between Jews and gentiles as something personally important. He had no cultural or religious ties to Judaism.[1] But he never tried to forget or to make others forget his Jewish extraction. He simply was able to establish natural human relations with people of all kinds and never felt himself hamstrung by racial barriers. Later in *The Neurotic Constitution* he would show how for so many Jewish children the fact of being a Jew became one of the most important factors in the development of intense inferiority feeling with its typical reactions. In the history of Adler's youth this factor played certainly no important, if any, role.

Adler went through elementary school and *Gymnasium* without difficulty and without special distinction. Outstanding was his interest for music, popular as well as classic. He had a good, strong, adaptable voice and a good gift for delivery. In later years there could be no friendly party in the Adlers' home without somebody's finally asking "the Doctor" to sing a Wagner aria, or sometimes it was a ballad by Loewe, Schubert, or Schumann.

Medical School

Adler became a student of medicine. Vienna's Medical School at this time was at the height of its splendor. Nearly every branch of the training which the future physicians had to go through was represented by a specialist of international renown. We have no information about the relationship between Adler and his teachers and we do

---

1. As a young man Adler adopted Protestantism, a small minority religion in Austria, because he considered it the most liberal, and he wanted his children to have some religious education. But otherwise there was no religious participation.

not know if there was an especially personal contact with any of them.

The most marked influence came, it seems, from Nothnagel, the famous internist. He was one of the specialists who nevertheless stressed that the physician must always look at the patient as a whole, not at an isolated organ or an isolated ailment, and that the emotional influence of the physician on the patient must be taken into account. "If you want to be a good doctor, you have to be a kind person," he told his students. It was this *Blick aufs Ganze* which became characteristic of Adler as a practitioner, as a psychiatrist, and as a philosopher.[2]

For the forming of a young man's spirit and character, life with his fellow students is usually as important as lectures, laboratories, and internship. In the eighties and nineties the student body of the University of Vienna was to an overwhelming majority nationalistic. Up to the Austro-Prussian War of 1866 an important part of the Austrian Empire had been a member of the German Confederation, and Austria the leading power in it. This tradition was still alive. Most of the Jewish students also took part in this German nationalism. The growing anti-Semitism split the nationalistic student groups into two camps: those who were anti-Semitic and those who accepted a restricted percentage of Jews into membership.

Socialist Movement

A very small minority of students went another way. They came under the influence of the emerging socialist movement; they studied

~~~~~~~~~~~~~~~~

2. Freud had closer contact with Hermann Nothnagel (1841–1905) than Adler, but reacted quite differently. We learn from Jones (1953 p. 64) that Freud had been an *Aspirant* in Nothnagel's clinic in 1882, and around 1900 wrote an article on infantile cerebral paralysis for his encyclopedia of medicine. But while Nothnagel "was idolized by students and patients alike," Freud could not emulate his enthusiasm for medicine. "He found no more interest in treating the sick patients in the wards than in studying their diseases. By now he must have been more convinced than ever that he was not born to be a doctor."

Adler (A1928l), in an interview, mentioned having studied with Theodor Meynert (1833–1892), the well-known neurologist and psychiatrist whom Freud greatly admired and whose assistant Freud had been in 1883 (Jones, 1953). The other teacher whom Adler included was Richard Krafft-Ebing (1840–1903); but Adler did not mention Nothnagel.

the books of Karl Marx—then still *terra incognita* for most of the professors of economy and sociology; and they opposed to the nationalism of the student majority a program of internationalism. They gathered for nightlong debates in the basements of cheap restaurants and coffeehouses, never able to find a permanent meeting place, for what these young men of very restricted means could spend was far behind the expectations of the innkeeper. But there was an intense intellectual life among the members of this circle, and an enthusiasm to prepare the world for a better future, very different from the superficiality with which the nationalist group handled political and social problems. A high percentage of this circle later played important roles in public life.

It seems that Adler's lack of interest in racial differences immunized him against nationalism. He stood rather aloof in his student days, and only personal friendship connected him with members of the socialist group. As a young doctor he joined the group, appeared in their debating meetings and was also seen now and then in big popular meetings, sometimes in the company of a small, very fair Russian student, Raissa Timofeyewna Epstein, who soon became Mrs. Alfred Adler.

Adler's participation in the group life was that of a listener, not of a speaker and debater. Nor did all sides of the Marxist theories, which his friends discussed passionately, stir him with equal interest. I think that the economic theories of Marx never got much of Adler's attention. In politics he was never active but a very eager, lucid observer, critically attentive toward all sides.

It was quite a different thing with the sociological conception on which Marxism is based. This had a decisive influence on the whole development of Adler's thinking. From Marx he learned how the established social situation, without the individual's knowing it, influences the individual's intellectual and emotional life. Here also Adler was not a Marxist in the orthodox sense. While his friends argued about the interpretation of difficult or ambiguous passages in Marx, this silent listener took in Marx's ideas, amalgamated them with his own personality, and gave them time. When *The Neurotic Constitution*[3] was written, the leading ideas were not from Marx but

3. (A1912a).

from Alfred Adler. They had rooted deep in Adler's soil, but they could come out only because the soil had been fertilized by Marx.

The Young Practitioner

There was another important consequence of Adler's connection with this group, a consequence which established as final something that had been already pre-built in Adler's boyhood. Responsive as Adler was to human contacts regardless of the other person's social stratum, his interest and sympathy centered in the "common man." The part of the city where a young doctor establishes his office depends on the kind of clients he is waiting for. Adler took an office and apartment in the Praterstrasse, a neighborhood of mostly Jewish and lower-middle-class population.[4] Nearby was the Prater, Vienna's famous amusement park, which brought him quite another type of patient—the waiters from the restaurants, and the artists and acrobats of the shows. All these people, who earned their living by exhibiting their extraordinary bodily strength and skills, showed to Adler their physical weaknesses and ailments. It was partly the observation of such patients as these that led to his conception of overcompensation. In general it was characteristic of Adler that through all the years of his general practice he was never only a general practitioner. Every case which was not utterly routine became for him a new link in the chain of his scientific research. Only in this way did it become possible for a general practitioner to publish a book like the *Study of Organ Inferiority*.[5]

.   .   .   .

Adler's bedside manner was unique. It was in the greatest possible contrast to any professional pompousness. He administered science to his patients as if it were as simple as scrambling eggs. Where there was a technical and also a popular term he would never use the technical one. Wherever it was possible he gave the patient or the family a clear

wwwwwwwwwwww

4. By examining all the cases reported by Adler and by Freud in their writings, the Polish psychiatrist, Isidor Wasserman (1958), found that 35% of Adler's cases came from the lower class, 40% from the middle class, and only 25% from the upper class. For Freud the corresponding percentages were 3%, 23%, and 74%. This has been discussed in relation to the personalities of Adler and of Freud, by Ansbacher (1959).

5. (A1907a).

interpretation of diagnosis and therapy. He knew what the doctor's visit meant for the patient's morale, and was sure to leave him more cheerful than he had found him. He told little stories out of daily life which brought the patient into contact with the outside world; he always had a little joke, not a routine medical joke tried out before at a hundred other sickbeds, but a word coming out of the given moment.

Had Adler followed the line of internal medicine, he undoubtedly would have become as important in this field as he became in psychiatry. His skill as a diagnostician was outstanding. He combined swift, sure judgment with extreme cautiousness. Often when he was told about the symptoms and diagnosis of a colleague's case he would say, choosing his words very carefully: "That is a mistake, or that may be a mistake." When he saw a patient himself, he was never satisfied with what seemed to be evident. He always tested the etiology of that particular case, carefully considering all possible concomitant causes, and often surprised his patients by seemingly faraway questions which no other doctor in a similar situation had ever asked them.

Family Life

In 1897 Adler married. His first child, a daughter, Valentine, was born in 1898. Alexandra followed in 1901, his only son Kurt in 1905, and Nelly in 1909. Adler did not react to his children like the average father. Each infant's character and the way of influencing it became a study for him. Thus out of his family life came much of the stimulation and some of the material leading to his theories on education and child guidance. Mrs. Raissa Adler had the task of integrating the application of these new theories, especially their abhorrence of inhibitions, with the exigencies of daily life and the resistance of nurses and cooks to these new methods. She did it all with unusual tact and calm firmness, and always knew how to render to Caesar the things which are Caesar's!

This was only one example of how she followed her husband's growth—always full of interest, sometimes full of admiration, but never giving up her own judgment and intellectual independence.

Mrs. Adler died on April 21, 1962, in her 89th year, in New York City. Three of the children are living in the United States. Alexandra and Kurt are both psychiatrists. Alexandra is also a neurologist. She continues her father's work and is president of the Individual Psychology Association in New York.

ASSOCIATION WITH FREUD

Original Meeting

Adler's meeting with Freud was a decisive fact not only in Adler's life but also in the history of psychotherapy and psychology. What first directed Adler's attention to Freud's theories was probably a general trait in Adler's personality. He hated prejudice and hackneyed opinions. He liked paradoxes himself and always had a weakness for those who had the majority against them. Thus when Freud, about 1900, developed part of his new theories in the Vienna *Gesellschaft der Aerzte* and faced the passionate and disdainful opposition of the bulk of his colleagues, Adler published a report in a medical periodical in which he asked for an objective, careful examination instead of *a-limine* rejection of Freud's statements.[6] Some time later, when Freud published his *Interpretation of Dreams*,[7] Vienna's leading newspaper, the *Neue Freie Presse*, in whose tradition it was to ridicule every new phenomenon in art, literature or science—beginning with Richard Wagner and not ending with Freud—poked fun at this new "Egyptian dream book." Again Adler took the defense.[8]

ᴧᴧᴧᴧᴧᴧᴧᴧᴧᴧᴧᴧᴧᴧ

6. This is not borne out by Freud's account of his relationship to the *Gesellschaft der Aerzte*. While Freud relates that he did give a report before this society and that he "met with a bad reception," the date was 1886, not "about 1900," and the topic was what he had "seen and learned with Charcot" (Freud, 1925, p. 23). Nor has Adler's "report in a medical periodical" to which Furtmüller refers been found as yet.

7. Freud (1900).

8. All of Adler's biographers agree with Furtmüller that Adler took up such a defense of Freud, although their various versions of this incident differ and it has to date not been possible to establish documentary proof of this defense (Ansbacher, 1962b).

In the interview cited before, Adler (A1928l) describes his first contact with Freud as follows: "At that time, nervous disorders. . . were treated simply symptomatically, through cold-water cures etc. . . . All these methods, to which hypnosis also belongs, seemed to me not to get at the root of the problem and to be essentially not more than miracle cures. . . . I searched deeper and deeper to get at the basis of the psychological connections, encouraged by the writings of Charcot and Janet. Then in 1899 I attended a

This, however, was only the beginning. Adler felt instinctively at first, then saw more and more clearly, that Freud's discoveries opened a new phase in the development of psychiatry and psychology. There was the idea that full insight into the elements of the patient's mental life and their connectedness was a basic prerequisite for a thorough cure. There was the conviction that methods could be found to achieve this scrutiny of an individual psyche. And there was the natural consequence that these new methods would cause a revolution not only in psychotherapy but in general psychology, too, by adding to the study of formal laws of psychic phenomena the study of the typical contents of the mind. In addition to these points of principle, Freud had already developed a series of scrutinizing methods and exemplified their application, particularly in the *Interpretation of Dreams.* Adler tested and used some of these methods, used them while changing them, since two persons are never able to use methods for contacting human beings in a completely identical way. This was especially true of Adler, who was so strong a personality and so different from Freud; he could not copy Freud's methods.

The later rift made it difficult for Adler and his friends to speak freely about his scientific relationship to Freud. Now that both great men are dead, it is no longer their personal differences but each one's contribution to the common treasure of human knowledge that is important. Here two things are clear: on the one hand, Adler's deep indebtedness to Freud; on the other hand, his independence from the beginning in formulating problems and looking for and finding solutions. There is not one of Adler's papers which would show him as a "Freudian" in the narrow sense of a school. On the contrary, everything he published during his collaboration with Freud shows that he had learned to use new tools, but the statue was of his chiseling and had been preformed in his own mind.[9]

lecture by Dr. Freud who, like myself, was attempting to find psychological connections of the various neuroses. I was a nerve specialist and was greatly interested in pathological anatomy and internal diseases. To recognize these in advance [or rule them out] is in my opinion one of the most important preconditions of any psychological treatment method. During 1901 and 1902 I was invited to discuss with Freud and some of his pupils the problems of neurosis." Unfortunately Adler did not clarify the interesting question of how Freud came to invite him.

9. See Ansbacher (1962b).

The Freudian Circle

In 1902 Adler joined the Freud circle.[10] Once a week a group of psychotherapists gathered in Freud's home to report on their work and studies and to discuss medical, cultural, and philosophical problems in the light of the new methods. Several writers, students of literature and history, and educators joined later. The members of the group varied greatly in weight of intellect and personality. Some of them used the impulse and inspiration coming from Freud for independent research; the majority preferred to handle their professional problems strictly under the guidance and advice of the master. Freud looked upon them, and they felt themselves, as his medical assistants. The debates of the circle, however, were always stimulating.[11]

What was judged as the pansexualism in Freud's theories brought upon him and his group passionate attacks from the medical profession and from the public, and the Freudians felt themselves in a struggle of life and death against what were, or what seemed to them to be, established prejudices. This struggle invited and made necessary a re-examination of standard theories not only in psychology and psychiatry but also in ethics, education, and different cultural fields. So, in a cloud of tobacco smoke and comforted by many cups of strong black coffee, they would try to demolish an old world of thought and build up a new one. If not all contributions to the discussion were equally satisfactory and interesting, there was always Freud's final résumé in which, with the same art of exposition that the world now knows from his writings, he would confront the speakers' experiences with his own enlightened one. Always a good reader, he would bring to a concrete problem parallels out of history or literature and often came to new, quite unexpected conclusions. The fundamental positions in everything that Freud or members of the circle published first went through the test process of a circle discussion.

〰〰〰〰〰〰〰〰

10. According to Jones (1955, pp. 8 & 459), in the autumn of 1902 Freud addressed postcards to Adler, Max Kahane, Rudolf Reitler, and Wilhelm Stekel, suggesting that they meet for discussion of his work at his residence. This was the beginning of the Psychological Wednesday Society, the name of which was changed to Vienna Psychoanalytical Society in April, 1908.

11. See Nunberg & Federn (1962).

What for many members added a special fascination to these group activities was the feeling of a kind of catacomb romanticism—a small and daring group, persecuted now, but bound to conquer the world.

Adler's Independence

For Adler this emotional element did not exist. We have seen that he had never felt himself a member of a racial minority group, but he had learned years before to be a member of a minority in the struggle against established opinions and vested interests. As a student and young doctor he had joined those who, a very small minority then, propagated new political and social ideals. His critical mind always made him suspicious of any idea which was accepted too lightly just because it had been accepted before. His activities in the Freud circle were strictly objective. He wanted, and was willing, to learn, but he understood that what he learned would be assimilated with his own way of thinking and used as an element in his own independent work. He was willing likewise to let the others take part in the results of his own studies. Unegotistic give-and-take seemed to him the basis of scientific cooperation.

When he joined the group he was already an independent thinker on the way to important discoveries. To sit at the feet of the master was not an attitude one could expect from him. Still less was Adler able or willing to *jurare in verba magistri* [to swear in the words of the master].

A warm relationship was never established with Freud or with most of the other members of the group. On the contrary, there were soon difficulties. These were bridged by Freud, who held Adler's collaboration desirable and useful. So Adler remained. His behavior in the group was always that of the scientist who is searching for truth. He could not restrain himself from speaking out what in his opinion was the truth, even if his words contradicted formulas established by a man who himself was proud of being in contradiction to "respectable" opinion. But he never forgot that Freud was the older man, the man who had achieved a historic progress in psychology, and the host. Where he disagreed he never stressed the disagreement. As far as possible he used the terms accepted by the circle for expressing his own thoughts.

Study of Organ Inferiority

That Adler was an independent thinker, not merely a negative critic but a man who was making positive contributions to the progress of science—this the members of the circle could see from the beginning if they wanted to. To the scientific public this became evident when in 1907 Adler published his *Study of Organ Inferiority*.[12] Such a monograph, coming from a young general practitioner, was quite unusual. And it was unusual that a book whose author had no other academic rank than the simple M.D. so swiftly won professional attention. With this small volume Adler stood at the cradle of the modern teachings on psychosomatic disorders. But that was only a detail in the complex of importance this book had for the development of Adler's theories. The principle of overcompensation—established here primarily for physiological functions, but already recognizable in its psychological effects, e.g., the stuttering Demosthenes—became one of the foundations on which the theory of the neurotic personality was later to be built.

The *Study of Organ Inferiority* was the only contribution of Adler's which received Freud's unqualified and frequently repeated commendation. There was a sting to the honey. Freud praised the book as a work of physiology and implied that Adler had better stick to physiology. He could not see its far-reaching consequences for psychology, and never understood that overcompensation in its psychological aspect covered far larger areas of the unconscious than the relatively narrow strata on which Freudian psychoanalysis directed its searchlight.

The Aggression Drive

The way Adler's own theories developed in the orbit of Freud's doctrines and terminology becomes particularly clear in Adler's use of what Freud taught about drives. Freud came to the development of

---

12. Before publication of this monograph Adler presented the material to Freud's Psychological Wednesday Society, which was followed by a discussion (Nunberg & Federn, 1962, pp. 36–47). According to the minutes, Freud "attributes great importance to Adler's work; it has brought his own work a step further" (p. 42).

his psychological theories from the discoveries he made as a practitioner of psychotherapy. He used basic theories of formal psychology and philosophical foundations as he happened to come on them in his reading. Thus he based his new system on a rather outmoded theory which saw in the drives basic and independent elements of the psychic life. Following Schopenhauer, who saw in sexuality the "genius of the species" in action, Freud opposed the sexual drives to all of the other drives as ego drives, without discussing the problem. How many elements of what he called sexuality, especially the erogenous zones of the infant, should be connected with this "genius of the species"? Finally, he accorded to the sexual drive the primacy, or rather a dictatorship, in the psychological development of the individual. Adler followed Freud's drive doctrine, without accepting the absolute preponderance of sexuality. For him there was a kind of democratic equality among the drives.

Drive terminology was used in the exposition of Adler's next step in building up his own theory of human behavior. In 1908 he wrote on "The Aggression Drive in Life and in Neurosis." [13] Reading this paper today we see clearly that the theory of *The Neurotic Constitution* was now on the way. Adler already saw several of the most important symptoms which betray the neurotic personality, but he still considered them as primary elements of the psyche, as expressions of a drive, and not as compensatory efforts reacting against an intense feeling of inferiority.

Adler was the first in Freud's circle to show active interest in problems of education. In this connection he discussed replacing material reward or punishment by giving or withholding demonstrations of love.[14] Here he used the conception of love as affection, which was far away from the libido theory, and—now that we can see the development of Adler's conception through all of its phases—rather to be understood as the first, just perceptible sounding of the social-interest theme.

∿∿∿∿∿∿∿∿∿∿∿∿

13. This paper (A1908b) was never translated in full. However, for significant excerpts of it see Adler (A1956b, pp. 30–39). Prior to its publication this paper also was presented and discussed before Freud's circle (Nunberg & Federn, 1962, pp. 406–410).

14. (A1908d). For excerpts of this otherwise untransla' `   ⌐r see Adler (A1956b, pp. 39–42).

RIFT WITH FREUD

Frictions

Meanwhile psychoanalysis, still the concern of a hard-fighting minority, was no longer confined to Vienna but had spread abroad into many countries. Psychoanalysts held their yearly conventions, and in 1909 Freud went to the United States, preparing there a field which was to bring rich harvest. In April 1910 the Psychoanalytical Convention in Nuremberg agreed to the foundation of an International Psychoanalytical Association. Its first president—under Freud's sponsorship, naturally—was C. J. Jung, professor at the University of Zurich. Adler became president, W. Stekel vice-president, of the Vienna organization. Freud, Adler, and Stekel took turns as moderators of the weekly discussion evenings. These weekly meetings now were no longer social evenings in Freud's home, but took on a more formal character. At the same time the new framework made it possible to admit a greater number of members.[15] Among them for the first time was a woman physician, an innovation at which some members of the old group looked with skepticism.

It would have seemed the natural thing to do for Freud to take the international presidency himself. That he preferred to place it outside of Vienna was a clear symptom of his uneasiness about the situation in the Vienna group. On the other hand, that his choice fell on Jung could be interpreted as a sign of his willingness to give the members of his Association, at least the members leading in research, freedom to follow their own line of thought. For, the impartial observer must assume, Freud could not seriously have expected that a man of so different a background as Jung, living in a different atmosphere, working with different kinds of patients, would be willing in the long run to accept the Freudian position as something unchangeable or changeable only by Freud himself.

Actually, for some time the tension in the Vienna group seemed to

15. Jones (1955, p. 130) comments with regard to this move that by the autumn of 1910 the meetings of the Society had grown too large for Freud's apartment and were therefore transferred to the auditorium of the *Medizinisches Doktoren-Kollegium*. This "perhaps conduced to a chillier and more formal atmosphere. I observed myself that it was very different from what I had witnessed in the earlier years of the Society."

be eased. Freud and Adler cooperated in founding the *Zentralblatt für Psychoanalyse.*[16] In the group the new surroundings, the more formal gatherings of a greater number, and the presence of new people who were not yet implicated in the old controversies, created a much more pleasant atmosphere. But not for long. Adler naturally used the new *Zentralblatt* to publish his papers,[17] and these papers naturally developed his ideas, which grew more and more into a system. In the group he liked to fall back into his old habit of being a silent listener.

Some of Freud's most enthusiastic disciples, however, could not stand Adler's silence. They urged him again and again to develop his criticisms of Freud's theories and his own findings, in lectures as well as participation in the discussions.[18] Freud, generally of impeccable calm outwardly, gave signs of growing nervousness. Not Freud, but these overenthusiastic followers of his turned the struggle for scientific insight into a fight for Freud's personal prestige. One of them went so far as to say that as Freud was the discoverer of psychoanalysis it was his exclusive privilege to decide what was right and what was wrong in psychoanalysis. So much incense bewildered the mind even of a giant like Freud; and what normally would seem exaggerated adulation was nevertheless little compared with what the disciples offered.

One evening, both Adler and Stekel expressed independent views—independent from each other's, as well. Freud answered with some irritation. Adler always strictly avoided deviations into the personal field, but Stekel thought that for once he would express the admiration everyone felt for Freud in the style established by the extremists. He compared himself to a sparrow which had been carried by an eagle skyward and when the eagle was at the top of its flight tried a few yards more for himself. Freud's answer was, he now saw that the vice-president was willing to accord him a first-class funeral while the

wwwwwwwwwwwww

16. This was in October, 1910, and Stekel was a cofounder. Adler and Stekel became the coeditors, with Freud editor-in-chief.

17. (A1910f, A1910h, A1911c, A1911d, A1911f).

18. This led to the two papers which Adler read on January 4 and February 1, 1911, in which he presented his critique of psychoanalysis, and which were discussed at length on February 8 and 22 (Jones, 1955, p. 132). They were subsequently published by Adler (A1911a, A1911b) and large translated excerpts of them as well as of the ensuing discussion can be found in Adler (A1956b, pp. 56–75).

president thought a routine funeral would be good enough. Freud was too self-controlled to let the inner fire often blaze out into the open in this way.[19] There were other meetings without fencing. The slightest incident, however, could reopen the heckling.

The Final Crisis

The final crisis came during the summer when the group was in recess. Freud wrote a letter to the publisher of the *Zentralblatt* announcing that he could no longer be editor together with Adler, so the publisher would have to choose between them.[20] The publisher communicated the letter to Adler, who spared him the embarrassment of choice by resigning.[21] As a logical consequence he also resigned from the presidency of the Vienna Society, and from membership in it. Among the members this news aroused excitement; except for the narrowest circle everybody was dismayed, and many expressed to Adler their sympathy and their disapproval of Freud's tactics. When it became clear that they for their part would have to choose between Freud and Adler, some of the protesters became silent.

Twelve members, however, addressed a letter to the group to protest against Freud's action and to state that they would find a way for further scientific collaboration with Adler.

In the first meeting of the Psychoanalytic Society after the summer vacation [22] Freud himself presented a motion which declared membership in any society founded by Adler to be incompatible with membership in his group. Adler's friends knew that the die was cast;

19. Jones's (1955, p. 136) version of this episode is: "Stekel was fond of expressing this estimate of himself half-modestly by saying that a dwarf on the shoulder of a giant could see farther than the giant himself. When Freud heard this he grimly commented: 'That may be true, but a louse on the head of an astronomer does not.'"

20. According to Jones (1955, p. 133), "Freud suggested to Adler that he resign his position as coeditor of the *Zentralblatt* and wrote to the publisher, Bergmann, to the same effect."

21. The following declaration by Adler (A1911g) appeared in the August issue of the *Zentralblatt*: "Herewith I should like to notify the readers of this periodical that as of today I have resigned from the editorship of this periodical. The editor-in-chief of the periodical, Professor Freud, was of the opinion that between him and myself there are such large scientific differences that a joint editorship would appear unfeasible. I have therefore decided to resign from the editorship of the periodical voluntarily."

22. October 11, 1911 (Jones, 1955, p. 133).

for the sake of principle, however, they put up a fight for freedom of research within the frame of Freudianism. Freud, in the chair, strictly banned every excursion into controversy over psychological and therapeutic doctrines by Adler's friends, while he allowed himself the freedom of repeated polemics against Adler. Nevertheless, the whole argument went on very courteously, and when the voting had the foreseen result Adler's friends left the assembly with words of thanks for what they had learned in the years of common effort.[23] They formed a new association, with Adler as president, which they called Society for Free Psychoanalytic Research.[24] Freud was angry at this name because he resented the implication, "as if in his group research were not free."

Personality Differences

What caused the rift between Freud and Adler and made it so deep? One fundamental reason was the difference in their personalities, or better, in certain sectors of their personalities.

There was, first, the difference in their approach to science and

23. According to Jones (1955, p. 134), it was Furtmüller who "made an impassioned speech" against a resolution "that members should decide between Freud's and Adler's societies." But the resolution was passed by eleven votes to five. David Bach, Baron Hye, and Stefan von Maday had already resigned with Adler before this meeting. After the passing of the resolution, the following also resigned: Carl Furtmüller, Franz Grüner, Gustav Grüner, Frau Dr. Hilferding, Paul Klemperer, and D. E. Oppenheim.

24. From psychoanalytic writings the myth has been created that this new group who had separated itself from Freud and followed Adler was formed along political lines. Wittels (1924, p. 151) wrote, "Adler and his nine friends were all socialists," and Jones (1955 p. 134), "Most of Adler's followers were, like himself, ardent Socialists." The fact is that three—Bach, Furtmüller, and Frau Dr. Hilferding—were indeed socialists. But the other six were in all likelihood not. According to Klemperer, the first secretary-treasurer of the new group, he himself had no political affiliation; neither did Franz and Gustav Grüner; and von Maday was certainly not a socialist (personal communication, January 23, 1963). Oppenheim was considered actually a conservative (Dr. Alexandra Adler, personal communication, June 1, 1961). Of Baron Hye, as a nobleman, we dare assume that he also was not a socialist. On the other hand, of those who remained with Freud there was at least one who subsequently became a socialist, Paul Federn, as pointed out in the introduction to this biography. We did not gather information on the others. But the evidence seems sufficient for the conclusion that the rift with Freud, rather than following political lines, was due to differences in theory and approach which crossed political lines.

research. The achievements of both men were based on an extraordinary gift for understanding other people's inner life, and thus finding keys in details of thinking and behavior which had previously been neglected as irrelevant. Freud was eager to bring the results of psychological intuition into forms corresponding to exact science. He liked systematization, classification, drawing blueprints of the psyche as of a machine or a building, detailed and standardized methods of analysis.

Adler, on the other hand, felt from the beginning that this approach threatened to give an independent value to the single symptom, the momentary psychic phenomenon, and neglected the possibility of its being just a drop in the broad stream of the personality's life and its expendability. Instead of a sophisticated symptomatology and classification he insisted on the "unity of the neuroses." That made his psychology appear much more "simple," much less "scientific." This difference in approach, however, does not explain the rift. On the contrary, what we ask ourselves is: "Why couldn't these two men with their different approaches work together peacefully as friends, or side by side, complementing instead of opposing each other?"

There was another difference which should have made it easier for Freud to go along with Adler: Freud was the man of the world, careful of his appearance; unsatisfactory though his university career was, knowing how to use the prestige of title and the dignity of a professor; as masterful and elegant with the spoken word as in writing, even in the small circle of his original group combining the ease of informal talk with some of the solemnity of the cathedra. In contrast, Adler was always the "common man," nearly sloppy in his appearance, careless of cigarette ashes dropping on his sleeve or waistcoat, oblivious of outer prestige of all kinds, artless in his way of speaking although knowing very well how to drive his points home.[25]

25. A few additional words about Adler's appearance would seem to be in place here. He was possibly a bit shorter than average, stocky and well rounded though not heavy. As to his face, the profile view of the frontispiece offers an excellent likeness, although it is at some variance from his other known portraits. The difference finds its explanation in the following passage from Hertha Orgler (1963, p. 208): "It was not easy to get a good likeness of Adler. Although he had a well-cut and prominent chin with a deep dimple, his nose offered difficulties. Broad in front, sharp in profile, it thoroughly changed

Shouldn't Freud have seen in such a person a foil rather than a competitor? The trouble was, Adler was a "common man," careless of prestige, simple in manner and speech, not by inferiority but by choice, so his artlessness worked as a catalyst for any tendency in Freud to pontificate.

Both men were domineering. It would be hard to decide whether originally Freud's "sadistic component" or Adler's "masculine protest" was stronger. The difference was that Adler had early made domineering a central problem of his research and so became particularly sensitive to tricks and disguises of this domination hunger, tricks which other people might overlook and the individual himself might use without being fully aware of it. He also understood that in the long run nobody can stand being the object of domineering by another person, whatever form it may take, without strong, often hostile reactions. This made him cautious about his own tendency to dominate, and he tried to control it.

This difference between Freud and Adler becomes striking in their handling of their patients. Freud made the patient lie down on a sofa while he sat behind, invisible. The procedure developed historically from his technique in hypnotism. Psychologically, in this way the patient was continuously reminded that he lay there as a patient and had to accept the doctor's superior position.

Adler and his patient faced each other in comfortable easy chairs and the treatment had the outward form of a friendly chat, even when the progress of the treatment made it necessary that the patient had to hear or find out for himself things which seemed to him unpleasant or cruel.

In the relationship between Freud and Adler, Adler was a clear-sighted, severe judge of all the different details in contacts where Freud's tendency to dominate made itself felt. Adler knew that an emotional reaction is proof for the domineering person that he is getting the upper hand. Adler's response, therefore, was cold ob-

---

his aspect according to the draftsman's point of view." Beyond the sharp nose profile, the frontispiece illustrates well Orgler's further description from life. "His underlip was full, his curved upperlip partly covered by a little dark moustache; his well-shaped ears lay close to his head. The growth of his hair, considering his age, was of a remarkable abundance, and his forehead was high."

jectivity without missing the moment and point when his opponent was not on guard. It was this method which wounded Freud deeply, and Adler knew it.

Freud's Frustrations

Nevertheless, this personal antagonism would never have led Freud to the extreme step against Adler, which was actually a kind of excommunication, if for many years his relationship to the surrounding professional world had not been that of distrust and seclusion. When he began to develop his new theories on sexuality, he and his followers found opposition which was not merely severe but passionate every time they tried to defend their cause in medical meetings and congresses. As a consequence Freud declared a kind of boycott against all such gatherings. That was justified insofar as many of the arguments directed against him were intellectually and ethically below the level fairly to be expected from debate in professional circles. But Freud and his group could not avoid the logical consequences of isolation. Tired of listening to the stupid, superficial criticisms of scientific ignoramuses he grew unused to taking any criticism. The uncritical admiration of the selected few had to compensate for the lack of public success which at that time he had still not won.[26]

There is another factor to consider. It is natural for every important scientist to want a group of disciples who will not only apply his methods and pursue his way of thinking but will also be teachers of others and so propagate his work to later generations. Ordinarily the scholar as a university professor has the opportunity to work in this direction by influencing the appointment of new faculty members in his own and other universities. Although nepotism, vanity, and egotism may so win influence in the academic machinery, at bottom it

wwwwwwwwwww

26. The belief of Freud's "lack of public success" at that time is now known to have been an oversimplification. A careful search of the literature has shown "the esteem in which Freud was held among many of his contemporaries *from the start* (eds.' italics) as a great man, psychologist, explorer, writer, and humanist" (Bry & Rifkin, 1962, p. 29). "The complexity in the scientific and cultural background makes it understandable that, although knowledge and appreciation of Freud's work spread widely and rapidly, the belief has persisted that Freud was ignored or opposed by virtually all but his direct followers and disciples" (p. 28).

is a sound idea. And even if for domineering characters this method also becomes a means to hold disciples under pressure, the contact and cooporation with scholars coming from other camps can never be completely shut out.

Now at the University of Vienna, Freud was in fact never more than a simple *Privat Dozent*, entitled to give lectures but without any influence on the academic administration. The title of Professor Extraordinary, which he received in the routine way, was never more than just a title.[27] The influence which other scholars exercise through the academic machinery, he could exercise only on the members of his group, and here again isolation removed many inhibitions, made his influence more direct and absolute.

The growing number of patients who wanted his help he could not possibly take care of personally, and this put material power into his hands. It is easy to understand that a man who had been outlawed for his genius by his colleagues a few years before, now felt satisfaction that he commanded not only intellectual but also worldly power. So it cannot be surprising that a man to whom his immediate surroundings conceded dictatorial powers finally decided to get rid of the voice of the critic who was beginning to stimulate other people also to criticism. This step, nevertheless, proved to be fatal for the further development of Freudianism and harmful for modern psychology and psychiatry as a whole.

Consequences of the Rift

The exit of Adler and his group did not bring to an end the uneasiness in the Freud circle. Whoever was inclined to independent research and to critical examination now felt that he had to protect

---

27. Since Furtmüller wrote this a different light has been thrown on Freud's professorship. It was not accomplished "in the routine way." He had been a *Dozent* since 1885. In 1897 he was first proposed as Professor Extraordinary, but was passed over. In 1902 he became discouraged, "and so I made up my mind to break with my strict scruples and to take appropriate steps, as others do, after all" (M. Freud, 1958, pp. 72–73). Actually the desired end was achieved thanks to the "amiable intrigue" of a grateful patient and friend, Baroness Marie Ferstel, who managed to sway the hitherto adamant Minister of Education by the "bribe" of a painting by Boecklin which was in her aunt's possession and which was handed over to the Minister for the gallery he was about to open (pp. 73–74).

his independence lest he be helplessly submerged by rigid conformism. On the other hand, Freud's extremists thought it had not been worth while to get rid of Adler if the hydra of independence was to be allowed to grow new heads. So, Jung left soon after Adler. Stekel was next; later came Rank, once Freud's son Benjamin, or beloved disciple John; then Horney, Fromm, and . . . I must apologize to the others I do not speak of.

Thus Freud lost the chance to see his further steps into the realm of the unconscious checked by experts who had intimate knowledge of his ideas and at the same time distance enough not to be simply scientific yes-men. He lost them just at the time when his tendency to become more fanciful and speculative threatened to overwhelm his empiricism, when he embarked on the dangerous sea of secondhand prehistorics, and some cautioning would have done good even if it led only to some rechecking.

Every student of Freudianism knows the many changes Freud's theories underwent in the decades after 1911. There is no doubt that had anyone in the group at the time of the Adler crisis anticipated one of Freud's later *volte-faces* he would have been declared a heretic, too. Orthodoxy in science is like orthodoxy in religion: at the time a heretic is cast out he is censured for having sinned against a dogmatic system established once and for all. But soon the official doctrine changes on its own part and accepts new dogmas which often in carefully changed wording take up ideas for which a heretic died at the stake.

Another consequence for Freudianism, besides the loss of all independent and original collaborators, was that development toward originality and independence was frustrated in those in whom such development would have been possible. While Freud's association could and did unite many eminent men in psychiatry and various other fields, independence and originality had become the privilege of one man. Instead of an Alpine region with many peaks, from Mount Everest to the inconspicuous hilltop, Freudianism became an island with a single holy mountain.

For the dissenters also there were harmful consequences. Freud's isolationism compelled them on their part to form separate groups of their friends, and in each group some of the sectarian spirit which had started in the Freud circle developed. There were jealousy and competition instead of cooperation. Differences had to be stressed, if it was only by using a different terminology. And whereas under other circumstances the originator of something new might have contributed one element in a whole, he now felt obliged to spin out whatever he had of originality into a whole system of his own. How Adler's group tried hard to avoid these dangers and how far it succeeded we shall see later.

Inevitably, in speaking about the rift between Freud and Adler, so much has to be said about Freud's weaknesses and so little about what made him great. Nevertheless, it is not a distorted picture; it is a sketch drawn from the point where our special task required us to stand, not a monument showing him from all sides.

Freud's angry mood made him imitate the tactics of his old enemy, the Vienna *Neue Freie Presse*. This newspaper, passionately attacked by the (later famous) Viennese writer, Karl Kraus, retorted by the most blighting exorcism it could command: under no circumstances was his name to appear in the paper. It was a joke in Vienna that if one day Karl Kraus should assassinate the old Emperor, the readers of the *Neue Freie Presse* would not be told of the Emperor's death, since this necessarily would have meant mentioning the name Karl Kraus. Such a proscription Freud now used against Adler. No paper published by a Freudian would quote Adler, until many years later Freud himself—more in an emotional outburst than in the spirit of a historian—told the story of his relations with Adler.[28]

Curiously enough, this wave of silence rolled forward over many of the sectarians, too. So it is that one may go through psychoanalytic literature without seeing Adler's name once. This silence takes on a more serious aspect because, in the progress of psychotherapy, others have been led to the study of problems first brought forward by Adler, with identical or analogous results. Whether they came to these problems and solutions by following their own line or in Adler's wake,

28. Actually it was only three years later that Freud (1914, pp. 338–347) published his paper "On the history of the psychoanalytic movement" in which he gave a lengthy account of his relations with Adler as well as Jung. This, however, does not contradict Furtmüller's statement that Adler was generally no longer quoted by the Freudians.

we will not decide. Certainly it was astounding for the well-informed reader when some pages or paragraphs of a paper made him turn to the index, and the name of Adler was not there.

In general, some of Adler's friends, particularly younger friends, were more shocked about this type of amnesia than was Adler himself. He did not enjoy it, but mostly his reaction was a bit of laughing and a joke. His most characteristic reaction can be best understood from a scene in Rostand's "Cyrano." To the aged Cyrano comes an admirer full of wrath. Last night, says the admirer, Molière brought out a new comedy which was an enormous plagiarism from Cyrano. Cyrano asks calmly: "And what did the public do?" "Oh, they laughed!" answers the admirer, infuriated. "They laughed," repeats Cyrano, and is pleased because he knows it was he himself who made them laugh. So it was with many pages in psychoanalytic papers. The readers did not learn Adler's name, but they learned some of Adler's ideas, unfortunately not always retouched with the art of a Molière.

EMERGENCE OF INDIVIDUAL PSYCHOLOGY

Adler's Reaction to the Rift

There is no doubt that Adler was deeply offended by Freud's actions against him, and the situation had rather unpleasant aspects. A year before, Freud had nominated Adler for the presidency of the Vienna group and founded the *Zentralblatt für Psychoanalyse* together with Adler, in full knowledge of the latter's independent and often dissenting views. Now he suddenly declared further cooperation impossible because Adler had not changed at all. Did that not mean that Freud had tried to play a bit of power politics in the ideal realm of science by offering Adler a modest share of influence and prestige on the understanding that he would accept the role of a satellite? [29]

29. Freud's playing of power politics is in fact confirmed in Jones (1955). Freud wrote to Ferenczi in April, 1910: "I will transfer the leadership to Adler, not because I like to do so or feel satisfied, but because after all he is the only personality there and because possibly in that position he will feel an obligation to defend our common ground" (p. 71). Freud's decision to put Adler and Stekel in charge of the newly founded *Zentralblatt* in the autumn of that year was reached in the same spirit. Jones calls this move and the handing over the presidency of the Society to Adler an "endeavor to appease the disgruntled Viennese" which, however, "was only partially and temporarily successful" (pp. 129–130).

Besides, for a year Adler had expended all the trouble and energy which are needed to get a new scientific journal started. But now he was no longer allowed to use it for himself.

It was surprising, and it showed Adler as an outstanding personality, that in this crisis he never lost his self-control. He spoke calmly when he informed his friends of what had happened. In the criticisms he directed against Freud's conduct he spoke with restraint and strictly avoided expression of emotion. To do so was a matter of personal dignity. It was also the best way to lead his friends not to fruitless resentment but to positive work.

Most of the friends who left the Freud circle with him did not do so as sworn followers of Adler's theories. Their collaboration in the Freud group had seemed highly useful to them just for the reason that they could take part in discussions of different solutions offered for the same problem and thus prepare themselves to make their choice and find their own way. They left with Adler because they believed him wronged and were indignant at Freud's treatment of him.

From the beginning Adler understood clearly how dangerous any fixation on the past and especially on Freud's feelings and reactions would be for such a group; it might become a mere flock of malcontents repeating endlessly the same complaints, and restricting their intellectual activity to negative and shabby criticisms of Freud's theories. Therefore Adler energetically insisted on an attitude which brought the group to look not back at the past but into the future. He cautiously avoided being didactic. Behind every suggestion he made in the many gatherings when the new group discussed its program stood the warning: you have left Freud because you did not want to tolerate infringement of your scientific independence; now show that you are able to do independent work.

The New Group

Immediately after their exit, the group which left the Freud circle felt a bit bewildered. Their participation in the Freud group had become part of their intellectual routine. With Freud they had been members of a minority, but it was an already well-entrenched minority. Now they had to begin from the beginning. But there was Adler's encouraging attitude, and there was much work to do. Thus came confidence and cheerfulness. Soon new and very active members were won, mostly relatively young men and women, physicians, philosophers, writers, and teachers. Letters were sent abroad, mostly by Adler himself, which told what had happened in the Freud circle and explained the plans of the new group. Very sympathetic and encouraging answers came. They showed that colleagues in Germany, in France, in Serbia, and in Greece were already well informed on the basic differences between Freud's and Adler's views. Freud's course of action was disapproved of or regretted in all these letters. The writers saw in Adler's and Freud's theories two ways of thought which were equally entitled to impartial study. Several wrote that they felt their own way of thinking was very near to Adler's and joined the group as corresponding members.

Adler had just changed his apartment and office, and at the same time he made a change in his professional activities. From the Praterstrasse he went to the Dominikanerbastei, a street in the center of the city near the Ringstrasse. While up to this time he had worked as a general practitioner, although more and more concentrating on psychiatric cases, he now specialized in psychiatry, reserving for the families of a few dear friends the privilege of his services as family physician.

At first the group met in Adler's new apartment. Soon, however, it had to look for more space and gathered in various clubrooms. There could not be any orthodoxy on principle, nor could there be any orthodoxy because the new members represented very different backgrounds. But there was the general eagerness to study Adler's ideas, to confront them with other doctrines, to try to find out what contributions they could add in different fields of thought. The necessary discussion of Freudianism thus became only part of a wider task of intellectual orientation. The former members of the Freud group soon sensed how much more stimulating the work was under the new circumstances. They could speak freely without fear that a daring word would evoke the dismay of a great, respected scholar. They could express their thoughts in their own way and look for terms which might best express what they wanted to say, whereas before, the Freudian terminology had unavoidably handicapped the free play of ideas.

By comparing Freud's and Adler's positions it became more and more clear that differences over specific problems were based on deeper differences in general attitude toward life as well as in the application of psychological methods. Here the philosophers took the lead and began to study the problems of methodology,[30] causality and finality, and of ethics.[31] There were students of Spinoza, Kant, the Neo-Kantians, Nietzsche,[32] and Bergson[33] in the group. Besides psychoanalysis, other schools of modern academic psychology were discussed, particularly the papers of Külpe's school of *Denkpsychologie*.[34] The contributions of great writers to a living psychology were appraised, with Dostoevski in the center,[35] and comparison of the artist's approach and work processes with those of the psychologist brought deeper insight into methodology. The psychological basis of current social phenomena was discussed, as of the German Youth Movement[36] whose influence was beginning to be felt in Austria.

From the beginning the hospitable atmosphere of the new group was in complete contrast to the strict seclusion of the Freud circle. This was to be characteristic of Adler's groups for the entire future. Never were there initiation rites, nor spoken or unspoken oaths of allegiance. Every member was entitled to introduce a guest who might be qualified by interest, experience, or ability to become a member.

〰〰〰〰〰〰〰〰〰〰

30. Discussing the problem whether Individual Psychology is possible as a science, Alexander Neuer (1914) aligned it with the primarily idiographic sciences (Windelband), calling it "the idiographic science *par excellence*." Accordingly, Neuer found it also related to "understanding" psychology (Jaspers), the phenomenological approach (Husserl), and personalistic psychology (William Stern). This is still today a very good delineation of Adler's systematic position, except for the absence of the social aspect which was not yet important in Adler's system in 1914.

In further outline of Adler's position it may be mentioned here that later he published in his journal contributions by John Dewey (1930) and David Katz (1930), both functionalists and the latter also a Gestalt psychologist, and by Jan C. Smuts (1932), the originator of holism (Ansbacher, 1961a).

31. Furtmüller (1912).

32. Freschl (1914, 1935).

33. Schrecker (1912).

34. The author of this discussion was Furtmüller (1914b). He explained the affinities between Individual Psychology and Külpe's Würzburg school of the psychology of thinking. Among the members of this school whom Furtmüller mentions we should like to point out Karl Bühler, who later formulated the concept of function pleasure in contrast to satiation pleasure, and Kurt Koffka, one of the three original Gestalt psychologists.

35. Adler (A1918c); Kaus (1926).

36. Wilken (1922).

When he had taken part in the meetings he might either stop coming or join the group. Psychiatrists, psychologists, and writers visiting Vienna were invited. By this openness of the circle over the years a very great number of workers in many different fields came in touch with the group, at least for temporary collaboration.

Naturally, most important for the activities of the group were the smaller number of those who worked with Adler through years and decades. These men and women kept such lasting contact with Adler because they felt stimulated by his thoughts and his personality, learned from his experience, found in his methods the right tools for their own research or their practical tasks. But they were never asked to be "Adlerians" in the sense that one had to be a "Freudian." Therefore, a former near friend could slip away more and more when experience and life turned him in another direction, but there could never be an "apostate." Actually, Adler was inclined to open the doors so wide that his friends sometimes thought he went too far. His optimism made him now and then overvalue the contributions of a newcomer and show a partiality toward him which might hurt older members. Particularly when he was introducing patients or former patients, his friends felt that he was apt to put a heavy load on the group by making it a party in encouragement therapy. But Adler knew the machine: the motor balked, but it brought the car over the hill.

Adler's Way of Teaching and Treatment

For Adler himself the months and years after the separation from Freud became a period of rapid inner growth. In the Freud group he had behaved like a safety valve; he could not hinder new ideas from expanding but he allowed them to escape into the open only when they had already accumulated the pressure of several atmospheres. Now he lived in free air. Not that he now had an uncritically admiring audience. Nearly all of the members who came from the Freud circle were at a lesser distance from Freud in their ideas than was Adler, so that he found here, either as a real or as a tentative criticism, every objection he might have met in the old circle. Here, however, these criticisms were not charged with emotion, and Adler could discuss them freely and use them to clarify his own and his listeners' conceptions.

He never stopped long with merely theoretical reasoning; he preferred to illustrate what he meant by facts. In the Freud circle he had been a clear but not too colorful speaker; now he began to develop his unique way of getting in touch with an audience, which later not only enabled him to stimulate and hold the attention of big new audiences of laymen as well as experts, but also made hundreds of auditors follow his courses regularly, semester after semester, without any academic compulsion.[37]

Even when he gave a prepared report there was at every moment a live current between him and his audience. He felt immediately when he was not completely understood, and he would make his point more clear, often using an anecdote out of practical life, or a case history. Doubt or opposition also only needed to be shown by the expression of the face or in a slight gesture, to be caught by him and answered with a short parenthetical remark, an aphorism, or, according to the circumstances, a friendly or sarcastic joke. Like the excellent listener he had always been, he followed the contributions of the other speakers in all details and shadings. Often when one of them made a good point which was not likely to get adequate attention or appraisal from the audience because it had been presented with too little stress or clearness, Adler took great pains to insist on its importance, to expose its connections with and consequences for the discussed problem, in this way helping the other to the honors of the evening.

Adler made the deepest, most lasting impression on his audience

~~~~~~~~~~~~~~~~

37. An eloquent confirmation of Adler's way of captivating an audience is found in a report of twenty years later: "Alfred Adler is an excellent speaker. He speaks completely without notes. It is a pleasure to follow his words as they are shaped in a process of creative thought, improvised yet with extraordinary scientific precision and clarity. At the same time he is an excellent teacher who presents his material in an unsensational manner, who is passionately yet factually captured by his subject matter, who mightily captures the listener, who develops even very complicated and abstract trains of thought with admirable simplicity, almost in a playful manner, and who always at the right moment illustrates a point with a striking example. In listening, one is almost seduced into following his thinking, and one follows willingly into new intellectual territory, fascinated and without stumbling." This account is taken from the German-language newspaper in Katowice, Poland, reporting on a lecture there by Adler (*Kattowitzer Zeitung*, April 20, 1932; quoted in *Mitteilungsbl. Indiv. Psychol. Veranstaltungen*, 1932, 1[5], 2).

when he reported in detail a case history, either giving the whole story of a patient including the results of the treatment, or returning to a current case at successive meetings to show how the progress of the treatment answered questions left open in his previous reports. The listeners came to see how an individual's personality, at first a maze of incoherent, contradictory traits, became understandable as a unity, how the symptoms of his neurosis came into line with what the patient and his neighborhood took for his normal behavior. They followed the efforts of the psychiatrist to understand the patient's behavior, and connect it with his experiences in the past and with the problems life made him face now.

They saw that then came the harder task of making the patient himself understand how experiences of early childhood and later life had influenced him in developing his present attitude, shunning real solutions of life's problems, looking instead for a fantastic, imaginary superiority.

Lastly came the still harder task of making the patient accept, not only by reasoning but also through deep personal insight, the necessity to change his style of life, to work out his problems, to abide by what Adler called the "logic of life" which asks for real cooperation in the real world instead of imaginary victories in a fantastically distorted world.

When Adler reached this point in his report of a treatment, his audience learned, as the patient had to learn, that the doctor's taking an equal instead of a superior position toward the patient did not make things so easy for the latter. For now Adler told the patient that he must cure himself, that the doctor could help him but could not take the job from his shoulders.

In this way the members of the group got an intimate knowledge of Adler's methods in tracking the aberrations of neurotic behavior to their source, and in helping the patient to understand and correct his mistakes.

From the start they were safe from the misunderstanding, frequent in critics but sometimes also in would-be followers of Adler, that encouragement at any price was the key of his treatment. Adler never encouraged without laying open the problem for the solution of which courage was to be used. Not encouragement in itself, but balance of encouragement and responsibility was Adler's formula, if formula there has to be. Therefore, he avoided pointing out to the patient tasks which he knew were too difficult for him. His encouragement, furthermore, never meant simply, "Go ahead, you are all right," but "Go ahead, if you try very hard you will do it."

To speak of Adler's "reporting" on his cases does not give the full picture. The liveliness, spontaneity, and openness of Adler's comments would be characterized better as trying to make the group witness, as far as possible, what happened between him and the patient. Thus they could watch his method in action, and see that it was much more than a theory. On the other hand, they perceived how intimately many details of his method were connected with his own personality. Consequently, no other psychotherapist could follow this method simply by taking it over in all its details. On the basis of the general principles each one had to build up his own individual method, using Adler's way as an inspiring guiding example. This also helped to avert the danger of sectarianism in the group.

The Neurotic Constitution

All his life Adler was a strenuous, indefatigable worker, but never more so than in the years after he left the Freud group. There was from morning until late in the afternoon, and often in the evening, the chain of his patients. There were papers to write and other people's papers to read. There was the work with the group; not only the weekly gatherings, but naturally again and again discussions with individual members who wanted to talk with him personally about specific problems of theory or practice, and always he found room in his overburdened schedule for such talks. There were the letters and guests from abroad; and reading. And there was a family of four growing children who asked for, and got, their share of their father's time and attention.

Never did Adler complain of fatigue, never did he look tired. As a true Viennese, his relaxation consisted mostly in one or two hours in a coffeehouse where he met friends and where generally he was soon again in the midst of "shoptalk," which often referred to difficult professional or theoretical problems. His vacations were never counted by months but by days, at most by weeks.

This frantic intensity of work made it possible for Adler to publish his book, *The Neurotic Constitution,* as early as 1912.[38] Whereas his earlier works showed him tackling problem after problem in the search for his own way, we see here the man who has found this way and is now able to unite the answers to specific problems into a well-organized system. All his thinking and research of former years are integrated in this book.

His old interest in Marx's sociology enabled him to understand how the development of an individual psyche is dependent on the facts, the opinions, and the values of the society in which he lives.[39] The psychological consequences of organ inferiority in combination with secondary inferiority feelings are shown as the initial impulse in the neurotic drama. The aggression drive is no longer in itself an independent psychic factor but a link in the chain of psychological dynamics.

Adler's contact with Freudianism had a positive as well as a negative side. Whoever had worked with Freud could not separate from him without offering his own answer to the problem of sexuality.

38. The original German title is *Über den Nervösen Charakter,* which Furtmüller translated as *The Nervous Personality.* The title of the English translation of the book is *The Neurotic Constitution* (A1917a), which is perhaps not a fortunate choice since the term constitution is often used to refer to innate characteristics. But since the book is now known by this name we have substituted it throughout for Furtmüller's translation.

39. Among the influences on Adler, Furtmüller singles out only Marx, in addition to Freud. Yet *The Neurotic Constitution* contains ample evidence of Vaihinger's (1911) influence and several sincere acknowledgments on the part of Adler (A1912a). E.g., he speaks of "a fortunate circumstance" by which he became acquainted with Vaihinger's work, "in which I found the trains of thought suggested to me by the neuroses set forth as valid for general scientific thought" (p. 30). "The scheme of which the child avails himself in order to enable him to act and orient himself is one common to and in accordance with the tendency of the human understanding to reduce that which is chaotic, fluid, and intangible in life to measurable entities by means of the assumption of fictions" (p. 36). Thus Adler adopted Vaihinger's "idealistic positivism," that is a form of transactional pragmatism, as his own philosophy of science. It made him keenly aware of his own assumptions and served as a continuously present memento against the reification of assumptions and constructs. It kept him methodologically on the operational level (see Ansbacher, 1965). It also made him appreciate the continuity between scientific theory and human thought processes in general. The importance of Vaihinger for Adler is well brought out by Lewis Way (1962, pp. 75–84). It is also shown in Adler (A1956b, pp. 77–87), where large excerpts from Vaihinger are included.

Adler's Freudian critics speak about his denying or belittling the role of sexuality. Neither is true. On the contrary, Adler first analyzes, then integrates the manifold reasons why sexuality plays an outstanding role in the development of personality, not as a strange force opposed to the ego drives but as a part of the personality itself. As a psycho-physiological factor it becomes implicated in the dynamics of inferiority and compensation like any other psycho-physiological factor. Furthermore, relations to other human beings are determined by sexuality more than by any other psycho-physiological factor, for there is not only the relation from partner to partner but also the attitude toward parenthood. Therefore, social opinions and evaluations of sexuality are especially intense and make themselves felt in the development of the individual's attitudes from a very early age. These are the components of the reaction complex which Adler described as the "masculine protest."

.   .   .   .

We shall see that in *The Neurotic Constitution* one of the pillars supporting Adler's final system is still missing. Nevertheless, it is his standard work. Nobody can understand Adler's work as a whole who has not studied the rich material of this book. Some of Adler's later formulations sound very simple, and it seems easy to accept them as common sense or disparage them as commonplace. *The Neurotic Constitution* shows how deep and how carefully constructed are the foundations of his doctrines.

Unluckily, this indispensable book is not easily readable. Adler, so inspiring and on the whole so clear in his speaking, never took time to worry over the necessary differences between the spoken and the written word. So many scholarly lectures are dull because their spoken language is the language of a dry and lifeless book. Adler's books so often make hard reading because what was lively and understandable when he addressed an audience lacks clearness and precision on paper. The spoken word may be supplemented by accent, intonation, a gesture, a smile, a significant pause. A rather cryptic word or sentence, thrown into the context as Adler liked to do, will either be instantly understood or else not brought into the focus of attention by the listener, who cannot stop but has to follow the speaker.

The conscientious reader, however, wants everything made completely clear and does not accept any ambiguity. The listener may overlook a missing link in a chain of demonstration; the reader, if he is the kind of reader such a book wants, will have to worry about supplying for himself what the writer was not careful enough to furnish him.

On the other hand, these difficulties and flaws contribute to the fascination of *The Neurotic Constitution*, and make it fruitful reading for those who are able and willing to overcome the difficulties. Reading Adler in this way means going back from the written to the spoken word, and thus behind the letters and the pages the personality of Adler comes to life again. Sometimes you will brood a quarter of an hour over a paragraph. But then you will get out of it more stimulation to pondering, agreement, opposition, and doubt than in many chapters of easy reading.

The Neurotic Constitution will never be a book for "required reading," eighty pages an hour, but we have no doubt that when many a book praised now for its limpid elegance will be forgotten, psychologists, psychiatrists, sociologists, and philosophers will still come back to some of the dark pages of Alfred Adler.

Academic Rejection

When *The Neurotic Constitution* was published, Adler submitted it to the Vienna Medical School in his application for the *venia legendi*.[40] He wanted to become a *Privat Dozent*. That was a big mistake, and Freud's fate should have warned him.

We have seen how Freud, himself a *Privat Dozent*, never rose higher in the academic hierarchy.[41] Even when he was at the height of his success, and scientific societies of the whole world honored him, the Vienna Medical School did not. And what is more, Freud was able to become *Privat Dozent* only because he received this appointment *before* he had made his revolutionary discoveries. His very

---

40. Permission to lecture at the university.

41. Furtmüller considered Freud's having received the title of *Professor Extraordinary* as "never more than just a title" (p. 349 above) by which the academic functions, rights, and privileges of the bearer were in fact not elevated above those of a *Privat Dozent*. Furtmüller means to stress here the fact that Freud never was appointed *Professor ordinarius*.

achievements in science would have banned him from even a modest place on the faculty.

There were scores of young physicians who received the *venia legendi* because they mastered the technique of their specialty without any indication that important contributions to scientific research could ever be expected from them. The majority of them wanted to be *Privat Dozent* not from scientific or academic ambition but because the title enabled them to ask higher fees from their patients. The relations between *Privat Dozent* and *Professor ordinarius* were the courteous relations between colleagues and scientists, on the tacit presupposition that the vast hierarchic gap between them would never be forgotten.

It is evident that a man who, as a nonconformist, had already built up his position in the scientific world by independent, original work did not fit into this system. Furthermore, the neurologist immediately responsible for the decision, an eminent scientist of international renown, was an expert on the neurological side of psychiatry but in his interests very far from psychotherapy. He was not aware that the requisites of research and demonstration in this field were different and did not depend in the same measure upon case material and statistics that were inaccessible to a private physician who did not have the facilities of a university hospital at his disposal.[42]

It was only natural that when the final negative answer came, in

42. Phyllis Bottome (1957) relates that Professor Otto Pötzl, whom she considers at least partially responsible for the rejection of Adler's application, explained to her his reasons as follows: "Had Freud brought us his *Dream Analysis* as a thesis, I am quite sure we should have refused him his *Dozentur* upon it, in precisely the same manner that we refused Adler his, for *The Nervous Character*. Psychology was, and still is in our academic circles, not considered to be a science in itself, nor should it be given a philosophical handling, such as Adler's *Nervous Character* presented. Freud received his *Dozentur* from a specialized thesis upon *Aphasia* in pamphlet form. . . . It was Adler's refusal to take a specialized basis that made it impossible for us to bestow this honour upon him" (p. 109). Bottome adds that in fairness to Wagner-Jauregg, who had to make the final decision, it must be remembered that *The Neurotic Constitution* "is by no means clear to read" (p. 110). The rejection of Adler's application, a document of over 3,000 words, signed by Julius Wagner-Jauregg, has been located and published in full by H. A. Beckh-Widmanstetter (1965) and reported by Ansbacher (1966). In the above quotation we substituted *Dozentur* for professorship since it is the former to which Pötzl was referring.

spite of the attempt to sweeten the pill with the sugar of flattering words, Adler was offended. But neither he nor his friends ever overemphasized this episode. Proof of this is that although it was never treated as a secret, many members of Adler's group heard only years afterwards of the university's rejection of a great opportunity.[43]

The Name "Individual Psychology"

In 1913 the group changed the name of the association. There was a negative and a positive reason for this. As Freud insisted that the term psychoanalysis should be reserved exclusively for the truths and errors which he personally endorsed, Adler's friends wanted to avoid being characterized as a rebellious sect instead of as a group of independent scientists.

On the positive side it seemed fitting that the name of the association should express, as far as a name could do so, the central idea of Adler's psychology. This central idea was the idea of personality; the working hypothesis was that the various actions and ideas of an individual could not be explained as caused by isolated psychic powers like drives, or motivated by certain isolated experiences like traumas, but only in connection with the whole of the individual's psychic picture. Thus the name of Personality Psychology would have been the most fitting. But unfortunately this had already been taken for the doctrine of another psychologist who approached the problem of personality by methods widely different from Adler's. The group

43. When Adler (A1922c) had the satisfaction of writing the preface to the 3rd edition of *The Neurotic Constitution,* he expressed himself about this episode in the following words: "On the occasion of the 3rd edition of this book the obligation to be frank oppresses me in a most tormenting way. Thus I wish to make a confession which certainly will deprive me permanently of the affection of my readers. After a detailed negative appraisal of this book my application for permission to lecture at the university was rejected by the Vienna College of Professors. By this decision I have up to the present been prevented from giving lectures to university students and physicians. Those who know understand how difficult the dissemination of my views became. Yet today this has nevertheless been accomplished. Perhaps the following circumstance has somewhat helped in this: The views of Individual Psychology demand the unconditional reduction of the striving for power and the development of social interest. Its watchword is the fellowman, the fellowmanlike attitude towards the immanent demands of human society. There may be more venerable theories of an older academic science. There may be newer, more sophisticated theories. But there is certainly none which could bring greater gain to all people."

discussed the problem thoroughly, the decision naturally resting with Adler. He finally chose Individual Psychology as the one term which seemed next best to characterize his method.[44]

There were two objections to this name. First, Individual Psychology was already in common use in contrast to social or group psychology. Here, however, misunderstandings were not likely to arise, since in the one use the name characterized a special field of research, in the other a special method. The more serious objection was that the name could suggest that the psychic reactions of the isolated individual should be studied, whereas it was just one of the central points of Adler's psychology that the individual could be understood only by studying his contacts with the social groups in which he lived. Nevertheless, the name expressed more of the system it covered than most scientific terms are able to do. And its ready acceptance by friends, opponents, and the general public has shown that it was not a bad choice.[44a]

Publications

The group soon felt that they had to offer their work to the inspection of the scientific public. They therefore looked for different opportunities to express themselves in print. In the first months after separation from Freud, the hospitality of several medical and psychotherapeutic journals had to be accepted. But they wanted to sail under their own flag. A series of monographs began to be published. These showed from the beginning that the group was trying the new

44. Introducing the first issue of the *Zeitschrift für Individualpsychologie*, of which he was coeditor with Adler, Furtmüller (1914a) wrote regarding the name: "The name of Individual Psychology intends to express the conviction that psychological processes and their manifestations can be understood only from the individual context and that all psychological insight begins with the individual." Even then he was aware of "the fundamental objections which are raised against the possibility of a psychology of the individual."

44a. On the positive side of the name Individual Psychology, it is to be said: When Adler introduced the name (A1912a, p. iii), he quoted Rudolf Virchow. This turned out to be from Virchow's paper on "Atoms and Individuals." Both terms actually mean the same, "indivisible"; but the former belongs to the physical sciences, the latter to the life sciences. It seems then that by the name Individual Psychology Adler wished to indicate also that his system predicates the organismic viewpoint, in contrast to Freud's physicalism. (Ansbacher, in press).

methods not only in psychotherapy but also in problems of philosophy and literature.[45]

A volume, *Heilen und Bilden*, brought together a number of papers by Adler and other group members.[46] It marked a development which was to be significant for the Adler circle for their whole future—the close collaboration of the psychiatrist with the teacher and educator.[47] The understanding of the psychological problems of childhood and adolescence which Individual Psychology offered and its special way of looking at human relations were to be made useful for daily life in the school and the family, and not reserved for the cases where child guidance needed the help of the psychiatrist.

In April 1914, the first issue of the *Zeitschrift für Individualpsychologie* was published.[48] Now the group felt sure that its voice would be heard continuously and listened to with growing attention. Everybody's activity and literary ambition were stimulated. Not only papers for the *Zeitschrift* but also quite a number of books were planned or already under way. Then came the outbreak of World War I, and almost immediately the group felt its harmful effects.

45. The name of the series was *Schriften des Vereins für freie psychoanalytische Forschung*, with Adler (A1912b) as editor. By 1914 four monographs had been published—Furtmüller (1912), Kaus (1912), Schrecker (1912), and Asnaourow (1913)—and six additional ones were announced.

46. The editors were Adler and Furtmüller (A1914a), as mentioned in the introduction. By the time of the second edition Furtmüller was apparently too busy with his work in education to take an active part, and Erwin Wexberg was added as a third editor (A1922a).

47. In his final words to this volume Adler (A1914a, p. 399) spoke of "the undeniable need for physicians and educators to work together." He concluded: "Individual Psychology is for us an artistic endeavor which enables us to regard all expressive movements in the context of a self-consistent becoming. The result is the following most important presupposition for the practice of education: to sharpen the sense of reality through illumination of the unrecognized life plan and through its revision, and to remove pathological and asocial aberrations through change of the self-created system." The idea of *becoming* had been introduced by Adler (A1912a, p. 445) when he quoted from Rudolf Hildebrand, "Throughout the great *being* which surrounds and deeply penetrates us, there extends a great *becoming* which strives toward the perfect being." Hildebrand (1824–1894) was a Germanist and professor at Leipzig whose philosophical writings anticipated Adler in a number of ways (Ansbacher, 1962a).

48. The subtitle of the journal was, "Studies in the area of psychotherapy, psychology, and education." Its editors were Adler and Furtmüller, as mentioned before. The very first paper was the one by Neuer (1914), which was soon followed by a paper by Furtmüller (1914b), both mentioned earlier.

Most members were young enough to be called up immediately. The weekly meetings were given up; the *Zeitschrift* was given up.[49] Some months later Adler, too, had to don the uniform of the army physician.

THE CONCEPT OF SOCIAL INTEREST

World War I

As an army doctor Adler worked for some time in a Vienna hospital. Then he was sent to a town in the province of Lower Austria, and finally, for the last months of the war, back to Vienna.

The stupor of the first weeks did not last. A smaller circle gathered around Adler as long as he was in Vienna, and again as soon as he came back. The process of winning new friends eager to study his theories came into action again. Also, wherever he went outside of Vienna he found himself the center of a friendly circle. His gregarious character attracted people personally. His way of getting into human contact with his patients, never blinded by routine in diagnosis and therapy; his objective, impersonal way of suggesting, where it seemed necessary, a new, unusual approach as a matter of common sense rather than a new discovery; these characteristics made even people who until then had not known anything about his scientific achievement see that here was a man from whom one could learn, who did not make it difficult to learn from him. Thus, in all the places where he worked during the war he left the mark of his personality.

For Adler, however, those years of war were not only a time when, often under circumstances of personal hardship, he developed fruitful professional activities, partly in fields new to him, such as treatment of shell shock.[50] They were also a time of important changes in his outlook on world affairs and on the problems of human personality.

When the war broke out he thought that for Austria it was a just war. Always inclined to paradox, in private conversation he liked to say: "You know, I always was critical toward our government and I

49. An attempt was made to continue the journal with Charlot Strasser, Zurich, as a third editor. But after August, 1914, only one further issue appeared, in September 1916, to complete Volume 1.

50. Adler (A1918f) wrote a paper on war neurosis which also contained a review of the current literature.

never expected that they could be right. Surprisingly, this time they are right!" An approval formulated in this manner had within itself the roots of reconsideration. This reconsideration took time and went on step by step; but long before the war was over Adler had definitely taken the opposite position. For those who are prone to underestimate Adler's skill as a writer it may be interesting to learn that he found means to tell of this change in his position which were understood by his friends and not by the military censor. He now wanted peace, what the war party called scornfully "peace at any price." When hostilities finally ceased, he accepted the dissolution of the Austrian monarchy and the establishment of the smaller Austrian Republic not as a defeat but as the beginning of a new, hopeful evolution.[51]

Social Interest

A second change was logically independent of the first, although psychological analysis would undoubtedly show an under-surface connection. During the war, Adler's psychological thinking took a new turn. He added the last pillar to his system—or maybe it would be more nearly correct to say, he placed his system on new foundations. During the war Adler discovered the basic, decisive importance of Gemeinschaftsgefühl, a term for which the best, although not completely satisfactory, English equivalent is social interest.[52]

This new element in Adler's theory made clear that the differences between Freud and Adler were more than differences regarding

51. At that time Adler (A1919a, p. 16) wrote an incensed pamphlet against the idea of collective guilt, ending with the words: "Only he could judge the guilt of this people who has lived among them. . . . He will acquit them of any war guilt. They were immature, had no guiding lines and no leader. They were pushed and driven to slaughter. . . . Let us rather ask forgiveness of the people and let us consult how the damage done them can be made good."

52. Actually, just before the war, Adler had introduced a very similar term, Gemeinsinn or Gemeinschaftssinn, which can be adequately translated as "social sense." One of his papers (A1914e) was entitled "The Psychological Life of the Child and Social Sense." In another paper (A1914f)) he stressed the necessity of the "advancement of the social sense." A certain "tendentious view of the world, originating in childhood, in its rigid one-sidedness causes the social sense to wither" (A1914e, p. 45). At a meeting of the Individual Psychology Society, Adler (A1914t) stated: "The ideal of social sense on which our life is based requires rest as well as mutual agitation." At another meeting he (A1914u) defined ethics as "the incarnation of the social sense." We owe the first two references to Miss Godelieve Vercruysse (1961).

psychological methods and hypotheses. Behind these differences lay a fundamental difference in philosophical attitude towards mankind. It was a rift which had gone through the philosophies and religions of all time and expressed itself also in the philosophers and moralists of the seventeenth and eighteenth centuries, the forerunners of modern ethics and psychology.

You may see in man a being originally completely egoistic; then "goodness" will appear as a victory of man over himself, and altruism must be explained as a complicated transformation of egoism, e.g., as a sublimation of drives. Or you may see altruistic as well as egoistic instincts as an original part of human nature; then human cooperation, in its most elementary and in its highest aspects, will appear not necessarily as the product of conflicts but as an evolution from the original basis.

The dilemma can hardly be decided by studying facts, especially the behavior of the infant. These facts need interpretation, and they will be interpreted differently by different scientists according to their basic philosophic positions. For Freud, man originally is a dangerous savage, and this dangerous savage still lurks in the unconscious of every individual. For him, absolute egoism is the starting point, and civilization takes on a negative aspect as a system of inhibitions. That Adler took the opposite position could have been seen, even before he spoke about social interest, from the difference in their therapeutic aims. Freud told the patient: "Accept the unavoidable inhibitions, then within their frame there will be the green light for your drives"; while Adler said: "Look at the 'logic of life.' It asks for cooperation." Freud's tendency to aristocratic individualism and Adler's choice to be the "common man" among common men are related to this difference in their basic positions.[53]

The new accent on social interest as a basic quality of the human mind now showed that what the patient had to learn from the logic of life was not something new, but only something covered over and forgotten in the struggle for imaginary superiority over inferiority feeling, so that the problem of therapy was not so much educating as re-educating.

~~~~~~~~~~~~~~~

53. While Furtmüller speaks of only two possibilities—either to regard man as originally completely egoistic, or "you may see altruistic as well as the egoistic instincts as an original part of human nature"—a third alternative exists. It is to

Contact with the Common Man

The concentration of Adler's thinking during the war on this problem of man's wish for human contacts and cooperation was not motivated by the broad, general aspects of the war. He did not accept the official declamations of patriotic rhetoric as true expressions of social interest, and the fact that war in itself is the ultimate negation of social interest on a wide scale could not make him hesitate.

What stirred his attention was again his contact with the common man, with the ordinary soldiers, with the wounded and sick in the army hospitals. For them war was not a political or social problem to be accepted or refuted; it was a disaster which breaks upon the individual, and the individual has to go through with it like other catastrophes of life. And before the prospect of being sent back to the front, their attitude, not of proud men playing the role of heroes, but of humble men thinking about themselves and their personal fate, could be either: "Others have to take it, so I shall take it, too," or "*sauve qui peut.*" [54]

Here the problem of malingering became very important for the development of Adler's thoughts. Just at a time when he was already

take the altruistic aspect out of the realm of instincts, or the conative realm, and to consider it instead as a cognitive quality. According to the Gestalt psychologist, Solomon Asch (1952, p. 334), man's capacity to relate himself in a positive way to others derives from our striving "to relate ourselves meaningfully to the surroundings." "One fundamental source of the need for society is the active and insightful relation of men to their surroundings. Our intellectual and emotional capacities urge us into the surroundings; they awaken our interest and concern" (p. 346). Thereby social concern becomes primarily a cognitive process, which only secondarily also acquires conative properties. This third alternative is a necessity for a truly holistic theory, because it cannot accept a basic dualism of egoistic and altruistic "instincts," but requires the recognition of only one master motive, which Adler eventually called striving for perfection or completion.

That Adler in fact took the social aspect out of the conative and into the cognitive realm is evidenced by his pointing to the "logic of life." Adler (A1929e, p. 31) implied quite clearly that he accepted the third alternative when he defined social interest as "an innate potentiality which has to be consciously developed." "We are unable to trust any so-called social instinct, for its expression depends upon the child's conception or vision of the environment." For a fuller discussion of this point see Ansbacher (1965).

54. His views on the attitudes of the common soldier towards the war are expressed in the pamphlet by Adler (A1919a) cited in footnote 51. Translated excerpts from this can be found in Adler (A1956b, pp. 457–459).

against the war and a partisan of "peace at any price," his judgment on malingering was nevertheless very severe. He did not accept excuses. When people reminded him that he himself was opposed to further bloodshed and therefore should not reproach poor devils who were trying to save their skins, he answered: "The malingerer knows very well that at a given time a regiment has to send a given number of men to the front, and so if he does not go it means another has to go for him."

The end of the war found Adler working in a Vienna army hospital. While most units of the Austro-Hungarian army dissolved themselves even before they were officially dismissed, most of the personnel of the hospitals stayed on because they understood that the patients could not be left without care. When the former military discipline was thus supplanted by a discipline of human cooperation, the enlisted men were not willing to respect the social barriers which had existed between officers and them. Especially did they insist that the food for the officers and physicians should be the same as for the men. That was hard for Adler's colleagues because social privileges for officers had become second nature for them. Adler himself, however, willingly accepted the diminished comfort because the new relationship to the noncommissioned personnel seemed to him so much more human and thus more dignified. With a smile he would say: "It's a pity that the new system wasn't established long ago. That certainly would have shortened the war considerably!"

Postwar Events and Brief Political Activity

The collapse of the Austro-Hungarian monarchy in October and November 1918 and the end of the war found the different layers of society in the German parts of Austria, soon to become the Austrian Republic, in very different moods. The industrial workers, who had suffered most from the economic hardships which came in the wake of the war and were passionately opposed to the military dictatorship which characterized the war period, greeted the end of hostilities and the establishment of a democratic government with enthusiasm. Large sections of the peasantry also preferred the new state of things to the old.

On the other hand, not only the heretofore ruling group but also nearly all career and reserve officers, the capitalists who were interested in the economic supremacy of Vienna over Central Europe, and a large part of the intelligentsia took the new developments very hard. Even those who later adapted themselves to the changed situation went through a long and painful period of transition. Not so Adler. For him the armistice was not a shock as it was for the ruling group, but a longed-for relief as it was for the suffering masses. The common man in him welcomed the changed social atmosphere.

The first period of the Austrian Republic was the only time when Adler took an active part in politics. In Austria Workers' Committees were organized, following the example of the Russian soviets but with quite different importance and functions. While in the Central Workers Committee of Vienna the leaders of the Social-Democratic Party argued over the basic political problems with the small Communist minority and the radicals of their own party, the local Workers Committees in the city districts took over some minor administrative functions, especially the adjudicating of housing facilities, and, furthermore, concentrated on political education.

The Workers Committee of the First District of Vienna, where Adler lived, elected him vice-chairman. The educational activities were what won his special interest. Such a position on one of the Workers Committees was considered by most of the incumbents as an important preparatory step in a political career, leading later to a seat in the City Council or in Parliament, or to some administrative appointment. Adler's ambition never faced in this direction. He was not the person to work under the conditions of party discipline, and he felt that in the long run he should give all of his time and energy to the field where he could not be replaced by anyone else.

Integrating the Concept of Social Interest

The activities of the Adler group became more regular and intense as soon as the war was over. As to persons it never became quite the same group it was before the war. Some members never came back home, others during those five eventful years had directed their intellectual interests elsewhere, and others were too much involved in practical activities to do much work in the group. But there were many valuable newcomers, especially—and that was of first importance for further development—a group of young, very enthusiastic teachers.

Soon the former development repeated itself. Adler's apartment became too small for the weekly meetings and they had to be held in clubrooms. Again, the formal sessions were followed by endless informal discussions in coffeehouses.

The first task for the group was to get acquainted with, to discuss, and to integrate the new trend in Adler's ideas which he had developed during the war. We have said already that his conception of an innate social interest in no way conflicted with his former position which showed the history of the neurotic personality as beginning with an intense feeling of inferiority. But nearly all of the old members, as well as the new ones who came to Adler after having studied *The Neurotic Constitution,* supposed that an absolute self-centeredness was basic to this inferiority feeling. For a time discussion of any special problem soon came back to this fundamental question.

As far as logical reasoning went, the new theory was accepted by most of the participants in these debates after a relatively short period of deliberation. It took more time, however, for them to see things in this new light for themselves, when they used Adler's theories as guidance for their own observations and their own thinking. And never did all of them adopt the new point of view with equal thoroughness.

Whoever studies the literature of Individual Psychology of the twenties will easily detect these differences in acceptance of social interest. That is not surprising. What is surprising, however, is that despite the ever-growing importance Adler gave to social interest, there are still numerous books which depict Adler as heralding the "will for power" like a second Nietzsche.

The attention which Adler gave to social interest had the result, too, that his case histories and reports of progress in individual treatments now sounded different. Hitherto, the crux of the treatment had been to make the patient understand by a convincing insight that in pursuing his old course he would not avoid defeats but on the contrary would be excluded from any real success in life. He had to see and to accept the "logic of life"; that for him there was no other way out than through compliance with this logic.

Now this intellectual work with the patient still remained, but it became combined with the strengthening of original potentialities in the individual which were only underdeveloped under the influence of the neurotic development. The principle of encouragement thus found a new application. The patient could now be shown that the new way of life which he had to choose if he wanted to become psychologically healthy did not mean something completely strange and opposed to all his former life; it only meant using aptitudes which he had always had within him but had neglected to acknowledge.

APPLICATIONS OF INDIVIDUAL PSYCHOLOGY

It was a good thing for the group, after the irregularity of work during the war and so many personal changes, that it was confronted with a new, widened point of view. This led to a thorough re-thinking and discussion of Adler's system and to a more profound understanding of the interrelation of its different parts. Along with the accrued confidence of the group that they were on the right track came the feeling that they now ought to make the new insight and the new methods useful to a wider circle. In Austria, and especially in Vienna, during the first decade after the war, in spite of so many material hardships, a strong will to work for a better future, a loving interest and sometimes enthusiasm for social advancement was widespread. No wonder the Individual Psychologists felt they should do their bit!

Adult Education

In this practical work Adler was also to become the leader. The first step was that he accepted an invitation to give regular lectures at the *Volksheim*, Vienna's most important adult education institute at that time. Here for the first time Adler became aware of his ability to get a large and not at all homogeneous audience to follow him, not as passive listeners but with active and creative attention. Attendance was surprisingly large from the beginning and, contrary to general experience in such lecture series, did not decrease but grew from lecture to lecture.[55]

---

55. These are the lectures on which the most widely translated book of Adler (A1927a and b), *Understanding Human Nature*, is based.

There were many teachers in his audience, parents (more mothers than fathers), men and women from different walks of life who had made psychology their foremost intellectual interest, and, characteristically enough, a number of university students who found in Adler's lectures the inspiration which their academic curriculum failed to give them.

Adler did not restrict himself to straight lecturing for long. The members of the audience were allowed to raise questions and submit special problems for discussion.[56] The *Volksheim* had a summer camp in the Alps near Vienna, and there for a week or more Adler lived with a small circle of especially interested students.

.   .   .   .

School Reform

The greatest challenge to Individual Psychology, however, lay in the possibility of influencing public education in Vienna, not through individual teachers and parents but in a much more comprehensive way. The Vienna of the first Austrian Republic was the city of School Reform, a radical change in organization, curricula, and methods, under the leadership of the socialist president of the Board of Education, Otto Glöckel.[57] From the beginning Individual Psychology had shown an interest in educational problems at least equal to that in the problems of psychotherapy. It now seemed that an opportunity

~~~~~~~~~~~~~~~~

56. There is a report by Dr. Alice Friedmann (1923–24) on seminars at the *Volksheim*. According to this report the first seminar was held during the winter 1919–1920, dealing with the young child. The next year was devoted to the school child, and the following year to problems of adolescence. During 1922–23 the topic was the life and work of important men, especially revolutionaries. During 1923–24 it dealt with social psychology; among those who read papers were a Dr. Rittersporn, and Manes Sperber, the later well-known author.

In the same year as the seminar on important men, Adler (A1923b) published an article on Danton, Marat, and Robespierre, in which he found that such men had in common an overriding ambition and at the same time were denied an appropriate place of activity by a deficient social organization. The same thought is expressed by Adler (A1926z) in connection with Mussolini: "Men and nations cannot bear to feel inferior. Strife for power develops. Robespierre, Marat, Mussolini sought the equation for their inferiority. Mussolini had no place in the world. The socialist party of Italy crushed him in November, 1914. . . . So he sought another outlet in his quest for power."

57. For a history of the School Reform see Papanek (1962).

not to be neglected was offered for each field to make use of the other.

Cooperation seemed even more possible since the basic principles of the Vienna School Reform regarding methods of education had much in common with the teachings of Individual Psychology. This was partly due to a sort of personal union, because some of the men who formulated the educational program were also Individual Psychologists.[58] Partly also—and this perhaps was still more important—the practical needs of progressive education in a large-scale school system led in the nature of things to a policy very near to some of the basic ideas of Individual Psychology.

Progressive education meant freedom for the child, meant encouragement of spontaneous activity instead of the merely receptive attitude demanded by old-time methods. But the public school system of a metropolis with nearly ten thousand teachers, all of them trained in teachers colleges to do their job in the old way, could not embark on unlimited experiments where freedom of teacher and freedom of children would threaten to create an interesting but dangerous chaos. So, from the beginning, the Vienna School Reform took care to avoid daring extremes which elsewhere, through some individual failures, often discredited the whole idea of progressive education.

Freedom could not be the opposite of, but had to be complemented by, order; and encouragement of the child seemed useful only when at the same time the child learned the meaning of responsibility. The old authoritative discipline could not be replaced by absence of discipline, but had to be replaced by a discipline whose rules the children themselves developed out of the necessities of the common work which was to be done in school. This combination of ideas of encouragement and responsibility formed the foundation on which cooperation between the Vienna educators and Individual Psychology seemed not only possible but natural.[59]

᠆᠆᠆᠆᠆᠆᠆᠆᠆᠆᠆᠆

58. Furtmüller was one of these, as mentioned in the introductory comments. According to Papanek (1962, p. 72), "others who worked right in the school system were Furtmüller's wife, Aline, Oskar Spiel, Ferdinand Birnbaum, and—among numerous others—the author of this study."

59. Eventually, in September 1931, an Adlerian experimental school (*Indivi-*

Nevertheless, this cooperation could not be established simply by making Individual Psychology the official psychology of the School Board. In the twenties Vienna became one of the most important, rather *the* most important, center of modern psychology. There was Freud with his already established, and Adler with his swiftly growing, international recognition. And there were two eminent representatives of the most advanced trend in academic psychology, Karl and Charlotte Bühler.

The Bühlers' was one of the very few progressive appointments made by the University of Vienna during the period of the first Austrian Republic, when the University in general was aggressively reactionary.[60] This appointment had been made possible only because the City of Vienna offered to the University a modern psychological institute on the condition that the chair of psychology be filled by a scholar of international rank. Thus the Bühlers were also the psychologists in Vienna's teachers college.[61] Besides the research work done under their direction, they were important for the training of teachers and student teachers in exact scientific methods. For the practical school life, however, and the solving of problems of organization and of methods of education their influence was negligible.[62]

<hr>

dualpsychologische Versuchsschule) was established in Vienna by Ferdinand Birnbaum, together with Oskar Spiel and Franz Scharmer. It was closed when the Dollfuss regime came to power in 1934, but resumed after World War II. Its functioning is described by Madelaine Ganz (1935, pp. 49–108). Subsequently, Spiel (1947) published a book about this school, which has now also appeared in an English version (1962). Furtmüller does not mention the experimental school, apparently because Adler was not personally connected with it.

60. Karl Bühler was appointed in 1922, Charlotte Bühler in 1923. Both were dismissed by the Nazis in 1938.

61. In further description of this appointment Charlotte Bühler writes: "The City of Vienna called directly on Karl Bühler to ask whether he, if appointed, would be willing to be the first university professor in Vienna to lecture to teachers directly at their own teachers college. Teachers had up to then only secondhand information of scientific psychology. We were to give them firsthand knowledge" (personal communication, November 7, 1962).

62. Charlotte Bühler sees the work of her husband and herself not as having been limited to the mere training of teachers in "exact scientific methods." She writes: "We taught them developmental psychology and its application to educational problems, awareness of social aspects of behavior in school and of

The establishment of the Bühlers' institute, however, was not the only reason which made it impossible to link the educational policy of the school board officially with Individual Psychology. The Freudians would have been influential enough to protest effectively against such a monopoly, and both Freud and Adler were considered dangerous influences by all conservatives, although Adler not to the same degree as Freud. For the school board it was hard enough to steer the ship of School Reform through a wild political sea, and it would have been unwise to provoke another storm. A similar consideration of caution also held Individual Psychology back. The school board was in the hands of the socialists, and although every effort was made to handle educational problems on a strictly nonpartisan basis, in the heat of political arguments an "official" psychology of the school board would undoubtedly have received the ridiculous stigma of a party psychology.

Teacher Training

A middle way was chosen, and Adler was asked to become a member of the faculty of the teachers college, the Pedagogical Institute of the City of Vienna.[63] Given Adler's prestige this step could not be criticized by anybody, for the lectures for teachers were not compulsory and it was up to the individual teacher whether he or she wanted to attend them. This contact between Individual Psychology and Vienna's teachers, however, once established, worked out in a marvelous way. Not through the school authorities, but by his influence on the thinking and the pedagogical methods of hundreds of teachers who came to him of their own will, Adler deeply affected the development of Vienna's schools, a rare and outstanding example of democracy at work.

Teachers who find their work getting difficult mostly do not

maturational factors, and gave them a psychological understanding of their educational procedures. We published a series of studies called *Wiener Arbeiten zur Pädagogischen Psychologie*. Beyond this, in the direction of influencing the 'practical school life,' we were not expected to go" (personal communication, December 18, 1962).

63. Adler lectured at the Pedagogical Institute, in the division of therapeutic education, beginning in 1924. The title of the lectures was The Difficult Child (*Schwererziehbare Kinder*) (H. Schnell, personal communication, December 17, 1962).

stumble over subject matter. Here information and advice are easily at hand. But how to get and hold the children's attention, make them work, handle disturbing elements, handle problem children? Here the teacher looking for help by following educational courses very often either gets a series of very wise, competent, general observations and rules, the application of which to a given individual case may not be easy; or he is advised to bring the causes of the difficulties into the open by a detailed study of the individual case, a method which not only would take much more time than the teacher could give but might also lead to meddling in family affairs.

The teachers who came to Adler's lectures realized that in discussing individual cases—and soon cases were also submitted by members of the audience—he taught them a method for using their own observations and implementing these by the information, often slight, which the parents gave them. From the way it was given they could make at least a fair guess at what was happening in the child's mind, a guess which would be tested in the child's reactions to the teacher's further handling of him.[64]

Adler's audience at the Pedagogical Institute learned about a new theory of human behavior and, at the same time, how to make immediate use of this theory in daily school and family life. What they heard in Adler's courses they afterwards brought up in faculty meetings and in talks with parents—groups and individuals. And many a child felt the climate surrounding him become more mild because in the Pedagogical Institute there was a man who knew how to change the moral atmosphere.

Responsibility was also a guiding idea here. Adler never advised minimizing asocial attitudes of youth under the slogan of "freedom." At the same time he also stressed responsibility on the part of the teacher by diagnosing fewer cases as the kind in which the child's unsociability was so severe that the influence of the teacher alone could not be considered sufficient to help.

~~~~~~~~~~~~~~~~

64. These lectures, like those at the *Volksheim*, were also published in the form of a book by Adler (A1929b). In the preface Adler states that the book contains specifically the lectures he gave at the Pedagogical Institute in 1928. "The reader will immediately recognize that I aim at a cooperation between psychiatrist, teacher, and family. . . . We are striving to improve the lot of the children, the teachers, and the family."

Child Guidance Clinics

This contact with a great number of teachers, and membership in the Individual Psychology Association of teachers who were thoroughly acquainted with the theory and practice of Individual Psychology, provided a very good opportunity for Adler's ideas to become the leading influence in a field which just at this time was opening up in Vienna. Under the name *Erziehungsberatungsstelle* the group established a number of child guidance clinics in public schools, with the consent of the school authorities but on a completely voluntary basis. Each clinic cooperated with a number of schools which had asked for this service.[65]

Children with educational problems could be brought to the clinic when the teacher suggested it and the parents agreed. A case was accepted only when the child was accompanied by a parent as well as by the teacher. Without any official pressure and without publicity these clinics soon won the confidence of teachers and families. Their most serious problem was that they could not handle all the applications. On principle, a psychiatrist and a teacher collaborated in each clinic. It was characteristic of Adler's way of applying Individual Psychology that he was always willing to offer his advice but he never recommended a stereotyped method. Each worker and each team in the clinics had to develop their own methods on the basis of the common principles.

Adler himself worked in one of these clinics. The method he chose for himself seemed a daring experiment at first, but it met with very significant success. Adler decided to use his work in the clinic as a demonstration, and therefore held his interviews with child and

65. By 1922 Adler had already established the first child guidance clinic in connection with his work at the *Volksheim*. Adler (A1922b, p. 120) mentions this in a paper in which he recommends the further development of such clinics and also the psychological training of special teachers to work with difficult children. He points out that such measures would be necessary to implement the School Reform which Glöckel had inaugurated. Adler, however, was well aware of the fact that he was not the first to establish child guidance clinics, as some believed. On the contrary, he lends strength to his recommendation for the establishment of such clinics by adding "as they also exist in Germany, in Switzerland, and in the United States." Adler's originality in child guidance was that he included the parent, the teacher, and an interested audience in his clinic sessions, thus practicing family therapy and social psychiatry.

parents not in privacy but before a restricted audience. The session began with an oral or written report from the teacher who was bringing the case to the clinic. Adler then analyzed this report and from it drew a picture of the child's character and problems and of the family situation. Then followed the interviews, first with the parent, then with the child. Or Adler might reverse the order when he felt that otherwise the child would be suspicious of some "conspiracy."

Adler's skill in handling people made the children as well as the adults soon feel at home with him, so they did not take account of, or soon forgot, the audience. That did not mean that Adler made it "easy" for the child. On the contrary, as time was precious, he liked to get to the center of difficulties with his first questions and remarks. Adler never gave authoritative advice but made the child study the problem with him and helped him to establish a plan to overcome the difficulties. Then a date would be set for a further interview when the child would tell him how the plan had worked out. Finally, Adler gave the teachers and parents a résumé of the case, often taking it as an example for elucidating more general problems. For the audience it was always striking to see how close Adler's sketch of the personality, taken from the initial report, came to the final picture offered by the interviews.[66]

The work of these child guidance clinics came to an abrupt end. When the Austrofascists overthrew the Austrian Republic in 1934, one of their first objectives was to kill the School Reform and every activity connected with it. These clinics, created by the spontaneous

~~~~~~~~~~~~~~~~~~

66. Detailed accounts of Adler's guidance work with children are to be found in three books of his (A1930a, A1930c, A1963) and one with associates (A1930f). The first gives the general theory and five case histories. The second reports twelve cases brought to the clinic which he conducted at the New School for Social Research in New York during his lecture series there in 1929. The third book, newly translated, consists of twenty case-study chapters. The fourth book covers the various aspects of Adlerian child guidance in twenty papers contributed by twenty-one of his Viennese co-workers: Alexandra Adler, Ferdinand Birnbaum, Paul Brodsky, Alice Friedmann, Friederike Friedmann, Arthur Holub, Martha Holub, Olga Knopf, Sophie Lazarsfeld, Ida Loewy, Alexander Müller, Alexander Neuer, Elly Rothwein, Regine Seidler, Lydia Sicher, Oskar Spiel, Theodor Vertes, Erwin Wexberg, Arthur Zanker, Theodor Zerner, and Ladislaus Zilahi. Finally, the study by Madelaine Ganz (1935, pp. 109–175), gives an account of the Adlerian child guidance clinics.

efforts of teachers and psychiatrists, were immediately closed by order of the new fascist school authorities.

International Acceptance

Adler at this time had already shifted most of his activities outside of Vienna. From the beginning the Vienna group was in contact with a quickly growing number of psychologists and psychiatrists abroad. After the war the international interest in Adler's theories became more and more lively, the network of friends and followers outside of Austria greater. When the *Zeitschrift* started again in 1923 it could add *Internationale* to its title and had a long list of collaborators from many countries.[67] More and more friends from abroad came to Vienna to stay for a shorter or longer period with Adler and his circle. Since Adler owned a comfortable country house with a beautiful garden in Salmannsdorf, a Vienna suburb, a numerous and varied company used to gather there, the Viennese often being outnumbered by people from England, Holland, the United States, and other countries.[68]

These visitors were not highbrow tourists who during their stay in Vienna wanted to get in touch with whatever might be the last word in intellectual development there. They were serious workers who back in their own countries tried to create centers for Individual Psychology. Groups and associations for Individual Psychology were organized in many cities. The groups in Germany were dissolved in

67. Adler was the sole editor, and there were 15 collaborators listed from Austria, 11 from Germany, and 17 from thirteen other countries. Soon two more were added: G. Stanley Hall, Clark University: and W. Ernest Hocking, Harvard University. In 1926 Leonhard Seif, Munich; Wilhelm Fürnrohr, Nuremberg; Fritz Künkel, Berlin; and M. Stam, The Hague, became coeditors. In 1927 Ladislaus Zilahi became managing editor. Beginning with 1932 the coeditors were: Seif and Fürnrohr; F. G. Crookshank, London; Stefan von Maday, Budapest; Lene Credner, Munich; Kurt Weinmann, Munich; D. G. Campbell, Chicago; Oliver Brachfeld, Barcelona; and the following from Vienna: Arthur Holub, Rudolf Dreikurs, Lydia Sicher, Ferdinand Birnbaum, Erwin O. Krausz, and Zilahi (managing editor). See also Wexberg (1926).

68. Adler acquired his country house in Salmannsdorf in 1926 (personal communication, Kurt A. Adler, November, 1962).

1933 when Hitler came to power.[69] When he came to Austria, in 1938, it meant the end of the association in Vienna. The international cooperation of the students of Individual Psychology remained active up to the time of World War II. When Adler died in 1937 there were groups organized and active in Belgium (Brussels), Czechoslovakia (Brno, Bratislava), Denmark (Copenhagen), England (London), France (Paris), Greece (Athens), Hungary (Budapest), Italy (Trieste), Yugoslavia (Zagreb), Netherlands (Amsterdam, Dordrecht, Rotterdam, Utrecht), Poland (Krakow), Rumania (Brasov, Cernauti), Spain (Barcelona), Switzerland (Zurich), Turkey (Oedemis), and the United States (Chicago). Literature on Individual Psychology was published in many languages, consisting partly of original papers of the workers in different countries and partly of translations of Adler's books or papers.

It was natural that these workers abroad wanted to see Adler in their own country, to have him speak to their friends and to wider groups of persons interested in psychotherapy and psychology, and so to secure a deeper and wider basis for the activities of their groups. Already for many years Adler had been invited to lecture in many, mostly Central European, cities. Even during World War I he lectured in Prague and Reichenberg. But now, beginning with 1926, lectures and courses abroad became a regular and important part of his program, a part which took a greater and greater portion of his time and energy, until finally Vienna became a place where he appeared, for months or weeks, rather as a visitor.

This work which led Adler from country to country, from city to city, was not simply the usual lecture-touring of writers and scientists who speak in the frame of a wide, varied program of lectures to an audience attracted by any well-known speaker, without professional or other special interest in his topic. Certainly Adler, too, lectured to such audiences. But the important thing always was to speak to

ᨆᨆᨆᨆᨆᨆᨆᨆᨆᨆ

69. At that time Individual Psychology groups existed in the following German cities: Berlin, Bremen, Breslau, Chemnitz, Dresden, Düsseldorf, Freital (Saxony), Freudenstadt, Giessen-Wetzlar, Halle, Hamburg, Heidelberg, Karlsruhe, Cologne, Magdeburg, Munich, Nuremberg, Stuttgart, and Wuppertal. In addition to conducting lecture courses and meetings, most of these groups maintained child guidance and counseling centers.

groups especially interested in the problems of Individual Psychology, and to discuss special problems with a smaller number of workers in the field. So his lecture tours gave new impulses to the activities of the different groups and served to coordinate them. Because of his warm, natural approach to people many who met him for the first time on these tours became his lasting personal friends.

United States

For a number of years these lecture tours were confined to places where Adler could address the audience in German because at this time he had only a reading knowledge of foreign languages. In 1926, however, he decided to accept an invitation to America and to deliver his lectures there in English. He worked the miracle of finding time in his overloaded schedule for daily English lessons, and after several months felt himself prepared for this daring undertaking. For it was daring to present himself, after a few months of preparation at an age which does not seem the best to begin the study of spoken foreign languages, to English-speaking audiences not only for prepared lectures but also for the possible heckling of question periods.

Adler's reaction to these difficulties was characteristic. He would have felt it to be a lack of courage and energy if he had renounced the opportunity to bring his ideas before wide new audiences. Shunning this task because his English was not perfect would have been in his opinion one of those pretexts which neurotics use to excuse their avoidance of real solutions to life's problems.

As to the audience, he thought that persons of good will would appreciate his effort to overcome the linguistic handicaps and they would meet him halfway in an effort to catch his ideas in spite of the difficulties of communication. Prejudiced people might use the imperfections of his language against him, but they would find grounds for criticism in any case. The events showed that Adler was right. His lectures in the United States were successful from the beginning.[70]

---

70. Adler's first trip to the United States was in all probability from December, 1926 to April, 1927. We give the following partial account of it to convey an idea of the scope of his activity, based on two contemporary reports of this trip ("Vortragsreise," 1927; Marx, Beatrice, 1927).

In New York he gave two series of six lectures each at the New School for

Adler now came to America year after year, dividing his work between the two continents but concentrating more and more on America.[71] In 1929–1930 he was lecturer at Columbia University, and, from 1932 on, visiting Professor for Medical Psychology at Long Island College of Medicine.[72] The language was soon no impediment for him. He was able to show in question periods his gift for sharp, witty improvisation in English as well as he had always done in German.[73]

Stressing Mental Hygiene

The extent and intensity of his lecturing, the challenge to make the essentials of his theories understandable to new and changing audiences in a single or a few lectures, began to influence importantly Adler's style of expressing his ideas and in a certain way the further development of these ideas.

wwwwwwwwwwwwwwwwwwwwwwwwwwwwwwwwwwwwwwwwwwwwwwwwwwwwwwwwwwwwwwwwwwwwwwwwwwwwwww

Social Research and at the Community Church. He also spoke before the Academy of Medicine, the Federation for Child Study, the Child Study Association, the Mental Hygiene Association, and the Cooper Union Institute. He held clinics at Mt. Sinai Hospital and at Beth Israel Hospital.

In Boston, Adler was the guest of William Healy. Among other lectures he gave one at Harvard University over which Morton Prince presided. Shortly thereafter, a paper by Adler (A1927k) appeared in the *Journal of Abnormal and Social Psychology* which was edited by Prince.

In Providence, Adler spoke at Brown University and the Providence Medical Association. He also addressed the parents and teachers of the Mary C. Wheeler School, where Miss Dey, the principal, was among his special friends (Bottome, 1957, p. 214).

In Chicago, the schedule included a series of six lectures to teachers, under the auspices of the Board of Education; numerous talks to various organizations; and an address before faculty and students of the University of Chicago. For the lecture series to teachers, 2500 applications for tickets had to be turned down.

Adler also went to Philadelphia, Culver Academy (Indiana), Cincinnati, Milwaukee, and visited various places in California, carrying on similar activities. Everywhere he was received with enthusiasm, drawing huge audiences so that frequently hundreds of people had to be turned away; and everywhere he was encouraged to return.

71. In 1928 he received an LL.D. degree from Wittenberg University, Springfield, Ohio.

72. The Long Island College of Medicine became the Downstate Medical Center, State University of New York, in 1950.

73. In 1934, after the Austrofascists had come to power, Adler left Vienna finally and made New York his home. During these last years he and Mrs. Adler lived at the Gramercy Park Hotel.

Always, from the time when he was a general practitioner, Adler stuck to the principle of showing patients and families the doctor not as a priest performing mysterious, esoteric rites but as a man who tried to make his knowledge and his therapy understandable to laymen just as far as possible. Now the tendency became more and more accentuated—to express himself simply; to renounce the prestige of the erudite if the intelligent but unsophisticated listener or reader had to pay the price of not possibly following him; to avoid complicated details and ingenious classification where they were a hindrance rather than a help for understanding basic ideas.

At the same time he felt increasingly that in addressing large audiences it was more useful and promised deeper results to stress, in addition to therapy of developed neuroses, the importance of mental hygiene, the prevention of neurosis. This meant especially leading children in the formative years to take their stand on the "useful side" of life. He liked to speak about the fundamental changes which would take place in life and in history when wise guidance of children on a universal basis would develop their socially useful tendencies and thereby make them secure against neurosis as well as against delinquency.

Naturally he knew that such an idea was Utopian because its realization would have to depend on the wisdom and socially sound attitude of at least the great majority of adults, which again depended on their, too, having had the benefit of such enlightened universal teaching; but nevertheless he found the idea useful because it made clear the interrelationship between the psychological attitude of the individual and the situation and development of society.

It was his experience that as a rule interested laymen were more open to his teaching than most professional people, psychiatrists as well as psychologists. Artful dissertations about details of his theories and defense of every single point against sophisticated attacks seemed to him less fruitful than awakening understanding for the main principles in men and women who could thus learn to solve their own problems better and help others in solving the problems of their respective spheres of life. He wanted to be understandable for the "common man" who was intelligent and open to new ideas.

It was a long way from the manifold and elaborate details of *The Neurotic Constitution* to the concentrated ideas of these lectures and writings of his American period. Hence he sometimes had to defend himself against the criticism that his teachings were too simple or even trivial. Proudly he answered that it had cost him years of hard work to learn to express in a simple way, without the barrage of professional patter, the results of a lifetime of observation and thinking.

This method, like every other, had its advantages and dangers. There were people who regarded themselves as Adler's disciples and thought that Individual Psychology was "easy." Because it was easy to remember the sentences into which Adler compressed the essence of his ideas, they overlooked the fact that behind them was the concentrated experience of decades. In order to understand a person's deepest problems after a few interviews one needed not only a divining gift like Adler's but also his thousands of hours of work, slowly and carefully unraveling the complicated and often entangled weavings of numerous human souls.

Differences with Followers

Not all of Adler's followers agreed with this shift in his interest to the general public. It meant that Adler wanted the work of the Association of Individual Psychology open for a wide range of interested people. He understood the necessity for physicians to discuss their special problems in professional meetings, but otherwise he did not like an inner circle of professionals or advanced students to gather separately from the whole group. Such esoteric exclusiveness seemed to him a contradiction of the spirit of Individual Psychology.

Many of Adler's friends resented this, several perhaps because they felt that their years of collaboration made them a kind of aristocracy among Individual Psychologists, others certainly because they felt that discussions of experts about specific problems were not helped by being combined with the training of beginners. Here also the different methods had advantages and disadvantages. In Vienna the weekly gatherings of the Adler association became one of the living centers of intellectual Vienna. The prestige of these evenings was based on the quality and interest of the lectures offered. For the old, intimate group work the audience was too big and too heterogeneous.

There were other, deeper reasons for the strain on Adler's relations with some of his old friends. We have seen how Marx's sociology influenced the growth of the roots from which Adler's psychology developed. Some of his followers overstressed this point and tried to make Individual Psychology as such a satellite doctrine of Marxism. Adler certainly did not deny to any political, philosophical, or religious group the right to amalgamate his teachings with their specific doctrines if they found this feasible and useful. He was always aware that common ideological indebtedness to Marx could relate Individual Psychology to other movements based on his sociology. But he declined to see Individual Psychology made a partisan affair. Its methods and results could be used by adherents of very different ideologies.

At the same time that enthusiastic leftist admirers of Adler tried to monopolize him for their political parties, Catholic scholars saw in Individual Psychology a scientific and educational instrument the use of which was completely in accord with Catholicism. While the scientist's work will always be influenced—consciously or unconsciously—by his own philosophical and ethical background, the practical results of his efforts may be used in different ways by the adherents of very different philosophies.

Ethics and Mental Health

It is not certain, however, whether Adler in the last period of his work would have agreed with this statement, at least as far as Individual Psychology is concerned. We have seen how the different elements of his theory were first integrated in *The Neurotic Constitution*, and how the whole system then got broader and deeper foundations through the doctrine of the basic social interest. From the later twenties on, without changing the elements of his theory, Adler shifted his interest more and more from the intricacies of inferiority feeling and the ever-varying reactions against it to the appeal to and the strengthening of social interest.

By and by the concept of social interest itself changed in character. When Adler first introduced the idea into his theory it was a biological fact, the preparedness of the individual from the first moments of his life to establish contacts, cooperating contacts, with other individuals. Now social interest became the mentally healthy direction for the innate striving toward perfection—for the individual as well as for mankind as a whole. Adler was fully aware that by this new definition social interest had left the borders of biology and entered metaphysics.[74]

One reason which led Adler to this development was that undoubtedly it is impossible to be a psychotherapist without offering the patient some guidance based on ethical principles. The guidance may seemingly be completely away from ethics; for example: "Follow your drives without inner inhibitions, only be careful to avoid dangerous conflicts with established laws or customs." Such guidance may be based on ethical nihilism, but that is also a philosophy. For the Individual Psychologist it will be clear that guidance must lead along the path of cooperation.

But that was not all. Individual Psychology had shown that in neurosis all the different activities of the individual become directed toward one over-all goal—fantastic personal superiority. It was only natural that the treatment should invite the individual to change his neurotic goal into one leading to the "useful side of life." This was concurrent with the theoretical position of Individual Psychology, which always had put special accent on the teleological character of all psychic activity.

As an ethical principle, metaphysical social interest or related conceptions are at the root of many ethical systems and religious creeds. That the underdevelopment of the innate potentiality for social interest, largely because of compensatory reactions against inferiority feelings, leads away from mental health is an insight for which we are indebted to Adler alone.

WORKING TO THE END

An indefatigable worker all his life, Adler labored harder than ever in the years he divided his activities between Europe and America. One may say that year after year he did a full year's job on each continent. What normally should have been times of vacation became periods of especially concentrated work for him. There were his numerous courses and lectures, his work at clinics and with private patients, and preparation of a long series of papers and books to be published. Most

~~~~~~~~~~~~~~~~

74. Adler used the term metaphysics in the sense of ontology, as basic assumptions about man.

of these were based on stenographic notes taken during his lectures.[75]
In the midst of all his activities Adler could not give much time to
editing. Thus some of his books and papers published in this period
do not always show the correctness in details, linguistic and otherwise,
which would correspond to their intrinsic value. This was due neither
to the author's laziness nor to any lack of respect for his readers, but,
given his overload of work, only to the choice between publishing the
papers this way or not publishing them at all. Here again Adler's
reasoning was right: whoever sincerely wanted to study his ideas
would get over these difficulties and catch the meaning of the author;
whoever was looking for a chance to criticize would find faults
anyway.

Unfortunately there were more serious consequences of his over-
working. Advancing age would have demanded economizing of his
forces. He did not care, confident of his seemingly unconquerable
physical health. During his whole life he had had only three attacks of
serious illness. But now, finally, the strain was too much. His heart
began to give out, and Adler, always an astute diagnostician, knew it.
Maybe he had set himself a term after which he would relax or at
least diminish his activities. For when friends warned him against
overdoing in the spring of 1937, he answered, smiling, that he would
take a real vacation the next year. That was not to be. In April 1937,
Adler went to Europe, and from April 26 to May 28 he gave lectures
in Paris, Belgium, Holland, and Scotland. At the end of May he went
to Aberdeen to give a course of lectures at the University for medical
students and student teachers. Other lectures were added to the
program. It was the concentration of work Adler was always used to,
and he enjoyed it as always. On the morning of May 28 he took a

75. Adler (A1927a, p. iii) confirms this method of working in the preface to
Menschenkenntnis, where he gives credit to a Dr. Broser, who held a law degree,
for having kept nearly complete notes of the *Volksheim* lectures on which the
book is based. "I am not exaggerating when I state that without his aid this book
would hardly have come into being." He also gives credit to his daughter, Dr.
Alexandra Adler, for proofreading and completing the book "during a time in
which I endeavored to win new friends for Individual Psychology in England
and the United States." Evidently Adler spoke at these lectures spontaneously,
without formal notes, and left it largely to others to set his thoughts down in the
form of a book, while he attended to what he considered more urgent matters.

walk. Suddenly he collapsed. He died in the ambulance which was taking him to the hospital.

REFERENCES[1]

Allport, G. W. *Becoming: basic considerations for a psychology of personality.* New Haven: Yale Univer. Press, 1955.

Ansbacher, H. L. "The significance of the socio-economic status of the patients of Freud and of Adler." *Amer. J. Psychother.*, 1959, 13, 376–382.

Ansbacher, H. L. "On the origin of holism." *J. Indiv. Psychol.*, 1961, 17, 142–148. (a)

Ansbacher, H. L. Review of R. B. Winn (Ed.) Soviet psychology: a symposium. New York: Phil. Libr., 1961. *J. Indiv. Psychol.*, 1961, 17, 229–230. (b)

Ansbacher, H. L. "Rudolf Hildebrand: a forerunner of Alfred Adler." *J. Indiv. Psychol.*, 1962, 18, 12–17. (a)

Ansbacher, H. L. "Was Adler a disciple of Freud?" *J. Indiv. Psychol.*, 1962, 18, 126–135. (b)

Ansbacher, H. L. Review of D. Müller-Hegemann. Psychotherapie: ein Leitfaden für Ärzte und Studierende, 3rd. ed. Berlin: VEB Verlag Volk und Gesundheit, 1961. *J. Indiv. Psychol.*, 1962, 18, 197–198. (c)

Ansbacher, H. L. "The Structure of Individual Psychology." In B. B. Wolman & E. Nagel (Eds.), *Scientific psychology: principles and approaches.* New York: Basic Books, 1965. Pp. 340–364.

[Ansbacher, H. L.] "Adler and the Vienna College of Professors." *J. Indiv. Psychol.*, 1966, 22, 235–236.

Ansbacher, H. L. "Alfred Adler: a historical perspective." *Amer. J. Psychiat.*, 1970, 127, 777–782.

Ansbacher, H. L. "Alfred Adler and G. Stanley Hall: correspondence and general relationship." *J. Hist. behav. Sci.*, 1971, 7, 337–352.

Ansbacher, H. L. "Adler's 'striving for power' in relation to Nietzsche." *J. Indiv. Psychol.*, 1972, 28, 12–24.

Ansbacher, H. L. "Rudolf Virchow's 'Atoms and individuals,' a key to the name of Adler's Individual Psychology." *J. Indiv. Psychol.*, 1973, 29, in press.

Asch, S. E. *Social psychology.* New York: Prentice-Hall, 1952.

Asnaourow, F. "Sadismus und Masochismus in Kultur und Erziehung." *Schr. Ver. freie psychoanal. Forsch.*, 1913, No. 4.

Bauer, R. A. *The new man in soviet psychology.* Cambridge, Mass.: Harvard Univer. Press, 1952.

Beckh-Widmanstetter, H. A. "Zur Geschichte der Individualpsychologie: Julius Wagner-Jauregg über Alfred Adler." *Unsere Heimat, Vienna,* 1965, 36 (10/12), 182–188.

---

1. For references to Adler see Part VII, Bibliography of Alfred Adler.

Bottome, Phyllis. *Alfred Adler: a portrait from life.* 3rd ed. New York: Vanguard Press, 1957.

Bry, Ilse, & Rifkin, A. H. "Freud and the history of ideas: primary sources, 1886–1910." In J. H. Masserman (Ed.), *Science and psychoanalysis.* Vol. 5. New York: Grune & Stratton, 1962. Pp. 6–36.

Dewey, J. "Individualität in der Gegenwart." *Int. Z. Indiv. Psychol.,* 1930, 8, 567–576. Engl. orig. "Individuality in our day." Now in *Individualism old and new.* New York: Capricorn Books, 1962. Chapt. 8.

Dreikurs, R. "Are psychological schools of thought outdated?" *J. Indiv. Psychol.,* 1960, 16, 3–10.

Ellenberger, H. F. *The discovery of the unconscious.* New York: Basic Books, 1970.

Federn, E. "The therapeutic personality, as illustrated by Paul Federn and August Aichhorn." *Psychiat. Quart.,* 1962, 36, 29–43.

Feuer, L. S. "The standpoints of Dewey and Freud: a contrast and analysis." *J. Indiv. Psychol.,* 1960, 16, 119–136.

Fischl, H. "Hofrat Dr. Carl Furtmüller: ein Siebziger." *Erziehung und Unterricht* (Vienna), 1950, 383–385.

Freschl. R. "Vorbemerkungen zu einer Individualpsychologie der Persönlichkeit Friedrich Nietzsche." *Z. Indiv. Psychol.,* 1914, 1, 110–115.

Freschl, R. "Friedrich Nietzsche and Individual Psychology." *Int. J. Indiv. Psychol.,* 1935, 1(4), 87–98.

Freud, M. *Sigmund Freud: man and father.* New York: Vanguard, 1958.

Freud, S. "The interpretation of dreams" (1900). In *Standard edition.* Vols. 4 & 5. London: Hogarth, 1932.

Freud, S. "On the history of the psycho-analytic movement" (1914). In *Collected papers.* Vol. 1. London: Hogarth, 1924. Pp. 287–359.

Freud, S. *Beyond the pleasure principle* (1920). New York: Liveright, 1950.

Freud, S. *Autobiography* (1925). New York: Norton, 1935.

F[riedmann], A[lice]. "Das Seminar für Massenpsychologie vom Oktober 1923 bis Jänner 1924." *Int. Z. Indiv. Psychol.,* 1923–24, 2(4), 30–31.

Fromm, E. *Sigmund Freud's mission: an analysis of his personality and influence.* New York: Harper, 1959.

Fromm, E. *Marx's concept of man.* With a transl. from Marx's *Economic and philosophical manuscripts.* New York: Ungar, 1961.

Fünfzig Jahre Volksheim: eine Festschrift zum 24. Februar 1951. Vienna 16, Austria: Volksheim, Ludo-Hartmann-Platz 7, 1951.

Furtmüller, C. "Psychoanalyse und Ethik." *Schr. Ver. freie psychoanal. Forsch.,* 1912, No. 1.

Furtmüller, C. "Geleitwort." *Z. Indiv. Psychol.,* 1914, 1, 1–3. (a)

Furtmüller, C. "Denkpsychologie und Individualpsychologie." *Z. Indiv. Psychol.,* 1914, 1, 80–91. (b)

Furtmüller, C. "Selbsterziehung als Berufsproblem des Lehrers." *Int. Z. Indiv. Psychol.,* 1930, 8, 70–78.

Ganz, Madelaine. *The psychology of Alfred Adler and the development of the child* (1935). Preface by P. Bovet. Trans. by P. Mairet. London: Routledge & Kegan Paul, 1953.

[Grün, H.] "Was wir wollen." *Aerztl. Standeszeitung* (Vienna), 1902, 1(1), 1–2.

Jones, E. *The life and work of Sigmund Freud.* Vol. 1. New York: Basic Books, 1953.

Jones, E. *The life and work of Sigmund Freud.* Vol. 2. New York: Basic Books, 1955.

Jones, E. *The life and work of Sigmund Freud.* Vol. 3. New York: Basic Books, 1957.

Katz, D. "Gespräche mit Kindern." *Int. Z. Indiv. Psychol.,* 1930, 8, 459–470.

Kaus, O. "Der Fall Gogol." *Schr. Ver. freie psychoanal. Forsch.,* 1912, No. 2.

Kaus, O. "Die Träume in Dostojewskys 'Raskolnikoff.'" *Indiv. Gemeinsch.* Munich: Bergmann, 1926. No. 4.

Lehrman, N. S. "Anti-therapeutic and anti-democratic aspects of Freudian dynamic psychiatry." *J. Indiv. Psychol.,* 1963, 19, 167–181.

Lichtheim. G. *Marxism: an historical and critical study.* New York: Praeger, 1961.

Marx, Beatrice. "Individual Psychology in America." *Int. Z. Indiv. Psychol.,* 1927, 5, xx–xxi.

Marx, K., & Engels, F. *Die deutsche Ideologie.* Berlin: Dietz Verlag, 1953.

Marx, K., & Engels, F. *Basic writings on politics and philosophy.* Ed. by L. S. Feuer. Garden City, N. Y.: Doubleday-Anchor Books, 1959.

Neuer, A. "Ist die Individualpsychologie als Wissenschaft möglich?" *Z. Indiv. Psychol.,* 1914, 1, 3–8.

Nunberg, H., & Federn, E. (Eds.) *Minutes of the Vienna Psychoanalytic Society.* Vol. 1. 1906–1908. New York: Int. Univer. Press, 1962.

Oliver, W. D., & Landfield, A. W. "Reflexivity: an unfaced issue of psychology." *J. Indiv. Psychol.,* 1962, 18, 114–124.

Orgler, Hertha. *Alfred Adler: the man and his work.* New York: Liveright, 1963.

Papanek, E. *The Austrian school reform: its bases, principles and development—the twenty years between the two World Wars.* New York: Fell, 1962.

Pestalozzi, J. H. *Sämtliche Werke.* Ed. by A. Buchenau, E. Spranger & H. Stettbacher. Vol. 12. Berlin: de Gruyter, 1938.

Riesman, D. *Individualism reconsidered.* Garden City, N. Y.: Doubleday-Anchor Books, 1955.

Rom, P. *Alfred Adler: und die wissenschaftliche Menschenkenntnis.* Frankfurt am Main: Kramer, 1966.

Schrecker, P. "Henri Bergsons Philosophie der Persönlichkeit." *Schr. Ver. freie psychoanal. Forsch.,* 1912, No. 3.

Schwartz, H. "Soviet encyclopedia—A to A." *N. Y. Times,* 1951, Aug. 5, VI, p. 19.

Smuts, J. C. *Holism and evolution* (1926). New York: Viking Press, 1961.

Smuts, J. C. "Das wissenschaftliche Weltbild der Gegenwart." *Int. Z. Indiv. Psychol.,* 1932, 10, 244–261. Engl. orig. "The scientific world picture of today." *Rep. Brit. Ass. Adv. Sci.,* 1931, 1–18.

Sperber, M. *Alfred Adler: der Mensch und seine Lehre; ein Essay.* Munich: Bergmann, 1926.

Sperber, M. *Alfred Adler: oder Das Elend der Psychologie.* Vienna, Munich, Zurich: Molden, 1970.

Spiel, O. *Am Schaltbrett der Erziehung.* Vienna: Jugend und Volk, 1947.

Spiel, O. *Discipline without punishment.* Ed. with introduct. by L. Way. Trans. by E. Fitzgerald. London: Faber & Faber, 1962.

Trotsky, L. *My life.* New York: Grosset & Dunlap, 1960.

Tucker, R. C. *Philosophy and myth in Karl Marx.* New York: Cambridge Univer. Press, 1961.

Vaihinger, H. *The philosophy of 'as if': a system of the theoretical, practical and religious fictions of mankind* (1911). Trans. by C. K. Ogden. New York: Harcourt, Brace, 1925.

Vercruysse, Godelieve. *Onderzoek naar de evolutie van Alfred Adlers opvatting over de "Levensstijl"; geschriften uit de jaren 1898–1917.* Louvain, Belgium: Cath. Univer., Inst. Appl. Psychol. Educ., 1961.

"Vortragsreise Alfred Adlers in Amerika." *Int. Z. Indiv. Psychol.*, 1927, 5, xix–xx.

Wassermann, I. Letter to the editor. *Amer. J. Psychother.*, 1958, 12, 623–627.

Way, L. *Adler's place in psychology: an exposition of Individual Psychology.* New York: Collier Books, 1962.

Wexberg, E. (Ed.) *Handbuch der Individualpsychologie.* 2 vols. Munich: Bergmann, 1926. Amsterdam: Bonset, 1966.

Wilken, F. "Die Jugendbewegung als neurotisches Phänomen." In A. Adler, C. Furtmüller, & E. Wexberg (Eds.), *Heilen und Bilden.* 2nd. ed. Munich: Bergmann, 1922. Pp. 251–264.

Wittels, F. *Sigmund Freud: his personality, his teachings, and his school.* New York: Dodd, Mead, 1924.

PART VII

Bibliography of Alfred Adler

Titles of books and periodicals are in italics; titles of papers are in quotation marks. Foreign-language titles are followed by an English translation in parentheses. Abbreviations are in accordance with the *World List of Scientific Periodicals* (Oxford, 1950).

In Adler's works, when a previous publication appeared in a volume of collected papers (e. g. A1914a, A1920a, A1930d), or in translation, the original source was most often not stated. One feature of the present bibliography is that the entries are supplied with cross-references, in brackets, to the original sources [Orig.], to reprintings [Repr.], and to translations [Trans.]. Where the language of the translation cross-reference is not stated, the translation is in English. Cross references all pertain to Adler publications, even where the A does not appear.

An asterisk (*) preceding an entry indicates that it is a reprint or a translation, in which case a cross-reference to the original is given.

To avoid the bibliography becoming too unwieldy, in the case of books that have appeared in English, only the American edition is listed, although English editions exist for all of them. Also, in the case of all books, generally only the first edition and a recent reprint are listed.

In addition to the standard reference works and numerous other sources, we have drawn on two theses from the Catholic University of Louvain, Belgium, by H. Cammaer and by Godelieve Vercruysse, containing extensive bibliographies of Adler up to 1914 and 1917, respectively. While our aim has been to list everything that has been *published under Adler's name, we do not expect that we have been completely successful.*[1]   *—Eds.*

A1898   *Gesundheitsbuch für das Schneidergewerbe.* (Health book for the tailoring trade.) Berlin: C. Heymanns. Pp. vi + 31.

A1902   "Das Eindringen sozialer Triebkräfte in die Medizin." (The penetration of social forces into medicine.) *Aerztl. Standeszeitung* (Vienna), 1(1), 1–3.

A1903a   "Stadt und Land." (City and country.) *Aerztl. Standeszeitung* (Vienna), 2(18), 1–3; (19), 1–2; (20), 1–2.

A1903b   "Staatshilfe oder Selbsthilfe?" (State help or self-help?) *Aerztl. Standeszeitung* (Vienna), 2(21), 1–3; (22), 1–2.

A1904a   "Der Arzt als Erzieher." (The physician as educator.) *Aerztl. Standeszeitung* (Vienna), 3(13), 4–6; (14), 3–4; (15), 4–5. [Repr.: 1914a, pp. 1–10.]

A1904b   "Hygiene des Geschlechtslebens." (Hygiene of sex life.) *Aerztl. Standeszeitung* (Vienna), 3(18), 1–2; (19), 1–3.

A1905a   "Das sexuelle Problem in der Erziehung." (The sex problem in education.) *Neue Gesellschaft* (Berlin), 8, 360–362.

A1905b   "Drei Psycho-Analysen von Zahleneinfällen und obsedierenden Zahlen." (Three psychoanalyses of ideas of numbers and obsessive numbers.) *Psychiat. neurol. Wschr.*, 7, 263–266.

A1906   "On the [organic] bases of neuroses." In H. Nunberg and E. Federn (Eds.), *Minutes of the Vienna Psychoanalytic Society.* Vol. 1. 1906–1908. New York: Int. Univer. Press, 1962. Pp. 36–41.

A1907a   *Studie über Minderwertigkeit von Organen.* (Study of organ inferiority.) Vienna: Urban & Schwarzenberg. Pp. 92. [2nd ed. 1927c; Trans.: English 1917c; French, 1956a.]

A1907b   "Entwicklungsfehler des Kindes." (Developmental defects of the child.) In *Heilen und Bilden,* 1914a. Pp. 33–40.

A1907c   "Zur Ätiologie, Diagnostik und Therapie der Nephrolithiasis." (On the etiology, diagnosis and therapy of nephrolithiasis [condition of renal calculi].) *Wien. klin. Wschr.*, 20, 1534–1539.

A1907d   "A psychoanalysis." In H. Nunberg and E. Federn (Eds.), *Minutes of the Vienna Psychoanalytic Society.* Vol. 1. 1906–1908. New York: Int. Univer. Press, 1962. Pp. 138–140.

ᴧᴧᴧᴧᴧᴧᴧᴧᴧᴧᴧᴧ

1. Some confusion has arisen over a book entitled *The Education of the Individual,* which was published in 1958 (New York: Philosophical Library) under the name of Alfred Adler. This book, however, is *not* by the founder of Individual Psychology and is therefore not included in this bibliography. The author, who previously published under the name of Charles A. Adler, is a distant relative of Adler and onetime lecturer and author in Individual Psychology; he eventually became an associate professor of education at Brooklyn College, New York.

A1908a   "Enuresis." "Lebererkrankungen." (Diseases of the liver.) "Nierenerkrankungen." (Diseases of the kidney.) In M. Kahane (Ed.), *Med. Handlex. praktiz. Aerzte.* Vienna: Urban & Schwarzenberg. Pp. 321–322, 578–580, 698–704.

A1908b   "Der Aggressionstrieb im Leben und in der Neurose." (The aggression drive in life and in neurosis.) *Fortschr. Med.,* 26, 577–584. [Repr.: 1914a, pp. 23–32.]

A1908c   "Über die Vererbung von Krankheiten." (On the heredity of diseases.) *Kampf* (Vienna), 9(1), 425–430. [Repr.: 1914a, pp. 41–49.]

A1908d   "Das Zärtlichkeitsbedürfnis des Kindes." (The child's need for affection.) *Monatsh. Pädag. Schulpol.,* 1, 7–9. [Repr.: 1914a, pp. 50–53.]

A1908e   "Die Theorie der Organminderwertigkeit und ihre Bedeutung für Philosophie und Psychologie." (The theory of organ inferiority and its significance for philosophy and psychology.) *Univ. Wien, Phil. Gesellschaft, Wiss. Beil.,* 21, 11–26. [Repr.: 1914a, pp. 11–22.]

A1908f   "Zwei Träume einer Prostituierten." (Two dreams of a prostitute.) *Z. Sexualwiss.,* 1, 103–106.

A1908g   "A contribution to the problem of paranoia." In H. Nunberg and E. Federn (Eds.), *Minutes of the Vienna Psychoanalytic Society.* Vol. 1. 1906–1908. New York: Int. Univer. Press, 1962. Pp. 288–292.

A1909a   "Über neurotische Disposition: zugleich ein Beitrag zur Ätiologie und zur Frage der Neurosenwahl." (On neurotic disposition: simultaneously a contribution to the etiology and problem of choice of neurosis.) *Jb. Psychoanal. psychopath. Forsch.,* 1, 526–545. [Repr.: 1914a, pp. 54–73.]

A1909b   "Myelodysplasie oder Organminderwertigkeit?" (Myelodysplasia [defective development of the spinal cord] or organ inferiority?) *Wien. med. Wschr.,* No. 45, 2631–2636. [Repr.: 1920a, pp. 214–220.]

A1909c   "A case of compulsive blushing." In H. Nunberg and E. Federn (Eds.), *Minutes of the Vienna Psychoanalytic Society.* Vol. 2. 1908–1910. New York: Int. Univer. Press, 1967. Pp. 125–138.

A1909d   "On the psychology of Marxism." In H. Nunberg and E. Federn (Eds.), *Minutes of the Vienna Psychoanalytic Society.* Vol. 2. 1908–1910. New York: Int. Univer. Press, 1967. Pp. 172–174.

A1909e   "The oneness of the neuroses." In H. Nunberg and E. Federn (Eds.), *Minutes of the Vienna Psychoanalytic Society.* Vol. 2. 1908–1910. New York: Int. Univer. Press, 1967. Pp. 259–265.

A1910a   [Editor, with S. Freud and W. Stekel.] *Zentralblatt für Psychoanalyse: medizinische Monatsschrift für Seelenkunde.* (*Zentralblatt* for psychoanalysis: medical monthly for psychology.) Until 1911.

A1910b   "Über den Selbstmord, insbesondere den Schülerselbstmord." (On suicide, especially among students.) *Diskuss. Wien. psychoanal.*

      Ver. No. 1. Wiesbaden: Bergmann. Pp. 44–50. [Repr.: 1914a, pp. 356–363. Trans.: 1967e.]

A1910c   "Der psychische Hermaphroditismus im Leben und in der Neurose." (Psychological hermaphroditism in life and neurosis.) *Fortschr. Med.*, 28, 486–493. [Repr.: 1914a, pp. 74–83.]

A1910d   "Trotz und Gehorsam." (Defiance and obedience.) *Monatsh. Pädag. Schulpol.*, 2, 321–328. [Repr.: 1914a, pp. 84–93.]

A1910e   "Über das materielle Substrat der psychischen Vorgänge." (On the material substratum of the psychological processes.) *Psychiat. neurol. Wschr.*, 11, 369–370.

A1910f   "Die psychische Behandlung der Trigeminusneuralgie." (The psychological treatment of trigeminal neuralgia.) *Zbl. Psychoanal.*, 1, 10–29. [Repr.: 1920a, pp. 54–69.]

A1910g   [Review] K. Pelmann. Psychische Grenzzustände. (Psychic border conditions.) Bonn: Cohen, 1910. *Zbl. Psychoanal.*, 1, 78–79.

A1910h   "Ein erlogener Traum: Beitrag zum Mechanismus der Lüge in der Neurose." (An invented dream: contribution to the mechanism of the lie in the neurosis.) *Zbl. Psychoanal.*, 1, 103–108.

A1910i   [Review] Anon. Hinter Schloss und Riegel. (Behind bars.) Munich: Langen. *Zbl. Psychoanal.*, 1, 112–113.

A1910j   [Review] F. Nadastiny. Untermenschen oder Narren? (Subhuman beings or fools?) Vienna: Konegen, 1910. *Zbl. Psychoanal.*, 1, p. 113.

A1910k   [Review] E. Wulffen. Der Sexualverbrecher. (The sex offender.) Berlin: Langenscheidt, 1910. *Zbl. Psychoanal.*, 1, 118–119.

A1910l   [Review] P. Schuster. Drei Vorträge aus dem Gebiete der Unfall-Neurologie. (Three lectures from the field of accident neurology.) Leipzig: Thieme, 1910. *Zbl. Pyschoanal.*, 1, p. 122.

A1910m   [Review] C. G. Jung "Über Konflikte der kindlichen Seele." (On conflicts of the soul of the child.) *Jb. Psychoanal. psychopath. Forsch.*, 1910, 2. *Zbl. Psychoanal.*, 1, 122–123.

A1910n   "Psychic hermaphroditism." In H. Nunberg and E. Federn (Eds.), *Minutes of the Vienna Psychoanalytic Society.* Vol. 2. 1908–1910. New York: Int. Univer. Press, 1967. Pp. 423–428.

A1910o   "On suicide." In H. Nunberg and E. Federn (Eds.), *Minutes of the Vienna Psychoanalytic Society.* Vol. 2. 1908–1910. New York: Int. Univer. Press, 1967. Pp. 503–504.

A1910p   "Vorwort." (Preface.) *Diskuss. Wien. psychoanal. Ver.*, No. 1. Wiesbaden: Bergmann. Pp. 3–4. [Trans.: 1967d.]

A1911a   "Die Rolle der Sexualität in der Neurose." (The role of sexuality in neurosis.) In *Heilen und Bilden,* 1914a. Pp. 94–103.

A1911b   " 'Verdrängung' und 'männlicher Protest': ihre Rolle und Bedeutung für die neurotische Dynamik." ("Repression" and "masculine protest": their role and significance for the neurotic dynamics.) In *Heilen und Bilden,* 1914a. Pp. 103–114.

A1911c   "Über männliche Einstellung bei weiblichen Neurotikern." (On masculine attitude in female neurotics.) *Zbl. Psychoanal.*, 1, 174–178. [Repr.: 1920a, pp. 76–80.]

A1911d   "Beitrag zur Lehre vom Widerstand." (Contribution to the theory of resistance.) *Zbl. Psychoanal.*, 1, 214–219. [Repr.: 1920a, pp. 100–105.]

A1911e   [Review] J. Langermann. Der Erziehungsstaat. (The state which stresses education.) 3rd ed. Berlin: Mathilde Zimmer-Haus, 1910. *Zbl. Psychoanal.*, 1, 258–259.

A1911f*   "Syphilidophobie: ein Beitrag zur Bedeutung der Hypochondrie in der Dynamik der Neurose." (Fear of syphilis: a contribution to the significance of hypochondriasis in the dynamics of neurosis.) *Zbl. Psychoanal.*, 1, 400–406. [Repr.: 1920a, pp. 106–112.]

A1911g   "Erklärung." (Declaration.) *Zbl. Psychoanal.*, 1, p. 433.

A1912a   *Über den nervösen Charakter: Grundzüge einer vergleichenden Individual-Psychologie und Psychotherapie.* (The nervous character: outline of comparative individual psychology and psychotherapy.) Wiesbaden: Bergmann. Pp. v + 195. [Trans.: English, 1917a; French, 1926b; Italian, 1950c; Spanish, 1959g.]

A1912b   [Editor] *Schriften des Vereins für freie psychoanalytische Forschung.* (Papers of the Society for Free Psychoanalytic Research.) Name changed to *Schriften für angewandte Individualpsychologie.* (Papers for applied Individual Psychology.) Munich: Reinhardt. Until 1917.

A1912c   "Organdialekt." (Organ dialect.) In *Heilen und Bilden*, 1914a. Pp. 130–139.

A1912d   "Psychischer Hermaphroditismus und männlicher Protest: ein Kernproblem der nervösen Erkrankungen." (Psychical hermaphroditism and masculine protest: a central problem of nervous diseases.) In *Praxis und Theorie*, 1920a. Pp. 11–15.

A1912e   "Zur Theorie der Halluzination." (On the theory of hallucination.) In *Praxis und Theorie*, 1920a. Pp. 36–40.

A1912f   "Zur Erziehung der Erzieher." (On the education of the educators.) *Monatsh. Pädag. Schulpol.*, 8. [Repr. as "Zur Erziehung der Eltern," 1914a, pp. 113–129. Trans.: Italian, 1914g.]

A1912g   "Vorwort des Herausgebers." (Preface of the editor.) *Schr. Ver. freie psychoanal. Forsch.*, No. 1, v–vii.

A1912h   "Das organische Substrat der Psychoneurosen: zur Ätiologie der Neurosen und Psychosen." (The organic substratum of the psychoneuroses: on the etiology of the neuroses and psychoses.) *Z. ges. Neurol. Psychiat.*, 13, 481–491. [Repr.: 1924j, pp. 168–176.]

A1913a*   "Individualpsychologische Behandlung der Neurosen." (Individual-Psychological treatment of the neuroses.) In D. Sarason (Ed.), *I. Jahreskurse für ärztliche Fortbildung.* Munich: Lehmann. Pp. 39–51. [Repr.: 1920a, pp. 22–35.]

〰〰〰〰〰〰〰

*Items 1911f, 1913a, 1913h, and 1913j appeared in Russian 1912–1914 and were available as of 1970 at the Lenin State Library, Moscow.

A1913b   "Zur Funktion der Zwangsvorstellung als eines Mittels zur Erhöhung des Persönlichkeitsgefühls." (Obession as a means for the enhancement of self-esteem.) In *Praxis und Theorie*, 1920a. Pp. 144–146.

A1913c   "Neue Leitsätze zur Praxis der Individualpsychologie." (New principles for the practice of Individual Psychology.) In *Praxis und Theorie*, 1920a. Pp. 16–21.

A1913d   "Individualpsychologische Ergebnisse bezüglich Schlafstörungen." (Individual-Psychological conclusions regarding sleep disturbances.) *Fortschr. Med.*, 31, 925–933. [Repr.: 1914c, pp. 336–340 (parts only); 1920a, pp. 119–126.]

A1913e   [Review] W. Stekel. Nervöse Angstzustände und ihre Behandlung. (Nervous anxiety and its treatment.) Vienna: Urban & Schwarzenberg, 1912. *Sex. Probl.*, 9(1), 62–64.

A1913f   "Der nervöse Charakter." (The nervous character.) *Sozial. Mschr.*, 19. [Repr.: 1914a, pp. 140–150.]

A1913g   "Individualpsychologische Bemerkungen zu Alfred Bergers *Hofrat Eysenhardt*." (Individual-Psychological comments on Alfred Berger's *Hofrat Eysenhardt*.) *Z. med. Psychol. Psychother.*, 5, 77–89. [Repr.: 1920a, pp. 183–194.]

A1913h*   "Zur Rolle des Unbewussten in der Neurose." (The role of the unconscious in the neurosis.) *Zbl. Psychoanal.*, 3, 169–174. [Repr.: 1920a, pp. 158–163.]

A1913i   "Erwiderung [an A. Maeder]." (Rejoinder.) *Zbl. Psychoanal.*, 3, 564–567.

A1913j*   "Traum und Traumdeutung." (Dream and dream interpretation.) *Zbl. Psychoanal.*, 3, 574–583. [Repr.: 1920a, pp. 149–157.]

A1914a   [Editor with Carl Furtmüller] *Heilen und Bilden: ärztlich-pädagogische Arbeiten des Vereins für Individualpsychologie.* (Healing and education: medical-educational papers of the Society for Individual Psychology.) Munich: Reinhardt. Pp. viii + 399. [Orig.: 1904a; 1907b; 1908b, c, d, e; 1909a; 1910b, c, d; 1911a, b; 1912c, f; 1913d, f; 1914c. 2nd ed. 1922a.]

A1914b   [Editor with Carl Furtmüller] *Zeitschrift für Individualpsychologie: Studien aus dem Gebiete der Psychotherapie, Psychologie und Pädagogik.* (Journal for Individual Psychology: studies in the area of psychotherapy, psychology and education.) Until 1916.

A1914c   * "Ein Beitrag zur Psychologie der ärztlichen Berufswahl." (A contribution to the psychology of choosing medicine as a vocation.) In *Heilen und Bilden*, 1914a. Pp. 336–340. [Orig.: parts of 1913d.]

A1914d   "Melancholie und Paranoia: individualpsychologische Ergebnisse aus den Untersuchungen der Psychosen." (Melancholia and paranoia: Individual-Psychological conclusions from investigations of psychoses.) In *Praxis und Theorie*, 1920a. Pp. 171–182.]

A1914e   "Kindliches Seelenleben und Gemeinsinn." (The psychological life of the child and common sense.) *Ann. Nat. Kult. Phil.*, 13, 38–45.

A1914f "Soziale Einflüsse in der Kinderstube." (Social influences in the nursery.) *Pädag. Arch.*, 56, 473–487.

A1914g "Per l'educazione dei genitori." (Education of the parents.) *Psiche*, 3, 368–382. [Orig.: 1912f.]

A1914h "Die Individualpsychologie, ihre Voraussetzungen und Ergebnisse." (Individual Psychology: its assumptions and results.) *Scientia*, 16, 74–87. [Repr.: 1920a, pp. 1–10.]

A1914i "The homosexual problem." *Urol. cutan. Rev.*, *Techn. Suppl.*, St. Louis, Mo., October.

A1914j "Zur Kinderpsychologie und Neurosenforschung." (Child psychology and the study of neurosis.) *Wien. klin. Wschr.*, 27, 511–516. [Repr.: 1920a, pp. 41–53.]

A1914k "Das Problem der 'Distanz': über einen Grundcharakter der Neurose und Psychose." (The problem of "distance": a basic trait of neurosis and psychosis.) *Z. Indiv. Psychol.*, 1, 8–16. [Repr.: 1920a, pp. 70–75.]

A1914l "Zur Sitophobie." (Fear of eating.) *Z. Indiv. Psychol.*, 1, 27–28. [Repr.: 1920a, pp. 147–148, as "Nervöser Hungerstreik," (Neurotic hunger-strike.)]

A1914m "Lebenslüge und Verantwortlichkeit in der Neurose und Psychose: ein Beitrag zur Melancholiefrage." (Life-lie and responsibility in neurosis and psychosis: a contribution to the problem of melancholia.) *Z. Indiv. Psychol.*, 1, 44–53. [Repr.: 1920a, pp. 164–170.]

A1914n [Review] T. Becker. Zur Diagnose paranoischer Zustände. (The diagnosis of paranoid conditions.) Munchn. med. Wiss., No. 12. *Z. Indiv. Psychol.*, 1, 62–63.

A1914o [Review] W. Astrow (Ed.) Petersburger Träume: eine unbekannte Erzählung von Dostojewsky. (Petersburg dreams: an unknown story of Dostoevsky.) Neue Freie Presse, Osternummer. *Z. Indiv. Psychol.*, 1, 63–64.

A1914p "Nervöse Schlaflosigkeit." (Nervous sleeplessness.) *Z. Indiv. Psychol.* 1, 65–72. [Repr.: 1920a, pp. 113–118.]

A1914q [Review] Engelen. Suggestionsfaktoren bei der Freudschen Psychoanalyse. (Factors of suggestion in Freud's psychoanalysis.) Deutsche med. Wschr., No. 19. *Z. Indiv. Psychol.*, 1, 92–93.

A1914r [Review] E. v. Koehler. Warum denken wir im Wachen in Worten, im Traume in Bildern? (Why do we think in words during waking, in images during dreaming?) Psychiat. neurol. Wschr., No. 46. *Z. Indiv. Psychol.*, 1, p. 142.

A1914s [Review] S. Meyer. Organische und geistige Entwicklung. (Organic and mental development.) Deutsche med. Wschr., No. 19. *Z. Indiv. Psychol.*, 1, p. 142.

A1914t In "Sitzungsbericht des Vereins für Individualpsychologie, March 7, 1914." *Z. Indiv. Psychol.*, 1, p. 96.

A1914u In "Sitzungsbericht des Vereins für Individualpsychologie, March 21, 1914." *Z. Indiv. Psychol.*, 1, p. 143.

A1916 "Die Frau als Erzieherin." (Woman as educator.) *Arch. Frauenk.*, Würzburg, 2, 341–349.

A1917a * *The neurotic constitution: outline of a comparative individualistic* *psychology and psychotherapy.* Intro. by Wm. A. White. Trans. B. Glueck and J. E. Lind. New York: Moffat, Yard. Pp. xxiii + 456. [Orig.: 1912a.]

A1917b   *Das Problem der Homosexualität.* (The problem of homosexuality.) Munich: Reinhardt. [Repr.: 1930d. Trans.: 1917d.]

A1917c   * *Study of organ inferiority and its psychical compensation: a contribution to clinical medicine.* Trans. S. E. Jelliffe. New York: Nerv. Ment. Dis. Publ. Co. Pp. x + 86. [Orig.: 1907a.]

A1917d   *"The homosexual problem."*Alienist Neurol.,38, 268-287.[Orig.:1917d.]

A1918a   "Über die Homosexualität." (Homosexuality.) In *Praxis und Theorie,* 1920a. Pp. 127-135.

A1918b   "Die Zwangsneurose." (Compulsion neurosis.) In *Praxis und Theorie,* 1920a. Pp. 136-143.

A1918c   "Dostojewski." In *Praxis und Theorie,* 1920a. Pp. 195-202.

A1918d   "Über individualpsychologische Erziehung." (Individual-Psychological education.) In *Praxis und Theorie,* 1920a. Pp. 221-227.

A1918e   "Bolschewismus und Seelenkunde." (Bolshevism and psychology.) *Int. Rundsch.* (Zurich), 4, 597-600.

A1918f   "Die neuen Gesichtspunkte in der Frage der Kriegsneurose." (The new viewpoints on the problem of war neurosis.) *Med. Klin.,* 14, 66-70. [Repr.: 1920a, pp. 203-213.]

A1919a   *Die andere Seite: eine massenpsychologische Studie über die Schuld des Volkes.* (The other side: a social-psychological study on collective guilt.) Vienna: Leopold Heidrich. Pp. 16.

A1919b   "Ehe und Kind." (Marriage and child.) In J. Spier (Ed.), *Die Schule der Ehe.* Munich: J. M. Müller. Pp. 348-385.

A1919c   "Geleitwort." (Preface.) In *Über den nervösen Charakter,* 2nd ed. Munich: Bergmann.

A1920a   *Praxis und Theorie der Individualpsychologie: Vorträge zur Einführung in die Psychotherapie für Ärzte, Psychologen und Lehrer.* (Practice and theory of Individual Psychology: introductory lectures in psychotherapy for physicians, psychologists, and educators.) Munich: Bergmann. Pp. 244. [Orig.: 1909b; 1910f; 1911c, d, f; 1912d, e; 1913a, b, c, d, g, h, j; 1914d, h, j, k, l, m, p; 1918a, b, c, d, f; 1920b, c, d. Repr.: 1924j. Trans.: English, 1925a; French, 1961a; Italian, 1949b; Polish, 1934c; Serbian, 1937a; Spanish, 1953.]

A1920b   "Über männliche Einstellung bei weiblichen Neurotikern. III. Versuch der Umkehrung als männlicher Protest." (On masculine attitude in female neurotics. III. Attempt at reversal as masculine protest.) In *Praxis und Theorie,* 1920a. Pp. 80-99.

A1920c   "Die individuelle Psychologie der Prostitution." (The Individual Psychology of prostitution.) In *Praxis und Theorie,* 1920a. Pp. 228-236.

A1920d   "Verwahrloste Kinder." (Wayward children.) In *Praxis und Theorie,* 1920a. Pp. 237-244.

A1921   "Wo soll der Kampf gegen die Verwahrlosung einsetzen?" (Where should the fight against waywardness begin?) *Soz. Praxis* (Vienna). [Repr.: 1922a, pp. 116-118.]

A1922a   * [Editor with C. Furtmüller and E. Wexberg] *Heilen und Bilden: Grundlagen der Erziehungskunst für Ärzte und Pädagogen.* (Healing and educating: foundations of the art of education for physicians and educators.) 2nd ed. Munich: Bergmann. Pp. viii + 330. [Orig.: 1914a; 1921; 1922b.]

A1922b   "Erziehungsberatungsstellen." (Child guidance clinics.) In *Heilen und Bilden*, 1922a. Pp. 119–121.

A1922c   "Geleitwort." (Preface.) In *Über den nervösen Charakter.* 3rd ed. Munich: Bergmann.

A1923a   [Editor] *Internationale Zeitschrift für Individualpsychologie: Arbeiten aus dem Gebiete der Psychotherapie, Psychologie und Pädagogik.* (International Journal of Individual Psychology: papers from the areas of psychotherapy, psychology, and education.) Until 1937.

A1923b   "Danton, Marat, Robespierre: eine Charakterstudie." (Danton, Marat, Robespierre: a character study.) *Arbeiter-Zeitung* (Vienna), December 25, 17–18.

A1923c   "Fortschritte der Individualpsychologie." (Progress in Individual Psychology). *Int. Z. Indiv. Psychol.*, 2(1), 1–7; (3) 10–12. [Trans.: English, 1924b, Part 1; Italian, 1925d.]

A1923d   "Die Tragfähigkeit der menschlichen Seele." (Degree of tolerance of the human soul.) *Int. Z. Indiv. Psychol.*, 2(2), p. 42.

A1923e   "Die Gefahren der Isolierung." (The dangers of isolation.) *Zbl. Vormundschaftsw.*, 15(3), p. 53.

A1923f   "Individualpsychologie und Weltanschauung." (Individual Psychology and world view.) *Int. Z. Indiv. Psychol.*, 2(2), 30–31.

A1924a   "Die Strafe in der Erziehung." (Punishment in education.) *Arbeiter-Zeitung* (Vienna), June 14, p. 12.

A1924b   * "Progress in Individual Psychology." *Brit. J. med. Psychol.*, 4, 22–31; also in German, pp. 12–21. [Orig.: 1923c, Part 1.]

A1924c   "Neurosenwandel und Training im Traum." (Change of neurosis and training in the dream.) *Int. Z. Indiv. Psychol.*, 2(5), 5–8.

A1924d   "Psychische Kausalität." (Psychic causality.) *Int. Z. Indiv. Psychol.*, 2(6), p. 38.

A1924e   "Neurose und Verbrechen." (Neurosis and crime.) *Int. Z. Indiv. Psychol.*, 3, 1–11.

A1924f   "Eine häufige Wurzel des Sadismus." (A frequent source of sadism.) *Int. Z. Indiv. Psychol.*, 3, 49–50.

A1924g   "Kritische Erwägungen über den Sinn des Lebens." (Critical considerations on the meaning of life.) In *Der Leuchter: Weltanschauung und Lebensgestaltung.* Vol. 5. Darmstadt: O. Reichl. Pp. 343–350. [Repr.: 1924n.]

A1924h   "Ein Fall von Melancholie." (A case of melancholia.) *Int. Z. Indiv. Psychol.*, 3, 103–105.

A1924i   "Schwererziehbare Kinder und nervöse Erwachsene." (Problem children and nervous adults.) *Int. Z. Indiv. Psychol.*, 3, 145–146.

A1924j   * *Praxis und Theorie der Individualpsychologie.* (Practice and theory of Individual Psychology.) 2nd ed. Munich: Bergmann, 1924. [Orig.: 1920a and 1912h.]

A1924k   "Über Weltanschauung." (On world view.) *Int. Z. Indiv. Psychol.*, 2(6), p. 38.

A1924l   "Kulturelle Einschränkung in der Erziehung der Frau zur Aktivität." (Cultural restriction in woman's education for activity.) *Int. Z. Indiv. Psychol.*, 2(6), p. 39.

A1924m   "Training?" (Training?) *Int. Z. Indiv. Psychol.*, 2(6), p. 39.

A1924n   * "Kritische Erwägungen über den Sinn des Lebens." (Critical considerations on the meaning of life.) *Int. Z. Indiv. Psychol.*, 3, 93–96. [Orig.: 1924g.]

A1924o   "Individualpsychologie und Weltanschauung." (Individual Psychology and world view.) *Int. Z. Indiv. Psychol.*, 3, 132–133.

A1925a   * *The practice and theory of Individual Psychology.* Trans. P. Radin. London: Routledge & Kegan Paul. Pp. viii + 352. [Orig.: 1920a. Repr.: 1959a; 1961b, Chapts. 1 & 3.]

A1925b   "Die Ehe als Aufgabe." (Marriage as a task.) In H. Keyserling (Ed.), *Das Ehe-Buch: eine neue Sinngebung im Zusammenklang der Stimmen führender Zeitgenossen.* Celle: Kampmann. [Trans.: 1926aa.]

A1925c   "Unerziehbarkeit des Kindes oder Unbelehrbarkeit der Theorie? Bemerkungen zum Falle Hug." (Uneducability of the child or incorrigibility of the theory? Comments of the case of Hug.) *Arbeiter-Zeitung* (Vienna), March 5, p. 6.

A1925d   * "Fondamenti e progressi della 'psicologia individuale.'" (Foundations and progress of Individual Psychology.) *Arch. gen. neurol. psichol. psychoanal.*, 6, 227–238. [Orig.: 1923c.]

A1925e   "Inschriften der menschlichen Seele." (Inscriptions of the human soul.) *Bereitschaft*, 6(2), 6–9.

A1925f   "Mitteilungen aus Erziehungsberatungsstellen." (Communications from child guidance clinics.) *Int. Z. Indiv. Psychol.*, 3, 201–203.

A1925g   "Diskussionsbemerkungen zum Vortrage des Prof. Max Adler." (Discussion comments on the lecture by Prof. Max Adler.) *Int. Z. Indiv. Psychol.*, 3, 221–223.

A1925h   * "Salvaging mankind by psychology." Interview with Eugene Bagger. *Int. Z. Indiv. Psychol.*, 3, 332–335. [Orig.: 1925j.]

A1925i   "Erörterungen zum Paragraph 144." (Discussion of paragraph 144 [making abortion illegal].) *Int. Z. Indiv. Psychol.*, 3, 338–340.

A1925j   "Salvaging mankind by psychology:" Interview with Eugene Bagger. *N. Y. Times*, September 20, IX, p. 12. [Repr.: 1925h.]

A1925k   "Über Neurose und Begabung." (On neurosis and talent.) *Int. Z. Indiv. Psychol.*, 3, p. 346.

A1926a   *Liebesbeziehungen und deren Störungen.* (Love relationships and their disturbances.) Vienna; Leipzig: Moritz Perles. Pp. 23.

A1926b   * *Le tempérament nerveux: éléments d'une psychologie individuelle* *et applications à la psychothérapie.* (The nervous character: elements of an individual psychology and its applications to psychotherapy.) Trans. Dr. Roussel. Paris: Payot. Pp. 366. [Orig.: 1912a.]

A1926c [Editor with L. Seif and O. Kaus] *Individuum und Gemeinschaft: Schriften der Internationalen Gesellschaft für Individualpsychologie.* (Individual and community: papers of the International Society for Individual Psychology.) Munich: Bergmann.

A1926d "Geleitwort." (Preface.) *Indiv. Gemeinsch.* (Munich), No. 1, ix–xi.

A1926e "Psychische Einstellung der Frau zum Sexualleben." (Woman's psychological attitude to sex life.) In A. Bethe *et al.* (Eds.), *Handb. norm. path. Physiol.*, Vol. 14(1). Berlin: Springer. Pp. 802–807. [Repr.: 1930d, pp. 89–97.]

A1926f "Psychosexuelle Haltung des Mannes." (Man's psycho-sexual attitude.) In A. Bethe *et al.* (Eds.), *Handb. norm. path. Physiol.*, Vol 14(1). Berlin: Springer. Pp. 808–812. [Repr.: 1930d, pp. 98–106.]

A1926g "Pubertätserscheinungen." (Puberty phenomena.) In A. Bethe *et al.* (Eds.), *Handb. norm. path. Physiol.*, Vol. 14(1). Berlin: Springer. Pp. 842–844. [Repr.: 1930d, pp. 85–89.]

A1926h "Homosexualität." (Homosexuality.) In A. Bethe *et al.* (Eds.), *Handb. norm. path. Physiol.*, Vol. 14(1). Berlin: Springer. Pp. 881–886.

A1926i "Sadismus, Masochismus und andere Perversionen." (Sadism, masochism and other perversions.) In A. Bethe *et al.* (Eds.), *Handb. norm. path. Physiol.*, Vol. 14(1). Berlin: Springer. Pp. 887–894. [Repr.: 1930d, pp. 67–78.]

A1926j "Sexualneurasthenie." (Sexual neurasthenia.) In A. Bethe *et al.* (Eds.), *Handb. norm. path. Physiol.*, Vol. 14(1). Berlin: Springer. Pp. 895–899. [Repr.: 1930d, pp. 78–84.]

A1926k "Die Individualpsychologie als Weg zur Menschenkenntnis und Selbsterkenntnis." (Individual Psychology, a way to understanding of human nature and oneself.) In J. Neumann (Ed.), *Du und der Alltag: eine Psychologie des täglichen Lebens.* Berlin: Warneck. Pp. 211–236. [Trans.: 1927n.]

A1926l "Schwererziehbare Kinder." (Difficult children.) In O. and Alice Rühle (Eds.), *Schwererziehbare Kinder: eine Schriftenfolge.* Heft 1. Dresden: Am Andern Ufer. [Trans.: Dutch, 1935n; French, 1958b.]

A1926m "Individualpsychologie." (Individual Psychology.) In E. Saupe (Ed.), *Einführung in die neuere Psychologie.* 4th & 5th eds. Osterwick-Harz: Zickfeldt, 1931. Pp. 399–407.

A1926n "Vorrede." (Preface.) In E. Wexberg (Ed.), *Handbuch der Individualpsychologie.* Vol. 1. Munich: Bergmann. Pp. v–vi.

A1926o "Vorrede." (Preface.) In H. F. Wolf, *Strategie der männlichen Annäherung.* Vienna: Ilos Verlag.

A1926p   "Die Ehe als Aufgabe." (Marriage as a task.) *Bereitschaft*, 6(7), 4–6.

A1926q   * "Die Ehe als Aufgabe." (Marriage as a task.) *Int. Z. Indiv. Psychol.*, 4, 22–24. [Orig.: 1926p.]

A1926r   "Die Funktion der Mutter." (The function of the mother.) *Gemeinschaft* (Berlin), 1(4).

A1926s   "Ein Fall von Karzinomangst." (A case of fear of cancer.) *Gemeinschaft* (Berlin), 1(5).

A1926t   "Ein Beitrag zum Distanzproblem." (A contribution to the problem of distance.) *Int. Z. Indiv. Psychol.*, 4, 141–143.

A1926u   "Neurose und Lüge." (Neurosis and lie.) *Int. Z. Indiv. Psychol.*, 4, 173–174.

A1926v   "Individualpsychologische Skizze einer Zwangsneurose." (Individual-Psychological outline of a compulsion neurosis.) *Int. Z. Indiv. Psychol.*, 4, 253–256.

A1926w   "Berufseignung und Berufsneigung." (Occupational aptitude and occupational interest.) *Jugend & Beruf*, 1, 89–93.

A1926x   "Die Individualpsychologie." (Individual Psychology.) *Scientia*, 39, 409–418. [Trans.: French, 1926y.]

A1926y   * "La psychologie individuelle, son importance au point de vue du traitement de la nervosité, de l'éducation et de la conception générale du monde." (Individual Psychology.) *Scientia, Suppl.*, 39, 115–123. [Orig.: 1926x.]

A1926z   "On Mussolini." Interview with George Seldes. *N. Y. World*, Dec. 26, p. 3E.

A1926aa   * "Marriage as a task." In H. Keyserling (Ed.), *The book of marriage: a new introduction by twenty-four leaders of contemporary thought.* New York: Harcourt, Brace. Pp. 363–372. [Orig.: 1925b.]

A1927a   *Menschenkenntnis.* (Understanding human nature.) Leipzig: Hirzel. Pp. vii + 236. [Repr.: 1947a; Trans.: Danish-Norwegian, 1930b; Dutch, 1932a; English, 1927b; French, 1949a; Greek, 1934d; Italian, 1954; Japanese, 1957b; Polish, 1948; Portuguese, 1945a; Serbian, 1934b; Spanish, 1931a.]

A1927b   * *Understanding human nature.* Trans. W. B. Wolfe. New York: Greenberg. Pp. ix + 286. [Orig.: 1927a. Repr.: 1927m, Chapt. 5; 1957a.]

A1927c   * *Studie über Minderwertigkeit von Organen.* (Study of organ inferiority.) 2nd ed. Munich: Bergmann. Pp. vii + 92. [Orig.: 1907a.]

A1927d   "Character and talent." *Harper's Mag.*, 155, 64–72.

A1927e   * "The feeling of inferiority and the striving for recognition." *Int. Z. Indiv. Psychol.*, 5, 12–19. [Orig.: 1927m.]

A1927f   "Zusammenhänge zwischen Neurose und Witz." (Relationships between neurosis and jokes.) *Int. Z. Indiv. Psychol.*, 5, 94–96.

A1927g   "Weiteres zur individualpsychologischen Traumtheorie." (More on Individual-Psychological dream theory.) *Int. Z. Indiv. Psychol.*, 5, 241–245.

A1927h   * "The cause and prevention of neurosis." *Int. Z. Indiv. Psychol.*, 5, 245–252. [Orig.: 1927l.]

A1927i   "Die Erziehung zum Mut." (Education for courage.) *Int. Z. Indiv. Psychol.*, 5, 324–326. [Trans.: English, 1928i; Spanish, 1927r.]

A1927j   "Individualpsychologie und Wissenschaft." (Individual Psychology and science.) *Int. Z. Indiv. Psychol.*, 5, 401–408.

A1927k   "Individual Psychology." *J. abnorm. soc. Psychol.*, 22, 116–122.

A1927l   "The cause and prevention of neuroses." *J. ment. Sci.*, 73, 1–8. [Repr.: 1927h, 1928h.]

A1927m   * "The feeling of inferiority and the striving for recognition." *Proc. roy. Soc. Med.*, 20, 1881–1886. [Orig.: 1927b, Chapt. 5; Repr.: 1927e, 1958c.]

A1927n   * "Individual Psychology: a new way to the understanding of human nature." *Psyche*, No. 28, 46–63. [Orig.: 1926k.]

A1927o   "A doctor remakes education." Interview. *Survey Graphic*, 58, 490–495.

A1927p   *Die Aufgabe der Jugend in unserer Zeit.* (The task of youth in our time.) Berlin: Laubsche. Pp. 41.

A1927q   "Alfred Adler über Amerika: das Geltungsstreben in Amerika." (Alfred Adler on America: the striving for significance in America.) Résumé with literal citations by L. Zilahi. *Int. Z. Indiv. Psychol.*, 5, 225–228.

A1927r   * "El valor: su importancia en la educacion del niño." (Courage: its importance in the education of the child.) *Nueva Era*, 8, 115–116. [Orig.: 1927i.]

A1928a   *Die Technik der Individualpsychologie. Vol. 1. Die Kunst, eine Lebens- und Krankengeschichte zu lesen.* (The technique of Individual Psychology. Vol. 1. The art of reading a life- and case-history.) Munich: Bergmann. Pp. iv + 146. [Trans.: 1929a.]

A1928b   "Feelings and emotions from the standpoint of Individual Psychology." In M. L. Reymert (Ed.), *Feelings and emotions: the Wittenberg symposium.* Worcester, Mass.: Clark Univer. Press. Pp. 316–321.

A1928c   "Erotisches Training und erotischer Rückzug." (Erotic training and erotic retreat.) In M. Marcuse (Ed.), *Verhandl. 1. Int. Kongr. Sex. Forsch., Berlin, 1926.* Vol. 3. Berlin, Köln: Marcus & Weber. Pp. 1–7.

A1928d   "Characteristics of the first, second and third child." *Children*, 3, 14 & 52.

A1928e   "Witwenverbrennung und Witwenneurose." (The burning of widows and widow neurosis.) *Int. Z. Indiv. Psychol.*, 6, 23–25.

A1928f   "Kurze Bemerkungen über Vernunft, Intelligenz und Schwachsinn." (Brief comments on reason, intelligence and feeblemindedness.) *Int. Z. Indiv. Psychol.*, 6, 267–272. [Trans.: 1964.]

A1928g   "Neurotisches Rollenspiel." (Neurotic role play.) *Int. Z. Indiv. Psychol.*, 6, 427–432.

A1928h   * "The cause and prevention of neuroses." *J. abnorm. soc. Psychol.*, 23, 4–11. [Orig.: 1927l.]

A1928i * "On teaching courage." *Survey Graphic*, 61, 241–242. [Orig.: 1927i.]

A1928j "Psychologie und Medizin." (Psychology and medicine.) *Wien. med. Wschr.*, 78, 697–700.

A1928k *Über den nervösen Charakter.* 4th ed. Munich: Bergmann.

A1928l "Besuch bei Dr. Alfred Adler." (Visit with Dr. Alfred Adler.) Interview with Artur Ernst. *Neues Wiener Tagblatt* (Vienna), July 1, 5–6.

A1928m "Psychologie der Macht." (Psychology of power.) In Franz Kobler (Ed.), *Gewalt und Gewaltlosigkeit: Handbuch des aktiven Pazifismus.* Zurich: Rotapfel-Verlag. Pp. 41–46. [Trans.: 1966b.]

A1929a * *The case of Miss R.: the interpretation of a life story.* Trans. Eleanore & F. Jensen. New York: Greenberg. Pp. xxii + 306. [Orig.: 1928a.]

A1929b *Individualpsychologie in der Schule: Vorlesungen für Lehrer und Erzieher.* (Individual Psychology in the school: lectures for teachers and educators.) Leipzig: Hirzel. Pp. viii + 114. [Trans.: Dutch, 1933a; Hebrew, n.d.a; Spanish, 1936b, 1941a.]

A1929c *Problems of neurosis: a book of case histories.* Ed. P. Mairet. Preface by F. G. Crookshank. London: Routledge & Kegan Paul. Pp. xxxvii + 178. [Repr.: 1964d; 1959e, 1967a, Chapt. 6; 1937e, Chapt. 7; 1937f, Chapt. 8. Trans.: French, 1969a.]

A1929d *The science of living.* Preface by P. Mairet. New York: Greenberg. Pp. 264. [Repr.: 1969b. Trans.: Portuguese, 1943.]

A1929e "Clinic for sick marriages." Interview with Helena H. Smith. *Delineator*, October, 115, 12 & 56, 59.

A1929f "Die Individualpsychologie in der Neurosenlehre." (Individual Psychology in the theory of neurosis.) *Int. Z. Indiv. Psychol.*, 7, 81–88.

A1929g "Eine Beratung: stenographische Aufnahme." (A guidance session: stenographic account.) *Int. Z. Indiv. Psychol.*, 7, 207–214.

A1929h "Übertreibung der eigenen Wichtigkeit." (Exaggeration of one's own importance.) *Int. Z. Indiv. Psychol.*, 7, 245–252. [Repr.: 1930e, Chapt. 1. Trans.: 1937c.]

A1929i "Unspoiling the spoiled child." *Parents Magazine*, May, pp. 19 + 72–73.

A1929j * "Les idées fondamentales de la psychologie individuelle." (The basic concepts of Individual Psychology.) *Rev. Psychol. concrète*, 1, 89–101. [Orig.: 1930n.]

A1929k "La psychologie individuelle dans la pédagogie moderne." (Individual Psychology in modern education.) *L'Avenir social* (Brussels), 1, 25–26.

A1929l "Sleeplessness." Manuscript. [Pub. A1944a.]

A1930a *The education of children.* Trans. Eleanore and F. Jensen. New York: Greenberg. Pp. 309.

A1930b * *Menneskekundskab.* (Understanding human nature.) Trans. O. Gelsted. Copenhagen; Oslo: Martins Førlag. [Orig.: 1927a.]

A1930c *The pattern of life.* Ed. W. B. Wolfe. New York: Cosmopolitan Book. Pp. 273.

A1930d   * *Das Problem der Homosexualität: erotisches Training und erotischer Rückzug.* (The problem of homosexuality: erotic training and erotic retreat.) 2nd ed. Leipzig: Hirzel. Pp. vi + 110. [Orig.: 1917b; 1926e, f, g, i, j. Trans.: French, 1956a; Spanish, 1936a.]

A1930e   *Die Technik der Individualpsychologie.* Vol. 2. *Die Seele des schwererziehbaren Schulkindes.* (The technique of Individual Psychology. Vol. 2. The soul of difficult school children.) Munich: Bergmann. Pp. viii + 188. [Orig.: 1929h, Chapt. 1. Trans.: English, 1963; French, 1952.]

A1930f   * [and Associates] *Guiding the child on the principles of Individual Psychology.* Trans. B. Ginzburg. New York: Greenberg. Pp. 268. [Orig. *Int. Z. Indiv. Psychol.*, 1929, 7, 161–243.]

A1930g   *The individual criminal and his cure: an address.* New York: Nat. Committee on Prisons and Prison Labor. Pp. 18. [Trans.: German, 1931h. Repr.: 1932e.]

A1930h   "Individual Psychology." In C. Murchison (Ed.), *Psychologies of 1930.* Worcester, Mass.: Clark Univer. Press. Pp. 395–405. [Repr.: 1965c, 1971d, n.d.c.]

A1930i   "First comes mother, next comes father." Interview with Lola J. Simpson. *Good Housekeeping,* November, 91, 36–37+.

A1930j   "Nochmals—die Einheit der Neurosen." (Once more—the unity of the neuroses.) *Int. Z. Indiv. Psychol.*, 8, 201–216.

A1930k   "Ein Fall von Enuresis diurna: stenographische Aufnahme einer Erziehungsberatung." (A case of enuresis diurna: stenographic account of a child guidance session.) *Int. Z. Indiv. Psychol.*, 8, 471–478.

A1930l   "The criminal pattern of life." *Police J.* (New York), 17(6), 8–11 & 22–23.

A1930m   "Individual Psychology and psychoanalysis." Manuscript. [Excerpts printed: 1964, Chapt. 14 footnotes.]

A1930n   "Grundbegriffe der Individualpsychologie." (Basic concepts of Individual Psychology.) In F. Giese (Ed.), *Handwörterbuch der Arbeitswissenschaft.* Vol. 1. Halle a/S: Marhold Verlag. Pp. 2428–2437. [Trans.: English, 1970b, French, 1929j.]

A1930o   "Something about myself." *Childhood and Character,* 7(7), 6–8.

A1931a   * *Conocimiento del hombre.* (Understanding human nature.) Trans. U. Bark. Madrid: Espasa-Calpe. [Orig.: 1927a.]

A1931b   *What life should mean to you.* Ed. A. Porter. Boston: Little, Brown. Pp. 300. [Repr.: 1958a.]

A1931c   "Rauschgift." (Intoxicants.) *Fortschr. Med.*, 49, 535–540; 571–575. [Repr.: 1932f.]

A1931d   "Wide, wide world." Interview with Lola J. Simpson. *Good Housekeeping,* October, 93, 40–41+.

A1931e   "The case of Mrs. A." *Indiv. Psychol. Pamphl.*, No. 1, 15–46. [Repr.: 1964.]

A1931f   "Zwangsneurose." (Compulsion neurosis.) *Int. Z. Indiv. Psychol.*, 9, 1–16. [Trans.: English, 1936i; French, 1958b.]

A1931g   "Der Sinn des Lebens." (The meaning of life.) *Int. Z. Indiv. Psychol.*, 9, 161–171.

A1931h   * "Die kriminelle Persönlichkeit und ihre Heilung." (The criminal personality and its cure.) *Int. Z. Indiv. Psychol.*, 9, 321–329. [Orig.: 1930g.]

A1931i   "Trick und Neurose." (Trick and neurosis.) *Int. Z. Indiv. Psychol.*, 9, 417–423. [Trans.: 1936g.]

A1931j   "The structure of neurosis." *Lancet*, 220, 136–137.

A1931k   "The meaning of life." *Lancet*, 220, 223–228. [Repr.: 1932d.]

A1931l   "Der nervöse Charakter." (The nervous character.) *Z. angew. Psychol., Beih.*, No. 59, 1–14.

A1931m   "Symptomwahl beim Kinde." (The child's symptom selection.) *Kinderärztl. Praxis*, 2, 398–409.

A1931n   "Individualpsychologie und Psychoanalyse. I. Individualpsychologie." (Individual Psychology and psychoanalysis. I. Individual Psychology.) *Schweiz. Erziehungs-Rundsch.*, 4(4), 59–61.

A1931o   "Individualpsychologie und Psychoanalyse. II. Die Unterschiede zwischen Individualpsychologie und Psychoanalyse." (Individual Psychology and psychoanalysis. II. The differences between Individual Psychology and psychoanalysis.) *Schweiz. Erziehungs-Rundsch.*, 4(5), 89–93. [Trans.: 1964.]

A1931p   "Was die Schule sein könnte." (What the school could be.) *Der neue Schulkampf, Prague*, 2(1), 5–7.

A1932a   * *Mensenkennis.* (Understanding human nature.) Trans. P. van Schilfgaarde. Utrecht, Holland: E. J. Bijleveld. Pp. 219. [Orig.: 1927a.]

A1932b   "Vorrede." (Preface.) In R. Dreikurs, *Einführung in die Individualpsychologie.* Leipzig: Hirzel. [Trans.: 1935d.]

A1932c   "The fear of woman: remarks." *Indiv. Psychol. Pamphl.*, No. 3, 11–13.

A1932d   * "The meaning of life." *Indiv. Psychol. Pamphl.*, No. 5, 9–22. [Orig.: 1931k.]

A1932e   * "The criminal personality and its cure." *Indiv. Psychol. Pamphl.*, No. 5, 46–59. [Orig.: 1930g.]

A1932f   * "Rauschgift." (Intoxicants.) *Int. Z. Indiv. Psychol.*, 10, 1–19. [Orig.: 1931c; pp. 15–19 are new.]

A1932g   "Persönlichkeit als geschlossene Einheit." (Personality as a self-consistent unity.) *Int. Z. Indiv. Psychol.*, 10, 81–88.

A1932h   "Die Systematik der Individualpsychologie." (The systematics of Individual Psychology.) *Int. Z. Indiv. Psychol.*, 10, 241–244.

A1932i   "Der Aufbau der Neurose." (The structure of neurosis.) *Int. Z. Indiv. Psychol.*, 10, 321–328. [Trans.: 1935g.]

A1932j   "Zum Thema sexuelle Perversion." (On sexual perversion.) *Int. Z. Indiv. Psychol.*,10,401-409.[Rep.:1933b,Chapt.11;trans.:1934f.]

A1932k   "Individualpsychologie und Erziehung." (Individual Psychology and education.) *Vjschr. Jugendk.*, 2, 1–6.

A1932l   "Technik der Behandlung." (Technique of treatment.) Manuscript. [Trans.: 1964.]

A1932m   "Failures in sex." *Modern Psychologist*, 1 (2), 55–60.

A1933a   * *De psychologie van het individueele op school en in het gezin.*

(Individual Psychology in the school.) Trans. P. van Schilf-gaarde. Utrecht, Holland: E. J. Bijleveld. [Orig.: 1929b.]

A1933b   *Der Sinn des Lebens.* (The meaning of life.) Vienna; Leipzig: Passer. Pp. 205. [Orig.: 1933f, Chapt. 12; 1933h, Chapt. 10; 1933j, Chapt. 4. Trans.: Dutch, 1935c; English, 1938a; French, 1950a; Spanish, 1935b; Swedish, 1934a; Yiddish, 1938b.]

A1933c   "Religion und Individualpsychologie." (Religion and Individual Psychology.) In E. Jahn and A. Adler, *Religion und Individual-psychologie: eine prinzipielle Auseinandersetzung über Men-schenführung.* Vienna; Leipzig: Passer. Pp. 58–92. [Trans.: English, 1964; French, 1958b.]

A1933d   "Individual Psychology and experimental psychology." *Charact. Pers.*, 1, 265–267.

A1933e   "Was kann die Individualpsychologie zur mathematischen 'Begabung' sagen?" (What can Individual Psychology say on mathematical "talent"?) *Int. Z. Indiv. Psychol.*, 11, 42–43.

A1933f   "Erste Kindheitserinnerungen." (First childhood recollections.) *Int. Z. Indiv. Psychol.*, 11, 81–90. [Repr.: 1933b, Chapt. 12.]

A1933g   [Review] W. B. Cannon. The wisdom of the body. New York: Norton, 1932. *Int. Z. Indiv. Psychol.*, 11, p. 154.

A1933h   "Was ist wirklich eine Neurose?" (What is really a neurosis?) *Int. Z. Indiv. Psychol.*, 11, 177–185. [Repr.: 1933b, Chapt. 10; Trans.: 1935f.]

A1933i₁   "Über den Ursprung des Strebens nach Überlegenheit und des Gemeinschaftsgefühles." (On the origin of the striving for superiority and of social interest.) *Int. Z. Indiv. Psychol.*, 11, 257–263. [Trans.: 1964.]

A1933i₂   "Über den Ursprung des Strebens nach Überlegenheit und des Gemeinschaftsgefühls." (On the origin of the striving for superiority and of social interest.) *Mitteilungsbl. Indiv. Psychol. Veranstaltungen*, 2(7), p. 1. [Trans.: 1964.]

A1933j   "Zum Leib-Seele Problem." (On the body-mind problem.) *Int. Z. Indiv. Psychol.*, 11, 337–345. [Repr.: 1933b, Chapt. 4.]

A1933k   "Die Formen der seelischen Aktivität: ein Beitrag zur individual-psychologischen Charakterkunde." (The forms of psychological activity: a contribution to the Individual-Psychological theory of character.) *Ned. Tijdschr. Psychol.*, 1, 229–235. [Repr.: 1934g. Trans.: 1964.]

A1933l   "Vor- und Nachteile des Minderwertigkeitsgefühls." (Advantages and disadvantages of the inferiority feeling.) *Pädag. Warte*, 40, 15–19. [Trans.: 1964.]

A1933m   "Individual Psychology." *Spinoza Quart.*, 2 (4), 14–19.

A1934a   * *Livets Mening.* (The meaning of life.) Stockholm: Bokfölaget Natur oog Kultur. [Orig.: 1933b.]

A1934b   * *Poznavanje Coveka.* (Understanding human nature.) Belgrade, Yugoslavia: Kosmos. [Orig.: 1927a.]

A1934c   * *Psycholgja Indywidualna.* (Individual Psychology.) Krakow, Poland: Gebethner i Wolff. [Orig.: 1920a.]

A1934d   * *Anthropognosia.* (Understanding human nature.) Trans. G. Paleologos. Athens: P. Dimikratos. [Orig.: 1927a.]

A1934e   "Lecture to the Medical Society of Individual Psychology, London, May 17, 1934." *Indiv. Psychol. Pamphl.,* No. 13, 11-24.

A1934f   * "Sexual perversions." *Indiv. Psychol. Pamphl.,* No. 13, 25-36. [Orig.: 1932j.]

A1934g   * "Die Formen der seelischen Aktivität: ein Beitrag zur individual-psychologischen Charakterkunde." (The forms of psychological activity: a contribution to the Individual-Psychological theory of character.) *Int. Z. Indiv. Psychol.,* 12, 1-5. [Orig.: 1933k.]

A1934h   "Körperliche Auswirkungen seelischer Störungen." (Physical effects of psychological disturbances.) *Int. Z. Indiv. Psychol.,* 12, 65-71. [Trans.: 1944b.]

A1934i   "Zur Massenpsychologie." (Mass psychology.) *Int. Z. Indiv. Psychol.,* 12, 133-141. [Trans.: 1937d.]

A1934j   "Über Kritzeleien." (On scribblings.) *Int. Z. Indiv. Psychol.,* 12, 201-203.

A1935a   [Editor] *International Journal of Individual Psychology.* Chicago: Int. Publications, Inc. Until 1937.

A1935b   * *El sentido de la vida.* (The meaning of life.) Trans. O. Brachfeld. Barcelona: Luis Miracle. [Orig.: 1933b.]

A1935c   * *De zin van het leven.* (The meaning of life.) Trans. P. H. Ronge. Utrecht, Holland: E. J. Bijleveld. Pp. 220. [Orig.: 1933b.]

A1935d   * "Foreword." In R. Dreikurs, *An introduction to Individual Psychology.* London: Routledge & Kegan Paul. [Orig.: 1932b. Repr.: 1959c.]

A1935e   "The fundamental views of Individual Psychology." *Int. J. Indiv. Psychol.,* 1(1), 5-8. [Repr.: 1964.]

A1935f   * "What is neurosis?" *Int. J. Indiv. Psychol.,* 1(1), 9-17. [Orig.: 1933h.]

A1935g   * "The structure of neurosis." *Int. J. Indiv. Psychol.,* 1(2), 3-12. [Orig.: 1932i. Repr.: 1964.]

A1935h   * "The prevention of delinquency." *Int. J. Indiv. Psychol.,* 1(3), 3-13. [Orig.: 1935m. Repr.: 1964.]

A1935i   * "Prevention of neurosis." *Int. J. Indiv. Psychol.,* 1935, 1(4), 3-12. [Orig.: 1935l.]

A1935j   "Der Komplexzwang als Teil der Persönlichkeit und Neurose." (The complex compulsion as part of personality and neurosis.) *Int. Z. Indiv. Psychol.,* 1935, 13, 1-6. [Trans.: 1964.]

A1935k   "Über das Wesen und die Entstehung des Charakters." (The nature and origin of character.) *Int. Z. Indiv. Psychol.,* 13, 29-30.

A1935l   "Vorbeugung der Neurose." (Prevention of neurosis.) *Int. Z. Indiv. Psychol.,* 13, 133-141. [Trans.: 1935i.]

A1935m   "Die Vorbeugung der Delinquenz." (Prevention of delinquency.) *Int. Z. Indiv. Psychol.,* 13, 197-206. [Trans.: 1935h.]

A1935n   * "Moeilijke Kinderen." (Difficult children.) In O. and Alice Rühle

(Eds.), *Moeilijke Kinderen*. 3rd ed. Trans. P. Dijkema. Amsterdam: Wereldbibliotheek. Pp. 16–26. [Orig.: 1926l.]

A1936a   * *El problema del homosexualismo*. (The problem of homosexuality.) Barcelona, Spain: Ed. Apollo. [Orig.: 1930d.]

A1936b   * *La psicologia individual en la escuela*. (Individual Psychology in the school.) Trans. J. Salas. Madrid, Spain: Rev. de Pedag. Pp. 134. [Orig.: 1929b.]

A1936c   "Introduction." In M. Maltz, *New faces—new futures: rebuilding character with plastic surgery*. New York: R. R. Smith. P. vii.

A1936d   "Are Americans neurotic?" *Forum*, 95 (January), 44–45.

A1936e   "Separate the Quins [Dionne quintuplets]: it must be done for their own good." *Hearst's Int.-Cosmopol.*, March, 89–90.

A1936f   "On the interpretation of dreams." *Int. J. Indiv. Psychol.*, 2(1) 3–16.

A1936g   * "Trick and neurosis." *Int. J. Indiv. Psychol.*, 2(2), 3–10. [Orig.: 1931i.]

A1936h   * "The neurotic's picture of the world." *Int. J. Indiv. Psychol.*, 2(3), 3–13. [Orig.: 1936l. Repr.: 1964.]

A1936i   * "Compulsion neurosis." *Int. J. Indiv. Psychol.*, 2(4), 3–22. [Orig.: 1931f; 1936m, pp. 193–195. Repr.: 1959f; 1964.]

A1936j   "Das Todesproblem in der Neurose." (The death problem in neurosis.) *Int. Z. Indiv. Psychol.*, 14, 1–6. [Trans.: 1964.]

A1936k   "Symptomwahl." (Choice of the symptom.) *Int. Z. Indiv. Psychol.*, 14, 65–80. [Trans.: 1946.]

A1936l   "Neurotisches Weltbild." (The neurotic's picture of the world.) *Int. Z. Indiv. Psychol.*, 14, 129–137. [Trans.: 1936h.]

A1936m   "Weiteres zur Zwangsneurose." (More on compulsion neurosis.) *Int. Z. Indiv. Psychol.*, 14, 193–196. [Trans.: English, 1936i; French, 1958b.]

A1936n   "Love is a recent invention." *Esquire* mag., May, pp. 56 and 128. [Repr.; 1971c.]

A1937a   * [*Practice and theory of Individual Psychology*.] Serbian. Belgrade, Yugoslavia: Geza-Don. A. D. [Orig.: 1920a.]

A1937b   "Psychiatric aspects regarding individual and social disorganization." *Amer. J. Sociol.*, 42, 773–780.

A1937c   * "A school girl's exaggeration of her own importance." *Int. J. Indiv. Psychol.*, 3, 3–12. [Orig.: 1929h.]

A1937d   * "Mass psychology." *Int. J. Indiv. Psychol.*, 3, 111–120. [Orig.: 1934i.]

A1937e   * "Position in family constellation influences life-style." *Int. J. Indiv. Psychol.*, 3, 211–227. [Orig.: 1929c, Chapt. 7.]

A1937f   * "Significance of early recollections." *Int. J. Indiv. Psychol.*, 3, 283–287. [Orig.: 1929c, Chapt. 8. Repr.: 1950b.]

A1937g   "Ist der Fortschritt der Menschheit möglich? wahrscheinlich? unmöglich?" (Is progress of mankind possible? probable? impossible?) *Int. Z. Indiv. Psychol.*, 15, 1–4. [Trans.: 1957c.]

A1937h   "Selbstmord." (Suicide.) *Int. Z. Indiv. Psychol.*, 15, 49–52. [Trans.: 1958d.]

A1937i   *Levensproblemen*. (Problems of life: new lectures on Individual

Psychology.) Trans. P. H. Ronge. Utrecht, Holland: E. J. Bijleveld.

A1938a   * *Social interest: a challenge to mankind.* Trans. J. Linton and R. Vaughan. London: Faber & Faber. Pp. 313. [Orig.: 1933b. Repr.: 1964e.]

A1938b   * *Der zin fun lebn* (Yiddish). (The meaning of life.) Trans. B. Bodluck and R. Lichstein. Wilno, Poland. [Orig.: 1933b.]

A1939   [Autobiographical notes.] ˆIn Phyllis Bottome, *Alfred Adler: a biography.* New York: Putnam. Pp. 9–12. [Repr.: 1947b.]

A1941a   * *La psicologia individual en la escuela.* (Individual Psychology in the school.) Trans. J. Salas. Buenos Aires: Edit. Losada. Pp. 174. [Orig.: 1929b.]

A1941b   "Failures of personalities" (1933). *Indiv. Psychol. News*, 1(8–9), 2–8.

A1941c   "Case interpretation" (no date). *Indiv. Psychol. Bull.*, 2, 1–9. [Repr.: 1964.]

A1943   * *A ciencia de viver.* (The science of living.) Trans. T. N. Neto. 2nd ed. Rio de Janeiro, Brazil: Jose Olympio editora. Pp. 304. [Orig.: 1929d.]

A1944a   * "Sleeplessness." *Indiv. Psychol. Bull.*, 3, 60–64. [Orig.: 1929l. Repr.: 1964.]

A1944b   * "Physical manifestations of psychic disturbances." *Indiv. Psychol. Bull.*, 4, 3–8. [Orig.: 1934h. Repr.: 1964.]

A1945a   * *A ciencia da natureza humana* (Portuguese). (Understanding human nature.) Trans. G. Rangel and A. Teixeira. Sao Paulo, Brazil: Editora National. Pp. 295. [Orig.: 1927a.]

A1945b   "The sexual function" (no date). *Indiv. Psychol. Bull.*, 4, 99–102. [Repr.: 1964.]

A1946   * "How the child selects his symptoms." *Indiv. Psychol. Bull.*, 5, 67–78. [Orig.: 1936k.]

A1947a   * *Menschenkenntnis.* (Understanding human nature.) Zurich: Rascher. Pp. vii + 236. [Orig.: 1927a.]

A1947b   * "How I chose my career." *Indiv. Psychol. Bull.*, 6, 9–11. [Orig.: 1939.]

A1948   * *Znajomosc czlowieka.* (Understanding human nature.) Lodz, Poland: Jaiolkowski. [Orig.: 1927a.]

A1949a   * *Connaissance de l'homme: étude de caractérologie individuelle.* (Understanding human nature: a study of individual characterology.) Trans. J. Marty. Paris: Payot. Pp. 191. [Orig.: 1927a.]

A1949b   * *Prassi e teoria della psicologia individuale.* (Practice and theory of Individual Psychology.) Rome: Astrolabio. [Orig.: 1920a.]

A1950a   * *Le sens de la vie.* (The meaning of life.) Trans. H. Schaffer. Paris: Payot. [Orig.: 1933b.]

A1950b   * "Significance of early recollections." In E. L. Hartley, H. G. Birch, and Ruth E. Hartley (Eds.), *Outside readings in psychology.* New York: Crowell. Pp. 361–365. [Orig.: 1937f.]

A1950c   * *Il temperamento nervoso.* (The nervous character.) Rome: Astrolabio. [Orig.: 1912a.]

A1952   * *La psychologie de l'enfant difficile: technique de la Psychologie In-dividuelle Comparée.* (The psychology of the difficult child: technique of comparative Individual Psychology.) Trans. H. Schaffer. Paris: Payot. Pp. 203. [Orig.: 1930e.]

A1953   * *Practica y teoria de la psicologia del individuo.* (Practice and theory of Individual Psychology.) Buenos Aires: Editorial Paidos. [Orig.: 1920a.]

A1954   * *Conoscenza dell'uomo.* (Understanding human nature.) Milan, Italy: Arnoldo Mondadori. [Orig.: 1927a.]

A1956a   * *La compensation psychique de l'état d'inferiorité des organes* suivi de *Le problème de l'homosexualité.* (Psychological compensation of organ inferiority, *followed by* The problem of homosexuality.) Trans. H. Schaffer. Paris: Payot. Pp. 247. [Orig.: 1907a and 1930d.]

A1956b   *The Individual Psychology of Alfred Adler: a systematic presentation in selections from his writings.* Ed. H. L. and Rowena R. Ansbacher. New York: Basic Books. Pp. xxiii + 503. [Repr.: 1964f. Trans.: Spanish, 1959b.]

A1957a   * *Understanding human nature.* Trans. W. B. Wolfe. New York: Premier Books, Fawcett World Libr. Pp. 224 paper. [Orig.: 1927b.]

A1957b   * [*Understanding human nature*] Japanese. Trans. & postscript by H. Yamashita. Tokyo: Nippon Kyobunsha. Pp. 356. [Orig.: 1927a.]

A1957c   * "The progress of mankind." *J. Indiv. Psychol.*, 13, 9–13. [Orig.: 1937g. Repr.: 1959d; 1964.]

A1958a   * *What life should mean to you.* Ed. A. Porter. New York: Capricorn Books. Pp. 300. [Orig.: 1931b.]

A1958b   * [and E. Jahn] *Religion et Psychologie Individuelle Comparée* suivi de *La nevrose obsessionnelle, Complement à l'étude de la nevrose obsessionnelle,* et *Les enfants difficiles.* (Religion and Comparative Individual Psychology, *followed by* Compulsion neurosis, Supplement to the study of compulsion neurosis, *and* Difficult children.) Trans. H. Schaffer. Paris: Payot. Pp. 172. [Orig.: 1933c, 1931f, 1936m, and 1926l.]

A1958c   * "The feeling of inferiority and the striving for recognition." In C. L. Stacey and M. F. DeMartino (Eds.), *Understanding human motivation.* Cleveland: Howard Allen. Pp. 466–473. [Orig.: 1927m.]

A1958d   * "Suicide." *J. Indiv. Psychol.*, 14, 57–61. [Orig.: 1937h. Repr.: 1964.]

A1959a   * *The practice and theory of Individual Psychology.* Trans. P. Radin. Paterson, N. J.: Littlefield, Adams. Pp. viii + 352. [Orig.: 1925a.]

A1959b   * *La psicologia individual de Alfred Adler: presentacion sistematica de una seleccion de sus escritos.* (The Individual Psychology of Alfred Adler: a systematic presentation in selections from his writings.) Ed. H. L. and Rowena R. Ansbacher. Trans. Nuria

Cortada de Kohan. Buenos Aires: Troquel. Pp. 570. [Orig.: 1956b.]

A1959c * "Foreword." In K. A. Adler and Danica Deutsch (Eds.), *Essays in Individual Psychology.* New York: Grove Press. P. xiii. [Orig.: 1935d.]

A1959d * "The progress of mankind." In K. A. Adler and Danica Deutsch (Eds.), *Essays in Individual Psychology.* New York: Grove Press. Pp. 3–8. [Orig.: 1957c.]

A1959e * "The drive for superiority." In H. Greenwald (Ed.), *Great cases in psychoanalysis.* New York: Ballantine Books. Pp. 175–186. [Orig.: 1929c, Chapt. 6.]

A1959f * "The compulsion to be big." In S. J. Beck & H. B. Molish (Eds.), *Reflexes to intelligence: a reader in clinical psychology.* Glencoe, Ill.: Free Press. Pp. 79–90. [Orig.: 1936i.]

A1959g * El caracter neurótico. (The nervous character.) Buenos Aires: Editorial Paidos. [Orig.: 1912a.]

A1961a * *Pratique et théorie de la Psychologie Individuelle Comparée.* (Practice and theory of comparative Individual Psychology.) Trans. H. Schaffer. Paris: Payot. Pp. 379. [Orig.: 1920a.]

A1961b * "The practice and theory of Individual Psychology." In T. Shipley (Ed.), *Classics in psychology.* New York: Phil. Libr. Pp. 687–714. [Orig.: 1925a, Chapts. 1 & 3.]

A1962   "Presentations and discussions." In H. Nunberg and E. Federn (Eds.), *Minutes of the Vienna Psychoanalytic Society.* Vol. 1. 1906–1908. Trans. M. Nunberg. New York: Int. Univer. Press. Pp. 36–41, 138–140, 288–292. [Orig.: 1906, 1907d, 1908g.]

A1963   * *The problem child: the life style of the difficult child as analyzed in specific cases.* Trans. from French by G. Daniels. Introd. by K. A. Adler. New York: Capricorn Books. Pp. xvii + 172. [Orig.: 1930e and 1952.]

A1964a *Superiority and social interest: a collection of later writings,* Eds. H. L. & Rowena R. Ansbacher. Evanston, Ill.: Northwestern Univer. Press. Pp. xxii + 434. [Orig.: 1928f; 1930m; 1931e, o; 1932l; 1933c, i₁&₂, l; 1934g; 1935e, g, h, j; 1936h, i, j; 1941c; 1944a, b; 1945b; 1957c; 1958d.]

A1964b * "Individual Psychology, its assumptions and its results." In H. M. Ruitenbeek (Ed.), *Varieties of personality theory.* New York: Dutton. Pp. 65–79. [Orig.: 1925a, Chapt. 1.]

A1964c "Letters to Lou Andreas-Salome" (1912, 1913). In Lou Andreas-Salome. *The Freud journal.* Trans. & introd. by S. A. Leavy. New York: Basic Books. Pp. 33, 35, 160–161.

A1964d * *Problems of neurosis: a book of case histories.* Ed. P. Mairet. Preface by H. L. Ansbacher. New York: Harper Torchbooks. Pp. xxvi + 180. [Orig.: 1929c.]

A1964e * *Social interest: a challenge to mankind.* New York: Capricorn Books. Pp. 313. [Orig.: 1938a.]

A1964f * *The Individual Psychology of Alfred Adler: a systematic presentation in selections from his writings.* Ed. H. L. and Rowena R. Ansbacher. New York: Harper Torchbooks. Pp. xxiii + 503. [Orig.: 1956b.]

A1965a "Fortune-telling and prophecy" (n.d.). *J. Indiv. Psychol.*, 21, 41–43.

A1965b * "Individual Psychology." In W. S. Sahakian (Ed.), *Psychology of personality: readings in theory*. Chicago: Rand McNally. Pp. 86–116. [Orig.: 1929d, selections from all chapts. but 6 and 7. Also 6 pp. from 1925a, Chapts. 1 and 3.]

A1965c *"Individual Psychology." In G. Lindzey & C.S. Hall (Ed.) *Theories of personality: primary sources and research*. New York: Wiley. Pp. 97–104. [Orig. 1930h.]

A1966a "Letters to a patient"(1911, 1913). *J.Indiv. Psychol.*, 22, 112–115.

A1966b * "The psychology of power" (1928). *J. Indiv. Psychol.*, 22, 166–172. [Orig.: 1928m.]

A1966c "Note to a clergyman" (1933). *J. Indiv. Psychol.*, 22, 234.

A1966d * *Menschenkenntnis.* (Understanding human nature.) Introd. by O. Brachfeld. Frankfurt am Main: Fischer Bücherei. Pp. 255. [Orig.: 1927a.]

A1967a * "The drive for superiority." In H. Greenwald (Ed.), *Active psychotherapy*. New York: Atherton Press. Pp. 27–35. [Orig.: 1929c, Chapt. 6; 1959e.]

A1967b "Presentations and discussions." In H. Nunberg and E. Federn (Eds.), *Minutes of the Vienna Psychoanalytic Society*. Vol. 2. 1908–1910. Trans. M. Nunberg. New York: Int. Univer. Press. Pp. 125–138, 172–174, 259–265, 423–428, 503–504, and passim. [Orig.: 1909c, d, e; 1910n, o.]

A1967c * "The style of life." In F. W. Matson (Ed.), *Being, becoming and behavior: the psychological sciences*. New York: Braziller. Pp. 205–209. [Orig.: 1929d, pp. 98–103.]

A1967d * "Preface." In P. Friedman (Ed.), *Discussions of the Vienna Psychoanalytic Society—1910: on suicide, with particular reference to suicide among young students*. New York: Int. Univer. Press. Pp. 29–32. [Orig.: 1910p.]

A1967e * "On suicide." In P. Friedman (Ed.), *Discussions of the Vienna Psychoanalytic Society—1910: on suicide, with particular reference to suicide among young students*. New York: Int. Univer. Press. Pp. 109–121. [Orig.: 1910b.]

A1968a * "Suicide." In J. P. Gibbs (Ed.), *Suicide*. New York: Harper & Row. Pp. 146–150. [Orig.: 1937h; 1958d.]

A1968b * *Superioridad e interes social: una colección de sus últimos escritos.* Compilados por H. L. y Rowena Ansbacher, con un ensayo biográfico de Carl Furtmüller. Trans. María Martínez Peñaloza. Mexico: Fondo do Cultura Económica. Pp. 365. [Orig.: 1964a.]

A1969a *Les névroses: commentaires, observations et présentation de cas.* Intro. P. Sivadon. Trans. Odette Chabas. Paris: Aubier Montaigne. [Orig.: 1929c.]

A1969b * *The science of living.* Introd. & ed. H. L. Ansbacher. Garden City, N.Y.: Doubleday Anchor Books. Pp. xxii + 138. [Orig.: 1929d.]

A1970a   *The education of children. Trans. Eleanore and F. Jensen. Intro. by
            R. Dreikurs. Chicago: Regnery Gateway Ed. [Orig.: 1930a.]
A1970b   *"Fundamentals of Individual Psychology." J. Indiv. Psychol., 1970,
            26, 36–49. [Orig.: 1930n.]
A1971a   Letters to G. Stanley Hall. In H.L. Ansbacher, "Alfred Adler and
            G. Stanley Hall: Correspondence and general relationship." J.
            Hist. behav. Sci., 1971, 7, 337–352.
A1971b   Letter to R.S. Stites. In R.S. Stites, "Alfred Adler on Leonardo da
            Vinci." J. Indiv. Psychol., 1971, 27, 208–212.
A1971c   *"Love is a recent invention." J. Indiv. Psychol., 1971, 27, 144–152.
            [Orig.: 1936n.]
A1971d   *"Individual Psychology." In S.R. Maddi (Ed.) Perspectives on
            personality; a comparative approach. Boston: Little, Brown.
            Pp. 249–259. [Orig.: 1930h.]
A no date a * [Individual Psychology in the school] Hebrew. Trans. A. Alkalay.
            Jerusalem: Publ. House "Ever." [Orig.: 1929b.]
A no date b * Sens Zycia. Krakow, Poland: Gebethner i Wolff.
A no date c * "Individual Psychology." Repr. Ser. Soc. Sci., P–3. Indianapolis,
            Indiana: Bobbs-Merrill. Pp. 395–405. [Orig.: 1930h.]

Index

428

INDEX